The World Made Otherwise

The World Made Otherwise

Sustaining Humanity in a Threatened World

Timothy J. Gorringe

CASCADE *Books* • Eugene, Oregon

THE WORLD MADE OTHERWISE
Sustaining Humanity in a Threatened World

Cascade Books
An Imprint of Wipf and Stock Publishers
199 W. 8th Ave., Suite 3
Eugene, OR 97401

www.wipfandstock.com

PAPERBACK ISBN: 978-1-5326-4867-0
HARDCOVER ISBN: 978-1-5326-4868-7
EBOOK ISBN: 978-1-5326-4869-4

Cataloguing-in-Publication data:

Names: Gorringe, Timothy J., author.

Title: The world made otherwise : sustaining humanity in a threatened world / Timothy J. Gorringe.

Description: Eugene, OR: Cascade Books, 2018 | Includes bibliographical references and index.

Identifiers: ISBN 978-1-5326-4867-0 (paperback) | ISBN 978-1-5326-4868-7 (hardcover) | ISBN 978-1-5326-4869-4 (ebook)

Subjects: LCSH: Human ecology—Religious aspects—Christianity. | Common good—Religious aspects—Christianity. | Christianity and culture.

Classification: BR115.P7 G578 2018 (print) | BR115.P7 (ebook)

Manufactured in the U.S.A.   11/02/18

For
Joseph and Danny
Ishaan and Kiran
Carenza and Kabir

There are two ways of looking at a revolution. We can observe the gestures which symbolize and focus whole ages of struggle . . . . But there are also the longer, slower, profounder changes in men's ways of thinking, without which the heroic gestures would be meaningless. These elude us if we get too immersed in detail; we can appreciate the extent of the changes only if we stand back to look at the beginning and the end of the revolution, if we can use such inaccurate terms about something which is always beginning and never ends. From the longer range we can appreciate the colossal transformations which ushered England into the modern world. And we can, perhaps, extend a little gratitude to all those nameless radicals who foresaw and worked for—not our modern world, but something far nobler, something yet to be achieved—the upside-down world.

—Christopher Hill

Contents

Preface

THIS BOOK IS THE outcome of an AHRC grant to look at the "The values which support constructive social change," which ran from 2010 to 2012. Thanks to: Stewart Barr, my co-investigator, an admirable colleague and splendid representative of political geography, with whom I wish I had been able to teach more; to Justin Pollard, our researcher, whose sense of the political was always refreshing; to Clare Keyte, who patiently helped us negotiate the shark-infested reefs of the AHRC and university politics; to Hugo Gorringe, who drip-feeds me articles on sociology from around the world; to Annette Kehnel, who gave me an opportunity to run the ideas by a lively group from three continents at the University of Mannheim in the winter semester of 2014; to the members of the Transition groups in Exeter, and Cheriton Bishop, one or two of whose ideas I share; and to Gill Westcott, who neglects her wifely duty of companionship in the interests of working tirelessly for the common good and for whom freedom is certainly "an endless meeting."

The book is dedicated to my grandchildren: beautiful, intelligent, and full of life (like everybody's grandchildren), who will have to put up with the mess their grandparents and great-grandparents made for them but who will, I hope, contribute to the creation of a more just and therefore sustainable world.

—Tim Gorringe

Michaelmas 2017

INTRODUCTION

Chapter One

A Coming Dark Age?

Because it knows of the kingdom and grace of God [the church] knows of human presumption and the plainly destructive consequences of human presumption. It knows how dangerous human beings are and how endangered by themselves. It knows human beings as sinners, that is, as beings who are always on the point of opening the sluices through which, if they were not checked on time, chaos and nothingness would break in and bring human time to an end.

—KARL BARTH[1]

IN THE SUMMER OF 2012 the Professor of Computational Science at the University of Cambridge put on a play at the Royal Court Theatre in London called *Ten Billion*. He heads a lab which researches into complex systems, including the climate system and ecosystems, as well as the impact of humans on the Earth. The set was his office in Cambridge, and he talked as he talks to his graduate students. He considered all the mutual implications of the various factors affecting our world: population, resource use, environmental impacts, and so forth. He argued that we face "an

1. Barth, *Against the Stream,* 20. Rebecca Solnit criticizes those who spoke of a return to a Hobbesian state of nature in the wake of Hurricane Katrina, with fears of looting and crime, but Barth was writing in 1945 in the light of the horrors of the Nazi regime. Solnit herself goes on record following the racist murders by white vigilantes after Katrina. *Paradise,* 241–42.

3

unprecedented planetary emergency." As a natural scientist work-ing on photosynthesis he is extremely sceptical of the possibility of a technical fix. In fact, his view is that "We're fucked."[2]

A few months late Brad Werner, another complex systems theorist, told a huge meeting of the American Geophysical union the same thing. There was, he said, a mismatch between short time scale market and political forces driving resource extraction/use and longer time scale accommodations of the Earth system to these changes. The only ray of hope he saw was in social movements resisting the dominant neoliberal economic model.[3] Why would they do that? Because they believed in the possibility of a world made otherwise. Because they had different values to those which currently run the world. This book is about those values and the practices that follow from them.

I write as a Christian theologian, but no theologian lives in an ecclesiastical and theological bubble. The complex systems which Emmot and Werner research include (though this is not their con-cern) cultural, economic, and political systems. Climate change is no distinguisher of persons: rich and poor, women and men, members of all faiths and every ideology, are affected. In most of what I write in this book I am therefore looking at values and political and economic practices that might speak to any human being. My stance is what Martin Buber called a "believing human-ism," represented amongst Roman Catholic theologians in an earlier generation by Jacques Maritain, by Karl Barth, and today by John de Gruchy.[4] All humanisms respond to Terence's famous dictum: "I am a human being, I count nothing human foreign to me."[5] Contrary to the view of the UK's "Humanist Association,"

---

2. Emmott, *10 Billion*, 196.

3. http://thinkprogress.org/climate/2012/12/09/1306051/agu-scientist -asks-is-earth-fked-surprising-answer-resistance-is-not-futile/.

4. Barth spoke of "the humanism of God." *Against the Stream*, 184.

5. *Homo sum; humani nil a me alienum puto.* Terence, *The Self Tormentor,* 187.

this "human" includes religion—at least, if surveys of adherents of the world religions count for anything. Although I am sure no religion, including Christianity, has *the* answer to the world's problems, I nevertheless believe that Christianity has a vital contribution to make in the construction of a truly human future. Theological comment therefore takes its place alongside political, philosophical, and economic commentary. Amongst the theologians on whom I draw the Dutch theologian Ton Veerkamp has a special place in this book. This is partly because he is little known in the Anglo-Saxon world and deserves to be better known, but more importantly because more than almost any other theologian or exegete he understands how theology is embedded in political and economic systems, and how, in turn, it bears on these. In seeking a response to the dangers posed by climate change he is therefore a valuable aid.

In the remainder of this chapter I examine Stephen Emmott's claim that climate change is likely to bring disaster and set up the argument that will be the basis of the rest of the book—that at the heart of the problem lie false values, and that it is these that must be addressed if we are to avoid the fate Emmott prophesies. I begin by looking at the literature of civilizational collapse, taking issue with Joseph Tainter's view that this has nothing to do with values; I then ask whether climate change is likely to bring about such a collapse, and why concern about it is so low a social and political priority. I consider what the political consequences of collapse might be and conclude by considering the suggestion that religion might play a key role either in averting collapse or in dealing with it if it comes.

Decline and fall

The decline and fall of Rome, which Gibbon called "the greatest, perhaps, and the most awful scene in the history of mankind," has had an enormous influence on the Western imagination that continues to this day in films and science fiction. Anticipating Nietzsche, Gibbon thought the decline of Rome followed from the enervating impact of Christianity.[6] Most writers, long before Alaric sacked Rome in 410 AD, traced the causes of collapse to moral decay. Clay tablets unearthed by archaeologists in the early twentieth century already claimed that the collapse of the Sumerian kingdom established by Sargon in the third millennium was due to the impiety of rulers.[7] The Deuteronomic history, probably written during the exile (587–538 BC), likewise traced the collapse of first Israel, and then Judah, to the idolatry of the whole people, but especially its rulers. "Idolatry" concretely meant the pursuit of a form of economy which was alien to Israelite traditions, with different property values.[8] The tremendous jeremiad of Revelation 18 foresees the fall of Rome on the grounds of idolatry expressed in trade—finally a trade in "human souls." Augustine's *City of God*, triggered by the sack of Rome, probably imagines that Rome will continue, but his critique of Rome focuses on its violence, which he sees at the heart of the earthly city.

The theme of civilizational collapse has continued to provoke comment ever since. Turning the biblical view on its head, Spengler thought the inner dynamism of any culture eventually ossified, leaving only the brittle and lifeless forms of bureaucracy.[9] Toynbee also thought civilizations eventually inevitably lost their creative power.[10] Contemporary commentators, by contrast, concentrate on economic factors. According to Joseph Tainter, one of the most celebrated contemporary anatomists of collapse, complex

6. Gibbon, *The Decline and Fall of the Roman Empire*, ch. 38. "The clergy successfully preached the doctrines of patience and pusillanimity; the active virtues of society were discouraged; and the last remains of military spirit were buried in the cloister: a large portion of public and private wealth was consecrated to the specious demands of charity and devotion; and the soldiers' pay was lavished on the useless multitudes of both sexes who could only plead the merits of abstinence and chastity."

7. Sargon ruled from 2270 to 2215. His kingdom began to disintegrate 200 years later.

8. All the Greek and Latin historians likewise have a narrative of moral decay and the need for social virtues if the polis is to flourish.

9. Spengler, *The Decline of the West*.

10. Toynbee, *Study of History*, vol. 4, 5.

societies are subject to increasing costs and diminishing marginal returns, so that productivity per unit of labor decreases and in his view this is what leads to collapse.[11] Today the cost of rising complexity is environmental destruction and resource depletion. Disagreeing with Gibbon, Tainter argues that Rome's fall followed from the excessive costs imposed on an agricultural population to maintain a far-flung empire in a hostile environment.[12] He is cautious about predicting the collapse of contemporary Western society, but believes that only the discovery of a new energy source can prevent a collapse that, today, "if and when it comes again will this time be global. No longer can any individual nation collapse. World civilization will disintegrate as a whole."[13]

In his widely read book *Collapse*, Jared Diamond focuses on resource depletion, although he makes more allowance for cultural factors than does Tainter. He points out that the failure of the Norse culture in Greenland was in part due to an inability to see that the Christian culture and norms that invaders had brought from their homeland were ill-adapted to survival in the new country. Similarly, on Easter Island, the wood necessary for survival was used up creating and transporting the vast stone statues that are all that remain of a once thriving culture.[14] With regard to the present, he notes that the prosperity the First World currently enjoys involves spending down its environmental capital (nonrenewable sources such as fish stocks, topsoil, forests, etc.) and earlier collapses show that a society's steep decline may begin only a decade or two after the society reaches its peak

---

11. Tainter, *Collapse,* 99. Tainter identifies eleven causes that have been proposed, from ancient times to the present: depletion or cessation of a vital resource or resources on which a society depends; the establishment of a new resource base; the occurrence of some insurmountable catastrophe; insufficient response to circumstances; other complex societies; intruders; class conflict, societal contradictions, elite mismanagement or misbehavior; social dysfunction; mystical factors; chance concatenation of events; and economic factors (40–90).

12. Ibid., 191.

13. Ibid., 215.

14. Diamond, *Collapse,* 267–79; 103–19.

numbers—because maximum wealth and population mean maximum environmental impact. In his view, at current rates of use, most or all of a dozen major sets of environmental problems will become acute within the lifetime of young adults now alive.[15] He does not argue that collapse will be global, but given the scale of the problems it is hard to see how it could be otherwise.

Tainter speaks derisively of those who point to what he calls "mystical causes" of collapse, which range from biological analogies—all created things sooner or later grow old and die—to ideas of the loss of intrinsic vitality, to those who identify moral collapse as the key issue. He lumps all these together, because they all imply value judgements. This will not work, in his view, because values are culturally plural: "The result is a global bedlam of idiosyncratic value systems, each claiming exclusive possession of the truth. No scientific theory can be raised on such a foundation, for the attempt will only lead to confusion and contradiction."[16] This dismissal of ethics is widespread in the literature I shall be examining, especially amongst economists, but we should not take it for granted. In the first place, it is viciously circular because the dismissal of value judgements itself rests on a value judgement. It looks back to Hume's distinction between fact and value, which itself arose from an impossibly simplistic epistemology, and then to nineteenth-century positivism that found its acme in Max Weber's notion of "value-free science." More importantly, it leaves us with what Marx called "a fragment of a man," whose economics apparently

15. Ibid., 513. Diamond specifies the destruction of natural habitats; destruction of wild fish stocks on which a third of the world's population depends; loss of biodiversity; loss of topsoil; loss energy resources; water shortages; the photosynthetic ceiling; pollution; the increase in alien species damaging lakes and waterways; global warming and the ozone layer; population; and the impact caused by the rise in living standards (486–96). By the photosynthetic ceiling he means that "'most energy fixed from sunlight will be used for human purposes, and little will be left over to support the growth of natural plant communities, such as natural forests" (491).

16. Tainter, *Collapse*, 85. Tainter does note that, with resource depletion, we have to ask what structural, political, ideological, or economic factors in a society prevented an appropriate response (51). In Marxist terms, this involves both base and superstructure.

enshrines no values, and whose culture (the bearer of values) has no influence on events. It fails to acknowledge what ought to be obvious, that biophysical and socioeconomic processes are fully interactive and that humans and their activities are fully part of the Earth. The material, the social, the cultural, the ethical, and, we should add, the spiritual, are fully intertwined: any analysis that fails to recognise this is hopelessly compromised.

A number of contemporary writers continue to maintain the priority of the moral in their analysis of the problems we face. Thus Wendell Berry argues that the basic cause of the energy crisis is not scarcity but "moral ignorance and weakness of character. We don't know how to use energy or what to use it for."[17] Our basic problems today, wrote Robert Bellah and his associates, in their examination of North American culture, "are moral and have to do with the meaning of life."[18] In their view a damaged social ecology, which left people without strong communities, would bring about collapse before any natural ecological disaster.[19] And Emmott offers "behaviour change" as the only real alternative to a technical fix.

I want to explore this suggestion, and to ask, if that is the case, what can be done to remedy it. But first I need to ask whether predictions of contemporary global collapse are plausible.

Is civilizational collapse likely?

As we have seen, prophecies of doom and gloom go back to the earliest accounts of human culture. It is easy for critics to have sport at the expense of alarmist scares, and, of course, doomsayers have often been wrong.[20] At the same time, there is an ancient fable about the dangers of assuming that because previous alarms were false, the next one will be.

17. Berry, *The Unsettling of America*, 32.
18. Bellah et al., *Habits of the Heart*, 295.
19. Ibid., 284.
20. Booker and North, *Scared to Death*.

Tainter's theory of collapse, in terms of diminishing marginal returns, is partly evidenced today in the increasing costs of extracting the oil on which our whole culture, and especially agriculture, runs. Many analysts have pointed out that the energy return on energy invested (EROI) has declined from 100 to 1 in 1930 (which means that the energy in one barrel of oil could pump out 100 barrels) to 30 to 1 in 1970 and 11 to 1 in 2000. In other words, more and more energy is needed to extract the same amount of energy content, as companies drill or dig deeper, or as they extract lower-quality resources that need to be processed more extensively. The breakeven EROI may actually be much higher than 1 to 1; it may be 3 to 1 after accounting for the energy needed to process fuel, and build the machinery to use it, and build and maintain the infrastructure needed by the machinery.[21] A declining EROI, Nathan Hagens argues, acts as a tax on the rest of society. Much attention is paid to the new surge in gross US oil production, failing to observe that capital expenditure requirements are rising faster than oil prices, or that exploiting shale formations requires an enormous increase in diesel use, or that the resulting oil has a higher API gravity, which exaggerates the energy content per barrel by 3.5 to 10.7 percent.[22]

Diamond's pointing to resource depletion is even more evident than diminishing returns, especially with regard to water, though also to phosphorus, on which agriculture depends. Yet reasons for believing that a global collapse might now be likely begin with neither of these positions, but with the vast increase in world population in the past century. World population has more than doubled in the past forty years to more than seven billion, and the UN currently predicts eleven billion by the end of the century. The UN figures assume the spread of education and increasing use of contraception but, as Emmott points out, both of these have been available in Niger for years, and the average birth rate is seven children per woman. If the current rate of global reproduction continues, there will not be eleven billion, but twenty-eight billion

21. Gardner, "Conserving non-nonrenewable resources."
22. Hagens, "Energy, credit, and the end of growth," 29.

of us by the end of the century.[23] Although one sixth of the present population still live in absolute poverty it remains the case that huge numbers mean huge impacts. Emmott argues that the pressures this size of population will generate can only end in complete collapse, in which the earth will become uninhabitable.[24]

Such arguments are premised on the fact that the planet is finite, and therefore cannot cope with unlimited demands, the argument made famous by *Limits to Growth* in 1972, and by the Brundtland Report, *Our Common Future*, fifteen years later. Both reports attracted ridicule and disbelief by mainstream economists but other studies have found that the predictions of the first report were almost exactly correct by the turn of the millennium.[25] Arguments by the likes of Julian Simon that human intelligence is our greatest resource, and that the more humans there are, the greater the potential creativity, and that humans will always come up with something, smack of the hubris that in classical Greece was the hallmark of tragedy.[26]

The obverse of Simon's argument is that it is precisely our ability to marshal the Earth's resources which has freed us from constraints, and this may be the biggest threat to human survival. Although climate scientists like James Hansen tell us that leaving fossil fuels in the ground is essential to survival, world coal extraction has climbed from 4,700 million tonnes in 2000 to almost 7,900 million tonnes in 2013—a more than tenfold increase since 1900. It fell by 6 percent in 2016 but was still 6,733 million tonnes in 2017, and President Trump wishes to increase US production. World oil production started only in the late nineteenth century, but grew rapidly from 20 million tonnes in 1900 to 3,260 million tonnes in 2000, and 4,382 million tonnes in 2016—a 219-fold expansion since 1900. The production of energy-intensive materials—cement, plastics, and steel—has more than doubled since

23. Emmott, *10 Billion*, 187–89.

24. Ibid., 196–97.

25. Turner, "A comparison of the Limits to Growth with thirty years of reality."

26. Simon, *The Ultimate Resource*.

1992, far outstripping overall economic growth. Global resource extraction—of fossil fuels, metals, minerals, biomass—grew 50 percent in the twenty-five years between 1980 and 2005, to about 58 billion tonnes of raw materials. With civilization itself hanging in the balance, Michael Renner argues, change in the face of climate chaos should be a no-brainer. Yet the politics of climate change shows how difficult it is, and how large a part big money plays in preventing action. "In the battle to do what is needed to ensure humanity's long-term survival, a combination of denial, short-term thinking, profit interests, and human hubris is proving hard—perhaps even impossible—to overcome."[27]

The likelihood of global collapse is also indicated by the transgression of what the Stockholm Resilience Centre outlined as nine "planetary boundaries." Three of these, they argued in 2009, had already been crossed, and four more were on the edge.[28] Five years later they have finessed the arguments but remain deeply concerned about the capacity of the earth to sustain life if current human impacts continue. They argue that the Holocene era, which began about 11,700 years ago, and has been the background to human history as we know it, has been succeeded by what has been called the Anthropocene, at the industrial revolution, a historical phase in which human beings and their demands are at the center.[29] This phase is associated with major mechanization of production, huge rises in population, and massive increases in energy consumption

27. Renner, "The seeds of modern threats."
28. Rockström et al., "A safe operating space for humanity." See also Steffen et al., "Planetary boundaries." The nine planetary boundaries they identify are climate change, change in biosphere integrity (biodiversity loss and species extinction), stratospheric ozone depletion, ocean acidification, biogeochemical flows (phosphorus and nitrogen cycles), land-system change (for example deforestation), freshwater use, atmospheric aerosol loading (microscopic particles in the atmosphere that affect climate and living organisms), and introduction of novel entities (e.g., organic pollutants, radioactive materials, nanomaterials, and micro-plastics). They believe three (climate change, disruption of nitrogen cycle, and biodiversity loss) are already crossed and four (ocean acidification, ozone depletion, land-use change, and freshwater use) are precarious.
29. The phrase is credited to Crutzen, "Geology of mankind."

both overall and per capita. It has been marked by "a supreme self-confidence about continued linear progress, the development of scientific and technical knowledge, expansion of production, the rational design of social order, the growing satisfaction of human needs, and, not least, an increasing control over nature (including human nature) commensurate with scientific understanding of natural laws."[30] The United States, which is at the forefront of this development, has provided the dream for much of the rest of the world: even its bitterest critics use its technology, its weapons, and ape its media. But the United States has 5 percent of world population, accounts for 22 percent of world energy consumption and 25 percent of its emissions. Americans drive a third of the world's cars and produce half of the world's transport-generated emissions.[31] As economists like Herman Daly have been insisting for years, this lifestyle cannot possibly be generalized. Cheap energy has been at the heart of this development that "required the breakdown of all previous constraints—logistical, political, moral, cultural—to maximize the present at the expense of the future, and to do so for the benefit of a very few at the expense of the many."[32] Wolfgang Streeck represents a variant of this complaint. He believes neo-liberal capitalism is displanting real democracy throughout the world, leaving governance in the hands of a tiny plutocratic elite. Since there is no readily available alternative, what is likely is a prolonged period of social entropy or disorder, a society "devoid of reasonably coherent and minimally stable institutions capable of normalizing the lives of its members and protecting them from accidents and monstrosities of all sorts."[33]

The Stockholm Centre continued the work of the *Limits to Growth* report, which focused on resource depletion as the next most important problem after population and this has indeed proved serious across the whole range of resources, including

30. Scott, *Seeing Like a State,* 89
31. Urry, *Climate Change and Society,* 53
32. Kunstler, *The Long Emergency,* 185
33. Streeck, *How Will Capitalism End?,* 36, 13. He invokes the specter of a new dark ages on page 14.

uranium, copper, phosphorus, rare earths that are vital for renewable energy, and above all water. Sixty percent of fresh water is found in just nine countries.[34] It is estimated that within twenty years almost half the world's population will experience water scarcity. Global consumption of water is doubling every twenty years, more than twice the rate of human population growth. Agriculture accounts for 65 percent (one ton of wheat requires one thousand tons of water), domestic use 10 percent, and industry accounts for the rest. Even now "the water table in major grain producing areas in China is falling at the rate of five feet per year. Of China's 617 cities 300 already face water shortages. 80 percent of their rivers no longer support fish life."[35]

Some analysts have been predicting peak oil for many years and if this were really the case it would have huge implications for farming and therefore for the capacity to feed seven or eleven billion. However, as Emmott notes, new reserves of oil and gas are constantly being found, and shale oil and gas is coming on stream. The problem, as he puts it, is not that there is not enough fossil fuels, but, to the contrary, that we will seek to use every last drop.[36]

The second Stockholm Report calls biosphere integrity a core boundary, but notes the difficulty in quantifying it. The history of evolution has seen a background rate of extinction of three species per year but this has now risen to 1,000 species per year. This is partly due to the widespread use of agricultural monocultures, and the use of toxic chemicals on plants, but also to global warming as species fail to adapt to changing temperatures. Biodiversity is not just an aesthetic issue. Currently bees are dying in huge numbers, making pollination more and more difficult—almost certainly due to the use of neo nicotinoid sprays,

34. Water-sufficient countries are those which have more than 1,700 cubic meters per person. Between 1,000 and 1,700 cubic meters there is water stress and below 1,000 cubic meters there is water scarcity.

35. Kunstler, *Long Emergency*, 163. Emmott (*10 Billion*, 74) also highlights the unsustainability of the water situation. He points out that four liters of water is used to produce a plastic bottle to hold water, and a hundred liters of water to produce one cup of coffee.

36. Emmott, *10 Billion*, 76.

a fact denied by industrial agriculture. Plankton, the basis of fish life, is being destroyed. Forests and wetlands that cleanse water are being cut down. "Had ocean dwelling organisms not seques-tered carbon into limestone and chalk over millions of years, our habitable planet would long ago have turned into Venus, which suffers blistering temperatures of 500° C thanks to an inhospi-table atmosphere composed of 96 percent of carbon dioxide."[37] In other words, biodiversity is a survival issue.[38]

The other core boundary, according to the two Stockholm Reports, is climate change. According to the Intergovernmental Panel on Climate Change (IPCC) the present carbon dioxide con-centration has not been exceeded during the past 420,000 years and probably not during the past 20 million years. Currently we are adding 6 billion tons of carbon to the atmosphere each year. All life on earth, and not just human life, thrives within a relatively narrow temperature band. The addition of just 1 degree may dra-matically raise the level of species extinction, and a few degrees could lead to irreversible damage. The mass extinction of the end Permian age was associated with a rise of 6 degrees Celsius which is within the range of what both the IPCC and the Chief Economist of the International Energy Authority consider possible.[39] In a paper delivered to the UK Department for International Devel-opment two scientists based at the Tyndall Centre in Manchester examine the claims that (a) 2 degrees of warming is the limit if the world needs to achieve to avoid runaway climate change and (b) that present policies are sufficient for that goal to be realized.[40] The problem with current analyses, they argue, is that they do not allow for cumulative emissions. Two degrees, they argue, "represents a

37. Lynas, *Six Degrees*, 106. Birol, *World Energy Outlook 2012*, 247.

38. Reviewing the science since 1990, Cardinale et al. are cautious but still conclude that "the impacts of diversity loss on ecological processes might be sufficiently large to rival the impacts of many other global drivers of environ-mental change." See their "Biodiversity loss and its impact on humanity," 61. Tudge notes that we cannot categorize all our fellow creatures as "biodiversity" and see biodiversity simply as a resource. *So Shall We Reap*, 355.

39. Lynas, *Six Degrees*, 244.

40. Anderson and Bows, "Beyond 'dangerous' climate change," 20–44.

threshold, not between acceptable and dangerous climate change, but between dangerous and 'extremely dangerous' climate change." Temperatures do not rise in a linear fashion but are likely to be accompanied by feedbacks and further temperature rises. In fact, already in 2010, "There is now little to no chance of maintaining the rise in global mean surface temperature at below 2° C, despite repeated high-level statements to the contrary." Avoiding dangerous (and even extremely dangerous) climate change is no longer compatible with economic prosperity, they argue. To avoid such change the world would need "a planned economic contraction . . . whilst allowing time for the almost complete penetration of all economic sectors with zero or very low carbon technologies."[41]

Kevin Anderson has since argued that the assumption that global temperature rise can be held to two degrees is a fantasy, insisted on because politicians find the truth completely unpalatable. Statistics on recent historical emissions, he argues, are sometimes "mistaken" or "massaged." Short-term emission growth is seriously downplayed. The choice of year when emissions are said to have peaked is "Machiavellian" and dangerously misleading. The reduction rate necessary is universally dictated by economists and not by climate scientists. Assumptions about "big" technology are naively optimistic. Those who argue that a two-degree future is possible have "a magician's view of time and a linear view of problems." For a rise of four degrees centigrade emissions would need to peak by 2020, which would require a reduction of around 3.5 percent per annum in CO_2 from energy. Even this would mean up to 40 percent reduction in maize and rice as the population heads towards 9 billion by 2050. As it is, in 2016 the Arctic Council has charted temperatures twenty degrees above the norm and highlights nineteen aspects of regime change, all of which may lead to tipping points that affect the world as a whole.[42] In fact, Anderson

41. Ibid., 41.

42. In August 2018 the Centre produced a further report, intensifying the warnings of a "hothouse earth" and calling for "a deep transformation based on a fundamental reorientation of human values, equity, behavior, institutions, economies, and technologies"—precisely what this book is outlining. Steffen et al, "Trajectories of the Earth System in the Anthropocene."

argues, four degrees of warming is incompatible with the continuance of an equitable and civilized global community and he is clearly worried that four degrees might not be the end of it but that a rise to six degrees might occur.[43] He cites Roberto Unger to the effect that "At every level the greatest obstacle to transforming the world is that we lack the clarity and imagination to conceive that it could be different." In other words, the problem is not fundamentally technical, but fundamentally moral and cultural.

In addition to the effect on food production, a rise of four degrees would mean an ocean rise of half a meter or more above present levels, causing major migration from coastal areas.[44] Ice sheets are already beginning to disintegrate in the Antarctic and this means there will not be a new stable sea level on any foreseeable time scale. Millions of people are likely to be displaced. Earlier civilizations collapsed in the wake of much smaller changes in climate. The impacts of climate change are already with us. In September 2015 the Meteorological Office in the UK issued a report which acknowledged that natural climate cycles in the Pacific and Atlantic oceans are reversing and will amplify the strong manmade-driven global warming. This will change weather patterns around the world. The lead researcher, Adam Scaife, believes, "We will look back on this period as an important turning point."[45]

43. Anderson, *Real Clothes for the Emperor*. In October 2014 Anderson wrote to David Cameron pointing out that an 80 percent reduction in carbon emissions was needed by the EU, not the 40 percent politicians were aiming at.

44. Hansen, *Storms of my Grandchildren*, 85. "If we burn all reserves of oil, gas and coal there is a substantial chance we will initiate the runaway greenhouse. If we also burn the tar sands and tar shale I believe the Venus syndrome is a dead certainty" (236).

45. Damian Carrington, "2015 and 2916 set to break global heat records, says Met Office," *The Guardian*, September 14, 2015. In his observations on the Paris climate negotiations of December 2015, George Monbiot argues that though the outcome was better than any that had preceded it nevertheless the emphasis on consumption, rather than production, means that the agreement will almost certainly be undermined, as governments seek economic "recovery" by exploiting fossil fuels. "Grand promises of Paris climate deal undermined by squalid retrenchments," *The Guardian*, December 12, 2015.

Kate Raworth finessed the Stockholm report by proposing that social boundaries such as jobs, education, food, access to water, health services, and energy need to be added to natural thresholds. In her model there are both social and biophysical boundaries, and the "safe operating space" for humanity lies between these.

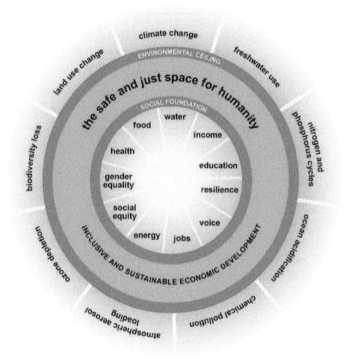

Figure 1

Moving into the safe and just space for humanity means eradicating poverty to bring everyone above the social foundation, and reducing global resource use, to bring it back within planetary boundaries. Social justice demands that this double objective be achieved through far greater global equity in the use of natural resources, with the greatest reductions coming from the world's richest consumers. And it demands far greater efficiency in transforming natural resources to meet human needs.[46]

A number of analysts emphasize the fragility of the globalized networks on which a greater and greater proportion of the world's population depend. The grid, IT and communications, transport, water and sewage, and banking infrastructure are all technologically complex and expensive and rely on economies of scale, open supply chains and general monetary stability over the world. "The tight coupling between different infrastructures magnifies the risk of a cascading failure in our critical infrastructure and thus a complete systemic failure in the operational fabric upon which our welfare depends. At the very least, a failing infrastructure feeds back into reduced economic activity and energy use, further undermining the ability to keep the infrastructure maintained."[47]

If we put these arguments together I think we have to say that civilizational collapse is likely. Two questions then arise: what we can do to prevent such a collapse, and were it to happen, what should be done? Before addressing these questions I ask why the dangers posed by crossing planetary boundaries occupy so small a place in popular and political consciousness.

Denial, complacency, and stupidity

Why have we come so close to the brink of extinction so carelessly and casually?, David Orr asks.

> Why do we still have thousands of nuclear weapons on hairtrigger alert? How can humankind reclaim the Commons of atmosphere, seas, biological diversity, mineral resources, and lands as the heritage of all, not the private possession of a few? How much can we fairly and sustainably take from the earth, and for what purposes?

46. Raworth, "Defining a safe and just space for humanity."

47. Korowicz, "On the cusp of collapse." I am not considering here the apocalyptic scenarios of Philip Bobbitt, which turn on terrorists obtaining either biological weapons, nuclear weapons, or disabling the internet. I shall say something about this in chapter four.

Why is wealth so concentrated and poverty so pervasive? Are there better ways to earn our livelihoods than by maximising consumption, a word that once signified a fatal disease? Can we organise governments at all levels around the doctrine of public trust rather than through fear and competition? And, finally, how might homo sapiens, with a violent and bloody past, be redeemed in the long arc of time?[48]

The answer to these questions is not obvious. In the Transition movement, which is one of the more hopeful civil society movements attempting to address the problems raised by the crossing of planetary boundaries, the favored explanation is "denial." Appealing above all to the work of Joanna Macy, the story goes that people, deep down, are aware of the danger and are repressing it—they are in denial. The hedonism of contemporary society is a form of displacement activity. What is needed to deal with it is "healing our rift with nature."[49] Part of this analysis is to insist that fear simply paralyzes, and that conveying terrifying information is no way to go about mobilizing people for dealing with problems. Rather, a picture of an alternative society has to be set out that is so attractive that people will want to opt for it.

In Norway Kari Mari Norgaard carried out more than a year's research on attitudes to climate change, and considered various reasons given for people failing to act: the claim that people do not have enough information (which Emmott endorses); that people are too selfish or greedy; that climate change comes well down in the hierarchy of needs, and the inverse relation between wealth and concern; the belief that technology will after all fix all our problems; and that people are so disempowered that they are not responding to anything. She, too, believes that denial stems not from greed or inhumanity but from the sense of guilt engendered by the contradiction of understanding the moral imperative to live differently but actually failing to do so.[50] In a sociological gloss to

---

48. Orr, "Governance in the Long Emergency," 291.

49. Macy, *Coming Back to Life.*

50. Norgaard, *Living in Denial,* 61.

this she notes that denial is socially organized, and that societies develop and reinforce a whole repertoire of techniques or tools for ignoring disturbing problems.[51] At the same time she allows that the poverty of political options is one of the key factors in producing apathy and her solutions, much closer to where I wish to look, are partly in regenerating democracy.[52]

A different explanation, more favored by cultural theorists, is that Aldous Huxley's dystopia is now our present reality. Marshal McCluhan's successor at New York University, Neil Postman, cites studies which found that 51 percent of viewers could not recall a single item of news a few minutes after viewing a news program; 21 percent of TV viewers could not recall any news item within one hour of broadcast.[53] He delivers what he calls "the Huxleyan warning":

> What Huxley teaches is that in the age of advanced technology, spiritual devastation is more likely to come from an enemy with a smiling face than from one whose countenance exudes suspicion and hate. In the Huxleyan prophecy, Big Brother does not watch us, by his choice. We watch him, by ours. There is no need for wardens or gates or Ministries of Truth. When a population becomes distracted by trivia, when cultural life is redefined as a perpetual round of entertainments, when serious public conversation becomes a form of baby-talk, when, in short, a people become an audience and their public business a vaudeville act, then a nation finds itself at risk; culture death is a real possibility.
>
> Huxley believed with H. G. Wells that we are in a race between education and disaster . . . in the end, he was trying to tell us that what afflicted the people in *Brave New World* was not that they were laughing instead of thinking, but that they did not know what they were laughing about and why they had stopped thinking.[54]

51. Ibid., 215.

52. Ibid., 225.

53. Postman, *Amusing Ourselves to Death*, 156.

54. Ibid., 168. In 2002 a BBC program on "Great Britons" drew up its list through a popular poll and ended up with either media personalities or people

"Pleasure" is our cultural dominant and even the counterculture seeks for "happiness" (without asking, in any particular case, whether we should be happy or sad). Lewis Mumford traced a connection between a money-centered culture and one based on the "pleasure principle": both, he argued, cannot recognize limits.[55] "Pleasure" becomes an addiction and is part of the trivialization of life in a consumer society. In seeking to analyze the relation between neoliberal economics and democracy Wolfgang Streeck speaks of a populace "stupefied by the products of a culture industry that Adorno could not have imagined in his most pessimistic moments."[56] Certainly in the affluent world we live in a society that takes cheap flights (in which the cost of damage to the environment is nowhere factored) completely for granted. The suggestion that one ought perhaps not to fly is regarded as absurd. George Monbiot spoke of the "love miles" people incurred to visit distant relatives. But in the academic community, at least, we have to speak of "ego miles," as tens of thousands of academics, including those who specialize in warning about the problems of climate change, jet off annually to vast conferences that are not primarily about the exchange of ideas but about establishing and maintaining reputations and providing the "esteem indicators" universities demand. Middle-class families take weddings in the West Indies, or foreign holidays, not simply for granted but as a basic human right. Rather than this papering over an underlying feeling of unease my experience is that a world of ease and pleasure is the stream in which we swim and that it makes fear, and unease, difficult, if not impossible to experience.

Like Postman, Mumford also referred to the amount of television American children watch and argued that this lessened human autonomy and the capacity for either critical thinking

who had recently featured on television programs. *Private Eye* 1066 1.11.02

55. Mumford, *The Pentagon of Power*, 169. He appealed to work on the "pleasure center" in the brain which, though no longer the focus of much media comment, has not been disconfirmed.

56. Streeck, *Buying Time*, 158. Crouch notes the way in which political language has changed and now models itself on advertising copy, which does not engage in rational argument, but seeks to persuade. *Post Democracy*, 26.

or for engaging with reality. Appealing to Milgram's famous experiment, he argued that this showed how effectively the blindly obedient response required of organization man had been built into the modern personality.[57]

Quite different from this, but likewise acting against any recognition of the problems of climate change, is the sense that the world is so taken for granted that massive changes, which might involve the end of human life on earth, are simply unimaginable.[58] This seems to be the "frog in the kettle" syndrome: the frog does not notice that the water is too hot until too late. Amongst the poor, meanwhile, whether in the rich world or amongst the one billion struggling to survive, Maslow's hierarchy of needs certainly kick in: the poor do not have time to worry about this because other worries are much more immediate.

Complacency of a different sort is manifested by those who believe, like Antony Giddens, that there is "no way back" from our high-tech present. Science and technology, he tells us, got us into this hole, and they will get us out of it.[59] Andrew Simms rightly describes this cohort as the "courtiers of Canute"—as if somehow our technological expertise puts us beyond reach of cultural collapse. This group believes we can deal with climate change by a mixture of appeal to the magic of the market, to the possibilities of increased energy efficiency, and geo-engineering. Giddens believes we should be seeking ways to deal with climate change through a mixture of taxes, "market mechanisms" (including derivatives and hedge funds), and business innovation. Unlike Emmott, who is actually working on such initiatives, he believes we are on the brink of a new technological revolution that will be able to stabilize emissions over the next fifty years. "The best way of keeping climate change policy in the forefront will be to work to keep it

57. Mumford, *Pentagon*, 279, 284.

58. Thus a farmer said to me, after a sermon in which I spoke about climate change: "You don't believe that do'ee? Us've seen it all before!" For him, running climate and weather together, it was simply nonsense to talk about the possibility of permanent climatic change.

59. Giddens, *The Politics of Climate Change*, 228.

THE WORLD MADE OTHERWISE: INTRODUCTION

at the cutting edge of economic competiveness, integrate it with wider political programmes and avoid empty moral posturing."[60] The sneer at "empty moral posturing" amounts to the refusal to admit to any alternative to the status quo—characteristic of many responses to the threat of climate change.

Dieter Helm's suggestions are likewise all based on current economic "realism." In a passage worthy of the Tea Party he argues that Green political proposals are radically egalitarian, authoritarian, go against the grain of human nature, and have not the slightest chance of being effected in the time period within which climate change needs to be cracked—if ever.[61] He agrees that ethics has its place, "But those ethics have to be grounded in resource allocation, demand and supply, and mediated through actual rather than ideal behaviour—in other words, in economics, although not determined by economics."[62] Ultimately self-interest rules. Though neither Giddens nor Helm are climate deniers, their proposed responses underwrite the policies of those who, overtly or by implication, most certainly are.

Tainter also thinks that we have allowed ourselves to become trapped in a competitive spiral from which we cannot escape. To opt for simpler societies would be as foolhardy as to opt for unilateral disarmament. "We simply do not have the option to return to a lower economic level, at least not a rational option. Peer polity competition drives increased complexity and resource consumption regardless of costs human or ecological."[63] This "no alternative" argument (a central tenet of neoliberalism, of course) contradicts the evidence of cultural collapse which he amasses throughout his book.

Kingsley Dennis and John Urry explore a hi-tech future, chiefly in regard to transport, and Roger Scruton pins his hopes partly on geo-engineering by the United States.[64] Dieter Helm

60. Ibid.,149.
61. Helm, *The Carbon Crunch*, 239.
62. Ibid., 67.
63. Tainter, *Collapse*, 214.
64. Dennis and Urry, *After the Car*; Urry, *Climate Change and Society.*

believes that we should be technological optimists: climate change is not an insuperable problem, and there is no shortage of potential energy. Developments over the past century give us every reason to hope that new sources of energy will be found, but it is an urgent matter to encourage research and development. His proposal is that every country ought to devote 0.5 percent of their GDP to a global climate mitigation R&D fund.[65]

To such arguments we have to object, first, that trying to deal with climate change through market mechanisms is trying to fight fire with fire, as I shall argue in more detail in chapter six. James Hansen objects that geo-engineering does not address ocean acidification problems and that sun shielding is more expensive and difficult than rational alternatives such as energy efficiency, renewable energy, and nuclear power.[66] The marine biologist Sally Chisholm notes that "proponents of research on geo-engineering simply keep ignoring the fact that the biosphere is a player (not just a responder) in whatever we do, and its trajectory cannot be predicted. It is a living breathing collection of organisms (mostly microorganisms) that are revolving every second—a 'self organising, complex, adaptive system' (strict term). These types of system have emergent properties and simply cannot be predicted. We all know this! Yet proponents of geo-engineering research leave that out of the discussion."[67] As James Kunstler remarks, "The idea of buying time until the tech demigods deliver a technology miracle is just another way of describing a cargo cult."[68] In fact, what the Stockholm paper outlines, in line with the earlier reports, are what John Greer calls predicaments rather than problems: a problem has a solution, a predicament does not.[69]

---

65. Helm, *Carbon Crunch*, 227, 244.

66. Hansen, *Storms of My Grandchildren*, 230.

67. Quoted in Klein, *This Changes Everything*, 267.

68. Kunstler, *Long Emergency*, 129. Tim Jackson agrees, arguing that "Simplistic assumptions that capitalism's propensity for efficiency will allow us to stabilize the climate or protect against resource scarcity are nothing short of delusional." *Prosperity Without Growth*, 86.

69. Greer, *The Long Descent*, 22.

The third group is different again. In his analysis of sin the Swiss theologian Karl Barth reads the traditional vice of sloth partly in terms of stupidity, which plays, he argues, "a leading role in world history." Stupidity is nothing to do with IQ. On the contrary, many very intelligent people might be profoundly stupid. Rather, it is "culpable relapse into self–contradiction; into incoherent, confused and corrupt thought and speech and action."[70] Hannah Arendt preferred not to talk of stupidity, but she traced much human evil to "not thinking." Nothing more is needed for disaster to happen, she argued, than to live in constant distraction and never to leave the company of others.[71]

This group is represented by the real climate deniers, those politicians and business leaders who, in the interests of profit, deny climate change and fund institutes and think tanks to challenge the findings of climate research. Naomi Klein documents them in the first chapter of *This Changes Everything*, but in the UK we can think of the dismissal of Green proposals as "a hindrance to business." We can also look at the popularity of *Top Gear*, a television program devoted to extolling fast, powerful cars and laddish behavior that takes a completely cynical view about the damage CO_2 emissions do to the planet. The program earns tens of millions of pounds and has 350 million viewers across the globe. A proposal to sack its popular presenter, Jeremy Clarkson, generated a million signatures in a few hours. And how else would we characterize Yale economist William Nordhaus's argument that climate has little economic impact upon advanced industrial societies because most people in "advanced societies" live in "carefully controlled environments" such as offices and shopping malls![72]

As Barth comments, "as one of the most remarkable forms of the demonic, stupidity has an astonishingly autonomous life against whose expansions and evolutions there is no adequate

70. Barth, *Church Dogmatics*, IV/2, 412. Franny Armstrong's 2009 film *The Age of Stupid* related this idea to climate change.

71. Arendt, *The Life of the Mind*, vol. 2, 80.

72. Nordhaus, "To curb or not to curb."

safeguard. It has rightly been said that even the gods are power-less in the face of it."[73]

But what are we to make of the Royal Dutch Shell "New Lenses" document of May 2015, which seems to anticipate a four-degrees rise in global temperature, with the possibility, given feedbacks, of rising to six degrees, in which case human life on the planet would be impossible? The CEO of Shell talks about the need to balance awareness of climate change with the need to provide energy for the poor of the world, but the company has just taken over the exploration arm of British Gas, in a move to boost growth. A spokeswoman said: "By combining BG's port-folio and skills set with Shell's capabilities we can deliver a step change in the growth priorities for both of our companies. This means more deep water and more LNG [liquefied natural gas] plays where we have strong profitability and capabilities." In the United States, the Union of Concerned Scientists has started a campaign against Shell over its continued involvement in the American Legislative Exchange Council (ALEC), a right-wing organization that has been criticized for drafting model legis-lation that denies any human contribution to climate change. Friends of the Earth in the Netherlands say of the CEO, "This is not an evil guy leading the world to destruction. He is just leading a company that is trying to find a way of maintaining this [fossil fuels] system."[74] The New Lenses document is written in corporate speak, but it shows some awareness of the realities of climate change. So how are we to read continued pursuit of growth (to meet the financial bottom line and keep shareholders happy)? If it is not ignorance is it cynicism? And how are we to understand Donald Trump's appointment of the heads of Exx-onMobil to head the US Environmental Protection Agency, and his proposal to cut funding to NASA's meteorological research unit—previously headed up by James Hansen? Is this stupidity? Or is it downright wickedness?

73. Barth, *Church Dogmatics*, IV/2, 414.

74. Terry Macalister, "The real story behind Shell's climate change rheto-ric," *The Guardian*, May 17, 2015.

The consequences of collapse

Were civilizational collapse to happen, what then? What would be the likely consequences? There is an extensive literature which discusses this, which proposes three possible scenarios: warlordism, authoritarian governmental response, and a reversion to simpler societies.

What climate scientists like Kevin Anderson and campaigners like Naomi Klein are concerned with is preventing collapse—bringing about present political, economic, and cultural changes to steer humanity off that course. Most of this book is concerned with that change. But suppose, as present political options seem to indicate, that collapse happens. What are the likely consequences? Tainter argues that collapse, which is recurrent in human history, involves a "sudden pronounced loss of an established level of socio-political complexity." Society becomes smaller, simpler, less stratified, and less socially differentiated.

> Specialization decreases and there is less centralized control. The flow of information drops, people trade and interact less, and there is overall lower coordination among individuals and groups. Economic activity drops to a commensurate level, while the arts and literature experience such a quantitative decline that a Dark Age often ensures. Population levels tend to drop and for those who are left the known world shrinks.[75]

Tainter here invokes the Dark Ages, and many commentators (most famously Cormac McCarthy in *The Road*) suspect that a new dark age of warlordism and anarchy might follow civilizational collapse. Emmott's play ends with the record of a conversation with a brilliant young scientist who works in his lab. If there was one thing you would do in the face of this situation what would it be?, he asks. The answer: "Teach my son to use a gun."[76]

It is currently fashionable to deny that the Dark Ages were truly "dark" but the French historian Jacques le Goff notes that in

75. Tainter, *Collapse*, 193.
76. Emmott, *10 Billion*, 198.

seventh-century Europe there was a decline in skills, and no one knew how to quarry, transport or work stone, or make glass. "Artistic taste underwent a regress, and so did morals . . . Not only did the old stock of peasant superstitions re-emerge, but all the sexual perversions ran riot and acts of violence turned nastier." Torture became worse. Structures of law broke down and, according to a contemporary, Gregory of Tours, "each saw justice in his own will."[77] Many suggest that after collapse conditions similar to those which Colin Turnbull claimed he found amongst the Ik, after they were moved from their traditional lands, would prevail. Only the strong survive, the weak are victimized, robbed, and killed.[78]

In parts of the world, and not only in Somalia, Syria, and Iraq, this is already a reality. Roberto Saviano, whose work on the Naples mafia, the Camorra, has driven him into hiding, says that in this part of Italy "cruelty is the most complex and affordable strategy for becoming a successful businessman."[79] It is, he says, an extreme form of neoliberalism. The Camorra define themselves as businessmen but each have their own armed band, and they kill without mercy. This is more or less the world that another Italian, the computer scientist Roberto Vacca, predicted forty years ago.[80]

Reversing the traditional argument, Diamond argues that moral collapse follows economic collapse.

> Today, just as in the past, countries that are environmentally stressed, overpopulated, or both, become at risk of getting politically stressed, and of their governments collapsing. When people are desperate, undernourished, and without hope, they blame their

77. Le Goff, *Medieval Civilization*, 33.

78. Turnbull, *The Mountain People*. Since the book was published other anthropologists have challenged his findings.

79. Saviano, *Gomorrah*, 46

80. Vacca, *The Coming Dark Age*. The increasing attacks on environmental activists around the world, often resulting in murder, may well presage the direction in which societies all around the world are moving. The driver of this violence is the protection of wealth and privilege. Jonathan Watts and John Vidal, "Environmental defenders killed in record numbers," *Guardian Weekly* July 28, 2017.

governments, which they see as responsible . . . They try to emigrate at any cost. They fight each other over land. They kill each other. They start civil wars . . . The best predictors of modern "state failures"—i.e. revolutions, violent regime change, collapse of authority, and genocide—prove to be measures of environmental and population pressure, such as high infant mortality, rapid population growth, a high percentage of the population in their late teens and twenties.[81]

Already, governments in the wealthy world are spending huge amounts of money on keeping immigrants out, and far right parties with ideologies of exclusion are on the rise.

This suggests a second possible scenario, namely the emergence of strong but illiberal states. "In richer countries, consumer led economic growth falters or is actively shut down by government policies to focus limited resources on food, fuel and climate security."[82] A more liberal alternative is "Environmental Keynesianism" in which a strong central government transforms societal infrastructure using an inclusive strategy that entails economic redistribution and the fostering of a culture of democracy. The consumer society would be abandoned, and there would be a wartime ethic with everyone working for the common good. Another option is suggested by the film *Children of Men*. Here we have a picture of strict government control, carbon rationing, immigrants kept out, and tight centrally planned forms of production and consumption. This has been described as a khaki green state, an ecological version of Hobbes's *Leviathan*.[83]

A third group thinks of reversion to simpler and more local societies that, according to Tainter, are the historical norm.[84]

---

81. Diamond, *Collapse*, 516. The struggle for a Tuareg homeland, crushed partly by France and partly by Al Qaeda, is driven in large part by climate change. Here as elsewhere climate change is a progenitor of widespread violence. http://www.aljazeera.com/programmes/orphans-of-the-sahara/2014/01/orphans-sahara-rebellion-20141810554727702.html.

82. Holmgren, *Future Scenarios*, 64.

83. Chatterton and Cutler, *The Rocky Road to Real Transition*, 38.

84. Tainter, *Collapse*, 24.

Reversion to such a society is a frequent theme in the literature of collapse. Kingsley Dennis and John Urry believe that "Eco communalism might emerge from breakdown. Under conditions of reduced population and rupture in modern institutions a network of societies guided by a small is beautiful philosophy conceivably could arise."[85] Richard Duncan argues that millennia of low-tech cultures *preceding* the industrial pulse will be balanced by millennia of low-tech cultures *after* the industrial pulse. Continental governments like the US will come apart to be replaced by regional or local governments.[86] Richard Heinberg believes that if national structures broke down some kind of decentralized bioregionalism might take its place.[87] The salient fact about life in the decades ahead, James Kunstler argues, is that it will become increasingly and intensely local and smaller in scale. It will do so steadily and by degrees as the amount of cheap energy decreases and the global contest for it becomes more intense.[88] John Greer believes that the best we can hope for is for some individuals, groups, and communities to do what they can to preserve essential culture and practical knowledge for the future out of which a new culture, or cultures, will emerge.[89] This recalls the famous closing paragraph of *After Virtue*, in which Alasdair MacIntyre talks of "the construction of local forms of community within which civility and the intellectual and moral life can be sustained through the new dark ages which are already upon us."

> A crucial turning point in that earlier history occurred when men and women of good will turned aside from the task of shoring up the Roman imperium and ceased to identify the continuation of civility and moral community with the maintenance of that imperium. What they set themselves to achieve instead—often not recognizing fully what they were doing—was the

85. Dennis and Urry, *After the Car,* 149.
86. Cited by Greer, *Long Descent,* 34
87. R. Heinberg, Muse Letter #186, October 2007.
88. Kunstler, *Long Emergency,* 239
89. Greer, *Long Descent,* 30

construction of new forms of community within which the moral life could be sustained so that both morality and civility might survive the coming age of barbarism and darkness . . . What matters at this stage is the construction of local forms of community within which civility and the intellectual and moral life can be sustained through the new dark ages which are already upon us. And if the tradition of the virtues was able to survive the horrors of the last dark ages, we are not entirely without grounds for hope.[90]

Three years later, and certainly completely independently, Rudolf Bahro made the same suggestion: we need, he said, a new Benedictine order. Like the first one it will come into being by people relating to "God."[91] Bahro was a deviant Marxist (expelled from East Germany, after being imprisoned for writing "The Alternative in Eastern Europe," in 1979), and a heretical Green, who left the German Green Party because of its compromises with the market system. He was no orthodox believer. But his attempt to find a workable response to what he called, following E. P. Thompson, "exterminism," led him to religion and talk of God.

Religion as a response to collapse

Do we really need to talk about God? Some argue that it is more likely that crisis will generate widespread anger, fear, conflict, and a deepening paranoia than a spiritual awakening and ecological reckoning. Crises, it has been argued, tend to erode democratic impulses and structures and produce dictatorial regimes.[92] However, Bahro is not alone in his appeal to religion and indeed both

90. MacIntyre, *After Virtue,* 263. Macintyre is concerned with what he takes to be the collapse of moral agreement in Western society but his analysis of character types shows that he grounds his analysis in an account of society. *After Virtue* is therefore an essay in moral philosophy grounded in social analysis. That analysis can be questioned but my previous argument is designed to show that social collapse may well be in the cards.

91. Bahro, *Building the Green Movement,* 90.

92. Maniates, "Teaching for turbulence," 264.

Gandhi and Martin Luther King, Jr. grounded their successful social movements in religion. David Holmgren thinks a renewed civic culture might be built on the basis of a transition towards a non-materialistic society combined with a resurgence in indigenous and traditional cultural values and the evolution of more spiritual "cultures of place."[93] Noting that Toynbee spoke of the downslope of civilizations as the great incubator of religious movements, Greer suggests that "the religious dimension will very likely play a massive role in the way that people adapt or fail to adapt to the world of harsh limits and harsher choices that the missed opportunities of recent decades have made inevitable."[94] Kunstler believes that the survivors of cultural collapse will have to cultivate a religion of hope, that is, "a deep and comprehensive belief that humanity is worth carrying on . . . I don't doubt that the hardships of the future will draw even the most secular spirits into an emergent spiritual practice of some kind."[95] He thinks that the Christian church may be one of the corporate organizations that survives, though Bahro's comment on a similar suggestion is, "Last chance for an established Christianity?! I'm sceptical."[96]

He has every reason to be sceptical. As Wendell Berry comments in relation to economic thinking, organized Christianity exists as "a respecter and comforter of profitable iniquities."[97] Organized religion, said Saul Alinsky, is materialistically solvent but spiritually bankrupt. He agreed with Harold Laski that the Christian ethic had accommodated itself to slavery at its ugliest, to capitalism in its most ruthless form, to every war that has been waged since Constantine made Christianity the official religion of empire—and, we have to say, continues to do so.[98] And if we look elsewhere, we find the State of Israel (which does not represent all Jews, or even all Israelis, but exists to offer a refuge to all Jews) is

93. Holmgren, *Future Scenarios*, 73.

94. Greer, *Long Descent*, 219.

95. Kunstler, *Long Emergency*, 21.

96. Bahro, *Avoiding Social and Ecological Disaster*, 68.

97. Berry, *Sex, Economy, Freedom and Community*, 100.

98. Alinsky, *Reveille for Radicals*, 201.

forced to defend a chauvinistic imperialism in Palestine, reducing Gaza to a concentration camp, periodically bombed to rubble, and the Muslim world rife with a nihilistic terrorism in the name of God, "the Compassionate, the Merciful." Even Buddhism does not have clean hands: Buddhist monks egged on savage ethnic cleansing in Sri Lanka and the Rohinga have been driven out of Myanmar. In India Hindu chauvinists murder people suspected of eating beef, as well as both Muslims and Christians, in the name of a belief—which would have appalled Gandhi—that India is only for Hindus. Any rationalist is well within their rights to dismiss a resort to religion as regressive nonsense.[99] Nevertheless, I believe Bahro is right that the life-germ of a different social order is spiritual, not economic. The idea of God, he says, is the essential starting point for a politics of salvation.[100] "The last chance for our existence and emancipation lies in our being able to free ourselves from the patterns of the old culture, and to risk again an appeal to the Godhead."[101] Mumford agreed: If humankind is to escape its programmed self-extinction, he argued, the God who saves us will not descend from the machine: he will rise up again in the human soul.[102]

Let me briefly explore this idea. First of all, we shall repeatedly come across suggestions in this book, like those already mentioned by Antony Giddens and Dieter Helm, which amount to rearranging the deck chairs on the Titanic. Tweaking the market system, reforming parliamentary democracies, hoping for a new technological breakthrough, will get us nowhere because the

99. The sharpest critique, it should be said, comes from faith. Buber says, "There is nothing so apt to obscure the face of God as a religion." *A Believing Humanism*, 115. According to Barth, "the deeper we go into the land of religion, the deeper we go into the land of the shadow of death." *The Epistle to the Romans*, 2nd ed., 276.

100. Bahro, *Avoiding Social and Ecological Disaster*, 16. Aloysius Pieris says, quite rightly, that every religion, including Christianity, is at once a sign and a countersign of the kingdom of God, a potential means of either emancipation or enslavement. *An Asian Theology of Liberation*, 88.

101. Bahro, *Avoiding Social and Ecological Disaster*, 304.

102. Mumford, *Pentagon of Power*, 413.

analysis of why we got into the present position in the first place is nowhere near radical enough. Old patterns of domination are simply reproduced. Bahro argued that the demands of an average consumer lifestyle (and this was in the 1980s!) were more dangerous than nuclear power stations and dioxins because "in face of monstrous differences in standards" such a lifestyle is a threatened luxury.[103]

Bahro learned from both E. P. Thompson and from Lewis Mumford, who coined the term "megamachine" to talk about the way in which human labor was organized for vast tasks, such as pyramid building, which meant that the prospect of a life without limits became possible.[104] In the modern version of the megamachine people are materially satisfied, but they stop deciding and thinking for themselves. Politics becomes entertainment. This organization of society structures human consciousness in violent and oppressive ways and underlies the whole technological and economic global culture.

Bahro argues, therefore, that fundamental change is needed at the spiritual level, at the level of values, and this is where the idea of "God" comes in. The Dutch biblical scholar Ton Veerkamp suggests that what we mean by the word "God" is whatever it is that provides the fundamental justification for rights of ownership, but we can extend this to include the fundamental narrative of order, of sense-making, in any given society. To speak of "God" is to speak of the foundational order of any society—and this includes the neoliberal global order. The question is not whether or not there is a God, for there is always a God in this sense. The question, rather, is how we understand "God." Is "God" the one who represents the politically and economically strong (as, for example "God" clearly is in the Anglican Book of Common Prayer) or YHWH, who frees people from the house of slavery and protects the weak?[105] The name YHWH, Veerkamp argues (and later he wants to follow Miskotte and the Synagogue and speak simply

---

103. Bahro, *Avoiding Social and Ecological Disaster*, 92.

104. Mumford, *The Myth of the Machine*, 206.

105. Veerkamp, *Autonomie & Egalität*, 101.

of The NAME), stood for a social order that contradicted the order of all the societies around, which were all based on exploitation and slavery. In this case the foundational order underwritten by the idea of "God" is a world made otherwise. The idea of God, I shall argue, functions either to reinforce or to resist prevailing hegemonies.[106]

Martin Luther already raised the question of what the word "God" signifies in his *Large Catechism*. Commenting on the first commandment he noted that "the faith of the heart makes both God and idol." He went on: "A God is that to which we look for all good and in which we find refuge in every time of need . . . Many a person thinks he has God and everything he needs when he has money and property; in them he trusts and of them he boasts so stubbornly and securely that he cares for no one. Surely such a man also has a god—mammon by name, that is, money and possessions—on which he fixes his whole heart. It is the most common idol on earth."[107]

Nowhere is this more true than in the contemporary affluent world, classically expressed by the notorious article of Victor Lebow in 1955:

> Our enormously productive economy . . . demands that we make consumption our way of life, that we convert the buying and use of goods into rituals, that we seek out spiritual satisfaction, our ego satisfaction, in consumption . . . We need things consumed, burned up, worn out, replaced and discarded at an ever increasing rate.[108]

Ultimately, Bahro wants to argue, it is this that lies behind exterminism. To survive, he argues, we need a fundamental reorientation of values, or, we can also say, a fundamental change in our idea of "God" (whether we believe this being exists or not). Veerkamp's account of "God" is purely Durkheimian: it does not presuppose any Being who exists beyond the created order. It is,

---

106. I argue this, in relation to Karl Barth, in *Karl Barth: Against Hegemony*.

107. Luther, *The Large Catechism*, 11.

108. Lebow, "Price Competition in 1955," 7.

in Norman Gottwald's phrase, a "socio-servo mechanism." But we can recognize the way the idea of God functions ideologically without concluding to atheism. Whichever way we use the word "God"—whether we believe that God exists or not—we are speaking of the origin and image of the values we live by. (Would that the faith of those who believe in the Triune God was as much in evidence as those who believe in the god of the market!) What marks the difference between God and idol, in this sense, is not the existence or non-existence of God so much as whether the understanding of God leads to life or death: in the biblical narratives, at any rate, death-dealing practices are always characterized in terms of idolatry. The "God" who is mentioned on the dollar bill was believed to be life giving for 200 years, and particularly for the last eighty. People pointed to rising standards of living: better food—for some, better medical care—for some, better housing—for some, and the claim was that this would be generalized, that a rising tide would lift all boats. But, in a savage irony, a literal rising tide is now eliminating Pacific communities, and is set to eliminate cities and harbors all around the world. Ultimately, it turns out, this "God" delivers death and not life. We need another account of God therefore, and this is what Bahro is asking for.

Bahro sought transformation through meditation and community living, drawing especially on Hindu and Taoist thought. What was needed, he believed, was a critical mass of integrated individuals. "No order can save us which simply limits the excesses of our greed. Only spiritual mastery of the greed itself can help us. It is perhaps only the Prophets and Buddhas, whether or not their answers were perfect, who have at least put the question radically enough."[109] But, we can ask, do Bahro's suggestions remain too individualistic? How are they to be understood in terms of the ongoing narratives that inform all cultures? On the one hand, we face, as Emmott insists, an unprecedented planetary emergency, which affects everybody, in every culture and creed. That means that narrow appeals to one particular faith tradition simply will not do. At the same time the relativism of

109. Bahro, *Avoiding Social and Ecological Disaster*, 25.

the postmodern West, which is the bad conscience of the global market, is no help. On the other hand, the narratives that inform our lives cannot be replaced, as the Enlightenment imagined, with generalizing appeals to ethics or principles: these, too, do not go deep enough. Some way has to be found to speak cogently to the whole human community, at a foundational depth (the depth represented by the word "God") whilst understanding that there is no getting around particularity, specific histories, and, indeed, the question of what is or is not true. What is needed is the kind of believing humanism Buber outlined, which is prepared to listen to other traditions, to learn from them, and to live in friendship and charity whilst at the same time celebrating and affirming the insights at the heart of its own tradition.

If we appeal to "God" (whether existent or not) this compels us to revisit some seemingly abstruse medieval theological controversies that have profound contemporary consequences. Both Christianity and Islam debated whether God engages with that which is not God through reason or through will. In Islam Ibn Sina (980–1077), known to the West as Avicenna, and Ibn Rushd (1126–1198) (Averroes) both expounded the idea of God drawing on Aristotle, and thus they put reason first, and this laid the foundation for work in mathematics, medicine, architecture and other sciences. They were opposed by Al Ghazali (1058–1111) who laid all the emphasis on God's omnipotence and will. A similar opposition was found in Christianity in the thirteenth century, between Thomas Aquinas and Duns Scotus. In Christianity, Thomism prevailed. Though this too became a dogma that obstructed scientific advance, in the seventeenth century, it also understood reality as rational and therefore open to rational exploration and this conviction made possible the scientific revolution of the seventeenth century onwards. In Islam, however, Al Ghazali, and the Ash'arite school, prevailed. This led, Robert Reilly has argued, to "the closing of the Muslim mind." To take three examples: first, it ruled out discussion in terms of cause and effect. The Pakistani physicist Pervez Hoodbhoy writes about the Islamization of science textbooks in which effect must not be related to physical cause, for to do so leads towards atheism.[110] Between 1983 and 1984 weather forecasts were suspended in Pakistan on the grounds that it is God's will that causes changes in the weather. After the 2005 earthquake, in which 90,000 people died, Mullahs interpreted it as God's wrath on a sinful nation and urged people to smash television sets. The result has been, as the UN Arab Development Report has highlighted year after year, that there is a huge knowledge gap in the Muslim peoples, which feeds their frustration and heightens their rage.

Second, this position makes moral reasoning impossible. What is right is what God wills: God does not will it because it is right. Al-Ghazali writes: no obligations flow from reason but from the shari'a.[111] A theologian like Karl Barth has a command ethic which is superficially similar to mainstream Islam's. He, too, believes ethics is rooted in the sacred text, and in what we learn of Jesus and the first disciples. The key differences are, first, that Barth's understanding of God is as "the One who loves in freedom." It is not will that is primary but a narrative of love in freedom and freedom in love which human beings are called to enter into. Second, the hermeneutical process of engaging with the Scriptures is quite different: hermeneutics is the task of the whole community, past and present, and involves a repeated listening and questioning. Scripture is not itself the Word of God, but the witness to the Word. For Barth, and for Christians more generally, the Word is Jesus of Nazareth, a life which cannot be reduced to a system but that invites continuous exploration.

Third, this has profound implications for politics. As Reilly puts it, if God is force then force becomes one's God. Within this view, power becomes self-legitimating. It is no accident that the embraced view of a tyrannical God produces tyrannical political orders. "The rule of power is a natural, logical outcome of a voluntaristic theology that invests God's shadow on earth—the Caliph or ruler—with an analogous force based on God's will. Within the voluntaristic outlook, man's only responsibility is to

---

110. Reilly, *The Closing of the Muslim Mind,* 67.
111. Ibid., 69.

obey."[112] Hobbes's belief that "the general inclination of mankind is a perpetual desire of power after power" followed from an account of power as ultimate. The pursuit of power, he said, "ceaseth only in death" and, as Robert Bellah comments, "if power is our only end, the death in question may not be merely personal but civilizational."[113] Much theistic belief—Muslim and Christian— tacitly deifies power in itself. There is little understanding that the view of God revealed, for example, in Scripture constitutes an outright challenge to all such ideas.

The idea of God is also closely bound up with identity. Hendrik Kraemer, the Dutch scholar of Islam, wrote in 1928 that he considered Islam to be "deified group solidarity." But in fact it is not only Islam of which this is true: it may apply to States, cultures, sects, religions, even football teams! It is an important warning, however (which we could also draw from the seventeenth-century religious wars in Europe, or from aspects of the conflict in Northern Ireland), that "God," especially an idea of God for which we are prepared to kill, may be an idolatrous projection of our own group identity. The State, country, class, wrote Julien Benda in 1927, "are now frankly God; we may even say that for many people (and some are proud of it) they alone are God."[114]

The idea of God stands for the ultimate source of value, often understood in a purely idealist way. But values are only actualized in practices: there is a dialectic between values and practices, about which I shall say more in the next chapter. This means that our ideas of what is ultimate, "God," are reflected in political and economic structures, and conversely these structures make clear what we really believe in, as Luther said. It follows from this that changing values is crucial to transformational politics, and this goes beyond changing individual priorities.[115]

112. Ibid., 131.

113. Bellah et al., *Habits of the Heart*, 295.

114. Benda, *The Treason of the Intellectuals*, 24

115. Webb, "Society Matters." Leonard points out that "people may decrease one environmentally destructive behaviour with good intentions, only to offset the gains by increasing a different and more destructive activity.

The relation between values and practices is what this book sets out to explore. I have outlined the warnings of Kevin Anderson, James Hansen, and many others, that if we continue on the same economic and political path we are following at present disaster—in the shape of civilizational collapse—is inevitable. What might avert this are the transformational values which, as Naomi Klein, Gustavo Esteva and many others recognize, are already to be found in social movements such as Transition Towns, Via Campesina, People's Organisations, and in hundreds of other similar initiatives around the world. The profound changes we need to see in order that a constructive and not a destructive future can be realized begin bottom up, and all involve radical value change. Unlike Helm I do not believe these changes are counter to human nature, or that they are impossible. Rather, I accept the mantra of the Transition movement:

If we wait for governments it will be too little too late

If we act as individuals it will be too little

If we act as communities it might be just enough, just in time.

Following this introductory chapter, which has sought to persuade readers of the seriousness of the problem, the book has three parts. The first part consists of two chapters on values and virtues. "Values" are everywhere, but what we mean by values is rarely clarified. It is rarely pointed out, for example, that there are not only values but disvalues, and that these latter can wreck whole cultures and may threaten the planet. Following Schweitzer and others, I argue that "life" is the foundational value but throughout the book I seek to understand what values and disvalues are in play in different political and economic systems, and to urge the values which "make for life."

Framing environmental deterioration as a result of poor individual choices removes these issues from the political realm to the personal, implying that the solution is in our personal choices rather than better policies, business practices, the structural context. The missing ingredient is not more information or more individual eco-perfectionists, it is collective engagement for political and structural change." "Moving from individual change to societal change," 251.

In the current discussion values and virtues are often opposed. What we need, we are told, are not values but virtues. I argue, to the contrary, in the third chapter, that virtues instantiate, or realize, virtues and I agree with the virtue ethicists of the past forty years that the tradition of the virtues is probably the best chance we have of furthering our humanity, of saving ourselves from disaster.

Values and virtues do not exist in the abstract, but are realized in practices. It is Alasdair MacIntyre who has introduced the notion of "practice" into ethical discussion. I have learned from him, but I extend his account of practices to include fundamental political and economic realities. The second section of the book deals with these "practices" and in each chapter I will ask what values and virtues these practices instantiate. In the fourth chapter I ask what kind of polity we should be aiming for in an increasingly dangerous world. There are resurgent nationalisms, new nationalisms, but also new imperialisms—new and noisy claims to provide the narrative of the world. Amidst all these I argue that a world of small, independent but federated states would give us the best chance of addressing climate change, and that the political conditions for such a world are at hand, though of course threatened by the nationalisms and imperialisms I have mentioned.

When it comes to the political organization of these states, "democracy" is still widely applauded but everywhere new authoritarianisms are on the rise. Democracy, as we know it today, is a very recent concept, but also not in especially good health. I argue, in the fifth chapter, that new forms and practices of democracy are essential if we are to address climate change realistically.

In chapters six and seven I address economic issues. The currently hegemonic economic model, neoliberalism, threatens democracy, and it constitutes, in my judgement, the single most serious threat to our planetary future. Establishing a different kind of economy, built on different values, is therefore imperative. This is the theme of chapter six.

Under neoliberalism industrial capitalism is replaced by finance capital, what the German economist Karl Heinz Brodbeck calls "the rule of money." Many anthropologists, but also theologians, have already called for money to be re-thought. Money, I argue, is a social convention, and can therefore be changed. How this could happen, in what direction, and how the value signified by money relates to more fundamental values, is the theme of chapter seven.

For Adam Smith agriculture was a primary part of economics. Today "agricultural economics" is a niche discipline. However, as I have argued in this chapter, if what Anderson, Hansen, and others argue is correct then famine will be the principal immediate threat to the human future. The production of food is therefore a crucial question that is not the concern just of farmers and the farming unions. Like everything else farming rests on values and the contest of values is perhaps nowhere so apparent as in farming. This is the theme of chapter eight.

In each of the chapters on practices one value or virtue is especially highlighted: freedom in chapter four, on the state; equality, in chapter five, on democracy; justice in chapter six, on the economy; mutual aid or solidarity in chapter seven, on money; and gratitude in chapter eight, on farming.

The final part of the book is called "Transition." The word is taken from the Transition movement, but the transition appealed to, and which is underway worldwide, goes far beyond that. I follow up Brad Werner and Naomi Klein's suggestion that social movements, and people's organizations, offer us the best hope of realising a different, sustainable, and truly human future. I end, however, with the question of what to do if, as seems likely today, "business as usual" prevails. In that case I think the Benedictine communities which both MacIntyre and Bahro invoked may have something to offer "in keeping the lamps of civilization alive in the new dark ages." But I turn now to the question of values.

VALUES
and
VIRTUES

Chapter Two

Value, Life, and Politics

The struggle to establish how value is to be defined is the heart of politics.

—David Graeber

In the previous chapter I argued that there are two tasks arising from what Emmott calls the "unprecedented planetary emergency" with which we are currently faced: one is to find ways of avoiding runaway climate change. This is primarily a political task, but politics and economics, I shall argue, ultimately rest on values. The other is to think how our humanity can survive if we fail to act now (and Kevin Anderson has said that a four-degree rise is incompatible with civilized life). I am approaching these two questions through the idea of value, and I ask first whether the language of values is coherent.

Questioning values

In our culture "values" are constantly invoked: United States Presidents go to war in defense of "Western and democratic values"; Asian dictators argue that democracy is not consistent with "Asian values." Terrorist outrages are routinely described in terms of a contest of values.[1] Politicians announce inquiries to see whether

1. In 2015 the reaction to the Charlie Hebdo murders was characterized in

shari'a law is compatible with "Western values." In his final speech as President, Barack Obama said he would continue to maintain "American values," but his successor claims to be doing just the same—though with diametrically opposite policies. Angela Merkel of Germany is described as the defender of "liberal and progressive values" over against the rise of insular nationalism. Right-wing politicians tell us they stand up for "family values."[2] Manufacturers of cakes and biscuits tell us their products show that they adhere to "traditional values." Leading charities join in common cause to make sure they appeal to values that promote empathy rather than competition and greed.[3] Social movement activists are concerned to reformulate their values in order to communicate more effectively with the sectors they wish to mobilize.[4]

The looseness with which the term *values* is used goes some way to explain the hostility of contemporary philosophy to this language, a hostility all the more ironic given the intense philosophical discussion of value from the mid-nineteenth to the mid-twentieth century, when "axiology" was cried up as a major new branch of philosophy. Today that discussion is almost entirely forgotten, replaced by a crude psychological and sociological determinism that confidently assigns values, "on empirical grounds," to "intrinsic" or "extrinsic" determinations, depending on the individual's response to the perceptions of others.[5]

Another reason for philosophical hostility to the concept of value is that many follow Hannah Arendt in assuming that the language of value derives from economics. Value belongs to the realm of exchange, she argues, and is necessarily alienating, as it reduces everything to a commodity. "Universal relativity, that a thing exists

---

terms of a contest between different values and the "Je suis Charlie" protests were said to stand for freedom of expression against those who deny that. After the November killings President Obama spoke of Paris as "symbolizing the values of progress." In 2017 the attack at Westminster was described in the House of Commons as "an attack on our values."

2. So F. Fillon in 2016 in France.

3. Crompton, *Common Cause.*

4. Della Porta and Diani, *Social Movements,* 68.

5. As in Crompton, *Common Cause.*

only in relation to other things, and loss of intrinsic worth, that nothing any longer possesses an 'objective' value independent of the ever changing estimations of supply and demand are inherent in the very concept of value itself."[6]

Charles Taylor makes the same complaint from another direction, arguing that "the relatively colourless language of values" tends to imply moral relativism because values language follows from the fact that no non-anthropocentric good, indeed nothing outside subjective goods, can be allowed to trump self-realization.[7] Taylor may be drawing on the work of Robert Bellah and his fellow researchers some years earlier, who found that practically everyone spoke about values, but what this meant was preferences. The language of values is self-contradictory, they argued, precisely because it is not a language of value, or moral choice. "It pursues the existence of an absolutely empty unencumbered and improvisational self. It obscures personal reality and social reality and particularly the moral reality that links persons and society."[8] Values "turn out to be the incomprehensible, rationally indefensible thing that the individual chooses when he or she has thrown off the last vestige of external influence and reached pure, contentless freedom . . . The improvisational self chooses values to express itself; but it is not constituted by them as from a pre-existing source."[9] The emptiness of values language is illustrated by Kristen Monroe's comment that in her interviews with those who rescued Jews and those who just stood by during the Third Reich, an unrepentant former Nazi, wife of the former head of the Dutch Nazi party, was the one who used the term *value* or *values* most frequently.[10] As she notes, what this

6. Arendt, *The Human Condition*, 166.

7. Taylor, *Sources of the Self*, 507. Cf. Gertrude Himmelfarb: "Values brought with it the assumptions that all moral ideas are subjective and relative, that they are mere customs and conventions, that they have a purely instrumental, utilitarian purpose and that they are peculiar to specific individuals and societies." *The De-Moralization of Society*, 11.

8. Bellah et al., *Habits of the Heart*, 79.

9. Ibid.

10. Monroe, "Cracking the Code of Genocide."

THE WORLD MADE OTHERWISE: VALUES AND VIRTUES

means is that it is not enough to talk about values in the abstract: we need to know the content of such values.[11]

Norbert Elias's study *The Civilizing Process* calls the language of values into question in another way. It traces the growth of a "pacified social space," in Europe, which gradually diminishes the delight people take in cruelty. The book was first published in Germany in 1939; the 1968 edition is dedicated to the memory of his parents, both of whom died at the hands of the Nazis, one in Auschwitz. The German state had a monopoly of force. It prided itself on its culture; it had the most distinguished musical tradition in Europe, arguably the best universities, the greatest philosophical tradition. There was a church in every village, and often two. It ought to have been a "pacified social space," but all this was turned upside down in a couple of years into a demonic parody of any civilizing process. We learn in this collapse, says Zygmunt Bauman, that "there is no moral-ethical limit which the state cannot transcend if it wishes to do so, because there is no moral-ethical power higher than the state."[12] But it is not just "the state" which can collapse in this way. The possibility for whole cultures to suffer moral collapse has been seen again in Cambodia and Rwanda, and today with Isis, and Boko Haram and their associated groups. It is in the very nature of things human, wrote Hannah Arendt, that every act that has once made its appearance and has been recorded in the history of mankind stays with mankind as a potentiality long after its actuality has become a thing of the past.[13] So where does this leave the language of value?

The social origin of values

The problem with much of the discussion of values in the first half of the twentieth century is that it did not make clear in what way values went beyond the subjective (nor indeed did it address

11. Ibid., 722

12. Bauman, *Modernity and the Holocaust*, 86.

13. Arendt, *Eichmann in Jerusalem*, 273.

Hannah Arendt's point that the language of value was rooted in commodification). That "values" mean "preferences" is an example of the "emotivism" that MacIntyre argues replaces the reasoned approach to ethics which characterised European thought from the fifth century BC to the eighteenth century AD.[14] MacIntyre seeks to reclaim the tradition of the virtues, in which I follow him, but I first want to outline an earlier attempt to give objective status to values by grounding them in social process. Thirty years before MacIntyre, John Findlay, who studied with, and translated, Husserl, proposed a phenomenology of value that begins with an analysis of consciousness, including belief, action, and willing. He took from Brentano the idea that consciousness is always directed to an object, whether physical, conceptual, or imaginary. The subtext of his argument is a deep disagreement with twentieth-century British empiricism and emotivism, and especially the ideas of G. E. Moore. Challenging the empiricist consensus since Hume, he argued for the intimate connection between epistemology and moral philosophy. If the former is inadequate, he suggests, the latter will also be. The poverty of much twentieth-century moral philosophy, on his account, owes much to the continuance of the supposed fact-value distinction, a distinction that plays a particularly crucial role in economic thought. Consciousness, the phenomenologists want to argue, is a much broader category than cognition, and is never a purely individual affair. On the contrary, consciousness is necessarily social, or as Findlay puts it, communicative. As human beings, he argues, we have on the one hand a tendency to impose our conscious orientation on others and on the other hand to conform our orientations to theirs. By either route we achieve the characteristic goal of consciousness, "*the having of an object which is more of an object because it is an object for many or for all.*"[15] "Mind is nothing if not a viewing of things in lights that are general, which extend themselves naturally to ever further cases, and the thought of things in an explicitly universal perspective."[16] This

14. In *After Virtue*, chs. 2 and 3.

15. Findlay, *Values and Intentions*, 88 (my italics).

16. Ibid., 92.

is another way of saying, what we would today take for granted on sociological grounds, that our knowing is culturally shaped.[17] It is true that the epistemology of Brentano and Husserl is by no means taken for granted but that knowledge is a social and not a primarily individual thing follows from any concession to the social construction of reality or the acknowledgement of the cultural blindfolds involved in all knowing.[18]

In an account of how values arise, Findlay argues that the objects of consciousness, those things diversely present to mind, are then articulated in explicitly entertained opinions, judgements, and beliefs. Knowledge, we can say, involves judgements of many kinds ("this is real"; "that is dangerous"; "that is beautiful" and so forth). Our consciousness is from the start structured by wants and these, for both an individual and a community, are "smoothed, polished and fitted together to construct a firmament of values and disvalues."[19] If this is the case then the objection that values are "merely subjective and relative" fails. They may be *culturally* relative but they are not relative from person to person. However, Findlay goes further in distinguishing (following Hume) between warm blooded and cold blooded wanting. There is elementary wanting, the wanting of the infant: I need food now! But, "It is of all distinctively human properties the most amazing and most rich in consequence that we can plan meals without being hungry, can buy pictures without being aesthetically stirred, can marry suitably without being ruttish on heat, and can consult our own good and that of our neighbours while stirred by neither fear nor love."[20] This is "cool choice," and it is the "reasons" by which our cool choice is guided that build up "a relatively fixed"

17. I shall revisit this in chapter 7, setting out Karl Heniz Brodbeck's account of money as a form of socialization.

18. Thus, for example, Leonardo made mistakes in his anatomical drawings because his reading of Galen led him to see things which were not there. Gombrich, *Art and Illusion*, 72.

19. Findlay, *Values and Intentions*, 159.

20. Ibid., 182.

firmament of values that are our reasons for choice and action.[21]
"Our 'values,'" says Findlay, "are the relatively fixed points of the
compass by means of which our choices are guided."[22] Findlay
speak of "drifts of consciousness," a drift towards the impersonal
that has its roots in the detachment from particular interests, a
tendency towards more and more open universality of attitude,
and towards the elimination of arbitrary kinds of interest, for
specific persons or classes of person etc. These "drifts" are not
individual but social. The process resembles Durkheim's account
of the establishment of law, which represents the collective consciousness of a particular culture. In effect a canon is established
by means of repeated comparison. This is a societal matter: "The
fixation of values depends supremely on the continued effort to
communicate our wants to others and to receive the impress of
theirs."[23] It is this process, according to Findlay, which establishes
moral values. In effect Findlay is arguing that over the millennia
values are rationally honed: they are neither purely subjective nor
the product of commodification. Their roots are in desire, but in
desire as apprised and tested, "emotion recollected in tranquillity."
They may begin with feelings and preferences but the process of
comparison and rational criticism is what gives us the field of values, which transcend such preferences. We can see this process in
action in the evolution of the law codes of the Ancient Near East,
and the way these are rethought in the teachings of Jesus.[24]

Findlay argues that our judgements necessarily tend to universality: "To love even fishing enthusiastically is to demand that
others should share this love, and to feel that only inexperience,
prejudice or perversity can prevent them from doing so. To be
measure setting, magisterial is . . . a feature of all our valuations."[25]
"There is no culture whose inhabitants treat their own norms

21. Ibid., 211.
22. Ibid., 204.
23. Ibid., 210.
24. As also in the changing moral commentary from Aeschylus to
Euripides, and Plato and Aristotle's response to that.
25. Findlay, *Values and Intentions*, 213.

and their own conceptions of the human good as having merely local significance and local authority," writes Alasdair MacIntyre. "When philosophers come to evaluate those norms and conceptions they confront the tasks of evaluating them as norms for which it is claimed that it would be right and best for all human beings to live by them and as adequate conceptions of the human good."[26] These norms, of course, may be values or disvalues. What are counted values for one group may be disvalues for another (for example the values of feminism versus the values of patriarchy, which claims that "we respect and protect 'our' women").

Values, on this account, are the revisable, but nonetheless tenacious, culturally constructed judgements that characterize our whole conscious life. They represent a culture or subculture's evaluation of what it means to be human, of what life is about. It makes no sense to speak of arbitrarily choosing them.[27] They represent what any particular culture means by "conscience." This is true even for cultures that want to replace the very idea of conscience by obedience to the will of God understood through revelation. What are understood to be the commands of God constitute the pattern of values that grounds that society. This account of the origin and meaning of value commends itself on the grounds of what we know of the social construction of reality but also as an account of an ongoing process of clarification that has close analogies with the development of law.

To speak in this way of values is to acknowledge that they come to us embedded in narratives or, in MacIntyre's term, in traditions. This is true even of seemingly rather formal discussions like Aristotle's *Ethics*, which in fact are part of an ongoing and very vigorous discussion which goes back at least to Pericles, and which frequently refers to recent Greek history. As Stanley Hauerwas argues, all significant moral claims are historically derived and require narrative display.[28] There is not, as Kant seems to have thought, a universal standpoint free of narrative, though this does

26. MacIntyre, "Politics, Philosophy and the Common Good," 246.

27. Findlay, *Values and Intentions*, 204.

28. Hauerwas, *A Community of Character*, 99.

not mean that there are not values that we rightly argue apply to all humans whatsoever and to that extent are universal. I shall take up this question in the next chapter.

On Findlay's account valuations are "the most serious of human activities." "The corruption of fundamentally 'wrong values' is arguably a worse corruption than an occasional, or even habitual, nonconformity to correct values duly acknowledged."[29] The sociologist Thomas Meyer rightly says that values "set down final standards for desired social relations, individual modes of behaviour, social and political structures, life-goals and ideals for the individual and the collective self. Furthermore, they also bind people's feelings and guide their moral judgement."[30] To that extent, those Muslim or Asian critics who decry "Western values" perceive rightly that changing values means changing society and this could challenge deeply held views of, for example, the role of women.

The collapse of values

Findlay argues that values are the culturally shaped accounts of the human good that are tenacious but also always in process. But what about the situation in which values collapse? During his brief ascendancy, wrote Mumford, Hitler and his agents succeeded in debauching human values and breaking down salutary innovations it had taken civilized peoples thousands of years to build up in order to protect themselves against their own destructive fantasies. None of the perversity Huxley had anticipated in his brave new world was out of order in the Third Reich.[31] In her book on Eichmann Arendt remarks that on the basis of the accumulated evidence "one

---

29. Findlay, *Values and Intentions*, 206. Cf. Rowan Williams on Dostoevsky, for whom "the question of the context from which we derive values is the most serious, life-and-death question we could possibly articulate." *Dostoevsky*, 228.

30. Meyer, *Identity Mania*, 71. Cf. Hedley Bull: "by a society's culture we mean its basic system of values, the premises from which its thought and action derive." *The Anarchical Society*, 64.

31. Mumford, *Pentagon of Power*, 251.

THE WORLD MADE OTHERWISE: VALUES AND VIRTUES

can only conclude that conscience as such had apparently got lost in Germany, and this to a point where people hardly remembered it and had ceased to realize that the surprising 'new set of German values' was not shared by the outside world."[32] Peter Haas argues, with regard to Auschwitz, that its most compelling lesson is the receptivity of ordinary people to new ethical discourse.[33] If ethical and moral matters really are what the etymology of the word (*ethos*) indicates, Arendt wrote at the end of her life, it should be no more difficult to change the mores and habits of people than it would be to change their table manners. The ease with which such a reversal can take place under certain conditions suggests indeed that everybody was fast asleep when it occurred.

> I am alluding, of course, to what happened in Nazi Germany and, to some extent, also in Stalinist Russia, when suddenly the basic commandments of Western morality were reversed: in one case, thou shalt not kill; in the other thou shall not bear false witness against a neighbour. And the sequel—the reversal of the reversal, the fact that it was so surprisingly easy to re-educate the

32. Arendt, *Eichmann*, 103.

33. Haas, *Morality after Auschwitz*, 232, 225. Tzvetan Todorov writes, "The question is often asked, how 'ordinary people', 'decent husbands and fathers', could have committed so many atrocities. Where was their conscience in all this?" His answer is that by usurping social goals and restricting people to instrumentalist thinking, the totalitarian power manages to have its subjects accomplish whatever tasks they are assigned without having to disturb the individual's moral structure at all. "Guards who committed atrocities never stopped distinguishing between good and evil. Their moral faculty had not withered away. They simply believed that the 'atrocity' was in fact a good thing and thus not an atrocity at all—because the state, custodian of the standards of good and evil, told them so. The guards were not deprived of moral sensibility but provided with a new one." *Facing the Extreme*, 129. There is also the vexed question of how vicious anti-Semites, who celebrated the death of Jews and of other hostages, could still write a great novel, or enjoy great art. Steiner instances Lucien Rebatet and the novel he wrote in prison, *Les Deux Etenards*. He writes, "The ability to play and love Bach can be conjoined in the same human spirit with the will to exterminate a ghetto or napalm a village. No ready solution to this mystery and to the fundamental questions it poses for our civilization lies at hand." *Extraterritorial*, 55. Of course Augustine had the category of original sin for precisely this reason.

Germans after the collapse of the third Reich, so easy
indeed that it was as though re-education is automatic—
should not console us either as it was actually the same
phenomenon.[34]

So—revisable but tenacious? Of course, much has to be allowed for
the impact of living under terror. The tiny White Rose group (which
opposed Hitler) proclaimed—"We are your conscience": they
were all very soon rounded up and executed. What appears to be
value change may be lack of courage. Again, most people, and most
cultures, also live with a conflict of values, so that broadly moral
commitments may coexist with deep-seated prejudices such as anti-
Semitism, which may then override other values. Or again, we all
know about *amour fou*—the infatuation that can sweep reason and
all other commitments before it. Perhaps there is a cultural version
of this insanity, and the reversal of the reversal, of which Arendt
speaks, corresponds to coming back to one's senses.

Though values are clearly fragile they are also undeniable,
and a strong reason for continuing to use this language is the challenge it mounts to the claim of the neoliberal market to provide
the fundamental standard of value for everything whatsoever.[35]
Wolfgang Streeck argues that the neoliberalism that currently
rules our world rests on a "moral re-education" that shapes school
and university curricula and that involves the "moral marginaliza-
tion" of those who disagree.[36] Current economic norms, as I shall
argue in chapter six, rest on a contest about values and therefore
need challenging on those grounds.

To pursue the question further I note that since values only
exist in societies—that is, in groups of people organized in families, tribes, cultures and so forth—this means that, as Marx argued,
they relate to specific modes of production.

34. Arendt, *The Life of the Mind*, vol. 1, 178.
35. So Graeber, *Toward an Anthropological Theory of Value*, xi.
36. Streeck, *Buying Time*, 59, 156.

Values and modes of production

The American sociologist Ron Ingelhart and a wide range of collaborators have attempted to map changing values in relation to changing modes of production over the past forty years.[37] Drawing on development theory they make a distinction between pre-industrial, industrial and post-industrial cultures corresponding to what they call survival values, secular rational values, and self-expression values. They do not define what they mean by value, but we can evaluate the argument bearing Findlay's account in mind.

Preindustrial cultures, but also cultures which for one reason or other lack security, have what they call "survival values," which repress aspirations for social mobility, justify acceptance of the existing social order by the poor, and seek to limit reproduction (by cultural norms relating to sexuality) in order to soften the competition for survival brought by overpopulation. Such cultures have strong "bonding capital" but discriminate against foreigners, outgroups, and sexual minorities.[38] Politics tend to be authoritarian and morality focused on the well-being of the group.

The industrial revolution was linked to a shift from traditional to secular rational values, which they do not elaborate, but we can

37. The questionnaires that are the basis of Ingelhart and his collaborators' work are fairly crude. In the first instance people were asked to say what their country's two top goals should be from amongst (1) maintaining order in the nation; (2) giving people more say in important government decisions (3) fighting rising prices; and (4) protecting freedom of speech. Those who select "maintaining order" and "fighting rising prices" are classified as materialists, and those who opt for the other two are classified as postmaterialist. Later eight other questions were added: Respondents were asked to choose the two top goals from (1) maintaining a high rate of economic growth; (2) making sure that the country has strong defense forces; (3) seeing that people have more say in how things are decided at work and in their communities; (4) trying to make cities and countryside more beautiful and then secondly (1) maintain a stable economy; (2) progress toward a less impersonal, more humane society; (3) fight against crime; and (4) progress toward a society where ideas are more important than money. Abramson and Ingelhart, *Value Change in Global Perspective*, ch. 1.

38. Ingelhart and Welzel, *Modernization, Cultural Change and Democracy*, 54.

certainly think of the value of free enquiry, opposition to hierarchy, support of egalitarianism, and opposition to what is regarded as superstition. Mumford and Adorno obviously have a very different take on these values than their defenders, though there is a real case for progress here, as Sean Sayers has argued.[39]

In the contemporary world, Ingelhart and Welzel argue (they mean the affluent world), we have a postmaterialist emphasis on personal and political liberty, civilian protest activities, tolerance of the liberty of others and an emphasis on subjective well-being reflected in life satisfaction.[40] Here we have the "self-expression values" of individual autonomy and free choice that give rise to a new type of humanistic society that is increasingly people centred.[41] The bonding ties characteristic of small intimate societies give way to the bridging ties that connect people across the boundaries of predefined groupings. Religious, ethnic, and sexual diversity is valued more highly. There is an emphasis on rights, consumer, environmental, and data protection, and the growth of concern for integrity in governance and administration. A cosmopolitan tendency favoring universal human rights joins up with a libertarian tendency that favors individual liberties. Gender roles, religious orientations, consumer tastes, working habits, and voting behavior all become increasingly matters of individual choice.[42]

39. Sayers argues that modernity should not be understood merely negatively but involves the creation of new forms of social relation and new—liberal—values connected with them: values of liberty, equality, individuality, and tolerance. "Relative to the conditions in the premodern world, it constitutes in some important respects an advance." Sayers, "MacIntyre and Modernity," 88. Paul Kahn talks of "the basic liberal values," which include respect for the dignity and equality of individuals, skepticism towards fixed hierarchies, broad acceptance of diverse social groupings whether religious or ethnic, and a demand for representative government limited by a doctrine of individual rights embodied in a rule of law administered by courts. However, he also includes, much more contentiously, "a general sense of the need for well regulated markets to satisfy material wants." Kahn, *Putting Liberalism in Its Place,*"10.

40. Ingelhart and Welzel, *Modernization*, 248.

41. Ibid.,1.

42. Ibid., 3.

There is clearly some explanatory power in this schema, especially in understanding why acceptance of sexual difference has grown in the contemporary West and not elsewhere. Ingelhart and his co-workers also emphasise that such tolerance cannot be taken for granted and that a regression to survival values can very easily happen in the wake of economic collapse or other pressures (for example, massive immigration).[43] People absorbed in sheer physical survival tend to place less emphasis on human emancipation, so that they more readily accept and sometimes even demand restrictions on the civil and political liberties that define democracy.[44] Already today, "Much of southern Italy shows many features of a society dominated by hierarchical patron-client relations, with mafia like clan structures. These structures are linked with scarce resources, which impose rigid constraints on human autonomy, pressing people into closely knit networks held together by strict group discipline and governed by rigid authority patterns."[45]

Although illuminating, Ingelhart's account is extremely crude in terms of historical analysis. Fourth-century Athens was not characterized by survival values, and Benedictine values were not determined by the Dark Ages in which they arose. A very different historical account was outlined by Mumford, who argued that the village was the home of ethics, but that its life-affirming values were taken over by organized power in the wake of the first consistent surpluses. Materialistic assumptions equated human welfare and the will of the gods with centralized political power, military dominance, and increasing economic exploitation. Then, in the axial period (a hypothesis Jaspers and Mumford came up

43 Ingelhart argues, for example, that if Weimar had enjoyed an economic miracle like Bonn's, Hitler would almost certainly not have come to power. Ibid.,161.

44. Ibid., 162. Karl Jaspers notes that through the ages the peasantry remained comparatively secure in immutable orders, even if they had to starve. They endured and submitted, and lived in a pervading religious faith. Jaspers, *The Origin and Goal of History*, 127. Such an argument could of course be challenged by Marxist historians like Rodney Hilton, who chart the history of peasant rebellions, always savagely put down.

45. Ingelhart and Welzel, *Modernization*, 163.

with independently), a new set of values was proclaimed: "Not power but righteousness . . . was the basis of human society: not snatching, seizing and fighting, but sharing, cooperating, even loving: not pride, but humility: not limitless wealth, but a noble self-restricting poverty and chastity."[46] What Mumford and Jaspers flag up here is the possibility of diverging from the *consensus universalis*. Findlay's account could suggest that the realm of values had no critical or constructive dimension but this is in fact not the case. In the prophetic tradition of the Hebrew Bible these new values are ascribed to revelation: they articulate a "theology of the Word" with which to distinguish the new claims, and also to make the point that values do not originate, as they do in Findlay's account, purely in human interaction but have a source beyond it. Given the emergence of new and critical moral codes at more or less the same time, if we were to make sense of this in terms of revelation we would have to follow the strategy of the second-century Apologists (very well aware of both the strength and weaknesses of the Greek achievement), and think of it in terms of the work of a "logos" that inspired all human communities.

Recognizing the origin of new values in prophecy Nietzsche assumed the mantle of Zarathustra. He wanted to replace what he took to be the degenerate values of Christianity with a return to heroic values and his writings played a large part in the enthusiasm for the language of values in the first half of the twentieth century. Nietzsche, like all "prophets," had the originality of genius, but he also captured the mood of the close of the nineteenth century in its revolt against the bourgeois sanctimoniousness of the age. Whether or not Nietzsche provided resources for the Nazis, there is no doubt that his idea of the übermensch was false prophecy grounded, MacIntyre argues, in the very same emotivism represented by a saccharine liberal like G. E. Moore.

For Alberto Melucci it is not individuals but social movements that are "prophets of the present." "What they possess is not the force of the apparatus but the power of the word. They announce the commencement of change; not, however, a change

46. Mumford, *Myth*, 258.

in the distant future but one that is already a presence. They force the power out into the open and give it a face and a shape. They speak a language that seems to be entirely their own, but they say something that transcends their particularity and speaks to us all."[47] Similarly, James Jasper has argued that these movements are a key way that modern citizens articulate their moral vision for themselves. The importance of protest lies in its moral vision.[48] Something like this understanding underlies the urgent appeal of Naomi Klein, and of those scientists like Stephen Emmott and Brad Werner who look to the possibility of addressing the threat to planetary boundaries in time.

Values, we can say (if Findlay is right), are hegemonic, but hegemony is always challenged, and the challenge to values comes from both right and left, for good and for evil, from individuals and groups who sense the inadequacy or injustice of the prevailing consensus. Such challenges, as the "axial age" indicates, can be profound and far reaching, embracing social, political, and economic realms. In order to address the global emergency it is to such changes that we look.

The struggle for values as the heart of politics

Drawing on the work of the anthropologist Terence Turner, David Graeber argues, in the passage I have used as the epigraph for this chapter, that the struggle to establish how value is to be defined is the heart of politics.[49] Like Findlay, his account of value is societal, though he does not concern himself with the origin of values. Humans measure the importance of their actions and they evaluate their experience, he argues, by being incorporated in some larger, social totality (where a "totality" can, amongst other things, such as religious or mythological systems, refer to society understood as

47. Melucci, *Challenging Codes*, 1.
48. Jasper, *The Art of Moral Protest*, 375.
49. Graeber, *Toward an Anthropological Theory of Value*, 115.

a whole).[50] Such totalities, "the stuff of meaning," are always fluid, never closed, which means that essentializations such as "the West," or "the Arab World," etc. are always doubtful and often downright misleading. Nevertheless, within any "totality" there is a question of what matters, more generally, the question of the meaning of life. For Graeber, the language of value refers to the way people represent the importance of their own actions to themselves; normally as reflected in one or another socially recognized form. "Rather than value being the process of public recognition itself, already suspended in social relations, it is the way people who could do almost anything (including in the right circumstances create entirely new sorts of social relations) assess the importance of what they do. This is necessarily a social process."[51]

Postmodernists argue that all totalizing systems—science, humanity, nation, truth, and so forth—have been shattered. One can no longer even imagine that there could be a single standard of value by which to measure things. However, this argument overlooks the fact that throughout the world the neoliberal the market supplies this standard. A creative politics, Graeber argues, will be about working out, in, and through social interaction of all kinds, a challenge to this hegemonic claim.

Graeber's claim that the struggle to define value is the heart of politics could appeal to Aristotle, who begins the *Politics* with the argument that humans are distinguished from other animals by the fact that they have speech, and they have this precisely in order to choose their polity. The very function of language, he argues, is to sort out good and evil, just and unjust, and thus to determine the kind of community we want.[52] Aristotle collected more than 150 constitutions for his students to help in this process. Of course, in point of fact only free male citizens in Athens could take part in this process, and even Aristotle, as a metic, a migrant working in Athens, could not participate.

50. Ibid, xi, 40.
51. Ibid., 47.
52. Aristotle, *Politics*, 1253a3.

The Jewish and Christian Scriptures can also be understood in terms of a struggle to define value. They represent *in toto*, according to Ton Veerkamp, a reimagining of values and therefore of society and economics. We find there, he argues, an account of a struggle between two systems of value—one based on absolute property rights and the other on freedom and solidarity. This suggestion is of more than "academic" interest because, as Streeck has argued, we currently have a struggle between the aspirations and power of Staatsvolk, citizens, on the one hand, and of Marktvolk, the beneficiaries of finance capital, on the other.[53] The latter have reshaped the global economy in their own interest and, on Streeck's view, are seeking to consolidate their power by reducing politics to harmless domestic issues, whilst all the key decisions are decided by the criterion of market profit.

There is a real analogy between the situation addressed by an ancient text like Deuteronomy and the present. This is important because ancient texts (think of Plato and Aristotle, the Bhagavad Gita, the Koran, Gautama) continue to shape our imaginaries and understanding of the world, often in subversive ways. They are not, as nineteenth-century positivists thought, irrelevant remnants from an obscure and superstitious past. Deuteronomy, which was written during the exile of the old elite in Babylon, is one of these texts. In it we have an account of a society which does things otherwise than the nations round about—a prohibition of the accumulation of property and of slavery. The order envisaged is "the radical contradiction of the ancient oriental order of exploitation."[54] In other words, its idea of God was counter-hegemonic. The group responsible for Deuteronomy edited the so-called "history books," or "former prophets," which put the difference between Israel and its neighbors in terms of a contest between YHWH and Ba'al. The hostility to the Ba'al cult should not be read either as chauvinism or as religious intolerance: in any case, the stories are not history but saga or legend, a way of

53. Streeck, *Buying Time*, 5.
54. Veerkamp, *Die Welt Anders*, 71.

telling truths through stories. What is condemned in the cult is, Veerkamp argues, the ruling pattern of relationships.[55]

According to the traditions of Ba'al, a name which means "owner," the king has absolute power; according to the traditions of YHWH, on the other hand, the king was under the ancient law of the tribes. This is the background to the Elijah story. The king, Ahab, had a palace in Samaria, where the Ba'al cult was dominant, and a palace in Jezreel, which was Yahwist. He tried to satisfy both constituencies but ran into problems with the obstinacy of the old Yahwist peasantry, represented by Naboth. Under Canaanite law land could be freely bought and sold. It was a commodity. According to the old Yahwist principles however, each family had a share, their *nachalah*, which guaranteed them both a living and freedom. It represented every family's stake in the means of production. Ahab wanted Naboth's land to extend his palace garden and made him an offer he couldn't refuse. But Naboth did refuse, not, on Veerkamp's reading, because he appealed to an older culture, but on the contrary because he stood for the future of Israel, in which class relationships would not indeed be done away with, but in which arbitrary property acquisition would be strictly limited by tight legislation.[56] The threat to Ahab is deadly: he turns his face to the wall, which is what one does when one prepares to die (2 Kgs 20:2) and Jezebel, Ahab's wife, the leading protagonist of the Ba'al cult, understands this.[57] She has Naboth murdered and presents the land to her husband. Her act reveals not only a different understanding of God, but also, and because of that, of the human. Little people are not there to get in the way. If they do, they must be removed. No laws stand in the way. At this point Elijah turns up: *have you killed and taken possession?* "The king who sought to be a big landowner at the cost of freedom and life of people meets the prophet of YHWH, who claims to be the Sovereign of the land which he has given to his people in order to protect its

---

55. Veerkamp, *Autonomie & Egalität*, 61.

56. Veerkamp, *Die Vernichtung des Baal*, 112.

57. Ibid.

freedom against usurpation."[58] The king is not above the law: he is charged with theft and murder. The Naboth story is symbolically about what Ba'alim, the gods of ownership, do: they kill and take possession. Elijah, the representative of YHWH, the God of life, has to oppose them for this reason. Killing and taking possession is the hallmark of idolatry.

Veerkamp thinks this contest over value continues in what he calls the Messianic Writings (the New Testament). On his account (following Jacob Taubes) Paul is a political radical whose key word is "all"—all are included in the vision of the new society. Romans 7, for him, is the account of what it means to try to live according to Torah under conditions of alienation (quite independently, Herbert McCabe once said that Romans 7 was about living in Cuba under Batista). To live according to the flesh is to live according to the status quo. To live messianically is to live so as to make the alternative real (Gal 3:28). The opposition of "flesh" and "spirit" is the opposition of a life lived "messianically," i.e., as a radical alternative to the way of things. Veerkamp argues that Paul in fact represents a faithful continuation of the grand narrative set out in Torah. Similarly, Hebrews is not a return to Platonism, as it was read in the nineteenth century, nor a return to a sacrificial cultus, as for Girard, but the end of religion in that Jesus has once and for all put an end to the need for sacrifice. Hebrews 13:4 ("Here we have no abiding city") is not about otherworldliness but longing for the great alternative. It promises us that Rome (which for us is neoliberalism) will not last forever.[59] In the Gospels, which we must understand to some extent as responses to Paul, the theme of the kingdom of God is the quintessence of Israel's "grand narrative" of freedom and equality. In Mark "the way to Galilee" is a continuation of Israel's "long road to freedom." Matthew extends this way to the nations, and Luke embraces the path to Rome as a promise of a new world order. John, "an uncompromisingly anti-Zealot text," is concerned with

58. Wielenga, *It's A Long Road to Freedom*, 135.

59. Veerkamp, *Welt Anders*, 290.

intraJewish relations and argues that agape, solidarity in the messianic community, is the one thing that helps.[60]

After Constantine this grand narrative was revised. Christianity came to have the role of making people settled—accepting their social position. The NAME was confused with the universal God who underwrote the social conditions of the empire. The God who counters hegemony was replaced by one who reinforces it. With Augustine, finally, we have the emergence of the grand narrative of Christendom—both criticism and justification of the world as it is. The possibility of a truly different society, for Augustine, belongs only to the next life.

If Veerkamp is right, the struggle to define value is, therefore, the leitmotif of one of the founding documents of Western civilization, just as it is of Greek philosophy. In the recent past the struggle between capitalism and communism could be described in this way, and today Samuel Huntington's thesis of the clash of civilizations thinks of geopolitics in these terms. If Streeck and Naomi Klein are right, then the current development of neoliberalism also involves a struggle between "two ways," resting on quite different sets of values—in Streeck's terms, social justice and market justice. I shall return to this in chapter six. This contest centrally involves the question of planetary boundaries.

Values, politics, and planetary boundaries

In his account of value Findlay does not make clear that, as John Cottingham puts it, valuation arises because reality presents itself to us as imbued with value and meaning.[61] The only world in which we would not have to use value language at all would be a world where nothing at all was of value. Such dystopias have been imagined, and even partly enacted, but they can only be imagined because we are familiar with the opposite, a world full of all sorts

---

60. Veerkamp, *Welt Anders*, 335.
61. Cottingham, *Why Believe?*, 19.

of worth. This is paradoxical because the ecological crisis seems to indicate precisely that creation is not valued. Why is that?

Nearly fifty years ago the medieval historian Lynn White suggested that the Christian emphasis on dominion lay at the root of the ecological crisis, but in the first place this is far too undialectical an account of the way in which ideologies work in history; it ignores all Mumford's work on medieval technics, which worked with, not against nature; and, even more surprisingly, it ignores the contribution of the Benedictine movement to European prosperity and stability.

Mumford himself drew attention to the fundamental value change that took place in the seventeenth century. The work of Galileo and Descartes implied a hostility towards nature and the suppression of the natural environment by geometric mechanical forms, and the replacement of natural products by artificial manufactured substitutes.[62] Before that, human needs were restricted by the means of energy available and also by a whole range of nonutilitarian factors. In the wake of the new forms of energy, however—coal, electricity, and finally nuclear energy—a new set of postulates took precedence:

> First: man has only one all-important mission in life: to conquer nature. By conquering nature the technocrat means, in abstract terms, commanding time and space; and in more concrete terms, speeding up every natural process, hastening growth, quickening the pace of transportation, and breaking down communication distances by either mechanical or electronic means. To conquer nature is in effect to remove all natural barriers and human norms and to substitute artificial, fabricated equivalents for natural processes. From these general postulates a series of subsidiary ones are derived: there is only one efficient speed—faster; only one attractive destination— further away; only one desirable size—bigger; only one rational quantitative goal—more. On these assumptions the object of human life, and therefore of the entire productive mechanism, is to remove limits, to hasten the

62. Mumford, *Pentagon of Power*, 210.

pace of change, to smooth out seasonal rhythms and reduce regional contrasts—in fine, to promote mechanical
novelty and destroy organic continuity. Cultural accumulation and stability thus become stigmatised as signs
of human backwardness and insufficiency.[63]

A culture built on the denial of limits arose based on the idea of
"conquering" nature. This meant, according to his analysis, that
human functions and values that had emerged over millennia—
gifts of love, mutuality, rationality, imagination, and constructive aptitude that had enlarged all the possibilities of life—were
replaced by subjection to the machine. Victor Frankl argued that
if human beings do not allow tradition to tell them what they
ought to do, very soon they will not know what to do. Mumford
agreed: "Empty affluence, empty idleness, empty excitement,
empty sexuality are not the occasional vices or misfortunes of
our machine oriented society but it's boasted final products."
The art of the sixties and seventies, Mumford argued, sufficiently
pointed to a cult of anti-life.[64]

As Mumford realized, the impact of technics had to be
placed within that of the rise of capitalism. There are two aspects
to this, which I will take further in chapter seven. The first is that,
as Marx argued in Capital, money becomes the standard of value
for everything. The immense damage this has caused can be seen
in forests, fish stocks, and populations of rare animals around
the world. For money all these are destroyed and turned into so
much trash. To allow the market mechanism to be sole director
of the fate of human beings in their natural environment, wrote
Karl Polanyi, would result in the demolition of society. Human
beings would suffer, but also, "Nature would be reduced to its elements, neighbourhoods and landscapes defiled, rivers polluted
. . . the power to produce food and raw materials destroyed."[65]
That was in part a commentary on what happened in nineteenth-
century Europe, but it was also prophecy.

63. Ibid., 173.
64. Ibid., 360.
65. Polanyi, The Great Transformation, 73.

Capitalism, therefore, meant value change. The calculation of quantity, the observation and regimentation of time, and the concentration on abstract pecuniary rewards, all of which were necessary for a successful capitalist enterprise, could be traced back, Mumford believed, to the pyramid age, except that, in understanding the need for life, health, and prosperity, rather than profit, the pyramid age was better grounded in organic realities.[66] Naomi Klein cites studies that connect materialistic values to carelessness not just about climate change but to a great many environmental risks. Climate skeptics have, over the past forty years, won the battle over which values would govern our societies. "The central lie is that we are nothing but selfish, greedy, self gratification machines."[67]

Second, and here this links with Mumford's argument from technics, capitalism has to grow to live. The need to pay off interest and to make a profit drives all capitalist enterprises to constant growth—but a limited planet cannot stand this.

Mumford makes clear that this development did not happen unopposed. The many different currents that we identify as "romanticism" already challenged these two drives from the late seventeenth century onwards, and in the nineteenth century were responsible for the foundation of the first conservation groups, such as the Sierra Club. William Morris opposed a monotechnics with a passionate appeal to restore an older polytechnics and over the past forty years the ecological movement has insisted on the intrinsic value of creation. Christianity rediscovered its ancient doctrine of creation as grace about the same time and has argued both for the holiness of creation and for Sabbath as a practice of resistance to the commodification of everything. These moves can be understood as part of the " immense increase in emotional alertness, moral concern, and practical audacity which will be necessary on a worldwide scale if mankind is finally to save itself," of which Mumford speaks.[68]

66. Mumford, *Myth*, 279.
67. Klein, *Changes*, 62.
68. Mumford, *Pentagon of Power*, 262.

However, these were only counter-currents to the main stream, which was the growth of capital. "Competitiveness for unlimited money accumulation," says Ulrich Duchrow, "is the objective and subjective structure, the 'god' of our market society, which determines the whole." It is this god, this Ba'al, which is driving the rise in global temperature that could lead to the end of human life on earth; that lies behind the sweat shops, and that can crucify whole nations through debt. "Accordingly," says Duchrow, "the core of what we must reject is the absolute value attributed to competition and the total absence of limits set on the cancerous growth of capital."[69] Absolute value and absence of limits are traditional attributes of deity. Idolatry is not about harmless "green eyed yellow idols to the north of Kathmandu," or anywhere else, but about making absolute that which is not God. The idol of Nebuchadnezzar is, as Veerkamp describes it, a "really existing god," with real power, who has to be celebrated in liturgies that internalize its lordship and to defy which means you have to be cast into the fire, as the opponents of Pinochet and the other Latin American dictators were cast into the fire.[70] "Every generation will be confronted with its own Ba'als, their own strange gods, who grab power over them and seek to devour them."[71] Our own Ba'al, in the West and much of the rest of the world, is the doctrine of necessary economic growth. Of course all of us in the "developed" world are beneficiaries of the growth that has taken place since 1750. Of course growth is necessary to raise the living standards of billions of the world's people. But if growth is at the expense of generations yet unborn then it is idolatrous, and this is the charge. The living God is known in the giving of life: death is the hallmark of idolatry. We have a global economy that, like Naboth, kills and takes possession. In this context, theology is, as Veerkamp puts it, about lie detection. The fact that the Name of God is unspeakable and the voice of God cannot be tied down (*Gestaltlos*) is about resistance to colonization by any

69. Duchrow, *Alternatives to Global Capitalism*, 234.

70. Veerkamp, *Autonomie*, 245.

71. Veerkamp, *Vernichtung*, 51.

Ba'al.[72] This, I take it, is one of the indispensable contributions of theology to discussions of value.

Life as the fundamental value

Writing in the fifth century BC the Deuteronomists urged their compatriots to choose life over death (Deut 30:19). On Veerkamp's reading "death" was a way of referring to a society based on debt slavery and hierarchy, and life was the opposite. Certainly, the same choice confronts us today. By "death" at least three attitudes or practices could be meant. Whole cultures can opt for death as Europe did in 1914, when those who stood for life, like the French socialist Herbert Jaures, were murdered. Germany allowed itself to be dragged into a culture of death with the ascendancy of Hitler in 1933, and Europe was again dragged after it: the death camps and the incinerated cities followed. A similar option was taken by the Khmer Rouge in Cambodia, by Hutus in Rwanda, and by Anwar in Indonesia. Today we are familiar with the threat of Islamic terrorism, with its rhetoric of hatred, and the attempt to destroy not just those belonging to "the corrupt bogland of Western culture" as one critic puts it, but all memory of a pre-Islamic past. Robert Reilly cites the Tunisian Muslim thinker Abdelwahab Meddeb, who speaks of an "insane, absolute theocentrism" directed at the death of humanity. Fundamentalism, he says, "is the kind of negation of life, the nihilism to which theoretical reasoning leads when it is not subject to the control of practical reasoning."[73] But, who-

---

72. Veerkamp, *Autonomie*, 373–74.

73. Reilly, *Closing*, 200. Roger Scruton cites many of Ayatollah Khomeini's fevered utterances that valorize death. In 1984 he said, "If one allows infidels to continue playing the role of corrupters on earth, the eventual moral punishment will be all the stronger. Thus, if we kill the infidels in order to put a stop to their corrupting activities, we have indeed done a service. For the eventual punishment will be less. To allow the infidels to stay alive means to let them do more corrupting. Those who follow the rules of the Koran are aware that we have to apply the laws of qissas [retribution] and that we have to kill . . . War is a blessing for the world and for every nation. It is Allah himself who commands men to wage war and to kill." Cited in Scruton, *The West and the*

ever condemns the attacks on New York, write Ulrich Duchrow and Franz Hinkelammert, also has to condemn the strategy of globalization that is directed towards the increase of capital property. "The indirect effects of this strategy have led to the point where the reaction to the system is as extremely irrational as the system itself. In the new terrorism the system raises contradictions against itself. The opposites conflate and become one. The mysticism of death rises up against the dignity of humanity." The issue is to defend the dignity of human beings beyond the status of being an owner so that civilization at last respects this dignity.[74]

The sinister backdrop to this option for death is the threat of nuclear war, which could wipe out human life on earth, and which was the focus of what E. P. Thompson called "exterminism."

But the option for death is also implied in Western consumerism, which is nihilistic in another way. As David Korten argues, the defining political struggle of the twenty-first century is not so much between political ideologies as between life values and financial values—between a civil society and a capitalist society.[75] The capitalist world, too, "no longer loves life," as Camus wrote about Europe after World War II.

If what James Hansen, Kevin Anderson, and others are saying is true then "the carbon spewing nations are embarking on the greatest violation of human rights the world's ever seen." Benefits and burdens are not equitably shared between generations or between nations; children are not protected from harm; we do not act with compassion.[76] Therefore, "a reversal in convictions and basic values is necessary as well as a reversal in the attitude to life and in the conduct of life" if we are not to be absorbed by exterminism.[77]

Rest, 118. These attitudes and utterances can only be described as depraved.

74. Duchrow and Hinkelammert, *Property*, 137.

75. David Korten, "Creating a Post-Corporate World," Schumacher lecture October 2001.

76. Moore and Nelson, "Moving toward a global moral consensus on environmental action," 328.

77. Moltmann, *Ethics of Hope*, 67.

How are these life-denying cultures to be countered? Not, we have to say, through Nietzschean vitalism, an identification of life with the will to power, which overtly grounds exploitation.[78] This approach to "life" underwrites a truly vicious politics.[79] Writing out of Africa, and in the context of the catastrophe of the First World War, Albert Schweitzer, to whom Rachel Carson dedicated *Silent Spring*, called for a quite different ethics of the will to life: "It is good to maintain and to encourage life; it is bad to destroy life or to obstruct it."[80] Life as such is sacred. Ethics are responsibility without limit to all that lives—this goes beyond compassion. Kant's essay on perpetual peace was mistaken in Schweitzer's view: "Only such thinking as establishes the sway of the mental attitude of reverence for life can bring to mankind perpetual peace."[81]

An understanding about the need to assert the intrinsic value of life, writes Naomi Klein, is at the heart of all major progressive victories, from universal suffrage to universal healthcare.

> Though these movements all contained economic arguments as part of building their case for justice, they did not win by putting a monetary value on granting equal rights and freedoms. They won by asserting that those rights and freedoms were too valuable to be measured and were inherent to each of us. Similarly there are plenty of solid economic arguments for moving beyond fossil fuels as more and more patient investors are realising. And that's worth pointing out. But we will not win the battle for a stable climate by trying to beat the bean counters at their own game—arguing, for instance, that it is more cost effective to invest in emission reduction now than disaster response later. We will win by asserting that such calculations are morally monstrous, since they imply that there is an acceptable price for allowing

78. In *Beyond Good and Evil* (259), Nietzsche writes: "'Exploitation' does not belong to a corrupt or imperfect and primitive society: it belongs to the essence of what lives, as a basic organic function; it is a consequence of the will to power, which is after all the will to life."

79. Stern, *Nietzsche*, 79, in opposition to W. Kaufman.

80. Schweitzer, *Civilization and Ethics*, 242.

81. Ibid., 280.

entire countries to disappear, leaving untold millions to die on parched land, for depriving today's children of their right to live in a world teeming with the wonders and beauties of creation.[82]

Taking up Schweitzer's theme Karl Barth spoke of respect as "astonishment, humility and awe at a fact in which human beings meet something superior—majesty, dignity, holiness, a mystery which compels humanity to withdraw and keep their distance, to handle it modestly, circumspectly and carefully." He grounded respect for life on the incarnation. Respect for life "becomes a command in the recognition of the union of God with humanity in Jesus Christ."[83] This respect has practical consequences. It means that human life must be affirmed and willed. "Indifference, wantonness, arbitrariness or anything else opposed to respect cannot even be considered as a commanded or permitted attitude."[84] Respect for life means "daily mercy and resolute justice to all human life."[85] It means refraining from senseless destruction of the plant world and understanding that killing animals to eat can only take place as "a deeply reverential act of repentance, gratitude and praise on the part of the forgiven sinner in face of the One who is the Creator of man and beast."[86] It means responsibility for living conditions generally. It means the will for joy. And whilst it recognizes that war may not be absolutely avoidable "it is certainly commissioned to oppose the satanic doctrine that war is inevitable and therefore justified"—a devastating comment on the work of Philip Bobbitt.[87]

82. Klein, *Changes*, 464. In her most recent book, *No is Not Enough*, 240, Klein again says that resistance to "the new Shock Politics" has to begin by "leading with values, not policies."

83. Barth, *Church Dogmatics*, III/4, 339.

84. Ibid., 343.

85. Ibid., 347.

86. Ibid., 355.

87. Ibid., 460. Bobbitt speaks of war as "sustaining the State by giving it the means to carry out its purposes of protection, preservation and defence." *The Shield of Achilles*, 780. That Anglican Archbishops can endorse this kind of thing is presumably the reason that the Church of England seems to be metamorphing into a Mars cult—replacing peace chapels with military chapels

Today in Latin America political movements have drawn on the Quechua notion of Samak Kawsay, translated into Spanish as *buen vivir*—an idea of the good life radically at odds with the current consumerist version. The criteria for discerning an ethical scale, writes Walter Mignolo, has no other reference than life itself: "anti-ethical is everything that kills life or that can, at the short and long run kill life. Ethical is every attitude that moves for life, the integrity of life."[88] The attempt is to build societies in harmony with nature in which everyone has enough rather than more and more, but, as Naomi Klein warns, "escalating industrial scale development and extraction is overtaking this promising rhetoric."[89]

For ancient Israel "life" meant, in Veerkamp's terms, freedom and autonomy—a "no" to slavery, to hierarchy and a class society, and a search for peace in which Israel could fashion its own policies free from overlords. In the mid-twentieth century "life" meant, for Beveridge, reacting to the Great Depression, and to nearly two centuries of industrial exploitation, countering the "five giant evils" of want, disease, ignorance, squalor, and idleness. This was the foundation of the welfare state. In 1948 the UN declaration on human rights specified rest and leisure, a standard of living adequate for people's health and well-being, including food, clothing, housing, and medical care and necessary social services, and the right to security in the event of unemployment, sickness, disability, widowhood, old age, or other lack of livelihood. To this day these conditions are not met, even in many of the wealthiest countries in the world, and where they are met what Streeck calls the "Hayekian world" seeks to undo them. Such desiderata are important in reminding us that "life" should not be understood idealistically, and especially should not be postponed to "the next life." Humans are body-soul-spirit unities, and the soul and the spirit do not thrive without the body. At the same time the

---

(Exeter Cathedral) and endlessly celebrating past battles, from Agincourt onwards. At present, under the impact of nearly twenty years of "the war against terror," peace witness is regarded as unpatriotic as it was in 1915.

88. Mignolo, "From human rights to life rights," 168.

89. Klein, *Changes*, 181.

"fullness of life" of which John's gospel speaks (John 10:10) goes beyond this in all the dimensions of care, joy, and celebration of culture. "That's not living" people say of a life spent working from dawn to dusk, or commuting for six days a week, and unable to enjoy family and friends. In the arts, in food, in loving relationships, people experience the fullness of life which, as Moltmann rightly argues, is a foretaste of the fullness of life in God here and now.[90] At Passover Jews read the major scroll—the account of the exodus from Egypt, but they also read the minor scroll, the Song of Songs, with its ecstatic celebration of erotic love, as the reason we seek freedom in the first place.

Can an option for life be made? Naomi Klein notes that the transformative movements of the past "all understood that the process of shifting cultural values—though somewhat ephemeral and difficult to quantify—was central to their work. And so they dreamed in public, showed humanity a better version of itself, modelled different values in their own behavior, and in the process liberated the political imagination and rapidly altered the sense of what was possible."[91] Like the Deuteronomists she envisages a "yes" and a "no," a "no" to the values that allow countries to disappear, millions to die of hunger and thirst, and deprive today's children of a future. "Yes" to a vision of a life that is more than an endless contest of greed and power. This struggle cannot be won by adopting the values of the opposition—by arguing, for example, in terms of cost effectiveness. Vaclav Havel argued that it was necessary to develop a new understanding of the true purpose of our existence on this earth. "Only by making such a fundamental shift will we be able to create new models of behaviour and a new set of values the planet."[92] And values are important because they motivate people. As Barrington Moore observed, "Without strong moral feelings and indignation, human beings will not act against the social order. In this sense moral convictions become an equally necessary

90. Moltmann, *Ethics*, 58.

91. Klein, *Changes*, 462.

92. Assadourian, "Building an enduring environmental movement," 296. Assadourian himself looks to deep ecology for inspiration.

element for changing the social order, along with alterations in the economic structure."[93]

The choice between life and death, outlined by the Deuteronomists, marks the whole of human history, and the balance often seems to tip towards death. Today human numbers and the technical means for destruction available, plus the threat of overstepping planetary boundaries, makes the Deuteronomic imperative starker than ever before. In the next chapter I turn to the question of how cultures and individuals might best be led to affirm life.

93. Moore, *Injustice*, 469.

Chapter Three

On Making and Keeping Human Life Human

> Though under conditions of terror most people will comply, some people will not, and though "[the Holocaust] could happen" in most places it did not happen everywhere. Humanly speaking no more is required, and no more can reasonably be asked, for this planet to remain a place fit for human habitation.
>
> —Hannah Arendt

CULTURES (AND CLASSES, PARTIES, movements) enshrine values and disvalues. Often, the values they trumpet are not the ones they live by ("freedom and democracy") and most cultures, most of the time, live by both values and disvalues. As we saw in the last chapter, some cultures have periods when civilized values—values affirmative of life—simply collapse. According to Jaques le Goff, this happened in Europe during the Dark Ages. Might it happen again under the pressures arising from climate change? How might we guard against that possibility? It is that question I want to probe in this chapter and I shall do so through the tradition of the virtues, central to Aristotle's account of what it means to be human, and to what has been called Alasdair MacIntyre's "revolutionary Aristotelianism." As I noted in the previous chapter, values are often contrasted unfavorably with virtues: "don't talk about values, talk about virtues!," we are told. But virtues, I shall argue, are the realization, or embodiment of values, just as vices are the realization of disvalues; and both are concerned with the question of what it means to be human. I noted that values can be culturally relative, and extreme views of cultural relativism deny that we can talk of any universal human nature. I consider this to be mistaken and begin by appealing to cultural anthropology to argue that we can talk of a universal human nature, and moreover (second section) that we can talk about a proper human end. That there are human ends presupposes education (third section), which culminate, for the Aristotelian tradition, in the virtues (fourth section). In outlining the virtues I consider objections to this tradition, including objections from within Christianity, and then pass on to law, which for both Plato and Aristotle was a way of dealing with the failure to deal with a virtuous life (fifth section). In the previous chapter I explored David Graeber's contention that the attempt to define value was the heart of politics, and in the same way I here discuss the relation of virtues and politics (sixth section) before summing up these reflections on what it means to live a fully human life.

Is there a universal human nature?

Can we speak, in a culturally invariant way, about "human nature"? In his *Short History of Ethics* Alasdair MacIntyre rejected the belief that moral concepts were a timeless, limited, unchanging, determinate species of concept that can be examined and understood apart from their history. Moral concepts, he argued, are embodied in, and partially constitutive of, forms of social life.[1] At the same time, although what it means to pursue common goods varies from social order to social order, and therefore different aspects of the virtues are prominent in different social contexts, we find shared features, which mean that in different contexts the same virtues are needed. For this reason, accounts of the virtues specific to this or that time and place provide us with grounds for

1. MacIntyre, *A Short History of Ethics*, 1.

making universal claims both about human nature and about the functioning of the virtues.[2]

In discussions of human rights it is often claimed that the very idea of rights proper to all humans is a form of Western cultural imperialism, and that there are very different accounts of what it means to be human. These arguments are dubious because we can point to the common characteristics all humans share, which include not simply rationality and language, symbolic inventiveness and individuality, but also—and here crucially—a capacity for affection and for humiliation. The cultural anthropologist Melford Spiro argues that the helplessness of the human infant means that children are everywhere raised in family or family-like groups. "As a result children everywhere have the following characteristics: the need to receive love from, and the motivation to express love for, the loving and loved objects; feelings of rivalry toward those who seek love from the same (scarce) love objects; hostility toward those who would deprive them of these objects, and so on. In short, everywhere (due to Oedipal struggles and conflicts with siblings) children's love is necessarily thwarted, as well as gratified, to some extent. This applies, too, to the fact that humans need to live in social groups which requires compliance with cultural norms."[3] Spiro argues that it follows from the fact that all cultures must cope with common biological features that human beings have a nature as well as a history. There are common social and cultural features across a narrow range of social and cultural variability that, in their interaction, produce a universal human nature.[4]

In a similar way the political theorist Bhiku Parekh argues that the term *human nature* refers to those permanent and universal capacities, desires, and dispositions that all human beings share by virtue of belonging to a common species. Human beings have a common physical and mental structure, possess identical sense organs, share a common mental structure and possess capacities such as rationality, ability to form concepts and to learn

2. MacIntyre: "Where we were, where we are, where we need to be," 309–10.

3. Spiro, *Culture and Human Nature*, 25.

4. Ibid., 27.

language; and they all share the capacity to will, judge, fantasize, dream, build theories, construct myths, feel nostalgic about the past, anticipate future events, make plans, and so forth.[5]

Both Spiro and Parekh argue on biological or sociobiological grounds. Martha Nussbaum, by contrast, argues for a universal human nature on the ground that all humans have to face the same existential dilemmas. All have to negotiate death, to regulate bodily appetites and make judgements in the areas of food, drink, and sex, and they have to take a stand about property and the distribution of scarce resources and planning their own lives.[6] These shared dilemmas enable us to talk of shared humanity, and derivatively of the values that promote human flourishing.

Apart from being extremely dubious on biological and social grounds, arguments against the existence of a universal human nature are dangerous because were human rights a purely Western concern (say) this would endorse different standards for treatment of humans across cultures (torture is all right for Arabs but not for Westerners, for blacks but not for whites, for Jews but not for Aryans, etc.).[7] A proper respect for difference quickly shades into a very improper kind of apartheid, the subtext of which is often a defense of patriarchy.[8]

We are accustomed, these days, on the one hand to affirm that culture goes "all the way down," and that all cultures demand respect, and in the very next breath to argue that no human should be tortured, or that female circumcision is always wrong.

5. Parekh, *Redefining Multiculturalism*, 116.

6. Nussbaum, *Cultivating Humanity*, 138.

7. Muslim feminists in Britain have appealed to universal rights as Chetan Bhatt notes. *Liberation and Purity*, 264.

8. One of V. S. Naipaul's interlocutors in Pakistan told him: "When people here talk about the emotional rejection of the West, they usually mean one thing: Women." *Amongst the Believers*, 115. Amartya Sen, a Bengali in origin, challenges the claim that Asian societies have less time for individual freedom than Western ones, pointing out the many authoritarian dimensions of Western tradition, but also noting that the presence of dissidents in every culture makes it impossible to speak of the values that uniquely characterize any particular culture. *Development as Freedom*, 247.

This paradox, I want to suggest, is artificial, and the priority of cultural construction easily masks the extent of crosscultural agreement. As Terry Eagleton points out, there are few cherished works of art that advocate torture and mutilation as a form of human flourishing, or celebrate rape and famine as precious forms of human experiences.

> This fact is so baldly obvious that we are tempted to pass over its curiousness. For why, from a culturalist or historicist standpoint, should this be so? Why this imposing consensus? If we really are nothing but our local, ephemeral cultural conditions, of which there have been countless millions in the history of the species, how come that artistic culture over the ages does not affirm almost as many different moral values? Why is it that, with some egregious exceptions and in countlesss different cultural modes, culture in this sense has not on the whole elevated rapacious egoism over loving kindness, or material acquisitiveness over generosity?[9]

The answer to this question I take to be that what human beings share, both across cultures and across time, is deeper than what culturally divides them.[10]

On human ends

I take it, then, that there is something we can call "human nature," and I want to go on to argue that we can speak of human ends. To begin at the most basic these include survival, and therefore procreation. As Aristotle suggests, sociality (which includes child rearing) is a proper human end, and beyond that are the

9. Eagleton, *The Idea of Culture*, 105. Norman Geras points out that the need to justify inhumanity suggests the force of universalizing reasons. *Solidarity in the Conversation of Humankind*, 59.

10. Jeffrey Stout challenges the possibility of a moral Esperanto, and to put it like that does indeed suggest a falsely universalizing procedure, but, to use his own example, if we accept that in an honor society justice is vengeance, we find ourselves unable to be outraged by honor killings, or to protest against them in the name of—what? A shared humanity? *Ethics after Babel*, 72.

spiritual, cultural, and imaginative dimensions of human life that issue in the practice of all the arts, of engineering and town planning, and all the dimensions of play. Taken together these give us a recognizable account of "human flourishing" that, I suggest, all cultures can sign up to.

In the first book of the *Nicomachean Ethics* Aristotle asks about the ultimate end or object of human life. Even the question would be disallowed by many contemporary thinkers, on the grounds that teleological questions are out of bounds, a remnant of a priori prescientific thinking, and also that such questions fail to recognize the irreducible difference amongst both human cultures and individuals. Bernard Williams, for example, argues that we learn from Darwin that there is no teleology and that "there is no orchestral score provided from anywhere according to which human beings have a special part to play."[11] The difficulties teleological thinking can lead us into are illustrated by the ban on contraception in the Roman Catholic Church, on the grounds that the "end" of sexual intercourse is always procreation and that any other "use" is therefore "against nature."

Do these difficulties mean that we have to abandon any notion of human ends? The problem with the contraception argument is that the account of what is truly natural is shaped by a deep suspicion of pleasure and an even deeper suspicion of sexuality. Take those suspicions away and the arguments about contraception fail. Rosalind Hursthouse challenges the rejection of all teleology first of all on the grounds that, "If we really are, by nature, just a mess, then we are beings for whom no form of life is likely to prove satisfactory at all."[12] Order in the world we inhabit underlies the possibility of being able to switch on an electric light, of music and of language, and by that very fact (the possibility of communication) suggests the possibility of order both for individual and society (Plato's point in *The Republic*).

What would we mean by that "order"? I suggest it is the creative fulfilment of the potentials—as sketched in the previous

11. Williams, *Making Sense of Humanity*, 110.
12. Hursthouse, *On Virtue Ethics*, 261.

section—a fulfillment that is both individual and social. This would constitute the human telos. Discussing this, Aristotle at once dismisses three accounts of human ends, two of which are still with us, as inadequate. He notes that some people regard pleasure as the aim of life, which I suggested in the first chapter was a contemporary cultural dominant. Related to that is wealth, another leading contemporary contender. For Aristotle it is self-evidently not an ultimate good but, according to some contemporary commentators, this is exactly what liberalism enthrones and this necessarily destroys any understanding of human equality, given the obvious differences in human strength and skill.[13]

In ancient Greek society cultured people thought honor was the goal, but Aristotle also considered that too superficial.[14] Today, although we recognize "kudos," honor is not widely recognized as a goal to aspire to. "With the triumph of the ideology of individualism toward the end of the eighteenth century," writes Tzvetan Todorov, "the heroic model falls rapidly out of favour. People no longer dream of glory and adventure but aspire to personal happiness or even to a life of pleasure."[15]

Aristotle's own suggestion is that the human goal is *eudaimonia*, often misleadingly translated "happiness." Because Aristotle regarded the summit of human satisfaction as contemplation, or reflection, when Aquinas took this over he naturally argued that contemplation of God was the supreme human end, the true source of human happiness, a view which was reproduced in the Westminster Confession's teaching that the true end of human beings was "to love God and enjoy God forever." This view is fine if it recognizes that the God witnessed to in Scripture loves and engages with that which is not God. In the Middle Ages the idea that the human end was contemplation of God was used to justify a two-tier view of Christian discipleship that, in a text like *The Imitation of Christ*, urged disengagement from the world.

13. Macpherson, *The Real World of Democracy*, 62.
14. Aristotle, *Nicomachean Ethics*, 1095b, 1096a.
15. Todorov, *Facing the Extreme*, 50.

A recent account of human ends by Robert and Edward Skidelsky prioritizes the ancient virtue of moderation, which Bernard Williams dismissed as "a substantive and tedious Aristotelian ideal, which we can ignore."[16] The Skidelskys do not defend it as essential in an age of planetary boundaries, but as critical to a perception of what life is really all about in an age of consumerism, when it is taken for granted that more is always better. The desire to have more of everything all the time, they rightly see, is destructive of humanness. For them the good life is constituted by seven basic goods: health, security, respect, personality (the ability to frame and execute a plan of life reflective of one's tastes, temperament, and conception of the good), harmony with nature, friendship, and leisure.[17] There is a strong overlap here with the 1948 Declaration of Human Rights, to which I shall return in the next chapter. However, this account still works within the terms of liberal individualism, and *eudaimonia* is more than this. It is, in fact, the rational (which for Aristotle includes the emotional) pursuit of goodness, or the good life, realized in action; a balanced, whole, and just life *held in common*, pretty much what Herman Daly and John Cobb argue for in their economic manifesto, *For the Common Good*.[18] It is political, in the sense that it contributes to the good of the human community (the *polis*); it involves a constructive account of "housekeeping" (*oikonomia*) for the community. It involves the arts and leisure, and of course, it has a contemplative, spiritual, or reflective dimension.

Veerkamp's account of the grand narrative of Scripture, which I summarized in the previous chapter, shows that he understands it

---

16. Williams, "Acting as a Virtuous Person Acts," 18. Plato problematizes it in the *Charmides*, one of his "definition" dialogues, as he problematizes courage in the *Laches*, but perhaps as a way of challenging an accepted piety. In his classic study of Greek Tragedy, George Thomson argues that *sophrosune* was an instrument of class oppression, a way of keeping the lower classes quiet (*Aeschylus and Athens*, 350) but Philip Vellacott argues, to my mind more convincingly, that for Euripides it was key to his plea for sanity in the Peloponnesian war—a real parallel with climate change. (*Euripides*, 30.)

17. Skidelsky and Skidelsky, *How Much is Enough?*, ch. 6.

18. See Aristotle, *Nicomachean Ethics*, 1098a.

in some such way: as the attempt to form and to sustain a community that lives on the principles of generosity and of what Aristotle calls distributive justice, but outside the logic of retributive justice. If we begin from Paul's correspondence with the Corinthians, and with the Christian group in Galatia, then we can say that one of the big differences with Aristotle is that everyone is included. As Jacob Taubes puts it, Paul's keyword is "all"—women and men, slaves and free, Gentile and Jew. Key differences between Aristotle and the Messianic Writings are that for the latter the understanding of all reality as gift, and therefore of virtue as the response to gift ("grace"), is key, along with an understanding of community, and the possibility of joy for the individual as based on forgiveness.

There are, then, constructive human ends in all societies but, as we all know, these are constantly frustrated. Disvalues take priority over values. Why? And what is it that above all frustrates human ends? In the tradition of the virtues this was spoken of in terms of vices. In Christian theology the word used was *sin*. If we are thinking of the possibility of cultural collapse, and of what we have to do to prevent that, we need to address the question of what it is that destroys our humanity.

The roots of inhumanity

Once upon a time, and for many thousands of years—perhaps 200,000—human beings lived in hunter gatherer groups of fifteen to fifty people related by kinship. The groups were relatively egalitarian and leadership tended to be by example and not by fiat. They tended to have a common property regime with sharing and reciprocity as the central rule of social interaction.[19] These groups lived by custom, not law.[20]

19. Lee and Daly, "Foragers and Others."

20. Many of these groups have the notion of the giving environment, the idea that the land around them is their spiritual home and the source of all good things. This view, some argue, is the direct antithesis of the Judaeo-Christian perspective on the natural environment as a "wilderness," a hostile space to be subdued and brought to heel by the force of will. These groups believe in

Slowly, over many thousands of years, humans learned to cultivate crops, which required a settled, rather than a nomadic, existence. Hunters, as Colin Tudge argues, quickly overplay their hand: kill too much and you destroy your resource base. With settled agriculture, however, the more you work, the more you produce. Hunter gatherers commonly spend much of their time at leisure, but with the advent of agriculture humans have to earn their bread by the sweat of their brow. Now surpluses become possible, as well as large increases of population and, according to Rousseau, followed by Marx and Engels, we have the world-historical "fall." Now we have the beginning of hierarchy, of slavery, of gender oppression, of the toiling masses exploited by the few.

As a matter of fact, it seems that women and men were not equal even in hunter gatherer groups, and these groups were not especially peaceful either—interpersonal violence is documented for most and warfare is recorded for a number of hunter gatherer peoples. Nevertheless it is true that it is only after the emergence of complex societies, and of cities, that we get law, the function of which is to limit the disintegrative force of certain types of human behavior. If we take the "ten Words" of Exodus 20, which bear a strong resemblance to other, more ancient, Middle Eastern codes, then murder, theft, slander, adultery, perjury are all proscribed, for the obvious reason that no society survives if these are the norm.

Aristotle contrasted the virtues—habits that shaped a truly human life—with vices—habits that did the opposite. These included things like vanity and pusillanimity, the excess and defect of magnanimity, or great spiritedness—which today we would rather regard as undesirable character traits than as vices. From the fourth century onwards the church drew up a list of "seven deadly sins"—pride, lust, gluttony, avarice, envy, sloth, and anger.

---

a "Trickster," who symbolizes the frailty and human qualities of the gods and their closeness to humans, in sharp contrast to the omnipotent, all-knowing but distant deities that are central to the pantheons of state religions and their powerful ecclesiastical hierarchies. See ibid., 5. Such a critique overlooks the theology of creation according to which the natural environment is a "garden" to be cultivated and cared for, and for which all created reality is gift. More on this in chs. 5 and 8.

Pride was deemed the key vice, the sense that one could manage on one's own, without God.[21] Correspondingly sloth (*acedia*) follows from lack of faith in what God can accomplish, leading us to give up on both human and divine ends. Lust (*luxuria*) is the perversion of desire. Desire—not just sexual desire, but desire for all sorts of goods—is proper to our humanity, but it can consume us and in so doing defeat the realization of human ends. Avarice does the same thing. Gluttony (*gula*) is a vice not primarily because it is self-indulgent, but because it fails to respect the needs of others. In our culture it is either a joke—represented by stock characters like Billy Bunter—or a misrepresentation of a socio-psychological problem that leads to obesity. In fact, if it is about failing to respect the needs of others, it could easily be represented as the crucial vice of capitalism leading to the grotesque inequalities recently highlighted by Thomas Piketty (as detailed in chapter six). Envy was condemned because it was taken to imply a desire to see others suffer, or to misappropriate their property. Anger was understood as the root of violence.

Today for many people (in the West at least) cruelty—the use of the imagination to devise tortures to humiliate and destroy opponents—is the worst vice, though it remains, as it has always been, plentiful.[22] In his account of the Russian revolution Orlando Figes argues that the sadistic cruelty that marked the behavior of both sides was a cruelty made by history: The violence and cruelty that the old regime inflicted on the peasant was transformed into a peasant violence that not only disfigured daily

21. This was either picked up from, or shared with, the Greek tradition, and especially the Tragedians, for whom hubris is the key failing that brings disaster on humans.

22. Recently the fighters of ISIS took a captured Jordanian pilot and burned him alive in a cage, an action that does not deter young Western Muslims from going to join them. In *A People's Tragedy* Orlando Figes argues that the savagery of the revolutionary struggle in Russia built on and was made possible by the level of violence already taken for granted in Russian peasant society. *A People's Tragedy*, 96. Appalling savagery was found on both sides in the Greek civil war, and apparently had deep roots in Balkan history. Gerolymatos, *An International Civil War*. These histories have to be weighed against anarchist accounts of human cooperation, as mentioned in chs. 6 and 9.

village life, but also rebounded against the regime in the terrible violence of the revolution.[23] Over against a civilizing process, we might say, is a brutalizing process.

What is the root of inhuman behavior? The English word *sin* translates a large number of Hebrew and Greek words that designate unrighteousness, injustice, offenses against morals or laws, and losing one's way. If one examines the uses of the various words translated as "sin" in Scripture they all describe forms of behavior that destroy or diminish life. In Paul sin is a "power" under which we are bound (Rom 7:17), and this is the root of the Augustinian account of sin, which has been the dominant doctrine in Western theology. As Alistair McFadyen rightly insists, the language of sin carries an inbuilt reference to God, "naming the pathological as the denial of and opposition to God."[24] In his account of the Augustinian tradition McFadyen first gives an account of original sin as a "field of force," which we necessarily share in and which "distorts the internal energies by which one orients and directs one's life from within."[25] It completely muddies our understanding of reality. Secondly, in his account, sin is fundamentally idolatry— the shaping of our energies by that which is not God. This leads to a "total disorientation of desire."[26]

This account is close to what the liberation theologians called "structural sin." Thus the Jesuit martyr Ignacio Ellacuria wrote, shortly before his death, "The original violence, the root and beginning of all other forms of violence in society, is what is called structural violence, which is simply structural injustice . . . sanctioned by an unjust legal framework and an ideologically based cultural framework."[27] Depriving people of what is needed for a fully human life is violence and it begets the violence of repression, the violence of revolution, and the violence of rage and frustration.

23. Figes, *People's Tragedy*, 96.

24. McFadyen, *Bound to Sin*, 11.

25. Ibid., 188.

26. Ibid., 225.

27. Ellacuria, "Violence and non-violence in the struggle for peace and liberation," 70.

Augustine notoriously thought sin was transmitted through procreation. This has analogies with the work of those biologists, like Konrad Lorenz and Desmond Morris, who understand human violence as part of our evolutionary heritage. Aggression, it is argued, would have been necessary for hunting, and for defending the group against the attacks of wild animals. Without it homo sapiens could not have survived and we are still living with this evolutionary fallout. Instead of speaking of a "fall," the Uruguayan theologian Juan Luis Segundo followed the second-century theologian Irenaeus (who thought that humankind grew from the image to the likeness in a process in which Christ played a crucial part) in thinking instead of a slow process of hominization. What is today taken for wicked behavior, he suggested, may once have been a force for good.[28]

The many psychological explanations of dehumanizing behavior likewise have analogies with the idea that there are structures or "fields of force" that shape us willy nilly. Thus, for example, Carol Gilligan finds the connection between violence and patriarchy to be that men are not socialized into the maintenance of human connection, but rather into its breakdown.[29]

McFadyen is quite right that "sin" is a strictly theological category, understanding the roots of inhumanity in terms of a fracture in the human relation to God, but whilst we can offer that as a contribution to the discussion or how life-denying behavior should be understood, if we are appealing to all human beings (since everyone is impacted by the transgression of planetary boundaries) we need a language that does not require that everyone share the Christian faith. In her advocacy of a liberal polity Martha Nussbaum draws on the child psychologist Donald Winnicott to redefine Kant's idea of radical evil. A child's helplessness and primitive shame, she argues, lead to rage and destructive tendencies, which can be surmounted in the direction of concern only by a strong emotion of love toward the object whose destruction is both feared and sought. But even when a child has managed to develop capacities for genuine

28. Segundo, *Evolution and Guilt*, 76.
29. Gilligan, *In a Different Voice*, 43.

concern, persisting insecurities make it prone to projective disgust and the subordination of others, as people learn to split the world of humans into favored and stigmatized groups.[30] For Kant, radical evil centrally concerned competitive ranking and the obstacle it poses to the recognition of equal human dignity. A tendency to form hierarchies, Nussbaum argues, is clearly a part of our evolutionary heritage, but narcissism, the desire for omnipotence, and what she calls "anthropodenial" (the denial of our animal natures) make hierarchy take a particular shape that threatens the life of any moderately just society. Anxieties associated with bodily vulnerability takes the shape of disgust, which is projected on to other groups. These forces are radical in the sense of being rooted in the very structure of human development—our bodily helplessness and our cognitive sophistication—rather than being the creation of this or that particular culture.[31] The combination of narcissism with helplessness—a helplessness that is resented and repudiated—is where radical evil gets its start, in the form of a tendency to subordinate other people to one's own needs.[32]

This is an account of the deep roots of inhumanity that does not presuppose faith. I shall consider some of the difficulties it poses when I discuss the nature of the virtues. I take the first step in that direction by examining the role of education in shaping our humanness.

Learning to become fully human

Plato and Aristotle display their Greek prejudices by assuming that the polis is the core institution for the realization of our humanity and both give a key place within it to education. As compared to Plato, Aristotle allows a greater role for habituation and family training as part of that. People who have not been well brought

---

30. Nussbaum, *Political Emotions,* 165.

31. Ibid., 191.

32. Ibid., 172.

up, he argues, do not even have a notion of what is noble and truly pleasant, since they have never tasted it.

> What argument indeed can transform people like that? To change by argument what has long been ingrained in a character is impossible or, at least, not easy. Argument and teaching, I'm afraid, are not effective in all cases: the soul of the listener must first have been conditioned by habits to the right kind of likes and dislikes, just as land must be cultivated before it is able to foster seed. For a man whose life is guided by emotion will not listen to an argument that dissuades him, nor will he understand it. And in general it seems that emotion does not yield to argument but only to force. Therefore there must first be a character that somehow has an affinity for excellence or virtue, a character that loves what is noble and feels disgust at what is base.[33]

Hursthouse argues that one of Aristotle's key advantages as a moral philosopher is that he never forgets that children are also part of society, and that we were all once children. The moral agent is not for him, as he or she seems to be for some philosophers, born fully fledged from the philosopher's brow.[34] Humans differ from other animals in their capacity for education, and a sound moral education issues in possession and exercise of the virtues.

Education is not equivalent to "schooling," though in their study of Holocaust rescuers the Oliners argue that schools need to become institutions that not only prepare students for academic competence but also help them to acquire an extensive orientation to others. We could think of the proposal to include conflict resolution as a standard component of primary education as a plausible and constructive way of tackling that. But, they note, "It is out of the quality of routine human activities that the human spirit evolves and moral courage is born. Such courage is available to all through the

---

33. Aristotle, *Nicomachean Ethics,* 1179b 15–30.
34. Hursthouse, *On Virtue Ethics,* 14.

virtues of connectedness, commitment and the quality of relationships developed in ordinary human interactions."[35]

Tocqueville drew attention to the role of family life, religious traditions, and participation in local politics. He regarded the variety of active civic organizations as the key to American democracy. "Through active involvement in common concerns, the citizen can overcome their sense of relative isolation and powerlessness that results from the insecurity of life in an increasingly commercial society."[36] In the civic republican tradition, Bellah et al. comment, "public life is built upon the second languages and practices of commitment that shape character. These languages and practices establish a web of interconnection by creating trust, joining people to families, friends, communities and churches, and making each individual aware of his reliance on the larger society. They form those habits of the heart that are the matrix of a moral ecology, the connecting tissue of a body politic."[37] These accounts of civic life very much illustrate what Aristotle meant by moral education and perhaps explain the emphasis on the role of "civic society" over the past forty years.

Nussbaum argues that a humane polity begins with good child rearing. The disgust that arises spontaneously from our infant rage and helplessness makes equal political respect impossible. We overcome it by encouraging the trust and joy that good child rearing enables, and through imaginative play. This develops the spirit of love, which needs encouraging for a whole lifetime. All of the core emotions that sustain decent society, such as compassion and hope, have their roots in, or are forms of, love. Love is what gives respect for humanity its life, making it more than the shell.[38] Love

35. Oliner and Oliner, *The Altruistic Personality,* 260.

36. Bellah et al., *Habits of the Heart,* 38.

37. Ibid., 251.

38. Nussbaum, *Political Emotions,* 15. By compassion we mean "a painful emotion directed at the serious suffering of another creature or creatures. There are three aspects of this. First there is seriousness, understanding someone else's suffering in a way that is important and nontrivial. Second is the thought of non-fault: we typically don't feel compassion if we think the person's predicament chosen or self-inflicted. Third is the thought of similar possibilities.

is cultivated partly through the culture promoting and encouraging the spirit of play and imaginative sympathy that we find in the arts, and in particular in both comedy and tragedy.[39] The former teaches us to see "the uneven and often unlovely destiny of human beings in the world with humour, tenderness, and delight, rather than with absolutist rage for an impossible sort of perfection." The latter "gives insight into shared vulnerabilities."[40]

I shall say a little more about tragedy in the final chapter but a word is in order on both comedy and on the role of music in our humanization. Iris Murdoch famously argued that art was a school of attention through which we learned how to love. It teaches us the "selfless attention" that cuts through the fantasy that blinkers us, limiting our attention to false accounts of ourselves and the world, and that enables us to love the neighbor.[41] George Steiner, however, argues that we learn from the Shoah that we cannot say that "the humanities humanize": the cycle of Beethoven chamber music recitals went on in Munich a few miles from Dachau, and made no difference at all to Nazi barbarity. Acutely aware of the power of music, Plato warned that not all, but only some, music humanizes, and there is no agreement whatever on what kind of music that is. At the same time, music and the other arts are indisputably part of our humanness, and politically speaking one must doubt whether there has ever been a humane polity without comedy, indeed whether there could ever be a humane polity without it. It not only ironizes our imperfections but even more importantly, the power that corrupts (Acton).[42]

The person who has compassion often does think that the suffering person is similar to him or herself and has possibilities in life that are similar." Ibid., 144.

39. Ibid., 191.

40. Ibid., 16, 21.

41. Murdoch, *The Sovereignty of Good*, 103.

42. Umberto Eco's *The Name of the Rose* is in part a parable about the hatred the totalitarian mind always has for laughter. (Hitler reportedly foamed at the mouth when he saw Chaplain's *The Great Dictator*.)

Virtues as ways of becoming human

Virtues, according to Aristotle, are learned dispositions. He distinguishes intellectual virtues, acquired through schooling, and moral virtues, learned through habituation (another form of education, of course). The idea that the way in which we judge and understand might itself be a virtue seems odd to us, who routinely split epistemology from ethics, but Aristotle judges them to be virtues because all virtues involve the need to reason correctly. Wisdom and *phronesis,* practical reasoning, ground our search for truth, control our purposive action *(praxis),* and shape our appetites, impulses, and desires. In terms of the argument of this book virtues represent the realization of values, and vices the realization of disvalues. Havel called for the rehabilitation of values like trust, openness, responsibility, solidarity, and love, and today movements looking to repristinate democracy speak of generosity, humility, and empathy.[43] Here ancient *values* are recognized as essential political *virtues.*

Aristotle argues that just as you only learn a trade by actually doing it, so you learn the virtues by practicing them, something it is the lawmaker's job to foster. As someone with an intense interest in the natural world, Aristotle was impressed by the way in which things realized their potential, for example the way in which acorns became oak trees. In some respects it seemed to him that human beings had this same kind of potential, and he spoke of this as being "by nature." The moral virtues, he said, are engendered in us neither by nature, nor contrary to nature, but we are constituted by nature to receive them.[44] "To act virtuously is not, as Kant was later to think, to act against inclination; it is to act from inclination formed by the cultivation of the virtues."[45] Virtues are not feelings (a crucial difference from contemporary accounts of therapy), nor are they simply potentials or capacities

---

43. Havel, *Power of the Powerless,* 93; cf. the discussion of core values in the Alternative Party in Denmark, http://alternativet.dk.

44. Aristotle, *Nicomachean Ethics,* 1103a.

45. MacIntyre, *After Virtue,* 147.

(*dunameis*) but conscious acts, the product of our practical rationality (*phronesis*). They are expressions of choice: we do not become good or bad "by nature," a suggestion that puts him at odds with some accounts of how genes function. Every virtue, Aristotle suggests, can be understood in relation to extremes on left and right, extremes of excess or deficiency. This is his famous doctrine of "the mean," best understood, in Hursthouse's words, as the attempt to "get things right."[46] The idea of the mean comes not from the metaphysician but from the craftsman, who tries things out, stands back, measures by eye as well as by rule, to find out what fits. On these lines, Julia Annas remarks that virtue has the structure of a skill: it requires reflection and understanding of the basic principles of a practical ability, and this means a virtuous person cannot become so without being critically reflective.[47]

Aquinas suggests that political and private virtues can be distinguished.[48] Following this suggestion Todorov argues that the traditional heroic virtues, of strength, courage, and loyalty, may be indispensable during grave crises, in times of life or death struggle, uprising, or war, but that in peace these virtues are transformed into the obsession with winning, the need to succeed at all costs. The moral value of these is nil. The ordinary virtues—dignity, caring, the life of the mind—are appropriate to times of peace. They also have their place in times of crisis when the aim is to remain human.[49] Vasily Grossman distinguishes ideals of the good on the one hand and of kindness on the other. The former can lead to the attempt to impose it on others at any cost. What really matters is "everyday human kindness." "The kindness of an old woman carrying a piece of bread to a prisoner, the kindness of a soldier allowing a wounded enemy to drink from his water flask . . . It is

46. Hursthouse , *On Virtue Ethics*, 12.

47. Annas, *The Morality of Happiness*, 70–71.

48. *Summa Theologiae*, 1a 2ae 60.3 Aquinas distinguishes four levels of virtue: Moral virtues are political virtues because human beings are "by nature" political animals; there are "purifying virtues" that characterize those on the way to the heavenly city; there are virtues of those already purified; and there are exemplary virtues that exist already in God. *Summa Theologiae*, 1a2ae 61.5.

49. Todorov, *Facing the Extreme*, 107.

the kindness of one individual toward another, kindness without ideology, a kindness that does not ask that its beneficiary deserve it that is most truly human in a human being."[50]

One can understand this but it is important not to miss the key role courage plays in everyday, and *therefore* political life.[51] Both Eva Fogelman and Hannah Arendt draw attention to the place of courage in helping Jews. In April 1933 the Nazis called for a boycott of Jewish businesses. A few individuals defied the boycott but "the universities were silent, the courts were silent; the President of the Reich, who had taken the oath on the Constitution, was silent." This day, says Fogelman, was "the day of greatest cowardice." Without that cowardice, all that followed would not have happened.[52]

The tradition of the virtues dropped out of philosophical discourse for getting on two centuries, in a process famously analysed by MacIntyre, and there remain real objections to it. Thus, with characteristic irony, Barrington Moore remarks that political talk about the need for a thoroughgoing moral regeneration tends to cover the absence of a realistic analysis of prevailing social conditions, because such an analysis would threaten vested interests. "Probably it is a good working rule to be suspicious about political and intellectual leaders who talk mainly about moral virtues; many poor devils are liable to be badly hurt."[53] One can think of the emphasis on "family values" of the Thatcher and Reagan administrations and today under "austerity" (i.e., making sure the bankers do not have to pay for their mistakes) we begin to hear again of Poor Richard's virtues of thrift, discipline, and hard work.

50. Grossman, *Life and Fate*, 407–8.

51. Jonathan Schell reminds us that Gandhi understood courage as a key virtue, essential to nonviolent direct action. *The Unconquerable World*, 112, 132. Based on her understanding of virtue as rooted in attention, Iris Murdoch speaks of the courage that could act unselfishly in a concentration camp as "steadfast, calm, temperate, intelligent, loving." *Sovereignty*, 95

52. Fogelman, *Conscience and Courage*, 24.

53. Moore, *The Social Origins of Dictatorship and Democracy*. He is talking about what he calls "Catonism" (after Cato the elder), the situation in which peasant society is under threat by urbanization.

The Augustinian tradition puts a question mark against the element of striving implicit in the virtues, setting it over against justification by faith. For ancient ethics once I am convinced that it is important to become virtuous I can take steps to enable myself to act virtuously—by thinking harder before the appropriate occasion and consciously resolving to do so. By making this into a consistent pattern I can bring it about that acting virtuously is less and less effort on each occasion and the more I get used to it the more comfortable I will feel with it and the more pleasant it will be.[54] The practice of the virtues, on this account, rather resembles the twelve steps used in countering addiction. Justification, on the other hand, implies that the new life of grace comes to us as a free gift of God. Talk of virtue seems to assume that the moral life is a kind of human achievement. Furthermore, as Luther insisted in *The Bondage of the Will*, and Augustine in his debate with Pelagius, our ethical choices are misdirected because we cannot, apart from God, tell what is good. Dostoevsky teaches us that the capacity for "perversion, addiction, self sacrifice, self destruction and a whole range of 'rationally' indefensible behaviours" are part of what it means to be human.[55] The suspicion is that the tradition of the virtues cannot make sense of this.

The language of justification, originated by Paul and made into a shibboleth by Luther, was directed at the way in which moral imperatives can function to dehumanize us, making us judges both of ourselves and our neighbour, robbing life of joy and freedom and producing a censorious culture (memorably satirized by Shakespeare in the figure of Malvolio). Paul's keyword, *charis*, ("grace"), was the recognition that human beings live by forgiveness and that therefore they are not committed to this repressive moralism. This is an important truth, but it does not mean we have to dispense with the language of the virtues (as Aquinas saw). Aquinas, like Augustine, presupposes that the whole of reality is sustained by the divine self-gift ("grace") and that it is possible for human beings to live in an engagement with that self-gift. Here

54. Annas, *Morality*, 56.
55. Williams, *Dostoevsky*, 17.

comes the difficult bit: for Augustine, the best virtues of good pagans are nothing but "splendid vices." For Aquinas, we put ourselves within the orbit of divine self gift through the sacraments. This leaves the bulk of humankind without the possibility of living a virtuous life—something common experience, not to mention the understanding of God derived from Scripture, shows to be nonsense. We therefore need to acknowledge that engagement with the divine self-gift, which both creates and sustains all reality, is possible outside the church. Cyprian is mistaken: it is not *extra ecclesiam nulla salus*, though it is *extra gratiam nulla salus*. What the church does (or claims to do) is to provide, in its narratives, a true account of the nature of the God who is self-gift in Godself, and therefore to help humanity discern where God is to be found. This will mean that sharp questions can be put, for example, to Aristotle's list of the virtues—not to mention Franklin's! As Hauerwas rightly notes, "If the trumpeted return to civic virtue involves the arming of virtue with the courage of the soldier and if Christians are committed to another sort of courage not formed on war, there is good reason to think that the Christian churches cannot nor should not underwrite a programme of return to civic virtue, at least not in all aspects."[56] That is well said. A Christian account of the virtues begins with Paul's account of "the fruits of the Spirit" (Gal 5), though I have already given reasons for thinking that Aquinas was right to include courage (not in Paul's list) as one of the virtues. Key amongst the virtues is forgiveness. To live "in grace," which is to live a virtuous life, is to live both by the receiving and giving of forgiveness.[57]

A quite different objection to the language of the virtues comes from Martha Nussbaum, who argues that neither the Christian nor the Aristotelian account of the virtues can be combined

56. Hauerwas and Pinches, *Christians among the Virtues*, 151.

57. In the Christian narrative justice is defined through it, rather than the other way around (a fact which has huge implications for discussions of criminal justice). As MacIntyre points out, Aristotle would have found the idea that forgiveness was an alternative to punishment incomprehensible. "There are no words in the Greek of Aristotle's age correctly translated by sin, repentance or charity." *After Virtue*, 174.

with erotic love, with all the vulnerability it implies. "If you admit such love you will almost surely be led outside the boundaries of the virtues. But if we leave love out we leave out a force of unsurpassed wonder and power."[58] One of the real marks of progress in twentieth-century thought was reincorporating erotic love within both moral philosophy and theology, something that owes a great debt to Freud. The reasons for the ancient exclusion of passion from the virtues are only too obvious: eros is fragile, self-reflexive and, as Nussbaum observes, uncomfortably close to anger and even rage. But recognizing that does not mean that it is incompatible with a consistent pursuit of moral goodness, or that a way cannot be found to include eros within such a pursuit. Novelists like George Eliot and Dostoevsky give us a picture of erotic love "contributing to the greater good of the world" (Eliot's Dorothea Brooke) or as being the agent of a murderer's redemption (Sonia in *Crime and Punishment*). The "unsurpassed wonder and power" that Nussbaum rightly talks of, for all its fragility, is probably for most people the lightning flash that illuminates landscapes of generosity and openness to otherness and these flashes of illumination are a vital part of that human education that results in the virtues.

Lastly, there are objections on the grounds of moral theory. Critics of virtue ethics have often complained that it is unable to specify how people should act and that act- rather than agent-centered ethics are far more helpful in spelling out what people have to do in given situations. But in Germany after 1933 it was perfectly obvious what ought to be done, but people lacked the courage to do it. The miserably small numbers of those who helped Jews means, says Todorov, that we can take no comfort from the tradition of the virtues. Against that we can set Eva Fogelman's findings, that the half of 1 percent of Europe's population who acted to save Jews did so out of their basic character, their core values and self-images.[59] They acted on the basis of virtue, the values developed and instilled in childhood. These childhood experiences and influences, she says, formed a leitmotif that played through

58 Nussbaum, *The Therapy of Desire*, 480.
59. Fogelman, *Conscience and Courage*, 169.

the histories of most rescuers.[60] Moreover, though no single group emerged with especial credit from the catastrophe it is interesting that strong traditions of teaching and discipline were over-represented. In Holland, for example, members of the 8 percent of the population who belonged to the Reformed church accounted for nearly a quarter of the rescuers.[61] Bruno Bettelheim noted that in the camps Jehovah's Witnesses "were generally narrow in outlook, wanting to make converts, but on the other hand exemplary comrades, helpful, correct, dependable . . . quite in contrast to the continuous internecine warfare among the other prisoner groups, the Jehovah's Witnesses never misused their closeness to SS officers to gain position privilege in the camp."[62]

During the Eichmann trial the court heard how a German sergeant, Anton Schmidt, helped escaping Jews, before being executed himself. The court fell into silence, and Arendt comments: "a single thought stood out clearly, irrefutably, beyond question— how utterly different everything would be today in this courtroom, in Israel, in Germany, in all of Europe, and perhaps in all countries of the world, if only more such stories could have been told."[63] The fact that even a few people were able to display this courage, Arendt thought, meant that the planet remained fit for human habitation. If we persist in defining ourselves as doomed, write the Oliners, "human nature as beyond redemption, and social institutions as beyond reform, then we shall create a future that will inexorably proceed in confirming this view. Rescuers refused to see Jews as guilty or beyond hope and themselves as helpless, despite all the evidence marshalled to the contrary."[64]

The idea that the virtues could be discounted wholesale, or that the vices might take their place, so that the world could be run

60. Ibid., 253.

61. Oliner and Oliner, *The Altruistic Personality*, 38. In Britain Quakers took half of the children who came over on kindertransport before the war.

62. Bettelheim, *The Informed Heart*, 123.

63. Arendt, *Eichmann*, 231.

64. Oliner and Oliner, *The Altruistic Personality*, 260.

on the lines of the Camorra, or the Mexican drug gangs, clearly does not make sense, as Hursthouse argues.

> If to be a good, non-defective human being is to be endowed with those character traits that manifest themselves in seizing and enjoying whatever one wants, unconstrained by law and morality, and one's desires have not been enriched and amended by any of the training that begins the inculcation of the (real) virtues, then a collection of good human beings do not have any law or morality, do not give their children any kind of moral training—and indeed, clearly, do not bother about children at all, who, we must suppose, all die of neglect shortly after they are born.[65]

Society doesn't work on the basis of the vices, as we see in the case of the Nazis, Somalia, the Camorra, and so forth, and if Mumford is right, and capitalism turns traditional vices into virtues, then it is hardly surprising that our current society is full of problems. The current attempt by right-wing commentators to dismiss the virtues by understanding them simply as hypocrisy—so called "virtue signalling"—is only the most recent in a long line of attempts to justify the cynical use of power and discredit all attempts to change society for the better.[66]

The argument for accepting the tradition of the virtues as a key part in what it means to be human, therefore, runs like this: there are proper grounds for agreeing that there is as universal human nature, and that this is shaped by ends. The end, broadly speaking, is "flourishing," the exercise by all of the creative potentials latent in human beings. True flourishing, Christian theology wants to affirm, is the result of "grace"—i.e., being open to the divine self-gift that sustains all reality. An education (understood in the broadest sense to include arts, crafts, trades, as well as learning through relationships) structured around

---

65. Hursthouse, *On Virtue Ethics*, 252.

66. James Bartholomew in *The Spectator* takes credit for inventing this phrase. http://www.spectator.co.uk/2015/10/i-invented-virtue-signalling-now-its-taking-over-the-world/.

virtues—those dispositions that promote life—is what makes human flourishing possible. Education (in the sense defined) can be good or bad: it can embody values or disvalues. If it embodies the latter, however, society collapses.

Virtues and political practices

Aristotle gave a key role to training in the inculcation of virtue. "A given kind of activity produces a corresponding character. This is shown by the way in which people train themselves for any kind of context or performance: they keep on practising for it. Thus, only a man who is utterly insensitive can be ignorant of the fact that moral characteristics are formed by actively engaging in particular actions."[67] Aristotle assumes that the contemplative, or philosophical, life is best because it most resembles the divine. However, he acknowledges that the political or active life is what makes this possible. The moral virtues—moderation (*sophrosune*), courage, generosity, patience and, above all, justice, as guided by practical reason (*phronesis*—knowing which actions are appropriate at a given time)—are the ground of political life, and without these all the goods of human flourishing are simply impossible.[68]

The same is true in the Christian tradition, something which becomes clear when we remember that the word *ekklesia*, in the Messianic Writings, is borrowed from the word for the secular assembly in Athens, the meeting of the citizenry to debate policy. When Jesus uses it, and Paul takes it over, it probably translates *quahal*, the meeting of the tribes to do exactly the same thing. In choosing twelve disciples Jesus refounds Israel—he recapitulates it. At the heart of his teaching is the "kingly rule of God," which is to come "on earth, as in heaven." The messianic ecclesia is organized around this prayer and this praxis. What are called "the virtues of Christ" in Galatians 5—love, joy, peace, patience, kindness, generosity, faithfulness, gentleness, and self-control—serve this project,

67. Aristotle, *Nicomachean Ethics*, 1114a4–10.
68. Ibid., 1144b15.

the seed bed, for both Jesus and Paul, of a new humanity beyond ancient divisions.

MacIntyre has taken this up in his account of "practices" that are "any coherent and complex form of socially established cooperative human activity."[69] The examples he gives of practices include productive activities (farming and architecture), intellectual activities (science and history), artistic pursuits (painting and music), and politics (creating a political community).[70] Practices, on his account, are the school of the virtues. Accepting this argument I have used it to structure the next section of the book, in which I explore a set of key practices—political, economic, and agricultural—which will determine whether or not we keep our humanity in the crises we are likely to face (according to Emmott, Anderson, and other natural scientists). Anything that does not promote justice, courage, and truthfulness within individuals, and anything that does not aim in this and other ways to promote the common good of society is not properly regarded as a practice.[71] The virtues are cultivated through participation in practices, as practitioners come to find in a practice something beyond themselves that may be valued for its own sake rather than as a mere means to satisfy their more immediate and selfish desires.

That the practices through which we learn and exercise the virtues are essentially political is the assumption of Aristotle's *Politics.* He begins with the pragmatic and, as far as it goes, empirically based, assumption that human beings cannot survive on their own.[72] First, he argues, there is the family that meets the

---

69. MacIntyre, *After Virtue,* 187.

70. He also includes games such as chess and football, but I confess I do not see how they foster the virtues, especially in our money-soaked world.

71. Knight, ed., "Introduction," *The MacIntyre Reader,* 10.

72. The background to Aristotle's account is the wrestling with the concept of virtue in Plato's Protagoras and Meno. In the first the sophist Protagoras tells a *mythos* according to which human beings are ultimately asocial, and not "by nature" disposed to political association, and this leads to their destruction. To save them Zeus grants them *aidos,* reverence, shame, or humility, and *dike,* justice or right. These two virtues make a life in common possible, and to lack them is to put oneself outside of the bounds of civilized society. Socrates,

THE WORLD MADE OTHERWISE: VALUES AND VIRTUES

needs of food, shelter, and procreation. Then families get together in villages, and finally villages unite to form a polis. "For all practical purposes the process is now complete; self-sufficiency (*autarkeia*) has been reached, and while the polis came about as a means of securing life itself, it continues in being to secure the good life . . . The aim and the end is perfection; and self sufficiency is both end and perfection."[73] Only in the polis, Aristotle believes, can human beings realize their true end. The polis is a fact of nature, and human beings are "by nature" made to live in a polis (they are *zoon politikon*). Because humans, unlike bees, have no pre-given way of organizing themselves, but have to decide this by using their reason, politics is an inevitable human task. Contrary to the assumptions of modern individualism, Aristotle takes it as an axiom that the whole is prior to the part, because parts cannot exist without wholes.[74] Politics, for him, is the science that studies the human good, and in it the community comes first: "For even if the good of the community coincides with that of the individual, it is clearly a greater and more perfect thing to achieve and preserve that of a community."[75] Contrary to our understandings of politics as "the art of the possible" he believes it is concerned with "morally fine and just conduct."[76]

Although humans are "by nature political" this does not mean that they end up with one form of the polis. Aristotle was well aware of this, and therefore, as already noted, collected

---

however, problematizes this story. In the Protagoras he argues that virtue is a response to pleasure and that the choice of harmful pleasures is actually ignorance—people are misinformed (cf. the account of denial, complacency, and stupidity in the first chapter). As Socrates refuses to distinguish between noble and base pleasures, the argument collapses, for what then is virtue? In the Meno, meanwhile, Socrates now argues that virtues cannot be known. The problem has an acute existential dimension, for Socrates, in many respects an ideally virtuous man, and one who puts the polis first, is put to death by the polis. So is the city inimical to virtue?

73. Aristotle, *Politics* 1252b 28–52.

74. Ibid., 1253a19.

75. Aristotle, *Nicomachean Ethics*, 1094b7–10.

76. Ibid., 1094.15.

different constitutions for his students to consider. However, to be truly virtuous a person must exercise practical reason, and it follows that the best state, the one that most truly enables virtue, is the one in which citizens take turns in exercising rule, because mere subjects simply obey, and thus fail to exercise practical rationality.[77] The true political community, in his view, puts the common good first, in accordance with strict principles of justice, and has to be understood as "a partnership of free and equal persons" in which people can both rule and be ruled.[78] In fact, justice has no application apart from the polis.

Roman republicanism took it for granted that civic virtue meant putting the good of the state above that of oneself. Cicero begins his essay on the Republic with a list of great Roman heroes who did just that and these examples of courage and integrity exercised a huge pull on the European imagination right up to the eighteenth century, and indeed they reappear in Robert Bellah's appeal to the American founding fathers.[79] For Cicero the most important field of practice for moral excellence (*virtus*) is in the government of a state.[80] The moral virtues were placed at the heart of the state, with the result that the state itself had a religious aura, and demanded sacrifice, a legacy with which we are still living.[81]

---

77. Aristotle, *Politics,* 1279a 8.

78. Ibid., 1279a 20.

79. This underlines the importance of narrative in fostering the moral imagination. A strong metanarrative of human ends is a necessary, though not sufficient, condition for the cultivation of the virtues. I agree with David Harvey that postmodernism, with its abandonment of metanarratives—visible in many aspects of contemporary Western culture—is "the cultural logic of late capitalism." However, as we saw at the end of chapter 1, strong (religious) metanarratives may be anything but liberating. Traditions are always contests for the recovery, or redemption, of what is life-giving within them.

80. Cicero, *The Republic,* 1.2.

81. "It is right that good sense (*mens*), devotion (*pietas*), moral excellence (*virtus*), and good faith (*fides*) should be deified; and in Rome temples have long been publicly dedicated to those qualities so that those who possess them (and all good people do) should believe that actual gods have been set up within their souls." Cicero, *On the Laws,* 2.28.

In the view of many critics this tradition, which brought the polis and the virtues together, has been lost. In the last two decades of the twentieth century Robert Bellah and Robert Putnam anatomized the decline of civic virtue in the United States. The growth of individualism, both argued, undermined the sense of community. We are facing trends that threaten our basic sense of solidarity with others, Bellah argued. "Yet this solidarity—this sense of connection, shared fate, mutual responsibility is what allows human communities to deal with threats and take advantage of opportunities."[82] Tocqueville had warned that individualism might undermine the conditions of freedom and this individualism, they suggest, has grown cancerous.[83] "Individualism is a calm and considered feeling which disposes each citizen to isolate himself from the mass of his fellows and withdraw into the circle of family and friends; with this little society formed to his taste he gladly leaves the greater society to look after itself."[84] This individualism, it is argued, goes together with political liberalism, which, in a political extension of Adam Smith's invisible hand, believes that the good of the whole is fostered by each one pursuing their individual interests.

For William Galston individualism is not a problem but has its own distinctive virtue of independence, which means that we take care of ourselves and seek not to become a burden on others. This independence rests on self-restraint and self-transcendence. The acceptance of diversity requires tolerance, which is not the equivalent of extreme cultural relativism, but the intention to educate and persuade rather than coerce.[85] In the liberal economy there are virtues of imagination, drive, initiative, and determination on the part of the entrepreneur, and of punctuality, reliability, and civility on the part of employees. The economy as a whole is sustained by the work ethic, a capacity to delay self-gratification and adaptability. In the liberal polity citizen virtues include the

82. Bellah et al., *Habits of the Heart*, xxxvi.

83. Ibid., xlviii.

84. Ibid., 37.

85. Galston, "Liberal Virtues," 1282.

capacity to discern, and the restraint to respect the rights of others. The virtues of leadership include patience, the capacity to forge a sense of common purpose, and resistance to populism. The limits of persuasion constitute the boundaries of political action. Optimism and excellence are required in the executive, deliberative excellence and civility in the legislator, impartiality and interpretive skill in the judge. "The value liberalism attaches to the fulfilment of individual purposes rests on a critique both of the otherworldliness that denigrates earthly striving in the light of the hereafter and of the nihilism that withdraws all moral significance from such striving in the name of the absurdity of existence."[86] Intrinsic liberal virtues center on human excellence and all are concerned with a vindication of the dignity of every individual and the practice of mutual respect.

Galston acknowledges that liberalism recognizes no duty to participate actively in politics, no requirement to place the public above the private, and no commitment to accept collective determination of personal choices. Nevertheless he thinks it is not simply reducible to the pursuit of self-interest, because it involves restraint and respect for others. At the same time it tends to reduce politics to the art of the possible, it reduces justice to fairness, and it lacks an overall vision of the human good. What is missing is an account of common ends, a common destiny, a common tradition, and a common future.[87]

Stanley Hauerwas and W. H. Willimon dismiss liberal virtues of the kind that Galston outlines on the grounds that they function as cover-ups that allow the powerful to maintain social equilibrium rather than to be confronted and then to change. They prefer honesty and confrontation.[88] MacIntyre's critique of the liberal argument is that since virtues are acquired only through, and within, communities, the tradition of the virtues is at odds with liberal individualism for which a community is "simply an arena in which individuals each pursue their own self chosen con-

---

86. Ibid.,1285.
87. Bellah et al., *Habits of the Heart*, 252.
88. Hauerwas and Willimon, *Resident Aliens*, 63.

ception of the good life, and political institutions exist to provide that degree of order which make such self determined activity possible."[89] Political liberalism makes the individual the unique source of moral value: "Politics is represented as a market, where responsible individuals can choose the best offer among available offers." This means, first, that political offers are determined by elites, and this leads to growing voter apathy, and secondly, individual responsibility is understood solely in terms of strategic action.[90] Because the tradition of the virtues is at variance with individualism it is also at odds with the central features of the modern economic order and its elevation of the values of the market to a central social place. For this very reason it requires a rejection of the modern political order.[91]

Nussbaum emphasizes the importance of "a robust training in independent thought, personal accountability, and critical dialogue." A vigorous critical culture is one of the key ways to avert the rise of a death-fixated culture such as Nazism. Milgram compared his findings to Hannah Arendt and agreed with her that evil is not found in a sadistic fringe, but in normal people under circumstances in which they surrender personal accountability and simply go along with someone else's directives—a situation he called the agentic state, in which people surrender personal agency and become simply the vehicle for another's plan.[92] Nussbaum cites studies that show the enormous effect one person who tells the truth can have within a group—making it easier for everyone else in the group to do so. "These experiments showed that all decent societies have strong reasons to nourish and reward dissent and critical thinking, both through its intrinsic importance and for its effects on others."[93] Such an insight lay

89. MacIntyre, *After Virtue*, 195.

90. MacIntyre, "How Aristotelianism can become revolutionary," 182.

91. MacIntyre, *After Virtue*, 255.

92. Nussbaum, *Political Emotions*, 195.

93. Ibid., 193.

at the heart of Václav Havel's argument that what was important in political renewal was "living the truth."[94]

The role of law

Is the cultivation of the virtues through practices adequate for maintaining our humanity? Both Plato and Aristotle argue that, in building a sustainable city, education is not enough. Plato argues that the supreme virtue in a just state is *sophrosune*, "which means a law-abiding disposition or a spirit of respect towards the institutions of the state and a readiness to subordinate oneself to its lawful powers."[95] Aristotle turns to the role of law at the end of the *Ethics* and it provides the bridge to the *Politics*. Even more so is this the case for Cicero, for whom "as the laws govern the magistrate, so the magistrate governs the people, and it can truly be said that the magistrate is a speaking law, and the law a silent magistrate."[96] In the Hebrew Bible the "ten Words" are part of Torah, teaching but often understood as a summary of the basic requirements of a law-abiding society. What this emphasis on the law indicates is that, as Philip Wogaman puts it, "Morality cannot be legislated, but behaviour can be regulated. Judicial decrees may not change the heart, but they can restrain the heartless . . . The habits, if not the hearts of people, have been and are being altered everyday by legislative acts, judicial decisions and executive orders."[97] In Western societies we have seen this writ large over the past fifty years in matters of race and gender discrimination and in relation to matters of health and safety. Though "health and safety" has

94. Havel, *Power of the Powerless*, 40.

95. Sabine, *A History of Political Theory*, 77. Thomson regards this as classic repression. *Aeschylus and Athens*, 368. In the context of the debacle in Syracuse, however, set out in Plato's seventh letter, respect for law can be taken as the minimum requirement for a socially sustainable society. In the *Politicus* (*Statesman*) Plato begins by arguing that law is far too blunt an instrument for human societies, but later concedes that it is a regrettable necessity.

96. Cicero, *On the Laws* III.1, 2.

97. Wogaman, *Christian Perspectives on Politics*, 230.

become a byword for officious and unnecessary meddling, legislation has in fact prevented much careless and dangerous practice. It is probably both true and necessary to say, therefore, that no humane society is imaginable without a robust and humanitarian law, independently administered.

The capacity of positive law for corruption, however, calls its significance into question, as Cicero already saw clearly.[98] Dwight MacDonald notes that what the crimes of the Nazis teach us is that those who enforce the law are more dangerous than those who break it. The predominant type among guards were the conformists, willing to serve whoever wielded power and more concerned with their own welfare than with the triumph of doctrine.[99] In the aftermath of the Holocaust, legal practice and thus also moral theory, faced the possibility that morality may manifest itself in insubordination towards socially upheld principles, and in an action openly defying social solidarity and consensus.[100] By itself, wrote Václav Havel in 1978, law can never create a better society. "It is possible to imagine a society with good laws that are fully respected but in which it is impossible to live." It was important to maintain legality, he argued (he was shortly to be imprisoned for his resistance to the Stalinist state), but what was really important was a moral relationship to life, "keeping one's eyes open to the real dimensions of life's beauty and misery."[101]

Because of this there was a recourse to "natural law" at Nuremberg, which, rather than an ancient or Scholastic mystification is actually a resumé of the things that promote human flourishing as applied to the account of humanity I outlined in the first section. The standoff between Islamism and "Western values" illustrates again how important this is. Only insofar as we acknowledge the authority of natural law are we able to engage

98. "Most foolish of all is the belief that everything decreed by the institutions or laws of the particular country is just. What if the laws are the laws of tyrants?" *Laws*, 1.42.

99. Todorov, *Facing the Extreme*, 123.

100. Bauman, *Modernity and the Holocaust*, 177.

101. Havel, *The Power of the Powerless*, 77.

together in rational deliberation aimed at the common good. Only conformity to those precepts enables us to trust each other and to listen to each other as rational agents rather than as the agents of money or of power.[102]

Becoming and staying human

No moral tradition can guarantee our humanness, neither does law, and neither does education. As Norman Geras comments, "There are appalling language games always in preparation somewhere, now as ever. They will be 'played' by those looking for the chance of using them in deadly earnest."[103] At the same time, the collapse has never been total and courage, kindness, compassion, and the other virtues have never been eradicated. The tradition of the virtues, "rescuer" literature, and the literature of the gulag, remains the best clue to how it is we become and remain human in dark times. This includes many of the virtues of the tradition since Aristotle—courage, compassion, moderation, and practical reasoning—the ability to work out what on earth to do in unprecedented situations. In addition the Christian tradition insists on the paramountcy of forgiveness "for without forgiveness we can only forget or repress those histories that proved to be destructive or at least unfruitful."[104]

For some such an appeal to the virtues represents an "insipid humanitarianism" (Fanon). The bourgeois and liberal tradition of secular humanism, says David Harvey, forms a mushy ethical base for largely ineffective moralizing about the sad state of the world and the mounting of equally ineffective campaigns against the plights of chronic poverty and environmental degradation.[105] To the contrary, I argue. The virtues I have outlined, and the practices through which they are learned and honed, represent a "revolu-

---

102. MacIntyre, "How Aristotelianism can become revolutionary," 13.

103. Geras, *Solidarity*, 143.

104. Hauerwas, *Community*, 69.

105. Harvey, *Seventeen Contradictions*, 286.

tionary humanism" that is at the heart of the biblical witness and of any realistic account of sustaining our humanity. Far from being insipid or ineffectual it is the heart of "witness" (*martus*, from which we get "martyr," means "witness") to what is truly human and truly life-giving. Wolfgang Streeck wonders whether there is any possibility of rescuing democracy given the power of the present plutocracy. Stephen Emmott believes there is no possibility of saving humankind as a species, given the blindness governments around the world are showing with regard to climate change, and it has to be granted that the worldwide political situation—the paramountcy of self-interest, or national interest, the short-termism, the lack of care for those in need—supports his pessimism. In the long term the virtues win out—but do we have "the long term" given the planetary emergency? If the virtues are to win out then our political and economic practices will have to change. In the second section of the book I turn to ways in which these practices could, and will have to, change if we are to sustain our humanity in the remainder of this century and for whatever time remains.

PRACTICES

Chapter Four

The Shape of the Human Home

To consider oneself, according to eternal civil law, as an associate member of the cosmopolitan society is the most sublime idea a person can have of his destination. One cannot think of it without enthusiasm.

—IMMANUEL KANT

I HAVE ARGUED IN the previous chapter that the tradition of the virtues is the most promising way to think about sustaining our humanity, but it is easily misunderstood in an individualist way. Through education, in the broadest sense (which includes family upbringing), I may become an admirable human being. But as we saw, both Plato and Aristotle understood that humans exist in groups—which they called "polities." Virtues and vices are acquired within societies, and we cannot think of them outside these social and political structures. At the same time I argued in the first chapter that the problems arising from crossing planetary boundaries are primarily moral and political—that neither technological fixes nor tweaking of the present economic system are sufficient to address them. The rich world is currently already experiencing high levels of immigration and there are attempts on all hands to pull up the drawbridge and keep migrants out: migration is currently the issue that is pushing politics to the right all over the world. But if current analyses of ice-level melt in Antarctica are correct, we can expect much greater migration by the end of the century. The question, then, is how we manage politically without a regression into barbarism—whether local warlordism or worse. The problems outlined in the first chapter are all global in scope— none of them can be solved, or even addressed, by states in isolation. What is the best political base from which to address them? This is a question about the most just and sustainable shape of the human home. In terms of the discussion of the past two chapters I am asking about what values inform political order, and what practices we should be pursuing. MacIntyre speaks of practices as the school of the virtues—but there are practices of the vices also, which are not individual, but embedded in structures. In this chapter and the next I am considering political structures in the narrow sense, though economic structures (the theme of chapters 6 to 8) are also profoundly political. In this chapter I consider the shape of the "state," and in the next the governance of the state, though in bringing about the necessary changes the same practices are required. Hence the practices sketched in this chapter will be elaborated in the next.

Hedley Bull noted forty years ago, in response to the question of how to address urgent problems, that if immediate action was necessary, it was not helpful "to maintain at the same time that effective action can only be taken by political institutions fundamentally different from those which obtain in the present world." In the short run, he argued, it was only national governments that have the information, the experience, and the resources to act effectively in relation to serious crises.[1] One can see the point, but I shall argue that the conditions for very different political structures are in place and in fact here and there are emerging, and that with good will they could become dominant and provide the structures necessary to deal with the planetary emergency.

It may seem odd to regard the shape of the state as a "practice" that shapes virtues or vices, but Plato and Aristotle thought of the polis of their day like this, and both proposed alternatives. In considering the accounts of Hobbes, Hegel, and today of Roger

1. Bull, *The Anarchical Society,* 294.

Scruton and Paul Kahn, I hope it will become clear how the nation state can be construed as functioning as a "practice" that shapes a moral stance. This practice I consider to foster idolatry, and therefore propose an alternative.

I begin with a discussion of order and freedom as fundamental values that underlie any polity. I go on to discuss whether "nation states" should be normative, and if not, what the alternative might be. I argue that the best base to address the crossing of planetary boundaries would be federations of small states, based on what I am calling "rights cosmopolitanism." I conclude by asking whether cosmopolitan democracies might emerge.

Polity, order, and freedom

Bull began his study of the international political order by observing that all complex societies fulfil three functions: they seek to ensure that life will be in some measure secure against violence resulting in death or bodily harm; they seek to ensure that promises, once made, will be kept, and that grievances will be addressed; and they pursue the goal of ensuring that the possession of things will remain stable to some degree, and will not be subject to challenges that are constant and without limit. Order in social life means a pattern of human activity that sustains elementary, primary, or universal goals of social life such as these.[2]

This account of the political goal is shaped by a pessimism about human nature, and the society it gives rise to, which goes back at least to Augustine, or perhaps the Plato of *The Laws*, and which finds its classic exposition in Hobbes. Driven by competition, diffidence, and glory, all human beings are prone to violence. "Hereby it is manifest, that during the time men live without a common power to keep them all in awe, they are in that condition which is called war; and such a war, as is of every man, against every man."[3] This view is instantiated by the violence inherent in

2. Ibid., 5.
3. Hobbes, *Leviathan*, 1.13.

many urban situations in Latin America, the Middle East, and Africa. A World Bank study, *Voices of the Poor*, found that crime, violence, and insecurity are the primary concerns of low-income populations. The long-term absence of legitimate authority, the authors argued, is a multiplier that transforms governance into a variety of other voids: a segmented or fragmented labor market, a standard career of income instability, and a disintegration of social protective networks associated with decency and human security.[4] Order, incontestably, is necessary for civility but, as J. S. Mill argued, order is a *condition* of government rather than its purpose.[5] And, critics can say, "order" actually means the maintenance of property rights, and bourgeois order is another form of class war.[6] From an anarchist perspective David Graeber argues that the order appealed to by liberal theorists from Locke to Nozick in fact rests on "primitive accumulation"—fundamental acts of violence in the distant or not-so-distant past. This puts into question the legitimacy of the force deployed to "keep order."[7] Shalom, the conditions for human flourishing, includes order but this needs to be built on truth, "for ultimately order which is built on lies must resort to coercion."[8]

An important way of thinking of the establishment of order is in terms of "governance." In his study of South American Indian society, Pierre Clastres spoke of "society against the state." He argued that, among the Tupi-Guarani, there were sophisticated ways of ordering society which did not require the state form. Outbreaks of violence were regarded as a failure on the part of the chief. John Hoffman points out that humankind has survived for most of its existence without the state—that is to say, it has conducted its affairs without the presence of an institution claiming a monopoly of legitimate force. He develops what he calls the "anthropological

4. Epilogue by the editors in Koonings and Kruijt, eds., *Fractured Cities*, 138–39.
5. Mill, *On Liberty Etc.*, 160.
6. Hay, Lister, and Marsh, *The State*, 66.
7. Graeber, *The Democracy Project*, 238.
8. Hauerwas, *A Community of Character*, 33.

argument," which makes a distinction between state and government. Government, on his definition, is a process which resolves disputes through a range of sanctions all of which fall short of the use of organized force. It is a process of securing order through social rather than state sanctions.[9] Disputes and quarrels are part of the social condition, but these can be reconciled without force by "settlement directed talking."[10] Order, in the sense of a degree of predictability, stability, and regularity, can be established and maintained without force. It is crucial to distinguish government on the one hand from having a monopoly of legitimate force on the other. "Radically different principles are at stake. If force is decisive in defining the state, order, community, and cooperation are central to identifying government. Government is a process of regulating social behaviour. This is its essence and therefore force, like the war chiefs' temporary monopoly of power, is at best incidental to this process."[11]

Today the language of governance is used at local, national, regional, and global levels to speak of regulation and control. It applies both to governments and international organizations.[12] However, Wendy Brown sees "governance" as a key part of neoliberalism's "stealth revolution." Governance, she argues, reconceives the political as a field of management or administration and, citing Elizabeth Meehan, reconceives the public realm as "a domain of strategies, techniques and procedures through which different forces and groups attempt to render their programs operable." Problem-solving replaces deliberation about social conditions and possible political futures, consensus replaces contestation among diverse perspectives and political life is emptied of robust expressions of different political positions and desires.[13] Democracy

9. Hoffman, *Beyond the State*, 152.

10. Ibid., 38.

11. Ibid., 42.

12. Hay, Lister, and Marsh, *The State*, 194.

13. Brown, *Undoing the Demos*, 127. Streeck agrees. He cites the German Finance minister, W. Schäuble, who wants to replace government with governance, meaning "a lasting curtailment of the budgetary authority of the

becomes purely procedural and loses touch both with justice and with struggles over the nature of the good.[14]

Brown makes an important point, which has close connections with Streeck's view of neoliberalism, which I will take up further in chapter six, but governance could be understood, less polemically, as the attempt to find a new way to realize democracy, which does not rely on the gladiatorial conventions of the Westminster model, where opposite sides get locked into barren slanging matches. I shall say more on this in the next chapter in considering consensus decision-making.

The idea that the state existed primarily to keep order was already challenged by Aristotle. For him its purpose was the realization of the good life: "the association which is a state exists not for the purpose of living together but for the sake of noble (*kalos*) actions."[15] This is the paradigmatic expression of the state as a "practice," or set of practices, which can inculcate virtues. It informed views of the state by thinkers as different as Burke and von Ranke and still informs liturgies and rituals of civic piety such as Remembrance Day, the singing of national anthems, and so forth. From the sixteenth century onwards the noble actions that the state exists to foster have been understood as being based on freedom.

It was the Reformation struggle over freedom of conscience that increasingly put freedom center stage. The freedom championed here is the freedom that ought to be guaranteed to dissident intellectuals in China, or secularist bloggers in Bangladesh. This freedom gave place, in the eighteenth century, to freedom of the press, and in the nineteenth to national freedom (which is still an issue, as both Tibet and the Kurds illustrate). Writing in the context of an increasingly illiberal despotism, Kant gave freedom the key place in his political ethics, and by it he meant "freedom to make

---

Bundestag." Cynically, Schäuble thought he could bring the Parliament round to this. *Capitalism*, 92.

14. Brown, *Undoing the Demos*, 129.

15. Aristotle, *Politics*, 1280b36, 1281a2.

use of one's reason in all matters."[16] Freedom, he wrote, is the keystone of the whole architecture of practical reason.[17] This freedom presupposes order: it involves obedience to the law because only thus is it ensured that my freedom does not compromise yours. "Every action which by itself or by its maxim enables the freedom of each individual's will to coexist with the freedom of everyone else in accordance with a universal law is right."[18] Although Kant thought in terms of the individual he understood that human beings only survived in society and that freedom was therefore mutually limiting. Amartya Sen's "capabilities approach" to freedom is an extension of this. Freedom is the ability to choose a life one has reason to value. Such freedom, he argues, lies at the heart of all successful development—citing especially the Southern Indian state of Kerala as an example.[19]

This mutually limiting understanding of freedom is today compromised in two ways. The "freedom" that is trumpeted above all by North American propaganda means first of all "free markets," but these are in fact anything but free, actually everywhere maintained by colossal use of force. Freedom for the corporations means servitude for millions of others, and paradoxically requires, for example, the erection of a policed and electrified security fence the whole length of the US-Mexican border. We cannot, Polanyi concluded, approach the question of freedom without first discarding the utopian vision of classical political economy and much of its cognate libertarian politics. Only then could we come face-to-face with the reality of society and its contradictions. Otherwise, as is today most spectacularly the case, our freedoms are contingent on the denial of social reality. The freedom to pillage resources from under the feet of local and indigenous populations, to displace and to spoil whole landscapes where necessary, to stretch the use of ecosystems up to and in some instances well beyond their capacity to reproduce all

16. Kant, "What is Enlightenment?," in *Kant's Political Writings*, 55.

17. Kant, *Critique of Practical Reason*, Preface.

18. Kant, *The Metaphysics of Morals*, in *Kant's Political Writings*, 133.

19. Sen, *Development as Freedom*, 74.

became a key part of capital's necessary freedoms. "In a world of limits certain kinds of freedom are either impossible or immoral. The freedom endlessly to accumulate material goods is one of them. Freedoms to achieve social recognition at the expense of child labour in the supply chain, to find meaningful work at the expense of a collapse in biodiversity or to participate in the life of the community at expense of future generations may be others."[20] Addressing climate change acutely raises the question of freedom. "If unfettered freedom unleashes a climate chaos that threatens to undermine the great systems that sustain our lives and nations, then what would be left to freedom? What the world faces is a choice between social constraints democratically chosen and the fierce, uncontrollable, lethally unleashed constraints of flood, fire, and the societal chaos that will accompany rapid ecological changes."[21]

This reduction of freedom to free markets has consequences at the personal level too. Freedom, Bellah and his co-workers found, turns out to mean being left alone by others, "not having other people's values, ideas, or styles of life forced upon one, being free of arbitrary authority in work, family and political life."[22] Such freedom makes cooperation, and therefore a real polity, impossible: the polity is a conglomeration of individuals and the state simply holds the ring between them. The irony of that in the United States, Hauerwas argues, is that the pursuit of freedom ended in an excessively legalistic society. The church has gone along with this. Christians, he argues, accepted the assumption that politics is about the distribution of desires, irrespective of the content of those desires, and any consideration of the development of virtuous people as a political issue seems an inexcusable intrusion into our personal liberty.[23]

20. Jackson, *Prosperity Without Growth*, 44.

21. Moore and Nelson, "Moving toward a global moral consensus on environmental action," 229.

22. Bellah et al., *Habits of the Heart*, 23.

23. Hauerwas, *Community*, 73.

The truth is that if the task of the polity is to enable freedom then we need a much richer definition of freedom than that provided by the market. When Paul wrote that "For freedom Christ has set us free," he was presupposing the story of Israel's escape from Egypt to a new land where it could be autonomous, but he went further than autonomy. Ultimately, freedom for Paul was the ability to live in response to the divine self-gift, a life of joy, gratitude, self-gift, and therefore of creativity. Karl Barth described God as "the one who loves in freedom," understanding that freedom and love imply one another. Because our humanity is constructed by the way in which we understand God (as defined in the first chapter) this applies analogically to human beings as well. To put this in a non-Barthian way, freedom is at the heart of life because only free beings can love, and love is the best one-word account of the meaning and purpose of life that we have yet come up with.[24] Barth prefers to say: Christ reveals the meaning and purpose of life, and he does this in a complex redefinition of love (which, for example, puts many questions against Eros). Love, as this is made known to us in Christ, implies not only self gift but decision, commitment, responsibility, action (the leitmotif of the First Letter of John). In Aristotelian and Thomist terms (and against both Augustine and Hobbes) we could say that polity ultimately comes out of the human capacity for creativity and self- gift, and that it exists to further that and make that possible. Order, whilst essential, cannot be the political end.

The Christian tradition has consistently asked what freedom might mean in conditions of unfreedom. The biblical concern with freedom begins (in Exodus) with the story of an escape from slavery, and Leviticus—according to Veerkamp a manifesto for a contrast society—prohibited slavery amongst Israelites. Paul argued (in Philemon) that a slave who was also a Christian must be respected as a brother. For most of Christian history, however, slavery has been taken for granted. Augustine argues that human

---

24. Compare Iris Murdoch's account of freedom as "disciplined overcoming of self" whilst love is "the energy and passion of the soul in its search for Good." *The Sovereignty of Good*, 95, 103.

beings were born free and that slavery is the result of sin (appealing to Daniel 9:3–15). Although slavery is not intended by God "it remains true that slavery is a punishment ordained by that law which enjoins the preservation of the order of nature, and forbids its disturbance . . . That explains the Apostle's admonition to slaves, that they should be subject to their masters and serve them loyally and willingly (Eph 6:5)." What he means is that if they cannot be set free by their masters, they themselves may thus make their slavery, in a sense, free, "by serving not with the slyness of fear, but with fidelity of affection, until all injustice disappears and human lordship and power is annihilated, and God is all in all."[25]

Luther's 1520 treatise, "On the Freedom of a Christian Man," followed Augustine in exploring the dialectic of bondage and freedom. Expounding Philippians 2:5f he writes: "Thus from faith flow forth love and joy in the Lord, and from love a cheerful, willing, free spirit, disposed to serve our neighbour voluntarily, without taking any account of gratitude or ingratitude, praise or blame, gain or loss."[26] Four years later the German peasants cited a whole string of texts, including Romans 13, to appropriate this dialectic somewhat differently: "We willingly obey our chosen and appointed rulers (whom God has appointed over us) in all Christian and appropriate matters. And we have no doubt that since they are true and genuine Christians, they will gladly release us from serfdom, or show us in the gospel that we are serfs."[27] In effect what they are doing is appealing to the dialectical argument of Paul in Philemon: "true and genuine Christians" cannot treat slaves as slaves. If they do not they need to justify their actions from Scripture!

In his exposition of Romans 13 Karl Barth argues that "Let every man be in subjection" means that we must be aware of the falsity of all human reckoning as such. "It is evident that there can be no more devastating undermining of the existing order than

25. Augustine, *City of God*, 19.15. Augustine's great opponent, Pelagius, interestingly, advocates human equality much more vigorously, appealing to 1 Corinthians 12. "On Riches."

26. *Luther's Primary Works*, 128.

27. Luther, *The Christian in Society*, 12.

the recognition of it which is here recommended, a recognition rid of all illusion and devoid of all the joy of triumph. State, Church, Society, Positive Right, Family, Organized Research, etc, etc, live off the credulity of those who have been nurtured upon vigorous sermons-delivered-on-the-field-of-battle and upon other suchlike solemn humbug."[28] What was meant by "subjection," Barth insisted, was the resolution to starve the authorities of their pathos. (There is an analogy here to Gandhi's tactic of noncooperation). Romans calls neither for revolution nor for the status quo, but for "the great positive possibility" of learning what it means to love. This underlay his mature account of God as "the One who loves in Freedom," who elects the creature and asks for response.[29]

Needless to say, a "state," which might comprise many millions of people, could not possibly help people to learn freedom and love in this complex sense. In general we only get glimpses of this freedom, sometimes through eros, and sometimes through faith. On the other hand, political community can make the realisation of true freedom less difficult, partly through the reimagining of democracy that I propose in the next chapter and partly through the reconfiguration of the state that I go on to explore in the remainder of this chapter.

Polity as nation state

Aristotle had collected 158 constitutions for his students to study, and as this implies, human beings have lived, and continue to live, under a wide variety of political forms. The word *state* comes from the Latin *status rei publicae*, which means "form of government," whatever that might be: it is not prescriptive. During the

28. Barth, *The Epistle to the Romans*, 483.

29. Barth's emphasis on freedom has led some to argue that his is a theology of revolution. See, for example, Lehman, "Karl Barth: Theologian of Permanent Revolution," and Marquardt, *Theologie und Sozialismus*. McFadyen describes Augustine's view of freedom as "unlimited and unimaginable joy in God." *Bound to Sin*, 186. This is quite right but could, of course, never be taught by a polity and is only very partially realized, or even witnessed to, by the church.

seventeenth century the word comes to mean that underlying political unity of the people that can survive the coming and going not only of governments but also forms of government.[30] The rise of the modern and now hegemonic political module of the nation state, remarks James Scott, "displaced and then crushed a host of vernacular political forms: stateless bands, tribes, free cities, loose confederations of towns, maroon communities, empires. In their place stands everywhere a single vernacular: the North Atlantic nation state, codified in the 18th century and masquerading as a universal."[31] It certainly masquerades as a universal in Western discussion but the briefest survey of current world disorder shows that this is far from the case. At the end of World War II there were sixty states that helped form the new United Nations. Today this figure is more like 200, but there are at least 3,500 languages, all of which might make a pitch for cultural autonomy or the "self-determination" which guided "nation building" in the decades after World War II.[32] At the same time many of the "nations" which appear on the contemporary map are extremely arbitrary, and their frontiers, as mapping cultural and linguistic realities, more arbitrary still.[33]

30. Arendt, *On Revolution*, 287.

31. Scott, *Two Cheers for Anarchism*, 53. Nussbaum thinks the nation remains central "on account of its pivotal importance in setting life conditions for all on the basis of equal respect, and as the largest unit we know until now that is decently accountable to people's voices and capable of expressing their desire to give themselves laws of their own choosing." She also appeals to Mazzini's view that that the nation is a necessary fulcrum for the leveraging of global concern, in a world in which the most intransigent obstacle to concern for others is egoistic immersion in personal and local projects. *Political Emotions*, 17.

32. "World nations cannot exist, only a world where some potentially national groups, in claiming this status, exclude others from making similar claims, which, as it happens, not many of them do." Hobsbawm, *Nations and Nationalism since 1780*, 78.

33. "The idea of Soviet republics based on Kazakh, Kirghiz, Uzbek, Tadjik, and Turkmen 'nations' was a theoretical construct of Soviet intellectuals rather than a primordial aspiration of any of those central Asian peoples." Ibid., 166.

Most contemporary commentators agree that the nation state is a product of the political, religious, and technological changes that clarify in the sixteenth century. At this time the word *nation* began to lose its medieval meaning of a group united by common kinship and becomes used of a sovereign entity such as France or England.[34] These sovereign entities were marked by the growing coincidence of territorial boundaries with the uniform system of rule; the creation of new mechanisms of lawmaking and enforcement; the centralization of administrative power; the alteration and extension of fiscal management; the formalization of relations among states through the development of diplomacy and diplomatic institutions; and the introduction of a standing army.[35] David Held remarks that nation states triumphed in war because, as warfare became more extended in scale and cost, it was larger national states which were best able to organize and fund military power. They were economically successful because the rapid growth of their markets from the late sixteenth century onwards sustained the process of capital accumulation. Their success limited the possibilities for smaller states to make war, and they gained in legitimacy to the extent that they garnered popular support, as the authority of "the people" came to replace older appeals to formerly authoritative voices such as the church. This process was self-reinforcing: states had to prove they were democratic in order to be legitimate.[36]

Conventionally, the era of nation states is dated from the Peace of Westphalia in 1648, but E. H. Carr considered that the modern nation state emerged only after the Napoleonic wars and Ernest Gellner tied it tightly to industrialization, and considered the monopoly of education more important than the monopoly of force.[37] The nation state, which today is assumed by many to be

34. Ingham, *The Nature of Money*, 124.

35. Held, *Democracy and the Global Order*, 36.

36. Ibid., 72.

37. Carr, *Nationalism and After*, 6. Gellner, *Nations and Nationalism*, 49. Hastings demurred, arguing that the term *natio* was used in the Vulgate and taken up by authors like Bede to apply to the peoples of England, but his

the natural or normal form of human community, just as Plato and Aristotle thought of the polis, comes to be the carrier of identity. From being a contingent form of government which might take any number of forms, "the state" comes to have mystical or mythological dimensions. For Hobbes, famously, the commonwealth (he does not use the word *state*) is a "mortal god" with absolute power, derived from contract, to keep the peace and make possible normal forms of human flourishing.[38] For him the contract follows from natural law, by which he seems to mean a set of commonsense observations about what makes peaceful enterprise possible.[39] The social contract is what gives sovereignty legitimacy, and Rousseau takes the step, which Locke had already edged toward, of vesting legitimacy in "the people" and thus lays the ground for the identification of people and nation.

Nearly a century and a half after Hobbes Edmund Burke understands the state as part of something eternal:

> Each contract of each particular state is but a clause in the great primaeval contract of eternal society, linking the lower with the higher natures, connecting the visible and the invisible world, according to a fixed compact sanctioned by the inviolable oath which holds all physical and/or moral lectures, each in their appointed place.[40]

So for Burke the state, which for him is the nation state, is the bearer of all the goods of civilization.

Hegel in his turn gives the state a metaphysical dignity. "The nation state is Spirit in its substantive rationality and immediate actuality and is therefore the absolute power on earth."[41] "The

account of "nations" sounds more like what Hobsbawm calls "proto-nations." Hastings, *The Construction of Nationhood.*

38. Hobbes, *Leviathan*, 1.17.

39. Ibid., 1.13. Hobbes's assumption that the North American Indians are "savages" living in a "brutish manner" is as distant from contemporary hunter gatherer research as possible. It is also the reverse of Rousseau's assumptions.

40. Burke, *Reflections on the Revolution in France*, 194.

41. Hegel, *Philosophy of Right*, 212. Knox translates "Geist" as "mind." In the *Phenomenology* it is usually translated "Spirit." Given Hegel's theory of the

state is the divine will, in the sense that it is Spirit present on earth, unfolding itself to be the actual shape and organization of a world."[42] World history is to be understood as the outworking of Spirit through the individuality of particular states, all of which are autonomous. "History is Spirit clothing itself with the form of events or the immediate actuality of nature."[43] Hegel distinguishes four world historical realms, which are the Oriental, the Greek, the Roman, and the Germanic. In this last moment (the Germanic) Geist "grasps the principle of the unity of the divine nature and the human."[44] The supreme duty of the individual is to be a member of the state.[45] "Preparedness to sacrifice oneself on behalf of the State is a universal duty."[46] All this was written before Germany or Italy became "nations" and before the development of a "nationalism of the masses," known in the Anglo Saxon world as "jingoism," but equally alive in other parts of Europe as well as in Russia. It was at this time that the historian von Ranke could speak of individual states as "thoughts of God." Sabine remarks on this development that "after the middle of the century the concept of the state detached itself from the philosophical technicalities of the dialectic. In substance it was an idealization of power that united curiously a Philistine contempt for ideals apart from force with a moral respect for force as almost self-justifying. It placed the nation on a metaphysical pinnacle above control by international law and even above moral criticism."[47] This is a key part of my objection to the idea of the nation state: a very important tradition of thought, voiced by such very different thinkers as Hobbes, Burke, and Hegel, all give the state a metaphysical and *therefore* a moral significance. They all argue we must be prepared to sacrifice ourselves for the state. Today Paul Kahn properly criticizes liberalism for failing to

---

world historical outworking of Geist this seems a better translation.

42. Ibid., 166.

43. Ibid., 217.

44. Ibid., 222.

45. Ibid., 156.

46. Ibid., 210.

47. Sabine, *A History of Political Theory*, 558.

recognize that the State demands sacrifice—it demands that people die in its defense. As opposed to Hobbes, Kahn argues that the power of the state is located neither in contract nor in the power to threaten but in this demand for sacrifice. In the act of sacrifice, polity and citizen, objective power and subjective faith, are one and the same.[48] The modern nation state, he comments, has shown itself to be an extremely effective instrument of sacrifice.

> It has been able to mobilise its population to make sacrifices in order to sustain the state's own historical existence. In this sense, the nation state stepped into the place of religious belief, offering the individual the hope of transcending the limits of his or her own finitude. Modernity has been a major political faith even more destructive than the age of religious faith that preceded it.[49]

Only the state, not the church, can demand sacrifice of the person in the modern age.[50] The structure of sacrifice as a giving up of the finite and taking on of the infinite remains just what it has always been.[51] Like Hegel, though not on the same grounds, he argues that the state is to be recognized as an end in itself. Like Hegel he recognizes, and apparently endorses, the violence inherent in the state. (Hegel believed that war was not to an absolute evil and that the perpetual peace of which Kant dreamed would lead to the corruption of nations.)[52] Kahn distinguishes sacrifice from violence and characterizes the former as "a creative act of destruction."[53] What he does not go on to say is that this is idolatrous.

---

48. Kahn, *Putting Liberalism in Its Place*, 233.

49. Ibid., 276.

50. Of course for radical Muslims their faith demands this sacrifice, though it seems their ultimate aim is the establishment of a theocratic state.

51. Kahn, *Political Theology*, 121.

52. Hegel, *Philosophy of Right*, 210.

53. Kahn, *Political Theology*, 158.

THE SHAPE OF THE HUMAN HOME

The idolatry of the state

The charge of idolatry was the heart of Karl Barth's critique of the state. In his first Romans commentary, written in 1917, Barth argued that Christianity does not agree with the state but negates it in both its presupposition and its essence. The important thing is to deny the state the pathos, seriousness, and importance of the divine.

> Fulfill your duties without illusion, but no compromising of God! Payment of tax, but no incense to Caesar! Citizens' initiative and obedience but no combination of throne and altar, no Christian Patriotism, no democratic crusading. Strike and general strike, and streetfighting if needs be, but *no* religious justification and glorification of it! Military service as soldier or officer if needs be but under *no* circumstances army chaplain! Social democratic but *not* religious socialist! The betrayal of the gospel is *not* part of your political duty.[54]

The love of Christ remains faithful to "the hope, the unquiet, the longing, the radical and permanent revolution."[55] In other words, the political practices we follow, vis à vis the nation state, involve a critical watchfulness.[56] After World War II he argued that all

54. Barth, *Römerbrief*, 520.

55. Ibid., 353.

56. Nussbaum helps to understand what this might mean in calling for a critical patriotism that seeks constantly to understand the position of minorities, examines the reasons for past wars without demonizing, and teaches love of historical truth. Nussbaum, *Political Emotions*, 251–54. She cites Herder's essay on "Furthering humanity" in which an apotheosized "Peace Woman" seeks to produce seven emotional dispositions in the citizens of the future. First is a horror of war: citizens should learn that any war not limited to self-defense is mad and ignoble, causing endless practical pain and deep moral degeneration. Second, they will learn reduced respect for heroic glory. Third, the peace woman will teach a horror of false statecraft. We must teach disobedience and disrespect to the sort of political authority that likes to whip up war to advance its own power interests. Fourth, peace will teach patriotism but a patriotic love that is purified of dross, above all purified of the need to define the lovable qualities of one's nation in terms of competition with other nations, and even war against them. Fifth, feelings of justice towards other nations.

133

claims for absolute allegiance on the part of the state are idolatrous. Stanley Hauerwas agrees. The church's first task, he writes, "is not to make the nation state system work, but rather to remind us that the nation, especially as we know it today, is not an ontological necessity for human living. The church, as an international society, is a sign that God, not nations, rules this world."[57]

The wariness of idolatry is not confined to Christians. Durkheim taught that in religious worship society adores its own camouflaged image. On a national stage, said Ernest Gellner, societies worship themselves brazenly and openly, spurning the camouflage.[58] It is deified group identity.

This is my first objection to the nation state as currently understood: it lends itself to idolatry, and idolatry always destroys. "I vow to thee my country, all earthly things above"—this is Sir Cecil Spring-Rice's famous hymn, revised in the final months of World War I, and sanctifying death in war as "sacrifice." To such sentiments we have to object—there are a great many things more important than "my country." How can a thinking person, asks George Steiner, be anything but the most wary and provisional of patriots? "The nation state is founded on myths of instauration and of militant glory. It perpetuates itself by lies and half truths (machine guns and sub machine guns)." Our true citizenship, he argues, lies in a critical humanism, called to conscientious objection to the vulgar mystique of the flag and the anthem. For him (in an argument that would have made sense for Erasmus) our homeland is the text, "which makes us conscientious objectors to

---

Sixth, the disposition to fair principles for trade relations, involving a ban on monopoly of the seas and the determination to make sure that poor relations are not sacrificed to the greedy interests of the rich. Finally, citizens will learn to delight in useful activity: the maize stalk in the Indian woman's hand is itself a weapon against the sword. All of these, Herder argues, are the principles of the great peace goddess Reason from whose language no one can in the end escape. *Political Emotions*, 49

57. Hauerwas, *Community*, 110.

58. Gellner, *Nations and Nationalism*, 56. "At Nuremberg, Nazi Germany did not worship itself by pretending to worship God or even Wotan; it overtly worshipped itself."

the pathos and eloquence of collective mendacities on which the nation state builds it power and aggressions."[59]

A second objection to the nation state is the contingency and lack of fit between cultural groupings and ethnicities, on the one hand, and nations on the other. As Hobsbawm puts it, the homogenous territorial nation is a program that could be realized only by barbarians, or at least by barbarian means.[60] The monopoly of force that was the identifying mark of the state for Weber followed precisely because in territory nationality is always to a greater or lesser degree contested, as Jim Scott points out.[61] The lack of fit between national boundaries and the cultural groupings these boundaries include has consistently spelled difficulties for minorities.[62] Nationalism, said Adrian Hastings, has everywhere meant the decline in wider loyalties and tolerances. The worst failing of the nation state, he argues, is so to highlight the rights of one particularity as to become blind to those of all others. Nationalism is to be justified as an appropriate protest against the universalizing uniformity and dominance by the other, but its consequence is too often precisely the imposition of uniformity, a deep intolerance of all particularities except one's own.[63] Two and a half thousand years ago a prophet in the Isaianic tradition registered a protest against the whole theology of group election—known today in theories of "manifest destiny"—arguing that "Egypt and Assyria" were also God's people (Isa 19:23–25). "For all times and

---

59. Steiner, *No Passion Spent*, 322.

60. Hobsbawm, *Nations and Nationalism*, 134.

61. Scott, *Two Cheers*, 68.

62. Schell, *The Unconquerable World*, 290. Scott writes: "The state has nearly always been the implacable enemy of mobile peoples—gypsies, pastoralists, itinerant traders, shifting cultivators, migrating labourers—as their activities are opaque and mobile, flying below the state's radar." He adds, "For much the same reason states at present prefer agribusiness, collective farms, plantations, and state marketing boards over smallholder agriculture and petty trade." *Two Cheers*, 87.

63. Hastings, *The Construction of Nationhood*, 34.

all peoples," commented Martin Buber, "it is thereby said that no 'Sacro egoismo' can and may exist."[64]

The Mexican writer Gustavo Esteva raises a third problem for the nation state by asking whose interests the state serves. For him the nation state, from the harshest dictatorships to the most genuine and pure democracies, has been and continues to be a structure of domination and control imposed on the people to put them in the service of capital. It was designed for this purpose and absorbed and perverted all the diverse forms of state and nation created before. The state is the ideal collective capitalist, guardian of its interests. Even in the most modern democratic states it operates at best as a benevolent dictatorship.[65]

A fourth problem is that nation states have, from the start, been a focus of conflict. David Held points out that from about the twelfth to the nineteenth century between 70 and 90 percent of the English state's financial resources were continuously devoted to the acquisition and use of the instruments of military force, especially in international wars.[66] The state in both its precapitalist and its capitalist incarnations, says David Harvey, has been preeminently a warmaking machine embroiled in geopolitical rivalries and geo-economic strategizing on the world stage.[67] Competition between nation states was there from the beginning and this underlay the economic doctrines that required growth to finance war. In the nineteenth and twentieth centuries political "realism" assumed that every state had not only the right but the duty to pursue its own interests. The current scramble for the Arctic, as well as the settlement imposed on Iraq by the United States under Paul Bremer, show that this process is still in place.

These objections to nationalism—that it is prone to idolatry, that it is bad news for minorities, that nations are controlled by

64. Buber, *Believing Humanism*, 176.

65. Esteva, Babones, and Babcicky, *The Future of Development*, 115.

66. Reliable annual sets of accounts are available after 1688, and state finances were dominated by foreign wars. Held, *Democracy and the Global Order*, 53–54.

67. Harvey, *Seventeen Contradictions*, 44.

and in the interests of tiny elites, and that nations always have been, and remain, prone to war—problematize Roger Scruton's argument that the nation state is the best base for a response to the global emergency. Scruton means by a nation "a people settled in a certain territory, who share a language, institutions, customs and a sense of history to regard themselves as equally committed both to their place of residence and to the legal and political process that governs it."[68] For him we are most likely to take action to save the planet when motivated by "oikophilia," shared love of shared place, which finds its strongest form in the nation state.[69] Human beings are creatures of limited and local affections, the best of which is the territorial loyalty that leads them to live at peace with strangers, to honor their dead, and to make provision for those who will one day replace them in their earthly tenancy. Scruton looks back to Burke, but he could equally look to Rousseau, who claimed that the idea of "the society of the whole human race" was "a veritable chimera." A race could not be a society because a society had to have common possessions such as a common language and a common interest in well-being, which is not a sum of private goods but the source of them. Abstract ideas of reason overlook the fact that we derive our ideas from the societies in which we live. Like Scruton, he scorned the "pretended cosmopolitans" who "make a boast of loving all the world in order to enjoy the privilege of loving no one."[70]

Now there is, of course, truth in the idea of attachment to place, and today it is put best by Wendell Berry, who denies "the

68. Scruton, *Green Philosophy*, 241. Even in the United Kingdom—much less in Spain!—there is not a shared language and the hegemony of English rests on brutal, not to say totalitarian, attempts to extirpate the varieties of Gaelic. Scruton's appeal is part of a worldwide regression to what Klein calls "nostalgic nationalisms." *No is Not Enough*, 131.

69. Scruton, *Green Philosophy*, 19. He could have added Hannah Arendt's point that the fundamental deprivation of human rights is manifested first and above all in the deprivation of a place in the world that makes opinions significant and actions effective. Arendt, *The Origins of Totalitarianism*, 296. For her, rights can only be made effective within nations.

70. Rousseau, *Political Writings*, vol. 1, 453.

easy, generalizing sense with which the phrase a 'world citizen'" is used.

> There can be no such thing as a global village. No matter how much one may love the world as a whole, one can live fully in it only by living responsibly in some small part of it. Where we live and who we live there with define the terms of our relationship to the world and to humanity. We thus come again to the paradox that one can become whole only by the responsible acceptance of one's partiality.[71]

This is well said, but it is not said of the nation state. Berry writes of his care for his corner of Kentucky. It resonates with the vision of Proudhon, Kropotkin, and Landauer that the way to a more peaceful and just society rests ultimately on small local cooperative groups that are prepared to federate, and where, as Proudhon argues, the competence of the central authority, which will certainly be necessary, will be limited to "the simple tasks of general initiative, mutual assurance and supervision."[72] Leopold Kohr advocated a small state on the ground that mass always generates power and the bigger the power the worse the conflict. Switzerland, which in 2015 reemerged as the place in which people are happiest to live, earned his plaudits because the canton system ensured "the physical and numerical balance of all participants on a small enough scale to enable even a weak central authority to execute its decisions." The insistence on unification he understood as a cancer.[73]

To some, a huge problem requires a huge body to deal with it. Thus David Orr believes that in the face of the contravention of planetary boundaries, "it will be necessary to enlarge governments domestically and internationally to deal with the nasty aspects of the long emergency, including relocating people from rising oceans

---

71. Berry, *The Unsettling of America*, 123.

72. Buber, *Paths in Utopia*, 32.

73. Kohr, *The Breakdown of Nations*, 101. Kohr inferred the virtues of small scale from the atomic structure of the universe that displayed an "anarchic freedom of movement granted to their component particles."

and spreading deserts, restoring order in the wake of large storms, managing conflicts over diminishing water, food, and resources, dealing with the spread of diseases, and managing the difficult transition to a post-growth economy."[74] But why should we assume that small units would be worse placed to deal with violence and terror than large ones? The logic of this seems to be that the bigger the weapon the more likely the ability to control—but history over the past sixty years has shown exactly the opposite.

In contrast to Scruton's account of oikophilia Luke Bretherton offers a much more nuanced account of what he calls "pietas," which is the gratitude I owe to the community on whose language and economic, cultural, and legal structures I depend. This gift, he notes, "should not be overvalued or sacralised and is not determinative of all relations; for example, one's religious, familial or professional loyalties may at times stand over against, chasten, or place limits on one's civic obligations. Pietas grows out of both the need for others—living in the same place one depends on them for one's flourishing—but also affection for those among whom one lives."[75] This kind of critical pietas goes beyond the critical patriotism adumbrated by Martha Nussbaum, not to mention Scruton's oikophilia.

Developments that challenge the nation state

Quite apart from the moral and political objections to the nation state there are a whole series of developments that make the sovereignty of the nation state questionable. At present, Hobsbawm

74. Orr, "Governance in the long emergency," 287.

75. Bretherton, *Resurrecting Democracy,* 96. This is essentially Julien Benda's argument in his famous attack on "la trahison des clercs." For 2,000 years, he said, the intellectuals, and especially theologians, did evil but honored good. "This contradiction was an honour to the human species, and formed the rift whereby civilization slipped into the world." Towards the end of the nineteenth century, however, the intellectuals, including theologians, had come to defend a vulgar nationalism, turned aggressively against other nations, the consequences of which were seen only too savagely in World War I and in the disaster that he foresaw coming. *Treason,* 28.

remarked, we are living through a curious culmination of the technology of the late twentieth century, the free trade of the nineteenth century, and the rebirth of the sort of interstitial centers characteristic of world trade in the Middle Ages. The ideology of nations and nationalism is irrelevant to any of these developments.[76] Hobsbawm thought nations would be caught between infranationality and supranationality. Nation states, he predicted, would retreat before, resist, adapt to, be absorbed and dislocated by this new supranational restructuring of the globe. "Nations and nationalism will be present in this history, but in subordinate, and often rather minor roles."[77] Held likewise considers that interdependence and interpenetration seems inescapable.[78]

Challenges to the nation state come from both above and below. I am thinking in the first instance of the many calls for devolution or for the fragmenting of large states into smaller units: Britain, Spain, Turkey, Syria, Iraq, Sudan, Nicaragua, India—the list goes on. Within unitary states, like Britain, there are many moves towards devolved regional power, which are already realities in countries like Germany, Switzerland, or the United States. Buber spoke of the need for the renewal of society, by which he meant human sociality, the organization of human affairs in work-related enterprises on a cooperative basis. Building on the insights of those whom Marx had dismissed as "utopian socialists" he argued that a genuine society would consist of a network of little societies whose mutual relations would be determined by the social principle—the principle of inner cohesion, collaboration, and mutual stimulation, "Only a structurally rich society can claim the inheritance of the State."[79] The historian Jakob Burkhardt had already argued that the small state exists "so that there may be one spot on earth where the largest possible proportion of the inhabitants are citizens of the world." The small state, said Max Fritsch, makes freedom possible because, weak as it is, it cannot become an

76. Hobsbawm, *Nations*, 182.

77. Ibid., 191.

78. Held, *Democracy and the Global Order*, 19.

79. Buber, *Paths in Utopia*, 80.

idol to which the individual has to be sacrificed.[80] Streeck ironizes this kind of thought as "kleinstaterei"—nostalgia for a small state. It is not nostalgia, however, but the question of how, culturally and politically, we make democracy realizable. It takes up the Greek insight of diocesism—splitting off when a city reached an optimum size. For reasons outlined above nations do not represent this optimum. Something new needs to evolve, which includes both the generosity and humane values of cosmopolitanism, and the importance of rootedness, as recognized by Berry and many others, but represented in a perverted form by nationalism. Kropotkin spoke of this evolution as building a new world in the shell of the old, of, as it were, outflanking the power of state and corporation, and of the bureaucratic mentality that they thrive on.

In terms of devolution there are also the developments that Hobsbawm alludes to, in which cities assume an importance on the global map—whether because of a particular technical expertise, or because they act as "hubs" in the global economic framework. London, Frankfurt, Freiburg, Singapore, Hong Kong, are all examples of this. In the United States the Carbon Cities network has introduced carbon-limiting legislation that contradicts federal policy. When Trump withdrew from the Paris Accord on climate change both states and cities across the country announced their own contravening policy. This implies that local democracy, and local decision-making, trumps federal policy.

In the other direction to devolution there is the development of the United Nations and of federations like the European Union. It is true, of course, that the United Nations is not especially effective, but on the other hand it provides a framework for Habermassian "communicative action" that could be refined and built upon. Held envisages that the principle of noncoercive relations would govern the settlement of disputes, and the use of force would remain a collective option of last resort in the face of clear attacks to eradicate cosmopolitan democratic law. There would be a general check on the rights of states to go to war. As in the EU, but in a more significant way, people would have membership in the

80. Cited by Rees, *Government by Community*, 187.

diverse communities that significantly affect them and accordingly access to a variety of forms of political participation. All member states would be committed to the entrenchment of cosmopolitan democratic law in order to provide shape and limits to political decision-making. There would be regional parliaments and the possibility of general referenda cutting across nations and nation states in the case of contested priorities concerning the implementation of democratic law and the balance of public expenditure. The full implementation of cosmopolitan democracy would also require the formation of an authoritative assembly of all democratic states and agencies—a reformed general assembly of the UN.[81]

In addition the sovereignty of the nation state is challenged by the economic architecture of neoliberalism, which is global, and exercised both in economic institutions like the World Bank, the IMF and the WTO, and in the location investment strategy of TNCs. The regulation of global financial markets, the threats to the tax base of individual countries in the context of the global division of labor, and the absence of capital controls all create problems for national economic policy. All nations have to coordinate their economies across their boundaries. Held comments:[82]

> In the context of these complex transformations, the meaning of accountability and democracy at the national level is altering. In circumstances where transnational actors and forces cut across the boundaries of national communities in diverse ways, where powerful international organisations and agencies make decisions for vast groups of people across diverse borders, and where capacities of large companies can dwarf those of many states, the questions of who should be accountable to whom, and on what basis, do not easily resolve themselves.

The CEO of the Coca-Cola company looked to a future in which the institutions with the most influence in the world would by and

---

81. Held, *Democracy and the Global Order*, 272–73.

82. Held, *Cosmopolitanism*, 39.

large be businesses.[83] Alan Greenspan expressed the neoliberal norm when he noted that it mattered very little who the American President was because "the world is governed by market forces."[84]

Given the reality of transnational markets some argue that the nation state has been replaced by the "market state," or, as mentioned in chapter two, that the neoliberal project everywhere subjects "Staatsvolk" (citizens with a right to vote) to "Marktvolk" (investors whose primary loyalty is to "the market" and who are integrated internationally). Friedrich Hayek's vision was of a world where economic "laws" were recognized as autonomous and could not be interfered with by politicians. As we shall see in chapter six, this opposed social justice to market justice.

Everyone agrees that the territorial nation state is not about to disappear but on the other hand the romantic and mythicizing visions of the nineteenth century are now, even more than when they were first articulated, obviously unrealistic, even if they are not objectionable on moral grounds. What then replaces them? For more than two millennia the priority of individual states has been challenged by cosmopolitan visions.

Stoic and Christian cosmopolitanism

Even whilst Aristotle was teaching in Athens his former pupil, Alexander, conquered the eastern world as far as India. He died before he could consolidate his conquests but he had still brought into being a new world. Hellenistic philosophy, and especially Stoicism, was a response to this, replacing the focus on the polis with a focus on a world society that was carried on into Christianity.

For the Stoics all human beings have a spark of the divine logos, and therefore in principle are equal. The eternal Logos governs all things and our share in this implies a belief in the value of social purposes and in the duty of good people to bear a share of them.

83. Rosenau, "Governance and democracy in a globalising world," 42.

84. Streeck, *Buying Time*, 85.

> Hence there is a world state. Both gods and men are citizens of it and it has a constitution, which is right reason, teaching them what must be done and what avoided. Right reason is the law of nature, the standard everywhere of what is just and right, unchangeable in its principles, binding all men whether ruler or subject, the law of God. Every person was subject to both the law of their own city and the law of the world city, the law of custom and the law of reason.[85]

The second of these had greater authority and enabled arbitration between cities based on an understanding of common or natural law. For Stoicism, the polis is no longer the precondition for civilized life for it is the natural law that governs all people. As Chrysippus puts it: "For all beings that are social by nature the law directs what must be done and forbids what must not be done."[86] Paul had absorbed these views, and they appear in the argument in Romans. This law can be appealed to in disputes between cities that come second behind the cosmos. The worldwide mission of Christianity, set out by Luke in Acts, was a Christian transposition of the Stoic cosmic vision. For Christians, commented the Letter to Diognetus, sometime around the end of the first century, "every native land is a foreign land and every foreign land a native land." Henceforth the whole world was subject to Christ and all were subject to his rule. Hauerwas notes that "we live in a mad existence where some people kill other people for abstract and unworthy entities called nations."[87] The idea of the image of God, or of the fact that all people are sisters and brothers of "the Human One" (Matt 25) had huge implications for history. For the Christian, wrote R. G. Collingwood, "all men are equal in the sight of God: there is

85. Sabine, *Political Theory*, 137.

86. Cited in ibid., 136. Aquinas's account of natural law as rooted in the God who is law in Godself, and applying to all reality and all cultures, was the most articulate Christian version of universalism. The reaffirmation of natural law at the Nuremberg Trials once again puts this idea center stage, though curiously it is the United States, above all, that refuses to agree to many demands of international law, especially in carbon reduction treaties.

87. Hauerwas, *Community*, 109.

no chosen people, no privileged race or class, no one community whose fortunes are more important than those of another."

> All persons and all people are involved in the working out of God's purpose, and therefore the historical process is everywhere and always of the same kind, and every part of it is a part of the same whole. The Christian cannot be content with Roman history or Jewish history or any other partial and particularistic history: he demands a history of the world, a universal history whose theme shall be the general development of God's purpose for human life.[88]

Of course, as it worked out politically, such an understanding was problematized in many ways—by the acceptance of social hierarchy, by the existence of non-Christian groups like the Jews, and by the standoff with Islam. It is also the case that whilst, ideologically, medieval Europe had doctrines of a universal church and empire, economic and political organization was effectively almost wholly local. This was an inevitable consequence of limitations on the means of communication. "A large political territory was not governable except by a kind of federalism that left to local units a large amount of independence."[89] Nevertheless there was some account of a common humanity and a common culture expressed paradigmatically by someone like Erasmus. The word *humanism* is properly applied to this view and it long predates the *oikophobia* which Scruton sees as the origin of our political and ecological ills. Rather than this being rooted in a repudiation of home it is rooted in a generosity that has been taught to see all humans—including Jews, gypsies, and other migrants—as neighbors. Cosmopolitanism stood for this far more than any nationalism, and to this extent Scruton's caricature is an exact reverse of the truth.

88. Collingwood, *The Idea of History,* 49–50.
89. Sabine, *Political Theory,* 285.

Enlightenment and rights cosmopolitanism

Christian cosmopolitanism was challenged (if not completely occluded) by the rise of the nation state but in the eighteenth century another version took its place, articulated classically by Kant. Kant did not challenge the existence of the state, but he looked forward to a world of a federation of republics in which any person would have the right not to be treated with hostility in someone else's territory. All people have this right "by virtue of their right to communal possession of the earth's surface." He looked forward to the day when relations between states would be regulated by public laws "thus bringing the human race nearer and nearer to a cosmopolitan constitution."[90] Unlike previous cosmopolitanisms, Kant's was avowedly individualist. The rights of man (today, "human rights") were, for Kant, "God's most sacred institution on earth."[91] People have rights to freedom, equality, and independence or autonomy (*selbständigkeit)* but these rights can only be found in a society administered according to law. For him the social contract is not a historical fact or a sociological reality but a principle of reason, part of what it is which makes human life possible at all. Like the Stoics, Kant believes that all humans share the same practical reason and all are bound to act as they would expect to be acted upon.[92]

90. Kant, *Kant's Political Writings*, 106.

91. Ibid., 101.

92. Today Kant's categorical imperative is recast by Habermas in terms of the need to allow every person to be heard. What Habermas calls "communicative action" is sketched as a realization of rationality and tolerance: inclusive, open, non-manipulative, power free, based on the unforced force of the better argument, and transformative, meaning that interests are not exchanged but enriched while working towards broad-based consensus. The structure is never more important than the process of common deliberation. Hendriks, *Vital Democracy*, 117. For Habermas, humans exist in dialogical encounter and all exclusionary practices, of the type implicit in the nation state, call this into question. Rules for dialogical encounter are therefore necessary, on the assumption that differences will be addressed primarily by dialogue rather than by violence. On those grounds Held considers that the principles of cosmopolitanism "are the conditions for taking cultural diversity seriously and for building a democratic culture to mediate clashes of the cultural good." Held,

Today David Held builds on Kant's cosmopolitanism. His assumptions include the principles that individuals are the ultimate unit of moral concern, that all people are of equal worth, and that no country or culture has a claim that trumps universal claims that are "principles upon which all could act."[93] Held recognizes, however, that cultural specificities have to be taken into account, and considers Kant's guidelines inadequate because they take no account of differential power relations, do not recognize that discourse is often shaped by sectional interests, and because the idea of hospitality is too weak to deal with the cases of refugees and asylum seekers.[94]

What I want to call "rights cosmopolitanism" is a vision of a cosmopolitan world of federated states where all people enjoy basic rights and freedoms simply in view of their humanity. Let me expand on this.

Precisely why "rights" should be ascribed to human beings has proved contentious. To vest them in human capacities like rationality seems dangerous, because that would make, for example, sufferers from Alzheimer's dispensable. Rowan Williams seeks to ground them in "the liberty to make sense as a bodily subject," which means that the inviolability of the body itself is where we should start thinking about rights.[95] Other theologians have grounded them in the incarnation or the doctrine of the Trinity, and Williams notes the difficulty of a purely secular ac-

---

Cosmopolitanism, 77. The communities that would be the product of this dialogical encounter would be "simultaneously far more universalist and far more open to difference than most modern states have been." Linklater, "Citizenship and sovereignty in the post Westphalian European State," 122. Citizenship is understood as a system of moral duties that, again as with the Stoics, applies both to a person's city and to the whole of humanity. Ibid., 126. In the world at present the need to be heard applies most obviously to refugees. It is precisely because refugees are citizens of nowhere that they are potential citizens of the world. The question whether citizenship can be based on universal rights alone is raised by the problem that refugees have rights but that existing communities are not ready to guarantee them these rights. Hassner, "Refugees," 274.

93. Held, *Cosmopolitanism*, 45–47.

94. Ibid., 53.

95. Williams, "Religious Faith and Human Rights," 77.

count. However, in an insight very close to Levinas, Simone Weil insisted that, "The object of any obligation in the realm of human affairs, is always the human being as such. There exists an obligation towards every human being for the sole reason that he or she is a human being, without any other condition requiring to be fulfilled."[96] This is to say that the very existence of moral beings, what Levinas calls "the face," makes a claim on us. The existence of a moral or emotional "other" constitutes an irreducible moral foundation, something which, as we shall see in chapter six, is denied by Hayek and other neoliberal thinkers. As I argued in the previous chapter in relation to the virtues, however, to deny this is to open up the ground for moral chaos, for the "war of all against all." This is justified, as with Hayek, on Nietzschean grounds, but then we see, in the case of the Camorra, or with Fascism, that society does not survive. What we are left with is the world of warlords, as outlined in the first chapter. This world is quite clearly less than fully human—it cannot be defended on any reasonable account of human ends.

Tom Paine already outlined "the Rights of Man" in 1791, followed the next year by Mary Wollstonecraft's "Vindication of the Rights of Women," but it is really the Universal Declaration of Human Rights of 1948 that put the idea of rights center stage.[97]

96. Weil, *The Need for Roots*, 4. Weil herself objected to rights language, but as Michael Ignatieff has argued, "The language of rights represents the extent of our agreement about human ends." "The Limits of Sainthood," 44.

97. It is widely assumed that the United Nations Declaration of 1948 was a response to the death camps, though Samuel Moyn disputes this, arguing that its principal concern was welfare rights. In his revisionist history he argues that the Universal Declaration was not a response to the Holocaust, provoked relatively little response in the decades that immediately followed, and that "the year of human rights" was 1977. Only since then has human rights come to occupy a central position, at least in North America, and this was a result of the failed utopias of both communism and social welfarism. His concern is that we need to broaden our understanding of justice beyond human rights, which is a perfectly fair point, but to argue that the Declaration was not a response to the Holocaust is much more questionable. Moyn, *The Last Utopia*. It is hard to believe that the Declaration would have come into being had it not been for the atrocities of World War II. The second sentence of the preamble runs: "Whereas disregard and contempt for human rights have resulted

In the seventy years that have followed, the Declaration itself and the various further UN declarations and covenants dealing with rights have been denounced as a form of Western imperialism, as an example of extreme individualism, and as having no real basis. It is also the case that, as Samuel Moyn argues, the cause of human rights has been damaged by the United States "pursuing low-minded imperial ambitions in high-minded humanitarian tones."[98] Can human rights be defended? It is true, of course that there has been "human rights inflation," and that there are now "second and third generation" rights that are rather far from what the signatories of 1948 envisaged. On the other hand, much of the critique is disingenuous, for what do the critics wish to affirm? That it is, after all, fine, for example, to flog and imprison people for critiquing the state, as happened recently in Saudi Arabia? Is it really so difficult to find a justification for treating people of all cultures equally?[99]

---

in barbarous acts which have outraged the conscience of mankind, and the advent of a world in which human beings shall enjoy freedom of speech and belief and freedom from fear and want has been proclaimed as the highest aspiration of the common people." What exactly were the framers of the Declaration thinking of? The first ten articles all refer to the kind of situation that Jews, Gypsies, and others found themselves in in Nazi Germany, and which millions of others have found themselves in since, right up to today.

Moyn appeals to Marc Bloch's warning that historical difference must be respected but his insistence on this is so extreme it becomes impossible to see how any kind of cultural or intellectual development takes place: history becomes a series of unrelated silos. The fact that what the Stoics meant by cosmopolitanism is not the same as what is meant in the twenty-first century does not mean that their ideas do not contribute to it.

98. Moyn, *Human Rights and the Uses of History*, 2.

99. For example, Asian countries meeting in Bangkok protested that human rights monitoring violated state sovereignty and that conditioning economic assistance on human rights performance was contrary to the right of development. This was tantamount to asserting the right to use child labor and so forth if a given state wanted to. Similarly, Muslim critiques rest on the view that ultimately only the Shari'a is true human law as argued in 1990 in the Cairo Declaration on Human Rights in Islam, signed by forty-five foreign ministers of the organization of the Islamic Conference. In Kuwait, Article 18 of the International Declaration of Human Rights was suspended because it teaches freedom of thought that includes freedom to change one's religion and beliefs.

Stuart Hall argues that the discourse of rights may have developed within the western liberal tradition but has now become cosmopolitan and is "as pertinent to Third World workers struggling at the periphery of the global system, women in the developing world up against patriarchal conceptions of a woman's role, or political dissenters subject to the threat of torture, as it is to western consumers in the weightless economy."[100] Michael Ignatieff points out that the global diffusion of rights language would never have occurred had these not been authentically attractive propositions to millions of people, especially women, in theocratic, traditional, or patriarchal societies.[101] Rights are universal because they define, in particular, the universal interests of the powerless. They are contentious because they challenge powerful religions, family structures, authoritarian states, and tribes.[102]

In defending and extending the remit of human rights as a true expression of cosmopolitanism at least three points need to be considered. First, as Maritain argued at the time of the framing of the Universal Declaration, rights do not apply to "the individual" but to "the human person" understood within their cultural and familial context. Moyn highlights the contribution Christian personalism made to the original framing and the difficulties this has caused—leading to the whole issue of human rights being understood as a form of "Western and Christian" cultural imperialism. But on the other hand, this personalism means that the idea of human rights cannot be dismissed, as it is by some Muslim critics, simply as an instance of "Western individualism" (Held's insistence on individualism as lying at the core of the idea leaves him a hostage to fortune in this respect).[103]

---

100. Hall, "The Multi-cultural Question," in Hesse, ed., *Un/settled Multiculturalisms*, 233

101. Ignatieff, *Human Rights as Politics and Ideology*, 70.

102. Slavoj Žižek finds an analogy with the way in which the Mexican poor took the religion of their conquerors and, in the image of the virgin of Guadalupe, found an image of their terrible plight. "This is perhaps the way human rights works today for the exploited and dominated people of the world." Žižek, "Welcome to the spiritual kingdom of animals," 318.

103. Harvey also believes that the UN declaration privileges the individual

Chantal Mouffe argues that the notion of human rights as for-mulated in Western culture is only one formulation among others of the idea of the dignity of the person.[104] She is extremely vague, however, about what other formulations of the dignity of the person entail, except that they lay greater stress on community. But does this, we have to ask, allow for the expression of difference, or does it occlude it? In most examples we can see it occludes it. Janna Thompson argues that one of the problems with the communitar-ian view of identity (which is what Mouffe is defending) is that it has no resources for understanding social change. According to the communitarian view, individuals have the identity that they are fated to have; either they identify with the community or they do not. And if they do not, then there is no way of understanding why they should come to do so—whether by democratic or other means.[105] In fact, Mouffe's argument seems to grant some kind of intrinsic authority to "hegemony." But why should that be? If Na-tional Socialist ideas (or neoliberal ideas for that matter) are hege-monic, is that a reason to respect them? As the defenders of rights cosmopolitanism argue, there are limits to the moral validity of particular communities—limits that recognize and demand that we must treat with equal respect the dignity of reason and moral choice in every human being.[106] What is called for is not the end of national identity but national identities open to diverse solidari-ties, and shaped by respect for general rules and principles—pretty much the agenda of Kant's "Perpetual Peace."[107]

Second, as Held correctly sees, insistence on human rights will be empty whilst economic rights are not addressed. "A bridge has to be built between international economic law and human rights law, between commercial law and environmental law, between state sovereignty and transnational law, and between

---

rights and private property of liberal theory at the expense of collective rela-tions and cultural claims. *Seventeen Contradictions,* 285.

104. Mouffe, "Democracy," 190.

105. Thompson, "Community, Identity and World Citizenship," 193.

106. Held, *Cosmopolitanism,* 70.

107. Ibid., 102.

cosmopolitan principles and cosmopolitan practices."[108] Without addressing the economic issue "the advocacy of cosmopolitan standards can descend into high-mindedness." As I shall argue in chapters six and seven, a credible cosmopolitan democracy rests on a radically different economic order.

Third, Moyn's critique is directed at the way in which human rights have turned out to be a substitute for self-determination.[109] The human rights agenda, he argues, has displaced other utopias. As a political goal they are inadequate: too private and too apolitical. "If human rights call to mind a few core values that demand protection, they cannot be all things to all people. Put another way, the last utopia cannot be a moral one."[110] He calls for greater political imagination, and indeed effectively asks for justice, and not simply outrage and compassion, to once more become the political lodestar. In this he is quite right but the problem is not the reduction of politics to morality, but of assuming that morality is the realm of the personal rather than the political. "Rights cosmopolitanism" would be a world of small and devolved, but often federated states, where economic and environmental rules would be worked out together and held to be binding by the United Nations and its agencies, and where the acceptance of human rights would be the moral glue that bound communities together, and in particular dictate the treatment of refugees and migrants. Given that most of the ingredients are in place we can ask: Will this emerge?

Will rights cosmopolitan emerge?

Leopold Kohr concluded his book advocating the small state with the question, "Will it happen?" and answered "No." In the second decade of the twenty-first century, approaching very quickly the moment when "extremely dangerous" climate change (Anderson) may be irreversible, we face a painfully divided situation. On the

108. Ibid., 61.

109. Moyn, *Human Rights and the Uses of History*, 74.

110. Moyn, *Last Utopia*, 227.

one hand, as Bull, Held, and others argue, many of the structures and practices for a global democracy are in place. With good will they could be extended in the direction of a beefed up and reformed UN, and the reversion of the Bretton Woods institutions to their original purpose.[111] There would be what Bull speaks of as "a structure of overlapping authorities and criss-crossing loyalties that hold all peoples together in the universal society, while at the same time avoiding the concentration of power inherent in a world government."[112] At the same time there is the rise of right wing populisms in the West, a retreat from the UN and from international treaties on human rights and climate change, and the rise of religious chauvinism in India and most Muslim countries—all of which make dealing with the transgressions of planetary boundaries more difficult, if not absolutely impossible. Put together these could suggest the "new dark ages" of which MacIntyre spoke nearly forty years ago.

On the other side is what Paul Hawken calls the "Movement Society," comprising more than a million civic organisations working on everything from climate change to hunger to peace and human rights. He argues that this constitutes the largest social movement in history, working from the ground up, eluding the radar of the so-called 'movers and shakers' and actually bringing about real change in our political and economic landscape.[113] It is true of course that not all these movements are pulling in the same direction but effectively in this book—with Naomi Klein, Brad Werner, and many others—I am putting my money on this out-flanking movement. The political and economic practices which

---

111. Brian Martin argues that international governance is particularly unsuited to dealing with crises. The United Nations, he says, might give the appearance of having a centralized response capability but in reality it's a tool of powerful governments that have their own agendas. There is little citizen participation and little capacity to skill development. "Effective crisis governance," 278. But this should be regarded as a call to reform and improve the UN, not to write it off. *Mutatis mutandis* the same goes for the European Parliament.

112. Bull, *Anarchical Society*, 255.

113. Hawken, *Blessed Unrest*.

such movements involve will be the theme of the next two chapters, and their chances of success considered in the final chapter.

The questions which need to be addressed to deal with the global emergency are, as Bull put it, "the very issues over which governments have control, and do not seem likely to be willing to relinquish control, in the absence of vast changes in human society."[114] Is even an emergency likely to bring these changes about? "Pessimism of the intellect, optimism of the will" (Gramsci). Much exhortation by Green activists is whistling in the dark, and Emmott and others are quite right to emphasize the scale of the problems human beings face. At the same time the situation is not hopeless. The movements Paul Hawken documents may have the capacity to avert climate disaster by changing the culture and politics of their respective polities. Doing this will require a profound repristination of democracy and it is therefore to that question I turn.

114. Bull, *Anarchical Society*, 87.

Chapter Five

Valuing Equality

Democratization is the imposition of the apparent requirements
of equality on the endlessly resistant material of human lives.

—JOHN DUNN

I HAVE ARGUED IN the previous chapter for the priority of small,
federated political units, and underlined the importance of the
social networks that constitute them. In this chapter I want to take
this further as an account of the political practices that sustain our
humanness.

We saw in chapter three that in Zygmunt Bauman's view it
was the failure of democracy that allowed the Nazi catastrophe
to happen. If that is the case, then maintaining decent forms of
community in the face of the disruption climate change brings will
crucially involve maintaining, and in fact deepening, forms of democracy. Amartya Sen's celebrated argument (already anticipated
by Polanyi in 1944) that famines do not happen in democracies
also underlines the point and is pertinent to the climate change
scenario, for which famine is probably the worst threat.

My concern in this chapter, then, is democracy, which I understand as a key practice in the creation and maintenance of a
sustainable world. I begin with an account of enthusiasm, or lack
of enthusiasm, for democracy, and go on to outline what I consider the main reason for advocating it, which is a belief in human

equality. I then consider democratic values before going on to a review of current democratic structures in Western society, and the democratic deficit that ensues, and I ask whether we should be content with "second-best democracy." Finally I turn to alternative democratic structures, which might realize democratic values more truly, and which would stand some chance of engaging effectively with the transgression of planetary boundaries.

Enthusiasm for democracy?

Today, in Western rhetoric, it is assumed that democracy is the best and the normal form of government, and Ingelhart's World Values Survey shows that over 90 percent of the world's people support it, but this is, of course, a very recent development.[1] Right up to the nineteenth century *democracy* was a term of opprobrium. This included the founders of the American Independence struggle and of the French revolution. James Madison thought democracies had always been "spectacles of turbulence and contention," short in their lives.[2] Polanyi highlights the opposition to universal manhood suffrage in Victorian Britain, when Lord Macaulay demanded, in the House of Lords, the unconditional rejection of the Chartist petition in the name of the institution of property on which all civilization rested. "Inside and outside England from Macaulay to Mises, from Spencer to Sumner, there was not a militant liberal who did not express his conviction that popular democracy was a danger to capitalism."[3] Streeck argues that the contest between capitalism and democracy remains fundamental to the way the world is presently constituted.

Even today nearly half of the world's countries are not democracies, including the world's most populous state, China, and many exclude women from the vote.[4] Many are run by what are

1. Ingelhart, "How solid is mass support for democracy—and how can we measure it?"

2. Madison, Hamilton, and Jay, *The Federalist Papers*, 122–27. Paper no. 10.

3. Polanyi, *The Great Transformation*, 225–26.

4. The twenty democracies that have been continuously democratic since

effectively criminal gangs, as Augustine called states without law, and those that are not are most adequately labeled semi democracies rather than democracies.[5]

After World War II Karl Barth argued that it was possible to speak of a nisus within Christianity for democracy, but it was not possible to say that democracy was *the* Christian political order.[6] "More nonsense and meaningless blather is talked in Western public discourse today about democracy," said Eric Hobsbawm in one of his last lectures, "and specifically about the miraculous qualities assigned to governments elected by arithmetical majorities of voters choosing between rival parties, than about almost any other word or political concept."[7] Implicitly disagreeing with Bauman, he pointed out that liberal democracy is compatible with

the 1940s or earlier are a rather homogenous group. They are all economically developed, industrialized, and urbanized; with the exception of Japan, they belong to the Western Judaeo-Christian world; and most are geographically concentrated in the North Atlantic area. Lijphart, *Patterns of Democracy,* 53. To my mind this says something about the impact of Christian views of the human, detailed below.

5. Beinen, Rittbeeger, and Wagner, "Democracy in the United Nations system: cosmopolitan and communitarian principles," in Archibug, Held, and Köhler, *Re-imagining,* 304

6. Barth, *Against the Stream,* 40. David Held believes that the antithesis of *homo politicus* is the *homo credens* of the Christian faith: the citizen whose active judgement is essential is displaced by the true believer, who shifted the source of authority and wisdom from this worldly to otherworldly representatives. *Democracy,* 8. But the struggle between pope and emperor over the ultimate source of authority, leading finally to Marsilius and Wycliffe, shows this is not the case. Rousseau (who may be behind Held's view) also believed Christianity was unfitted for practical politics. Rousseau argued that Christianity has a number of fatal flaws from the point of political order. First it teaches people to hope for salvation that is otherworldly and spiritual, rather than political; thus "it leaves laws with only the force the laws derive from themselves, without adding any other force to them." Second, Christianity turns people's thoughts inward, as each is urged to examine his own heart; this teaching produces indifference to political events. Third, Christianity teaches nonviolence and even martyrdom, thus teaching people to be slaves. Its spirit is "too favourable to tyranny for tyranny not to take advantage of it at all times." *Social Contract,* book I, ch. 8.

7. Hobsbawm, *Globalisation, Democracy, Terrorism,* 5.

mass slaughter and displacement, as in Colombia. The solution or mitigation of the problems raised by transgressing planetary boundaries, he argued, would find no support by counting votes or measuring consumer preferences. In his view freedom and toleration for minorities were often more threatened than protected by democracy.[8] "The case for democracy is essentially negative. Even as an alternative to other systems, it can be defended only with a sigh."[9] Here he pretty much agrees with Plato and Aristotle right at the beginning of the discussion of democracy.[10] Christopher Achen and Larry Bartels mount a withering critique of what they call the "folk theory" of democracy—the idea that people rationally assess the options, based on the best evidence available, and find by contrast that group identity is what determines democratic outcomes. "Proponents of mind-numbing clichés about giving power to ordinary people bear considerable responsibility for the domination of government by narrowly self-interested groups."[11] The Dutch scholar Frank Hendriks notes that the core package of competitive elections with civic liberties is only elementary democracy: thin, flimsy democracy. We need a lot of things on top of that, he argues, before you can even begin to call it true democracy.[12]

This does not mean that we should give up on democracy, concluding that it is a fraud, but it does mean that it is essential to

8. Ibid., 97.

9. Ibid., 99.

10. Plato argues that oligarchy tends to give way to democracy, but democracy to tyranny because it gets drunk on the idea of liberty and breeds an anarchic culture. *Republic*, 562e. For all that he agrees with his pupil Aristotle that some form of modified democracy is the best we can actually do. *Laws*, 6.757. Aristotle considers rule by the mass of the people in the common interest the best form available. Following his principle of the mean between extremes he argues that the best constitution will be one where the middling class, those who are neither rich or poor, predominate, and where laws are made in their interest. Though democracy prioritizes the needy at the expense of the common good, it remains "the safest of the imperfect forms of government." *Politics*, 1302a.15.

11. Achen and Bartels, *Democracy for Realists*, 327.

12. Hendriks, *Vital Democracy*, 24.

think what might constitute a more realistic and effective form of democracy. I pursue this question here, and in chapter nine, but I begin with what I take to be the foundation of democracy, which is a belief in human equality

Democracy and equality

What relaunches democracy's career, after a gap of nearly 2,500 years, is a new understanding of human equality, expressed both in the American Declaration of Independence and in the French Revolution. "EQUALITY! The first wish of nature, the first need of man, the first knot of all legitimate association!," goes Sylvain Marechal's *Manifesto of the Equals* in 1796, trying to recapture the ideals of the revolution. "Are we not all equal? This principle remains uncontested, because unless touched by insanity, you can't say it's night when it's day. Well then! We claim to live and die equal, the way we were born: we want this *real* equality or death; *that's* what we need. And we'll have this real equality, at whatever price."[13] "Each individual . . . has the right to a say in the laws by which he is governed," said Robespierre. "Otherwise it is not true to say that all men are equal in rights, that all men are citizens."[14] "The principle of democratic rule is equality," says John Dunn, "the presumption that, when it comes to shaping a community and exercising power, everyone's judgement deserves as much weight as everyone' else's."[15] For David Graeber democracy is not a mode of government but "just the belief that humans are fundamentally equal and ought to be allowed to manage their collective affairs in an egalitarian fashion, using whatever means appear most

13. Translated by Mitchell Abidor, marxists.org 2004, 2016.

14. Cited in Dunn, *Democracy*, 115.

15. Ibid., 45. George Thomson says of ancient Greek democracy that it was "essentially the reassertion by the common people of their lost equality." *Aeschylus*, 43. On his account tribal society was egalitarian. War and conquest led to kingship, but a long period of peace made monarchy redundant and in these conditions democracy emerged.

conducive."[16] The philosopher Thomas Christiano calls democracy "the constitution of equality." The public realization of equality requires that each person be given a say in how the society he or she lives in is organized.[17] Since all or nearly all of the fundamental interests of each person are at stake, there is a kind of fundamental equality of stake in that world.[18]

But why should we consider equality important? After all, the most obvious fact of experience is that people are not equal in strength, intelligence, creativity, beauty, and, since the widespread adoption of agriculture, they have not been in property either—a fact that Rousseau saw as the root cause of inequality. The writers of the American Declaration appealed to "self evidence." Unfortunately this did not include either their slaves or the native American population, and the idea of human equality still needs arguing. Justin Dart, a member of Reagan's kitchen cabinet, contemptuously dismissed "crappy issues like equal rights."[19] The idea of equality, Keith Sutherland tells us, matters to no one but members of political science departments in liberal arts colleges.[20]

There are anthropological grounds for believing in human equality that I set out in chapter three, namely that all humans share the same basic needs and potentialities, including the potential for humiliation. We could, then, argue that these factors override obvious differences in talent, strength, beauty, etc., though that is a far cry from "self evidence."

The Stoics believed that all human beings contained a spark of the logos and are thus metaphysically equal, though Stoicism never led to a political movement for equality, probably because the belief in *pronoia* (providence) was implicitly fatalistic.[21] Chris-

16. Graeber, *Democracy Project*, 184.

17. Christiano, *Constitution*, 77.

18. Ibid., 80.

19. Bellah et al., *Habits of the Heart*, 264.

20. Sutherland, *The Party's Over*, 154. James Buchanan, a neoliberal winner of the Nobel Prize for economics, likewise detested equality and sought an oligarchic world run by billionaires. See MacLean, *Democracy in Chains*.

21. The consequences of this are most clearly seen in Aurelius's *Meditations*,

tiano grounds human equality in the dignity that follows from the fact that all persons are authorities in the realm of value. Democracy follows from this because "the fitting response to this dignity is to enable persons to exercise their distinctive authority and to enjoy that exercise."[22]

The pragmatic grounds for equality are set out by epidemiologists Richard Wilkinson and Kate Pickett in their celebrated book *The Spirit Level*. They adduce a mass of evidence to suggest that more equal societies have less crime, less violence, less mental illness and better overall health than unequal societies.[23] The howls of rage, and furious rebuttals that greeted their book—all from "democrats"—were revealing, because they were all in favor of retaining the present massive and growing degree of inequality worldwide. But, as Rousseau already argued, inequality is destructive of democracy.

In hunter gatherer societies equality is a form of group insurance, in that no member of the group knows when he or she may be likely to be in need, and it is linked to what Barrington Moore calls the "dog in a manger taboo," which condemns those who keep resources that are in short supply without use. Social equality in "primitive" societies has often been taken as a datum since Rousseau.[24] Alasdair MacIntyre, on the other hand, arguing that Christianity is the main protagonist of equality in Western discourse, believes that "the distinctive values of equality and of the criteria of need which Christianity in large part begot could not possibly commend themselves as general values for human life until it began to appear possible for the basic material inequali-

---

humane but, as regards the generation of a world made otherwise, hopeless.

22. Christiano, *Constitution*, 20.

23. Wilkinson and Pickett, *The Spirit Level*.

24. "From the moment one man began to stand in need of the help of another; from the moment it appeared advantageous to any one man to have enough provisions for two, equality disappeared, property was introduced, work became indispensable, and vast forests became smiling fields, which man had to water with the sweat of his brow, and where slavery and misery were soon seen to germinate and grow up with the crops." Rousseau, "Discourse on the Origin of Inequality," in *Social Contract and Discourses,* 215.

ties of human life to be abolished."[25] One can agree with this to the extent that the existence of material inequalities must appear as a problem, and not a part of the natural order of the universe, for the attempt to bring about change to start.[26] This is a very different matter from the argument that perceptions about equality arise only with material progress, something the historical record contradicts. As soon as we have class-divided, unequal societies, we have "meaning in the service of power," but we also have counter-myths and ideologies, of a primitive golden age where there was no inequality, where humankind was one, or perhaps of androgyny. These myths and ideologies shape society, at the very least by providing it a goal. This Christianity has done, in the West at least. Although the church has, probably from the beginning, compromised, and sometimes inverted, the gospel, the texts rise up against it. It is questionable whether there is a secular argument for equality that is as powerful as the theological. What I call "the gospel of equality" is, in fact, implicit in each article of the creed, itself a kind of thumbnail sketch of the biblical narrative. John Ball, broken on the rack at Smithfield for daring to challenge the social consensus of the fourteenth century, appealed to Genesis 3. He could equally have gone to Genesis 1—the doctrine of the image of God. It follows from the doctrine of the image of God that all human beings are created equal. "Equality is ascribed by God in the work of creation; it is not a human achievement or an empirical characteristic of human beings."[27] It is, in other words, grace, pure gift. As Kierkegaard put it, every person is equal simply in virtue of being loved by God.[28]

Equality follows, too, from the second article of the creed. If God takes flesh in Christ, if Christ is "the human one," then, as the parable in Matthew 25 depicts it, all human beings are his sisters and brothers. He is encountered in all. There is, as Paul says, "no distinction." The fourth-century Fathers understood

25. MacIntyre, *Short History*, 115.

26. Moore, *Injustice*, 468.

27. Forrester, *On Human Worth*, 84.

28. Ibid., 148.

this in terms of Christ's assumption of a universal humanity, so that all human beings were saved because all were included in his humanity. If this metaphysic is strange to us we can reinterpret it in terms of solidarity, so that in the incarnation God expresses solidarity with all humans.

The centrality of flesh to the doctrine of the incarnation also means that if we try to neuter the doctrine of equality by restricting it to "equality of opportunity," or "equality before the law," we make it of no effect. The key question is life chances, and these are greatly diminished by poverty. In the light of the incarnation, equality must mean equality of outcome and this means, in practice, legislation that restricts the possible extent of economic disparities, as Herman Daly has argued.

Equality follows, finally, from the doctrine of the Spirit, which understands the church as what Fiorenza calls "a discipleship of equals." The earliest church, she argues, was an egalitarian *koinonia* in which women and other people marginalized by the surrounding culture found a place, dignity, and were widely welcomed into discipleship roles.[29] Even when it sponsors no social or political program, the church is to be understood as showing in its life, fellowship, and worship an egalitarian alternative to "the way of the world."[30] The great study of the impact of mission on the southern Tswana by Jean and John Comaroff shows how this worked itself out in nineteenth-century Africa, and the same could be said about the impact of mission on Dalit groups in southern India.[31]

If this is the case we have to ask why, for most of its existence, Christianity has been happy with hierarchy and class society. Without pretending that these are exhaustive, two answers suggest themselves. Unlike Stoicism, Christianity had an eschatology, and this was potentially revolutionary. It was part of Augustine's genius to neuter this—partly in response to the challenge of the Donatists. In terms of defusing the radical potential of the gospel

29. Schüssler Fiorenza, *Discipleship of Equals*, 104.

30. Forrester, *On Human Worth*, 105.

31. Comaroff and Comaroff, *Of Revelation and Revolution*.

163

(evident, for example, in Ambrose and Chrysostom, Augustine's contemporaries), Augustine can be regarded as the greatest bomb disposal expert in history! Augustine pushed hope for the messianic conditions into the next life; here and now, under conditions of sin, the best we could do would be to keep evil in check. Secondly, in the centuries after Augustine a Neoplatonic ontology was absorbed into the Christian bloodstream through the sixth-century monk who has come to be known as Pseudo Dionysius: Aquinas cites him more than a thousand times. In this ontology we have the great chain of being—all the way from God to the humblest microbe. Humans are not situated on this chain as a class, but rather as classes. According to this ontology kings, nobles, commoners, and serfs simply exist on different parts of the great chain. In other words, it functions as an ideological justification of inequality. The big problem for this ideology was Scripture, which clearly believed no such thing. John Wycliffe, at the end of the fourteenth century, believed that "Holy Scripture is the highest authority for every Christian and the standard of faith and of all human perfection."[32] When the Peasants Revolt broke out in 1381 Wycliffe, though he opposed it, was widely blamed. John Ball, the priest who was one of its leaders, shared many of Wycliffe's views on church reform. More significantly he argued for social structures that reflected what he took to be a fundamental human equality that could be derived from Scripture. A good many clergy were involved in the revolt: "The better they knew the Bible and the writings of the fathers of the church, the more explosive the mixture of social and religious radicalism was likely to be."[33] Both clergy and laity were used to moralizing at the expense of each of the three estates, with especial attacks on the rich. John Ball's, "When Adam delved and Eve span, who was then the gentleman" was already a commonplace.[34] His social and political program envisaged "A regime of family ownership of peasant holdings and

32. Wycliffe, *De Veritate sacra Scripturae*, Introduction, 25.

33. Hilton, *Bond Men*, 210.

34. It appears in East Prussia in 1525: "Do Adam rent und Eva span,Wo war der Edelman? Im Kustal war er . . ." Hilton, *Bond Men*, 212.

artisan workshops, with the large scale landed property of the church and the aristocracy divided among the peasants."[35] The chronicler Thomas Walsingham tells us that Ball "tried to prove . . . that from the beginning all men were created equal by nature and that servitude had been introduced by the unjust and evil oppression of men against the will of God."[36]

When Lutheran ideas began to make an impact on Britain in the early sixteenth century those in authority worried that access to Scripture might cause rebellion. The bishops and "religious," said Tyndale in 1528, say that Scripture "causeth insurrection and teacheth the people to disobey their heads and governors, and moveth them to rise against their princes and to make all common and to make havoc of other men's goods."[37] He wrote *The Obedience of a Christian Man* to show that this was not so, picking up on Luther's *Freedom of a Christian Man*, and seeking to show that Protestantism had nothing to do with the Peasant War in Germany. Nevertheless readers, who included Henry VIII, found the disconcerting sentence: "The most despised person in his realm is the king's brother and fellow member with him and equal with him in the kingdom of God and of Christ."[38] Although he put the Bible into churches Henry soon found it necessary to pass an act prohibiting women, artisans, husbandmen, laborers, or servants from reading it.[39] Henry complained that the Bible was "disputed, rhymed, sung and jangled in every alehouse and tavern."[40] The cheapest Bible available was the Geneva Bible, available as a whole in 1560, and copiously annotated. James the First regarded the notes as "very partial, untrue, seditious and savouring too much of dangerous and traitorous concepts"—it high-

35. Ibid., 229.

36. Ibid., 222. It is interesting that Sidney Carter's 1960s song, "John Ball," has emerged in the second decade of the twenty-first century as a rallying cry for people who refuse to accept neoliberal duplicities.

37. Tyndale, *The Obedience of a Christian Man*, 26.

38. Ibid., 63.

39. MacCulloch, *Reformation*, 203.

40. Hill, *The English Bible and the Seventeenth Century Revolution*, 15.

THE WORLD MADE OTHERWISE: PRACTICES

lighted the biblical warrant for unseating tyrants.[41] The Geneva
Bible remained the Bible of the poor, and was the version used by
Cromwell's army during the civil war. This Bible was the ground
for Leveller and Digger arguments for both equality and democracy. "In the beginning of Time," wrote Gerrard Winstanley, appealing to the first chapter of Genesis, "the great Creator Reason,
made the Earth to be a Common Treasury, to preserve Beasts,
Birds, Fishes, and Man, the lord that was to govern this Creation;
for Man had Domination given to him, over the Beasts, Birds, and
Fishes; but not one word was spoken in the beginning, That one
branch of mankind should rule over another."[42]

It is no surprise that liberation theology in part rested on a
rediscovery of Scripture, beginning with literacy classes in Latin
America, where the Bible was often the only text available.

However, no matter how cogent the arguments for equality
we have to note how, in, for example, Mao's cultural revolution,
or with Pol Pot, "the rage for equality becomes something very
close to a rage against the reality of other human beings or the
very idea of a society." John Dunn therefore argues that "Untram-
melled and complete equality is not even a coherent idea. It appeals to too few emotions for much too little of the time and is
swamped by the immediacy and impact of its incessant collisions
with far too many other emotions."[43]

David Held distinguishes between ideal, attainable, and
urgent realizations of equality. An attainable level allows participation in political communities without systematic disadvantage
and arbitrary constraint. Urgent needs address lacks in health,
education and welfare that result in serious harm. The ideal remains something to aim at.[44] Martha Nussbaum affirms the value
of equality but wants to keep some inequalities on the side of
wealth and income, "in order to give incentives for striving and

41. Ibid., 64.

42. Winstanley, "A Declaration to the Powers of England," in *The Complete
Works of Gerrard Winstanley*, vol. 2, 4.

43. Dunn, *Democracy*, 143, 145.

44. Held, *Democracy and the Global Order*, 213.

innovation that raise the level of the whole society."[45] In response to this one would have to ask, first, what are meant by "some inequalities" because as soon as you get, say, the present degree of inequality, you get the reintroduction of hierarchy.[46] But second, why should we assume that material and financial incentives are necessary to persuade people to strive and innovate? Notoriously, this has played next to no role in the arts—actually rather the reverse has been the case, and in the history of scientific invention it has also played an absolutely minor role. Nussbaum seems to have allowed herself to buy the line of the corporations, and the overweening justification of inequality pushed by the financial masters of the universe.

Democratic values

If we believe in equality then, it might seem, we ought to have democracy because that treats all citizens as equal members of the polity, but equality alone is not enough. James Fishkin argues that not just equality, but deliberation and participation, which can also be glossed as inclusion and thoughtfulness, are the fundamental values of democracy.[47] The key here is deliberation. People can be required to vote, as in Australia, but if the vote does not reflect informed preferences then it can be carried by those who own the media, or by those with the most money. It expresses what Fishkin calls "raw" public opinion, opinion not tested by the consideration of competing arguments and information conscientiously offered. Mass democracy, he finds, has increased the weight of raw public opinion.[48] To these three values

45. Nussbaum, *Political Emotions*, 123.

46. Hahn and Hart remark that "There is a great lie at the heart of modern political economy. We live in self-proclaimed democracies where all are equally free as a universal principle. Yet we must justify granting some people inferior rights; otherwise functional economic inequalities would be threatened." Hahn and Hart, *Economic Anthropology*, 117.

47. Fishkin, *When the People Speak*, 159.

48. Ibid., 14, 48.

he adds "non tyranny"—that is, ensuring that the tyranny of the majority is avoided. In any democracy respect for minorities is key. As Schumpeter argued, "there are ultimate ideals and interests which the most ardent democrat will put above democracy" (for example the need to resist anti-Semitism, xenophobia, or the advocacy of torture or indeed mass extermination through nuclear weapons).[49] Structures for allowing freedom of belief and of (reasonable) practice have to be in place for democracy to work (we don't need to enshrine the right to torture and enslave, for example). As Kant argued, there needs, therefore, to be a rule of law which is not biased in favor of those with money or those otherwise in power. There have to be structures to help those who fall by the wayside through illness or other misfortune. There have to be safeguards against the exercise of power of "overmighty subjects," whether these be the press, corporations, or party or mafia bosses. An ethos of respect would not, as Nietzsche feared, lead to the emasculation of a culture but would underwrite a society built on cooperation (more on this in chapter six). This in turn requires an understanding that society is bound together in weal and woe, and is not a collection of disparate, competing atoms.

David Van Reybrouck argues that every political system needs to balance efficiency and legitimacy. Efficiency is about finding successful solutions to problems and legitimacy is about the degree to which people give their assent to these solutions. Democracy seeks to find a balance between these two.[50] In fact the degree to which people feel that their voices count is what provides legitimacy in the constitution of equality. What makes this possible are the key values of fairness and respect, and an ethos of participation. Democracy cannot flourish where natural inequalities of ability solidify into class and caste systems and where wealth differentials are too high (the point made by Wilkinson and Pickett, and by economists like Herman Daly). David Orr believes that democracy may be the best way of dealing with the long emergency but it will have to address its age-old nemesis: economic oligarchy.

49. Schumpeter, *Capitalism, Socialism, and Democracy*, 242.
50. Van Reybrouck, *Against Elections*, 5–6.

He agrees with Daly that beyond some threshold rising inequality divides society by class, erodes empathy, hardens hearts, undermines public trust, incites violence, saps our collective imagination, and destroys the public spirit that upholds democracy and community alike.[51] Structures such as tax regimes are needed to make sure this does not happen.

Aristotle argued that people do things together "by nature." We are suspicious of such arguments, knowing that "nature" is socially constructed, but what these arguments point to is suggested, for example, by the research of Herbert Gans who found, in his study of the vast "anonymous" suburb of Levittown, that it was actually honeycombed by interest groups of all kind.[52] The same result was found in a survey of my city, Exeter, where, in a population of 120,000, there were 640 societies and interest groups, representing everything from chess, Appalachian clog dancing, and postcard collecting to radical and conservative politics. These structures are often "apolitical" but they form the tilth which makes a healthy political culture possible. The main objective of democracy, according to David Held, is "the transformation of private preferences via a process of deliberation into positions that can withstand public scrutiny and test."[53] Respectful participatory practices are what allow this to happen. This presupposes in turn educational policies that foster critical and informed thinking and promote a culture of respectful debate.

Existing democracies

How well are these values represented in the relatively small number of countries, mostly Western, which are identified as "democracies"? We need to outline the way in which these democracies function in order to answer that question. The Dutch

---

51. Orr, "Governance in the long emergency," 288.
52. Gans, *The Levittowners*.
53. Held, *Cosmopolitanism*, 218.

scholar Frank Hendriks outlines four different ways in which these polities organize themselves.

The first form, with which Anglo Saxons are most familiar, is representative democracy. In the United States, after independence was attained, the participatory democracy that Jefferson wanted was headed off for three reasons. First, Madison argued that direct democracy was bound to lead to factionalism. Second, and relatedly, he argued that it simply could not work for very large populations. Third, it threatened private property. Direct democracy, John Adams warned, would mean that

> Debts would be abolished first; taxes laid heavy on the rich, and not at all on others; and at least a downright equal division of everything be demanded and voted. What would be the consequence of this? The idle, the vicious, the intemperate, would rush into the utmost extravagance of debauchery, sell and spend their entire share, and then demand a new division of those who purchased from them. The moment the idea is admitted into society, that property is not as sacred as the laws of God, and that there is not a force of law and public justice to protect it, anarchy and tyranny commence.[54]

Madison and Adams won the day and what has emerged, more or less worldwide, is "representative democracy," the delegation of power to an executive for periods of four or five years and, as Madison noted, "the total exclusion of the people in their collective capacity from any share" in executive power.[55]

J. S. Mill argued that representative democracy was the best form of government on the grounds that, although in a democracy everyone should participate, in practice this was impossible, even in a small town. Representation was the only way to assure participation, though he wanted major changes to the voting patterns and was extremely suspicious of party democracy.[56]

54. Graeber, *Democracy Project*, 165.

55. Dunn, *Democracy*, 79.

56. Mill, *On Liberty*, 198.

Thomas Christiano endorses the Madisonian argument. Most citizens, he says, simply would not have the time to devote to the complicated issues involved in making legislation. The process would inevitably be hijacked by elites with axes to grind. That is why a division of labor is necessary. It would also substantially undermine the power of citizens to decide on the structure and organization of society. Without the division of labor that the representative system supplies, citizens would be capable of doing a lot less than they would with such a division of labor. Hence, citizens would have much less power and thus power would inevitably be transferred to other sectors of the society. Hence, representative democracy is superior to direct democracy on the score of equality.[57] Achen and Bartels assemble a mass of evidence to show that Christiano's view (shared by Hendriks) is justified: people's electoral choices are driven neither by rational choice, nor even by a desire to punish governments for bad policies, but by things like bad harvests, shark attacks, and economic downturns for which governments may bear no responsibility. Elections, they say, "are capricious collective decisions based on considerations . . . that will . . . soon be forgotten."[58]

Representative democracy is often, also, "pendulum democracy" as in the United Kingdom, where there are two main parties; the result is calculated on a majority of seats, and government oscillates between two parties. Fishkin, following Schumpeter, calls it "competitive democracy"—the competitive struggle for the people's vote.

Representative democracy has always had its critics. England, said Rousseau, regards itself as free: "it is free only during the election of members of parliament. As soon as they are elected, slavery overtakes it, and it is nothing. The use it makes of the short moments of liberty it enjoys shows indeed that it deserves to lose them."[59] Hannah Arendt thought that the consent of the people that is presupposed in representative democracy was en-

57. Christiano, *Constitution*, 105.
58. Achen and Bartels, *Democracy for Realists*, 16.
59. Rousseau, *Social Contract*, 3.15.

tirely fictitious. "Representative government itself is in a crisis today, partly because it has lost, in the course of time, all institutions that permitted the citizens' actual participation, and partly because it is now gravely affected by the disease from which the party system suffers: bureaucratisation and the two parties tendency to represent nobody except the party machines."[60] Martin Buber argued that representation disabled community life. Only "the common active handling of the common" allowed community to flourish.[61]

The second way of organizing state democracy Hendriks calls "voter democracy." This works through referenda, plebiscites, and so forth. This form of democracy is mostly combined with other kinds (in the UK, for example, there are occasional, but important, referenda, for example on Scottish devolution, or on membership of the EU) but, "In California, where voter democracy has progressed more than anywhere else, the point has been reached where voter democracy instead of serving the individual has become a threat to the individual. Californian voter democracy has increasingly become the playground of well-to-do interest groups and other Pied Pipers, who have the funds and organisation to make the initiative-industrial complex work for them and to buy individual referendums and citizens initiatives. As a consequence we have a state verging on anarchy."[62] Recent referenda in Britain, Hungary, and Colombia all illustrate the difficulty of this form of democracy: it can be a way of validating anti-immigrant prejudice, or a refusal to bury the hatchet in relation to well-established wrongs. Referenda represent gut

60. Arendt, *Crises of the Republic*, 89.

61. Buber, *Believing Humanism*, 87.

62 Hendriks, *Vital Democracy*, 103. Looking at the North American debate on fluoridation of water, Achen and Bartels note that the "more democracy" people had the more likely people were to harm themselves and their children. "Crackpots, rogue doctors, and extreme right wing interest groups all fought fluoridation, and many voters, including a substantial fraction of those with college educations, could not sort out the self-appointed gurus from the competent experts." *Democracy for Realists*, 54.

reactions rather than deliberation based on argument.[63] Recent history shows only too clearly the dangers that this kind of political practice can involve. As Keith Sutherland points out, the Nazis employed devices like citizens' movements in plebiscites to undermine Weimar democracy. They also peddled the contempt for elites, which characterized both the Brexit referendum in Britain and the Trump election. For the Nazis, Sutherland writes, "traditional politicians . . . were an out of touch elite who could no longer retain the respect of the 'people'; the Nazi movement was able to subvert and eventually abolished democracy—all democracy, representative and direct—by exploiting popular dissatisfaction with the established political class and using direct means of consulting the masses which seemed to bypass conventional political system and reach the people without mediation." He points out that this was the reason that in post-war West Germany the establishment of a political class with integrity was a key part of rebuilding the political landscape.[64] Arguably Switzerland has found a way around this problem: more about this shortly.

Hendriks then speaks, somewhat confusingly, of "consensus democracy," which can be found in countries like the Netherlands, Belgium, Switzerland, and Austria. This is actually a version of representative democracy where representatives of parties or interest groups "go about their business in an integrative and consensus seeking way usually in a conference room or roundtable type setting."[65] This best represents what Fishkin, following Madison, calls "elite deliberation." Madison was sure that direct democracy would be a disaster. People's opinions needed to be filtered, and this would happen through the election of intelligent and able representatives who could better pronounce on "justice and the common good than could the people themselves if convened for the purpose."[66]

63. Van Reybrouck, *Against Elections*, 124.

64. Sutherland, *The Party's Over*, 80.

65. Hendriks, *Vital Democracy*, 28.

66. Fishkin, *When the People Speak*, 70.

Arend Lijphart argues that consensus democracies of this type perform better than majoritarian democracies across the board.[67] They are, he says, strongly correlated with a lower degree of violence.[68] They are more likely to be welfare states; they have a better record with regard to the protection of the environment; they put fewer people in prison and are less likely to use the death penalty; and the consensus democracies in the developed world are more generous with their economic assistance to the developing nations.[69]

Consensus democracy of this kind really enshrines Saul Alinsky's dictum that compromise lies at the heart of a free politics. "In the world as it is, 'compromise' is not an ugly but a noble word. If the whole free way of life could be summed up in one word it would be 'compromise.' A free way of life is a constant conflict punctuated by compromises which then serve as a jumping off point for further conflict, more compromises, more conflict, in the never ending struggles toward achieving man's highest goals."[70]

Hendriks's fourth form, participatory democracy, is found most commonly in social movements but a form of it is also found in Porto Allegre in Brazil, and in its participatory budgeting process. Local fora are responsible for about 20 percent of the total Porto Allegre budget. More than 85 percent of the population is familiar with the process and in the 2001 financial year the total number of participating citizens was estimated at 20,000; the participation of disadvantaged neighborhoods was above average, whereas as a rule

67. Lijphart, *Patterns of Democracy*.

68. Ibid., 270.

69. Ibid., 275.

70. Alinsky, *Reveille for Radicals*, 225. Cf. Achen and Bartels, who write that "politicians with vision who are also skilled at creative compromise are the soul of successful democracy." *Democracy for Realists*, 318. The formal consensus decision-making method distinguishes three levels of decision-making, each ending in a call for consensus, and has several formulas for coping with dissent: proposal shelved; proposal reconsidered by committee; or proposal carried forward because the objector stands aside. Special circumstances may require a proposal being put to the vote, which is subject to the rule that it takes an overwhelming majority of more than 75 percent to accept it. Hendriks, *Vital Democracy*, 110.

this tends to be below average anywhere else.[71] This practice is now being taken up in other parts of the world.[72]

Switzerland is also often cited as an example of direct and participatory democracy.[73] There are three tiers of government at the municipal, cantonal, and federal level. Subsidiarity is written in to the constitution and nearly 70 percent of all expenditure is managed at cantonal or municipal level, and their responsibilities include education, social security, and public health. All constitutional amendments are subject to referenda, and parliamentary decisions can be challenged by referenda initiated by any citizen. Most cantons and municipalities have a first past the post system. However, deliberation is a normal part of the process and the arguments of the losing minority are heeded, and minority or "losing" parties are included at each level of government. Given this structure Andreas Ladner argues that what looks like "direct" democracy (government by referenda) turns out in fact to be participatory, deliberative, and non-majoritarian.[74]

71. Hendriks, *Vital Democracy*, 123.

72. Exeter tried it, but has since dropped the experiment.

73. Colin Ward cites Herbert Luethy, who notes that in Switzerland "every Sunday the inhabitants of scores of communes go to the polling booths to elect their civil servants, ratify such and such an item of expenditure, or decide whether a road or a school should be built; after settling the business of the commune, they deal with cantonal elections and voting on cantonal issues; lastly . . . come the decisions on federal issues. In some Cantons the sovereign people still meet in Rousseau like fashion to discuss questions of common interest. It may be thought that this ancient form of assembly is no more than a pious tradition with a certain value as a tourist attraction. If so it is worth looking at the results of local democracy. The simplest example is the Swiss railway system, which is the densest network in the world. At great cost and with great trouble, it has been made to serve the needs of the smallest localities and most remote valleys, not as a paying proposition but because such was the will of the people. It is the outcome of fierce political struggles. In the 19th century the Democratic railway movement brought the small Swiss communities into conflict with the big towns, which had plans for centralisation." Ward, *Anarchy in Action*, 56.

74. Ladner, "Switzerland: subsidiarity, power-sharing, and direct democracy," 215

The democratic deficit

Most established democracies are the subject of intense critique. Van Reybrouck speaks of "democratic fatigue syndrome." Surveys in both Europe and United States show that confidence in the institutions of democracy is falling steadily. This fatigue draws on many dissatisfactions.

The problem with representation, it is often said, is that representatives do not reflect the perspectives of their constituents. Politicians represent their party to their constituents rather than the other way round. In constituencies with large minorities these minorities are never represented. Competitive democracies are competitions for which elites will run the country. "By denying the meaningfulness of public will formation, Competitive Democracy keeps the mechanism of democracy without its soul."[75] Amongst the general populace, levels of information about social and political matters are routinely low, partly because people believe their vote simply does not count. People's opinions are often "'top of the head', vague impressions of sound bites and headlines, highly malleable and open to the techniques of impression management."[76] When people engage on social media they often do so with the like-minded or "troll" those they disagree with.

Second, many of the institutions that govern our affairs are unelected—the European commission, the World Bank, the IMF, and of course the corporations. There has been what van Reybrouck calls "a far-reaching technocratisation of decision-making: bankers, economists and monetary analysts that got their hands on

75. Fishkin, *When the People Speak*, 179. Within representative democracies many advocate proportional representation. This has the virtue that people's political views are more nearly represented, so, for example, a small party for which 10 percent of the electorate voted might get no representation in a first past the post system, but might get 10 percent of all available seats under proportional representation. The disadvantage is that the smaller parties may often be xenophobic, racist, or represent extreme right-wing nationalist views and these can then hold the ring in coalition governments.

76. Ibid., 2.

the levers of power."[77] I have already mentioned Wolfgang Streeck's distinction between "Staatsvolk" and "Marktvolk." In his view the latter have effectively displaced the former, and democracy is in danger of being reduced to a combination of the rule of law and public entertainment.[78] The state exists only to safeguard market relations. Democracy is tamed by the market rather than the other way around.[79] He thinks declining electoral participation is a sign of resignation. People see that their vote makes no difference. "The political resignation of the underclasses consolidates the neoliberal turn from which it derives, further shielding capitalism from democracy."[80] When government becomes a process by which the super rich become even richer a pervasive cynicism is bred that undercuts all appeals to trust and shared values.[81] Colin Crouch calls this situation "post-democracy." The democratic movement peaked, he argues, after World War II, but what we now have is a return to pre-democratic models of power and influence, based largely on the role of "business" and in particular the transnational corporation. The fact that business lobbies effectively control public policy, and the whole realm of public provision is privatized, leads to democratic entropy.[82]

Third, the media are owned by a few powerful individuals who push their own political line. This means, according to Crouch, that "public electoral debate is a tightly controlled spectacle, managed by rival teams of professionals expert and the techniques of persuasion, and considering a small range of issues selected by those teams. The mass of citizens plays a passive, quiescent, even apathetic part, responding only to the signals given

77. Van Reybrouck, *Against Elections*, 23. Streeck comments: "Turning the economy over to a combination of free markets and technocracy makes political participation run dry." *Capitalism*, 141.

78. Streeck, *Buying Time*, 5.

79. Ibid., 116.

80. Ibid., 55.

81. Streeck, *Capitalism*, 34.

82. Crouch, *Post Democracy*, chs. 2, 5.

them."[83] There is a great deal of misinformation or misleading information. The rise of social media amplifies this. Social media can be mobilized to impersonate the public will, so that opinion appears to be representative of the general public but is really only from well-organized interest groups.[84] The result is the creation of a fog in which informed choices about elections can no longer be made because of the hysteria and media frenzy.[85] What we call "the public," says Graeber, is created, produced, through specific institutions that allow specific forms of action—taking polls, watching TV, voting, signing petitions or writing letters to elected officials or attending public hearings, and not others.

> These frames of action imply certain ways of talking, thinking, arguing, deliberating. The same public that may widely indulge in the use of recreational chemicals may also vote to make such indulgence illegal; they may make completely different decisions if organized into a parliamentary system, a system of computerized plebiscites, or a system of direct democracy. In fact the entire anarchist project of reinventing direct democracy is premised on assuming this is the case.[86]

For him, "Voting booths, TV screens, office cubicles, hospitals, and the ritual that surrounds them" are the very machinery of alienation. "They are the instruments through which the human imagination is smashed and shattered. Insurrectionary moments occur when this bureaucratic apparatus is neutralized."[87]

Relatedly, Václav Havel felt that parliamentary democracies "offer no fundamental opposition to the automatism of technological civilization and the industrial-consumer society, for they, too, are being dragged helplessly along by it." The omnipresent

---

83. Ibid., 4.

84. Fishkin, *When the People Speak*, 1.

85. Van Reybrouck, *Against Elections*, 54.

86. Graeber, *Direct Action*, 528.

87. Ibid., 530.

dictatorship of consumption and advertising could not be regarded as the source of humanity's rediscovery of itself.[88]

Fourth, big money, and the revolving door between politics and big business, is widely seen to corrupt politics. In the contemporary United States, Graeber points out, 1 percent of the population control 42 percent of the wealth and this makes democracy impossible. It is assumed that democracy is the market, freedom is the right to participate in the market, and the creation of an ever-growing world of consumer abundance is the only measure of national success.[89] Gopal Balakrishnan speaks of "a frothy, money soaked, soundbite politics, fruit of an ongoing privatisation and neutralisation of public power."[90]

All of these objections, which are common, underwrite the lack of enthusiasm for representative democracy, and the cynicism about politicians, widespread in democracies.

By and large, democracies do better in protecting the environment than totalitarian regimes, but they too have problems that prevent them from addressing planetary boundaries. The first is the short-termism characteristic of five-year election cycles. Governments will play a populist card, and put the demands of the local electorate before those of multilateral agreements. Added to this is the fact that local or national electorates are not very aware of, and care less about, cross border effects—problems which are not directly affecting them—like the radiation that Norway detects as originating in Sellafield. Third, democracies are vulnerable to lobbying from wealthy interest groups, such as the CBI in Britain, which reduces the provision of public goods.[91]

88. Havel, *Power*, 91.

89. Graeber, *Democracy*, 110. Commenting on President Obama's inability to implement social reform, Gary Younge notes that "The will of the people only gets a look in if it coincides with the will of the wealthy and the agenda of the party zealots. . . . Obama has quite a lot to cry about these days." "How the far right has perfected the art of deniable racism," *Guardian Weekly*, January 15, 2016.

90. Balakrishnan, *The Enemy*, 264.

91. Held, *Cosmopolitanism*, 209–10.

Given these difficulties could we do better or should we simply accept that we have to do with "the second best"?

Second best democracy

Those who live in representative democracies often hold up participatory democracy as the Holy Grail but Hendriks warns that expectations for active citizenship can be excessively idealistic (the same worry that Christiano and Achen and Bartels express). How high up in the pyramid of human needs is democratic self-fulfilment, really?, he asks. "Some think that average citizens have better things to do. They are happy to leave policy-making to the professionals, just as they like to leave bread making to the baker. Not counting exceptions, the average citizen has no need for endless nights of democratic participation and deliberation, most certainly not if the decision-making process is as protracted and time-consuming as it is in participatory democracy."[92] To Anglo Saxon eyes, direct and consensus democracy appears a great improvement on the Westminster model, but in his review of his four forms Hendriks insists there are virtues to each. Vital democracy, in his view, needs "a healthy dose of pollution and efficacious forms of hybridity and pluralism."[93] There will always be a democratic deficit. "You can have good governance, in the sense of good enough governance, but never perfect governance, as in democratic government without failings."[94] In a vital democracy there will always be dissatisfaction.

Dahl distinguishes between democracy as a guiding ideal and democracy as a sustainable practice. We should continue to pursue the ideal even if we know that this ideal can never be entirely realized in large-scale systems. What can be achieved and sustained is not ideal democracy—the government of all by all—but realistic

92. Hendriks, *Vital Democracy*, 126.
93. Ibid., 182.
94. Ibid.,187.

democracy or "polyarchy," government of many, alternating and correcting one another.[95]

Like both Plato and Aristotle, Dunn opts for the second best, the best that we can realistically achieve. Democracy as a political value, Dunn argues, constantly subverts the legitimacy of democracy as an already existing form of government. As a value it constantly probes the tolerable limits of injustice, in a permanent and sometimes very intense blend of cultural inquiry with social and political struggle.[96] In Held's terms democracy is an unfinished journey, not achieved in any country, presently; an endless journey, a process of interaction between civil society and political institutions; its meaning needs to be viewed comparatively not absolutely.[97]

But can something better be achieved? Might a democracy that was not just "second best" be realized? I shall outline two sets of proposals, the first of which takes further the suggestions of the previous chapter, that the "polis" that educated us in the virtues, and that would stand the best chance of combating climate change, would begin at the local level. This is the concern of the next section.

Subsidiarity

Key to many proposals for a better democracy is the notion of subsidiarity, the idea that "Everything that can be passed down for more local decision making must be."[98] Citizens can participate better in less remote communities. "Only a community of communities deserves the name of 'commonwealth,'" remarked

95. The minimum requirements of such a realistic democracy, sustainable in the long term and on a larger scale, Hendriks argues, are the following: 1, elected officials; 2, fair and frequent elections; 3, alternative sources of information; 4, freedom of expression; 5, freedom of assembly; 6, inclusive citizenship civil rights. Ibid., 24.

96. Dunn, *Democracy*, 171.

97. Archibugi, "Principles of cosmopolitan democracy," 200.

98. Day, *Consensus Design*, 127.

Buber. The union of persons and families into communities, and communities into associations is what will displace the state and enable a genuinely cooperative and democratic future.[99]

As we saw in the last chapter, David Held argues that economic, cultural, legal, and political processes already constitute overlapping networks within which we have to work. From both above (e.g., the UN or the European Parliament) or below (parish and town councils) participatory democracy can be the rule.[100] On the same lines Dahl and Tufte remark that rather than conceiving of democracy as located in a particular kind of inclusive sovereign unit we must learn to think of it as spreading through a nest of interrelated political systems like Chinese boxes.[101] Any polity is in reality a community of communities and if we are to encourage participation this has to begin at the lower levels where people feel their voice makes a difference. "Only to his immediate community is the average man capable of contributing a first-hand opinion," argued Ioan Rees. "In a sense it is from his immediate community that he derives his humanity."[102]

This idea is not new. Jefferson wanted a ward system where each ward would contain one hundred citizens, which would function as "small republics." "The further the departure from direct and constant control by the citizens the less has the government of the ingredient of republicanism."[103] Tocqueville noted that "the strength of free peoples resides in the local community. Local institutions are to liberty what primary schools are to science; they put it within the People's reached; they teach people to appreciate its peaceful enjoyment and accustom them to make use of it. With-

---

99. Buber, *Paths in Utopia*, 48, 137. Stephen Shalom's proposals for "nested councils" are a variation on these proposals. Building on Michael Albert's ideas of economic democracy (which I review in the next chapter), Shalom has proposed that even a country as big as the United States could be organized into a set of nested councils, where delegates are sent up from the bottom level to the top level. Albert, "The Politics of a Good Society."

100. Held, *Democracy*, 234.

101. Dahl and Tufte, *Size and Democracy*.

102. Rees, *Government by Community*, 104.

103. Cited by Arendt, *On Revolution*, 251.

out local institutions a nation may give itself a free government but it is not got the spirit of liberty."[104]

In Britain the local government act of 1894 created urban district, rural district, and parish councils. I have already mentioned the Swiss model of democracy. This model, Rees notes, tends to shatter any confidence one may have had in the importance of creating bigger units, of controlling them strictly from a center and seeing that real power is in the hands of officials you can trust rather than of a bunch of ignorant laymen.[105] It is by the cultivation of community in depth in small units that one begins to counteract the undermining of democracy by big money and vested interests and create a world society that has some hope of living within the world's resources. A small community, Rees argues (drawing on Tocqueville), is the world on such a scale that no one can escape their responsibility for replacing triviality with pride, humanity, humor, and taste and for rooting out as much misery as possible within the human condition.[106]

Educating people for democracy

Anyone with experience of (in Britain) parish or town councils might draw breath at this point. Do we escape triviality at the local level? Do we encounter taste, fairness, maturity of judgement? Surely, often the opposite is the case! Here the question of political education arises, and it is here that the "people's organizations" founded by Saul Alinsky have the most to offer. The job of building people's organizations, said Alinsky, "is the job of educating our people so that they will be informed to the point of being able to exercise an intelligent critical choice as to what is true and what is false."[107]

---

104. Tocqueville, *Democracy in America*, 1.61.
105. Rees, *Government by Community*, 159.
106. Ibid., 206.
107. Alinsky, *Reveille for Radicals*, 203.

The real democratic program, he said, is a democratically minded people—a healthy, active, participating, interested, self-confident people who, through their participation and interest, become informed, educated, and above all develop faith in themselves, their fellow men, and the future.[108] He also believed that unless ordinary people were aroused to a higher degree of participation, democracy would die at its roots—the withering disease of apathy at the roots of democracy would eventually cause its death.[109]

Alinsky's method was to identify local issues and then use nonviolent tactics to embarrass or shame authorities into action (for example, holding a prayer meeting outside the door of a recalcitrant mayor). It is only when the other party is concerned or feels threatened that he will listen, Alinsky argued. In the arena of action, a threat or a crisis becomes almost a precondition to communication.[110]

Respect for ordinary people was at the heart of his method—he believed a successful meeting was one where the organizer listened 60 percent of the time. He insisted on using "little Joes"—natural leaders in any community (and this included women)—in all of his campaigns. He also believed in starting where you are and mocked the need to change values before you started.[111]

Alinsky did not deny the accusation of being interested in revolution but, he said, "if it is a revolution it is an orderly revolution."

---

108. Alinsky, *Rules for Radicals*, 55. Macfadyen's "flatpack democracy" is another way of achieving this at local level.

109. Alinsky, *Reveille*, 184.

110. Alinsky, *Rules*, 89.

111. "To the appeal to organize for bread the modern young revolutionary replies, Before we move I think we ought to think over some basic values. It is this kind of reaction and thinking which makes the far left appear to be infinitely more intelligible when viewed from the perspective not of current political scene but of our space programme. These political astronauts have gone beyond the third world are now orbiting well into a mystical fourth world." Alinsky, *Reveille*, 224.

To reject orderly revolution is to be hemmed in by two hellish alternatives: disorderly, sudden, stormy, bloody revolution, or a further deterioration of the mass foundations of democracy to the point of inevitable dictatorship. The building of People's Organizations is orderly revolution; it is the process of the people gradually but irrevocably taking their places as citizens of a democracy.[112]

These organizations, says Heidi Swarts, are clearly working class.[113] People involved in them do not identify with "activists" and are more likely to spend time in church, the PTO, or the Boy Scouts than protest the WTO.[114] In the United States networks like ACORN (Association of Community Organizations for Reform Now) drew many thousands of poor and working-class citizens into a meaningful civic engagement that bridged racial boundaries in the service of poor and working class unity.[115] The ideology is down-to-earth, nonsectarian populism. It challenges corporate power and champions "the people" in energy policy, health care, housing, work, rural issues, community development, banking, taxes, and more.[116]

In the United States many of these organizations are church based. Church-based community organizing, says Swarts, integrates the public and private spheres by harnessing three discourses to the goal of redistributive politics: It draws on Christian discourse for political action; applies the language of private emotion to public problems; and harnesses family and values to a progressive rather than a conservative politics. Its innovation, she argues, is to intertwine the discourses of liberal Christianity, emotion, and family values with the discourses of politics and policy so that they seem naturally bound to each other.[117]

112. Alinsky, *Reveille*, 198.

113. Swarts, *Organizing Urban America*, xiv.

114. Ibid., xxx.

115. Ibid., 31.

116. Ibid., 33. Populist rhetoric, and the claim that tiny majorities represent the will of "the people" illustrate the danger of any populist appeal, however.

117. Ibid., 65.

The religious culture of the United States and Europe, and perhaps particularly of the United States and Britain, are notoriously different, but Luke Bretherton has recently offered a compelling account of the work of the British version of people's organizations, Citizens UK. From his richly documented, and in part ethnographic, work I shall highlight just four themes which bear on the nature of grassroots democracy and social change.

In the European context, majority Christian publics cannot be taken for granted, and in many cities there are large Muslim or Hindu populations, and sometimes majorities. One difference from the US scene, therefore, is the need to work across religious boundaries. Rather than "Church Based" Bretherton talks of "Broad Based" Community Organisations (BBCOs). He understands the practice of engaging in particular actions for social justice as a way of building a common life between people who otherwise share very different base commitments. "Common life politics is distinct from an identity politics, and from multicultural approaches, because recognition and respect is not given simply by dint of having a different culture or identity. Rather, recognition is conditional on one's contribution to and participation in shared, reciprocal, and public work."[118] Politics is a way of paying attention to others and hospitality is given and received between multiple traditions.[119] What emerges from community organizing is a heterogeneous society in which there is no one dominant group, faith, or ideology. This vision is close to Nussbaum's account of political liberalism.[120] It is an account of politics that does not idealize com-

118. Bretherton, *Resurrecting Democracy*, 92.

119. This was also the experience in Indian "Action groups" in the eighties, where shared commitments to political action generated a strong sense of trust and mutuality between people of different faiths.

120. "Political liberalism requires a public culture to be both narrow and thin: narrow in that it does not comment on every single aspect of human life but only those of most pertinence to politics; thin in that it makes no commitments on divisive metaphysical matters, such as eternal life or the nature of the soul. It must be such as to become over time the object of an overlapping consensus among the many reasonable overall views of life that the society contains." Nussbaum, *Political Emotions*, 387.

munity. The body politic, says Bretherton, is a constructed, fractious, and fragile artifice that requires something like the practices of community organizing in order to constitute and reconstitute itself out of its disparate elements. It is a constant work in progress rather than a spontaneous, natural phenomenon.[121]

Following on from this, Bretherton highlights the need, in such a democratic movement, to allow both for difference and for what he calls, picking up from Carl Schmitt, the existence of the friend–enemy distinction. Rather than moving beyond this distinction he suggests that the embrace of real difference functions like an immune system. "Analogous to an immune system, democratic politics is partially constituted by that which it opposes: that is, undemocratic and often vicious people inhabiting undemocratic and often dictatorial institutions. Democracy's paradox is that its pathogens are the source of its new life. Community organising embodies a means through which such pathogens as antipolitical and antagonistic friend-enemy relations can be metabolised into a faithful, hopeful, and neighbourly politics of the common life."[122] This is a very interesting suggestion, but looks implausible in the light of all the fascist and other totalitarian developments of the past century. Schmitt himself, of course, was the jurist of the Third Reich, and never disowned his positions. The classic Voltairean position of listening to your opponent no matter how vile their views has its limits, and this is important in the extraordinarily urgent need to address the transgression of planetary boundaries. Perhaps the most important thing, which Bretherton insists on, is that vehement opposition does not mean demonizing your opponent—a key temptation in climate activism.

At the same time, drawing on Jeffrey Stout, Bretherton depicts a politics of passion that is not a politics of hatred. According to Stout a politics of just anger aims to restore the spirit of democracy to democratic culture. "A spirit disposed to become angry at the right things in the right way and use this passion to motivate the level of political involvement essential

121. Bretherton, *Resurrecting Democracy*, 211.
122. Ibid., 298.

to striving for significant change. A politics completely emptied of the vehement passions, of spiritedness, tends in practice to be antidemocratic. It cedes the authority of decision-making to elites—experts and social engineers—who characteristically present themselves as disinterested and rational agents, intent only on maximising fairness and efficiency."[123]

Third, Bretherton offers an illuminating account of the rationale behind Alinsky's action-based method that finds a way to move beyond a mere politics of protest. The method begins by listening to what local people have to say and identifying an issue on which to act. This issue can then move beyond "both the rivalries of competitive group interests and the popular consensus to an expansive vision of a common life in which all may flourish."[124]

Fourth, Bretherton emphasizes the importance of political humility. "When democracy ceases to be ironic and its proponents proclaim their righteousness then a foolhardy and undemocratic politics quickly ensues." We have to recognize, he argues, that everyone in Western society is formed and involved in capitalism. "We cannot posit an un-tainted cultural politics of resistance from below. These postures presume forms of human speech and action capable of operating from a spatial and temporal register unconditioned by sin and patterns of domination. We must also resist the attempt to clothe an immanent political programme in messianic robes and thereby claim for it a false innocence and innovation."[125] This is well said, though whether it means that we have to seek a conversion of capitalism, or whether we need to replace it, as Naomi Klein and David Graeber believe, is another matter.[126] Recognition that we, too, are part of the problem is

123. Ibid., 124.

124. Ibid., 147.

125. Ibid., 106.

126. There is a rabbinic parable that bears on this. A Rabbi's disciples burst in to his room and say, "Rabbi, Rabbi—the world is so evil! There is so much injustice! The rich get the gravy and the poor get the blame! What can we do?" The Rabbi says, "Well, there's a natural solution and a supernatural solution." Oh, say the disciples. "We're not interested in supernatural solutions. Tell us the natural one." The natural one, says the Rabbi, is for the Holy One, blessed

clearly vital, though this does not have to end in a reprise of the Augustinian deferral of messianic vision.

Going beyond elections

Suppose we agree with the idea of subsidiarity—that, as in Switzerland, power should be arranged bottom up rather than top down. Suppose the work of people's organizations was so widely diffused that political education spread amongst the majority of people. Would elections still be (as they are in the UN Charter) the lodestone of democracy? There are a number of important voices that urge us to go back to the practice of sortition—choosing by lot—which was used in ancient Athenian democracy. In Athens both processes of election and sortition were used, the first for jobs that required expertise and the second when what was needed was good sense and integrity. Effectively sortition is already involved in jury service when what is needed is not expertise but representation of the common moral sense of the citizenry—based on the understanding that justice cannot be administered by "experts" but is the concern of the whole population.

The presupposition of the proposal to use sortition is what I mentioned earlier as a key democratic virtue, namely deliberation.

Deliberative democracy has been James Fishkin's concern in the United States. The conditions for a properly deliberative discussion are, he argues, first, reasonably accurate information; second, the presentation of arguments from different perspectives; third, diversity—the extent to which the major positions in society are represented in the discussion; fourth, the extent to which participants sincerely weigh the merits of the arguments; and finally the extent to which the arguments are weighed on their merits.[127] Ideally he would like a "decision day" before a general or presidential election, in which all citizens would be paid to spend

---

be He, to send his angels and to utterly consume the rich and cleanse the world of their villainy. The disciples are aghast. "Then what is the supernatural one?" "That," says the Rabbi, "is for the rich to be converted."

127. Fishkin, *When the People Speak*, 34.

a day discussing issues in small groups, informed by speakers from different perspectives. Experience over two decades has shown that when people are given this opportunity minds and priorities change. "The process is deliberative in that it provides informative and mutually respectful discussion in which people consider the issue on its merits. The process is democratic in that it requires the equal counting of everyone's views."[128] Failing such a national day, people's assemblies have been convened, in which people are randomly chosen, as in the jury process, given a chance to listen to experts in the field, and then allowed to deliberate. These assemblies function rather like juries, with the people present acting as pars pro toto for the rest of the population. Although not ideal these assemblies offer a picture of what everyone would think under good conditions.[129] In Ireland in 2013 this process was used to review the Constitution and it led to the acceptance of gay marriage in the country. In Texas randomly chosen citizens' assemblies had the effect of vastly increasing the amount of renewable energy in a state built on oil.[130]

Opponents of this process argue that all it does is to further empower the more educated and advantaged who are better able to present their case. This often goes together with the view that the mass of people are incompetent to deliberate or too disengaged with politics. To such views Fishkin responds, first, that in practice, when measured in deliberative events, opinion often moves away from the views of the advantaged. Second, such consultations show that people are more than able to deal with complex issues—once they believe their voice matters.[131] Further, such events have been shown to have lasting effects—leading to a public that is routinely better informed. His research leads to the view that such processes change policy attitudes, voting intentions, levels of information,

128. Ibid., 11.

129. Ibid., 194.

130. Van Reybrouck, *Against Elections*, 112.

131. Fishkin, *When the People Speak*, 119. A consultation in Omagh, Northern Ireland, led to significant increases in trust between Protestant and Catholic populations.

public dialogue, and public policy. In short, they produce better citizens. Here is another form of education in democracy which stands alongside Alinsky's ideas.

Again in the United States Terrill Bouricius, who had been an elected representative for twenty years in the state of Vermont, has proposed a complex system of government using sortition.[132] In his proposals there are six levels of legislation. The process begins with "interest panels," which consist of twelve citizens who propose topic-related legislation and who are not remunerated. There are also interest panels of experts whose views are considered by review panels. Together these interest panels feed up to an agenda council consisting of between 150 and 400 people, chosen by lot, who serve a three-year term without extension and who are salaried. This compiles the political agenda and chooses topics for legislation. Next, a policy jury, made up of adult citizens chosen by lot, decides on legislation. Above this a rules council made up of around fifty people chosen by lot from amongst volunteers decides on rules and procedures of legislative work. People can serve for a year and are salaried. Finally an oversight council regulates the legislative process and deals with complaints. This is made up of around twenty people and is salaried. Van Reybrouck writes:

> The policy jury hears the various legislative proposals put together by the review panel, listens to a formal presentation of arguments for and against, and then votes in a secret ballot. So there is no further discussion, no party discipline, no group pressure, no tactical voting, no political haggling and no backscratching. Everyone votes according to their conscience, according to what he or she feels best serves the general interest in the long term. To avoid charismatic speakers influencing the mood, the legislative proposals are presented by neutral staff members. Because the verdict is that of a good

---

132. He seeks to address problems including the overrepresentation of the educated, the dangers of group thinking, the difficulties involved in powerful individuals and in the need for people to have growing experience in the process (which would be lost if people only served short terms). Van Reybrouck, *Against Elections*, 140.

> cross-section of society as a whole the decisions of the
> policy jury have the force of law.[133]

This proposal will doubtless seem unnecessarily bureaucratic to many, and to involve a great many people in time which could be better spent elsewhere. On the other hand, it is an opportunity to overcome the democratic deficit, to move beyond the "second best" and to escape the toxic fog that currently surrounds elections. At the very least the proposal to *combine* elections (as in Athens, for jobs which require technical competence) with processes based on sortition deserves consideration. The work of people's organizations and the use of people's juries could, together, be practices that instill those virtues, and develop that level of citizenship, which could effectively address climate change.

Democracy and economy

It ought to be clear to any citizen in a "democratic" country that we cannot sit back and regard first past the post systems as the be all and end all of democracy. They fail both humanity and the planet. If we ask, Why?, we have to recall John Dunn's contention that the market economy is "the most powerful mechanism for dismantling equality that humans have ever fashioned."[134] In North American rhetoric, especially, democracy and markets are taken as coterminous, but as Held argues, it is far from obvious that markets are able to address the problems of planetary boundaries. Taxes are more effective than cap and trade schemes, for example. "What is required are representative institutions armed with the capacity and legitimacy needed to translate policy commitments into

---

133. Ibid., 146.

134. Dunn, *Democracy*, 137. In *And the Weak Suffer What They Must?*, Varoufakis also shows that there is a struggle between democracy and financial institutions, and that the latter will displace the former unless tightly controlled. Reviewing Nancy MacLean's book *Democracy in Chains*, George Monbiot argues that "The choice we face is between unfettered capitalism and democracy. You cannot have both." "A despot in disguise," *Guardian Weekly*, July 28, 2017.

real-world outcomes."[135] Held considers that a return to planning is needed which will be "push and pull between the political centre, regions and localities, which can only be resolved through deliberation and consultation."[136] The post-World War II institutions are no longer intact but "addressing the issue of climate change successfully holds out the prospect of re-forging a rule-based politics, from the nation state to the global level."[137] Because political change is impossible without economic change I turn, in the next chapter, to the shape of the economy in a threatened world.

135. Held, *Cosmopolitanism*, 233.
136. Ibid., 235.
137. Ibid., 238.

Chapter Six

Economics as If the Planet Mattered

We can't change ecological limits. We can't alter human nature.
But we can and do create and recreate the social world. Its norms
are our norms. This is where transformation is needed.

—Tim Jackson

IF WE ASK WHY we have the problems outlined in the first chapter,
the answer, above all, is that we have an economy committed to
non-stop growth (an idea which was unheard of before 1950).[1]
Currently every economy, in every country in the world, seeks to
grow to meet the spiralling needs of an ever greater number of
people. A vision of the good life drives this growth (try googling
images for "the good life"!). Basically, the whole world wants to
live like California (before the water began to run out and the
agriculture to shrink). But the planet is finite. For half a century
some economists have been insisting that this requires a different economic paradigm, but so far they have not been listened to.
If they are not heeded, however, the disaster predicted by James

1. Heinz Arndt argues that economic growth as a policy objective only
emerged after World War II as an effort by governments to achieve full employment for their citizens. Within a few years, driven by the Cold War and the
global arms race, economic growth became an objective its own right. Victor
and Jackson, "The Trouble with Growth," 39.

Hansen and Kevin Anderson will certainly come to pass. This is a political, and therefore a moral, issue. Economy is, as Adam Smith, Ricardo, and J. S. Mill all recognized, "political economy": the division between politics and economics on the basis that the latter is an independent "science" with its own norms is specious and disastrous. What is needed are democratic ways in which to realize alternative visions to the present neoliberal ascendancy. Values and disvalues, practices of life and practices of death, attend these understandings, and I will trace them out in this chapter beginning with the question of what we mean by "an economy," and how the effectiveness of an economy is measured. I consider the centrality of values to economics and then examine some of the key values and practices of the present economic disorder: privatization, competitive individualism, free markets, necessary growth and consumerism, the question of justice, and the relation of global and local, in each case considering the shape of a more sustainable alternative. In my arrangement I am following a theological rather than an economic logic although, as I hope to show, theological first principles have immediate consequences for our understanding of economics. I begin, however, by examining the values which underpin any economy.

The purpose of "the economy"

The words *the economy* appear in every newspaper, and are heard on every news broadcast, every day, everywhere in the world. It is the drumbeat of reality as we know it, and we simply take it for granted, but we only have to go back seventy or eighty years to find a world where this was not the case, and where such an emphasis on "the economy" would have seemed very surprising. Of course every society has regular ways of producing what it needs, an economy. But what does it need? Aristotle, a "genius of common sense" as Polanyi called him, gives us our first systematic reflection on economic matters, and he begins by asking whether there is a distinction between acquiring goods or things (*chrematistike*), on the one hand, and household management (*oikonomia*) on the other. The question turns on what it is people need in order to live well—in other words, the question of "the good life."[2] Wealth in the true sense, he says, consists of goods that we need to live, which provide a livelihood, or which are needed by the state or the household. *Oikonomia*, writes Herman Daly, is the science or art of efficiently producing, distributing, and maintaining concrete-use values for the household and community over the long run. Confusing *oikonomia* and *chrematistics*, misdefining the proper subject matter of economics, has deadly consequences, but this is what "free markets" are supposed to do, alchemically transmuting the dross of *chrematistics* into the gold of *oikonomia*.[3] The result is a depraved version of economy, "a ramshackle, propped-up, greed-enforced anti-economy that is delusional, vicious, wasteful, destructive, hard hearted, and so fundamentally dishonest as to have resorted finally to 'trading' in various pure-nothings." There is, says Wendell Berry, the author of these remarks, "no partition between economy and morality, and morality is long-term practicality."[4]

Throughout the European middle ages Scholastic thinkers put the question of the purpose of economic activity at the forefront. According to Schumpeter, at least, this was not the thinking of Neanderthals who had not realized the miracle of circular flow or Say's law, but of sophisticated people who lacked only an understanding of marginal utility.[5] The key thing was, however, as Polanyi argued, that in all societies prior to late eighteenth-century Europe, economy was submerged in social relationships. There was no separate and distinct institution based on economic motives. Production and distribution were ensured through reciprocity and redistribution. The subordination of economics to social

2. This in turn goes back to the discussion of human ends in chapter three.

3. Daly, Foreword in Berry, *What Matters?*, xi. Daly is an economist who has included theological reflection in his work, and Berry a poet and essayist who writes about economics. I draw on Berry especially in this chapter precisely because, as I argue below, economics is fundamentally a moral science.

4. Berry, *What Matters?*, 19.

5. Schumpeter, *History of Economic Analysis*, 98.

ECONOMICS AS IF THE PLANET MATTERED

norms changed with the growth both of trade and the factory system in the eighteenth century, and in theorizing this Adam Smith is taken to have inaugurated the modern "science" of economics. The suggestion that self-interest, rather than the common good, was the motor of the economy and that "the market," that is, a non-centrally planned series of actions, is the way in which goods and property are properly coordinated, is what marked the subordination of social norms to "economics."

The rejection of teleology was part and parcel of the European rejection of scholasticism and of course, when Aristotle's thinking about causation had become a dogma it had indeed obstructed scientific thought (as the trial of Galileo showed), but the baby was now thrown out with the bathwater. Already in the nineteenth century Ruskin protested this account of economics. As he put it (in opposition to J. S. Mill), "The real science of political economy, which has yet to be distinguished from the bastard science, as medicine from witchcraft . . . is that which teaches nations to desire and labour for the things which lead to life; and which teaches them to scorn and destroy the things which lead to destruction."[6] What Ruskin is effectively doing is raising the question of "the good life," meaning, the question of what life is for, what it means to be human—the question of human ends, which we discussed in the third chapter.

Taking up this question, Richard Murphy defines economics as concerned with the achievement of human potential—material, emotional and intellectual—alongside a sense of purpose. This constitutes "well being"—Aristotle's *eudaimonia*.[7] What this definition lacks, of course, is any attempt to situate human beings in their environment, any understanding that humans are bound up with, and dependent on, the nonhuman (or so-called "natural") world. Wendell Berry (a farmer as well as a writer) understands this better. He goes back to Aristotle's *oikonomia* and defines economics as "the ways of the human household, the ways by which the human household is *situated and maintained within the household of*

6. Ruskin, *Unto this Last*, 84.
7. Murphy, *The Courageous State*, 118, 153.

nature.[8] In an account of "the ways of the human household" the question of ends is primary. The failure to distinguish *oikonomia* from *chrematistics* rests on a refusal to distinguish wants from needs, a "particularly inept value judgement" that leaves the only goal that of having more than, or as much as others, a goal which infinitely recedes into the distance.[9]

Berry suggests that Jesus' phrase "the kingdom of God" might be translated as "the Great Economy." The great economy is the giftedness of all reality, our ultimate dependence on photosynthesis, the fact that we do not, and cannot—not even with the most advanced genetic science—create the raw materials of life out of nothing. The great economy, theologically God's creation of all things, or grace, sustains all that is. We are part of it, bound up in the bundle of life with all that is. The economy of which mainstream economics thinks is marked by the hubristic idea that it creates its own value, but, "That we can prescribe the terms of our own success, that we can live outside or in ignorance of the Great Economy are the greatest errors. They condemn us to a life without a standard, wavering in inescapable bewilderment from paltry self-satisfaction to paltry self-dissatisfaction."[10]

This idea of the kingdom of God is close to Barry Commoner's idea of ecology—that everything is related to everything else—but it includes a principle of humility, that "humans do not and can never know either all the creatures that the kingdom of God

---

8. Berry, *Sex, Economy, Freedom and Community*, 100 (my italics). "Probably the most urgent question now faced by people who would adhere to the Bible is this: 'What sort of economy would be responsible to the holiness of life? What, for Christians, would be the economy, the practices and restraints, of 'right livelihood'? I think [the church's] idea of a Christian economy is no more or less than the industrial economy—which is an economy firmly founded on the seven deadly sins and the breaking of all ten of the Commandments. Obviously, if Christianity is going to survive as more than a respecter and comforter of profitable iniquities, then Christians, regardless of their organizations, are going to have to interest themselves in economy—which is to say, in nature and work." Ibid.

9. Skidelsky and Skidelsky, *How Much is Enough?*, 41

10. Berry, *Home Economics*, 68.

maintains or the whole pattern or order by which it contains them."[11] This is the overarching understanding of "the economy" I presuppose in what follows.

How is the effectiveness of an economy measured?

The French economist Thomas Piketty has recently argued that the discipline of economics has yet to get over its childish passion for mathematics—born of the attempt to pretend that it was a "pure science," and thus "value free," and had none of the woolly subjectivity of the humanities. The obsession with mathematics, he says, is an easy way of acquiring the appearance of scientificity, without having to answer the far more complex questions posed by the world we live in. "The truth is, economics should never have sought to divorce itself from the other social sciences and can advance only in conjunction with them. The social sciences collectively know too little to waste time on foolish disciplinary squabbles."[12]

The childish preoccupation with arithmetic (rather than mathematics) helps explain why the main way of measuring the performance of an economy is through measuring "Gross Domestic Product"—the total amount of goods and services of a particular country. But, as has long been pointed out, all sorts of negative facts, such as car accidents, oil spills, or wars, contribute to GDP. Herman Daly proposed forty years ago replacing this with an "Index of sustainable economic welfare" (ISEW). This subtracts the value of unwanted side effects of economic activity from GDP and adds in the value of activity that advances well-being and is overlooked by GDP, such as unpaid housework or much social care. Daly concluded that ISEW per capita increased

11. Ibid., 55.

12. Piketty, *Capital in the Twenty-First Century*, 32. Ann Pettifor appropriately describes neoliberalism as the economic equivalent of "creationism" and notes that this is what most university departments of economics teach! *The Production of Money*, xvii.

far more slowly than GDP per capita and that in the decade from 1980 to 1990 it actually declined.[13]

The negative facts contributing to GDP include such "externalities" as acidification of the oceans, loss of biodiversity, and climate change. Externalizing environmental costs—shifting the cost of depletion and pollution from the producer to the general public, the future, and other species—is, says Daly, probably the most common and most disastrous chrematistic maneuver.[14] For Royal Dutch Shell, or the US coal industry, the end of human life on earth might be an "externality"—a price worth paying to keep its shareholders happy.

Trying to measure economic performance by GDP, says Kate Raworth, is like trying to fly a plane by its altimeter alone: "it tells you you're going up or down but nothing of where you are headed or how much fuel you have left in the tank."[15] It also has nothing to say about social justice. Around 13 percent of the world's population is undernourished, 19 percent of people have no access to electricity, and 21 percent live in extreme poverty.[16] People are properly concerned with the burgeoning size of the world's population but "the biggest source of stress on planetary boundaries is the excessive consumption levels of roughly the wealthiest 10 percent of people in the world and the resource intensive production patterns of companies producing the goods and services that they buy."

> The richest 10 percent of people in the world hold 57 percent of global income. Just 11 percent of the global population generates about half of global CO_2 emissions. And one third of the world's sustainable budget for reactive nitrogen use is used to provide meat for people in the European Union, just 7 percent of the world's population.[17]

13. Victor and Jackson, "The Trouble with Growth," 40.
14. Daly, Foreword to Berry, *What Matters?*, xii.
15. Raworth, "Defining a safe and just space for humanity," 28.
16. Ibid., 32.
17. Ibid., 34.

This led Raworth to produce the now-celebrated diagram of social and planetary boundaries that we saw in the first chapter. This, she says, ought to be on the first page of every economics textbook, and economics students should be told that their job was, in the light of social and planetary boundaries, to design economic policies and regulations that help bring humanity into a safe and just space between the boundaries and that enable us all to thrive there.[18] In other words, the way to measure the effectiveness of an economy is to ask questions like: what percentage of the population are in meaningful and constructive work? How are people housed and fed? How are the sick dealt with? How equal is this society? These questions rest on fundamental values.

Values and economics

At the beginning of the eighteenth century the Dutch physician Bernard Mandeville mischievously called into question the moral foundation of economics in *The Fable of the Bees*. The important thing, he argued, is to increase the sum of public happiness—but it turns out that this might include many things traditionally reckoned as vices, and particularly the priority of self-interest. In recent times we were told—by supposedly "socialist" politicians, no less—that "greed was good," "the best engine of betterment known to man," according to William Safire. But, as Berry points out, once you have made greed a virtue it will crowd out other virtues such as temperance, justice, or charity. "The greedy consume the poor, the moderately prosperous and each other with the same relish and with an ever growing appetite." By contrast, Berry insists the economic virtues would be "honesty, thrift, care, good work, generosity, and (since this is a creaturely and human, not a mechanical, economy) imagination, from which we have compassion." That primary value and these virtues, he argues, are essential to sustainability.[19]

18. Ibid., 35.
19. Berry, *What Matters?*, 18.

Adam Smith held no brief for Mandeville, but the effect of his endorsement of the leading role of self-interest was the same. The replacement of the tradition of the virtues with the calculus of pleasure and pain followed later in the century, and some form of utilitarianism has underlain economic theory ever since.

What was the reason for this change in the understanding of economics? Was it the rise of the factory system, enclosures, the increase of trade? Or did changes in ideology and the structure of feeling come first? In his great history of civilization and capitalism from the fifteenth to the eighteenth century, Fernard Braudel ironizes the idealist histories of Max Weber and Werner Sombart, the one linking capitalism to the Protestant ethic, the other to increasing rationality, and in particular to double-entry book-keeping.[20] He prefers a twofold account of the rise of capitalism, partly in terms of long-distance trade, and partly in terms of the rise of the bourgeoisie who, in the course of the sixteenth to the nineteenth centuries, finally displaced the old landed gentry as the real power in society. Braudel does not espouse a rigidly historical materialist point of view, however, and, like Marx, is happy to concede a dialectical relation between modes of production and ideologies of all kind, including religion and value systems.[21] Because it is a dialectic we can see both how changes in modes of production change ideas, but also the reverse. Keynes famously remarked that practical men were usually the slaves of some defunct economist and in his recent study of injustice Daniel Dorling concludes that there is no orchestrated conspiracy to prolong injustice but that "unjust thoughts have seeped into everyday thinking out of the practices that make profit. Ideologies of inequality have trickled down." In his view, "beliefs . . . underlie most injustice in the world

20. Braudel, *The Wheels of Commerce*, 563, 572.

21. Braudel notes that he does not believe that capitalism can be explained by material or social factors, and that "culture and civilization played a part." Ibid., 402. Cf. Marx's third thesis on Feuerbach: "The materialist doctrine that men are products of circumstances and upbringing, and that, therefore, changed men are products of other circumstances and changed upbringing, forgets that it is men who change circumstances and that the educator must himself be educated." Marx and Engels, *Collected Works*, vol. 5, 7.

and this means that changing the way we think is crucial."[22] Marx himself, followed by many commentators, including theologians, despised moral commentary on social events. What was important was analysis, and it was this that would help change things, not moralizing. But of course what prompted the analysis in the first place was passion against injustice. In fact this reaction to ethics was a positivist prejudice characteristic of a good deal of mid-nineteenth-century thought and repeated unthinkingly ever since. As George Sabine notes, the purpose of the Marxist theory of value was ethical and not purely economic:

> It was a theory of social good not a theory of prices, and the fundamental difference between Marx's theory and the Ricardian theory of value from which he derived it was a difference of standard for measuring social justice and well-being. Essentially Marx's criticism of capitalist economics was that it construed human relations in terms of the cash nexus which conceals the human problems involved.[23]

We cannot do without analysis, but the relation of ethics and economics can be put like this: analysis without ethics is blind; ethics without analysis is empty.

The assumption that economics has nothing to do with ethics found classic expression from Lionel Robbins in 1932, when he described economics as "the science which studies human behaviour as a relationship between ends and scarce means which have alternative uses."[24] Drawing partly on nineteenth-century

---

22. Keynes wrote: "Practical men who believe themselves to be quite exempt from any intellectual influences, are usually the slaves of some defunct economist. Madmen in authority, who hear voices in the air, are distilling their frenzy from some academic scribbler of a few years back." Keynes, *A General Theory of Employment, Interest and Money*, 383. Dorling, *Injustice*, 308, 320.

23. Sabine, *History*, 660.

24. Robbins, *An Essay on the Nature and Significance of Economic Science*, 15. As Hahn and Hart note, the utilitarianism Robbins espouses "cannot grasp how the 'preferences' that shape economic behaviour are formed in society and are necessarily subject to normative regulation designed to modify rational egoism." Hahn and Hart, *Economic Anthropology*, 173.

positivism and partly on Max Weber, he argued that economics is a value-free science. Economics, he wrote, deals with ascertainable facts, ethics with valuations and obligations. The two fields of enquiry are not on the same plane of discourse. "Between the generalisations of positive and normative studies there is a logical gulf fixed which no ingenuity can disguise and no juxtaposition in space or time bridge over." All that economics does is to inform our preferences. It makes clear to us the implications of the different ends we may choose.[25]

The bracketing out of the question of value ultimately goes back to Hume, and the attempt to free human thought once and for all from religious dogma. Epistemologically it was always flawed, as it overlooks the point that "facts" are always interpreted and the perverse consequence was to enthrone a very parochial account of human reason as ultimate, basically the "reason" of the early eighteenth-century European entrepreneurial class. It is this parochial form of reason that, unbeknownst to its practitioners, still lies behind the nostrums of neoliberalism. The elementary error on which it is based both blinds its adherents to its nature as ideology and in so doing makes any discussion of ends and means an act of pure dogma. Values are not evaded, but simply concealed. One set of values, those of the entrepreneurial class, are enthroned as sovereign.

Defining economics as the attempt to deal with scarcity looks back to Malthus, and, though still currently widely accepted, is an unargued assumption. But why should we accept it? In fact, the concealed assumption is that there is scarcity because human desire is infinite, but we cannot all have what we desire. The option of redistribution is not considered.[26]

The assumption of scarcity has bizarre effects. Thus Kenneth Arrow, a Nobel laureate in economics, writes: "I do not want to rely

25. Robbins, *Essay*, 155.

26. Hauerwas writes: "Scarcity is a necessary social creation when men are defined as having unlimited desires. The genius of liberalism was to make what had always been considered a vice, namely unlimited desire, virtue." *Community*, 80.

too heavily on substituting ethics for self-interest. I think it best on the whole that the requirement of ethical behaviour be confined to those circumstances where the price system breaks down. Wholesale usage of ethical standards is apt to have undesirable consequences. We do not wish to use up recklessly the scarce resources of altruistic motivation, and in any case ethically motivated behaviour may even have a negative value to others if the agent acts without sufficient knowledge of the situation."[27] Thus not only are resources limited but so is altruism! We only invoke it when the market system breaks down. We only invoke ethics *in extremis*.

By contrast Keynes, Herman Daly, and now Thomas Piketty have all argued that economics is a fundamentally moral science— a view which links them with Aristotle and the Scholastics, as well as with Adam Smith, as a matter of fact.[28] Daly insists that there are problems of political economy that have no technical solution but do have a moral solution, especially that of redistribution.[29] Absolute limits are absent from the economists' paradigm, he argues, because we encounter absolute limits only in confrontation with ultimates, which have been excluded from our tunnel vision.[30] Our refusal to reason about the Ultimate End merely assures the

27. Arrow, "Gifts and Exchanges," 355.

28. In an address at Cambridge in 1928 Keynes wrote: "I set us free to re- turn to some of the most sure and certain principles of religion and traditional virtue—that avarice is a vice, that the exaction of usury is a misdemeanour, and the love of money is detestable, that those walk most truly in the paths of virtue and sane wisdom who take least thought for the morrow. We shall once more value ends above means and prefer the good to the useful. We shall honour those who can teach us how to pluck the hour and the day virtuously and well, the delightful people who are capable of taking direct enjoyment in things, the lilies of the field, who toil not neither do they spin." Keynes, *The Collected Writings*, vol. 9, 321–23. In the Preface to the *General Theory* Keynes speaks of economics as belonging to "the other moral sciences." In a letter to Harrod, July 6, 1938, he writes: "Against Robbins: economics is essentially a moral science and not a natural science. That means it needs introspection and judgements of value." Cited in Brodbeck, *Die Herrschaft des Geldes*, 108.

Piketty believes that it is the "political, normative and moral purpose" that sets economics apart from the other social sciences. *Capital*, 574.

29. Daly, *Steady State Economics*, 10.

30. Ibid., 19.

incoherence of our priorities. Moral first principles would include some concept of enoughness, stewardship, humility, and holism.[31] What today is referred to as "the Market" cannot decide about specific proposals because "the decision is ethical."[32] As James Quiggin puts it, the economy is not a simple machine for aggregating consumer preferences and allocating resources accordingly.[33] People who have profited from the no-holds-barred neoliberal economy, like Warren Buffet and George Soros, have seen that the economy does not function without social trust, and that the economy, as currently conceived, saws off the branch on which it sits. Fritz Schumacher, Chief Economist for the British Coal Board, called for a return to wisdom. The problems of spiritual and moral truth, he said, are central: "From an economic point of view, the central concept of wisdom is permanence . . . Nothing makes economic sense unless its continuance for a long time can be projected without running into absurdities . . . Permanence is incompatible with a predatory attitude which rejoices in the fact that what were luxuries for our fathers have become necessities for us." The incorporation of wisdom into economic thinking, he argued, would exclude technological "solutions" that poisoned the environment or degraded the social structure or increasingly huge machines, entailing ever bigger concentrations of economic power.[34]

Daly notes that sustainable development will require a change of heart, a renewal of the mind, and a healthy dose of repentance. "These are all religious terms, and that is no coincidence, because a change in the fundamental principles we live by is a change so deep that it is essentially religious whether we call it that or not."[35]

I turn now to examine some of the key assumptions and practices of economic thinking, beginning with the idea of the commons.

31. Ibid., 47.
32. Ibid., 65.
33. Quiggin, *Zombie Economics*, 125.
34. Schumacher, *Small is Beautiful*, 26.
35. Daly, *Beyond Growth*, 201.

The commons

In the Christian tradition Patristic writers from Clement of Alexandria to John Chrysostom picked up Stoic arguments about the commonality of all creation, in which human beings share. The Greek words for that which is common, and sharing things in common, *koinos* (common), *koinoneo* (to have a share of), *koinonia* (fellowship, communion, sharing), were important in Stoic philosophy and found their way into the Messianic Writings. In Acts we learn how the early community devoted itself to *koinonia* and because of that had all things in common (*koinos*). Paul speaks of the Christian community as a *koinonia*, a fellowship, and demands therefore that a better off part must share its goods with a poorer part in an act of *koinonia* (sharing—2 Cor 8:4, 9:13). The Stoics used *koinonia* to speak of the whole inherited earth, and the early Fathers followed them in this. Thus Clement writes in his book, *The Teacher*:

> It is God himself who has brought our race to a *koinonia*, by sharing Himself, first of all, and then by sending His Word to all alike, and by making all things for all. Therefore everything is common, and the rich should not grasp a greater share. The expression, then, "I own something and I have more than enough; why should I not enjoy it?" is not worthy of a human nor does it indicate any community feeling (*koinonikon*).[36]

In his great treatise on Naboth's vineyard, Ambrose declares that "The earth was made in common for all" and derives this truth from the fact that we are born and die with nothing. In his commentary on 1 Corinthians, John Chrysostom likewise notes that "all this about 'mine' and 'thine' is mere verbiage, and does not stand for reality. For if you say the house is yours, it is a word without reality: since the very air, earth, matter, are the Creator's; and so are you too yourself who have framed it; and all other things also." Not to enable the poor to share in our goods, he said, "is to steal from them and deprive them of life. The goods we possess are

36. In Avila, *Ownership*, 37.

not ours but theirs."[37] These arguments—Stoic and Christian—still apply: that the resources of the earth belong to all people and that to privatize them is a form of theft.

The belief that the earth was a common treasury sat uneasily alongside ideas of private property, enshrined in Roman law, which became the common currency of Europe through the rediscovery and dissemination of this law from the tenth century onwards. Aquinas, in the thirteenth century, could assume that the right to common use was always prior. "Stealing," he taught, was not stealing if you were meeting needs for life.[38] This set of assumptions changed in the sixteenth and seventeenth centuries. John Locke on the one hand agreed with the ancient tradition that "God . . . hath given the World to Men in common . . . all the Fruits it naturally produces, and Beasts it feeds, belong to Mankind in common."[39] However, the benefits of creation have to be appropriated and this is done through labor. What we produce through our labor we own, and this is not held in common. "Thus the Grass my horse has bit; the Turfs my servant has cut; and the Ore I have digged in any place where I have a right to them in common with others, become my Property, without the assignation or consent of anybody. The labour that was mine, removing them out of that common state they were in, hath fix'd my Property in them."[40] The key point comes, however, in the introduction of money, which allows people to own more property than their labor can actually work. Money is a device that allows property to accrue to the industrious and the rational. In

37. Hutchinson, *What Everybody Really Wants to Know about Money,* 169. Today David Orr agrees. Some things, he says, should never be sold—because the selling undermines human rights; because it would violate the law and procedural requirements of openness and fairness; because it would have a coarsening effect on society; because the sale would steal from the poor and vulnerable, including future generations; because the thing to be sold as part of the common heritage of humankind and so can have no rightful owner; and because the thing to be sold—including government itself—should simply not be for sale. Orr, "Governance in the long emergency," 282.

38. Aquinas, *Summa Theologiae,* 2a.2ae 66.7—citing Ambrose.

39. Locke, ch. 5 in *Two Treatises of Government,* 286.

40. Ibid., 290.

Locke's view it is plain "that Men have agreed to disproportionate and unequal Possession of the Earth, they having by a tacit and voluntary consent found out a way, how a man may fairly possess more land than he himself can use the product of, by receiving in exchange for the overplus, Gold and Silver, which may be hoarded up without injury to anyone, these metals not spoiling or decaying in the hands of the Possessor."[41]

This argument now overturns the common treasury. In the state of nature all things were common, but not all people were rational and industrious. Some (like the North American Indians, according to Locke) were quarrelsome and contentious, and did not make a proper use of their land. The earth belongs then, not to all, but to those whose wit and industry allows them to exploit it. This idea was to have a long history, being the father of the neo-liberal argument that capitalism rests on people (entrepreneurs) using their wit and intelligence (caput). That his arguments led not only to class division but to slavery did not worry Locke. He himself profited from the slave trade. Beginning with the axiom of human equality, therefore, Locke has by simple steps ended up with private property, ownership, class, and even slavery. That it was Locke who argued thus was hugely important for he was the epitome of the mild-mannered liberal gentleman, and a Christian apologist to boot. From the dangerous Hobbes these arguments might have engendered suspicion, but from Locke they seemed only evidence of sweet reasonableness.

Locke's arguments justified the process of enclosure, which was already underway, but which was now massively speeded up and that led to the dispossession of the British peasantry.[42] Far from being of only antiquarian interest, the enclosure movement is more vigorous than ever. Today we know it as privatization. The root of the verb "to privatize" is the Latin *privare*, to bereave, deprive, or rob. The past participle *privatus* means "belonging to one individual" as opposed to the commons. For Ambrose the very word *private* "is not according to nature":

41. Ibid., 302.
42. Massingham, *The Wisdom of the Fields*, 12.

> For nature has brought forth all things for all in common.
> Thus God has created everything in such a way that all
> things be possessed in common. Nature, therefore, is the
> mother of common right, usurpation of private right.[43]

Private property rights favor the conversion of ecosystem stocks into market products regardless of the difference in contributions that ecosystems and market products have to human welfare. The incentives are to privatize benefits and socialize costs.[44]

If the Patristic and Scholastic arguments about the earth as a common treasury are right—and I believe they are—then, in the face of this movement of enclosure we need strategies—practices—for once again recognizing that, as Winstanley put it, "the earth is a common treasury for all." Nationalization was one way of dealing with this, and is probably still the best way to deal with structures such as railways, but Martin Large argues persuasively that mutualization is a better model for most things, as it retains the best aspects of free enterprise—personal initiative and the personal connection with capital. Utilities should be mutualized to take them back into common ownership.[45] He proposes a new capital commons sector where community capital trusts (CCTs) might be an alternative vehicle for trusteeship, rather than corporate ownership of capital. The purpose of a community capital trust, which would be nonprofit-making, would be to receive, acquire, hold, and invest capital for enduring economic, cultural, and social benefit. In any event, whether through CCTs, or through nationalization, or through the creation of cooperatives, or though land reform, ways need to be found to reverse the increasing enclosure or privatization of the earth's resources

43. In Avila, *Ownership*, 74.

44. Costanza et al., "Building a sustainable and desirable economy," 134.

45. Large, *Common Wealth*, 254. The Marxist David Harvey argues that land, resources, and the amortized built environment should be categorized and managed as a common property resource for the populations that use and rely upon them. Private property rights need to be absorbed into a comprehensive project for the collective democratic management of the commons. Harvey, *Seventeen Contradictions*, 50.

and to recognize them as a gift, a common resource, not only for all people but for all creatures.

An acceptance of the reality of the commons would be the first article of an alternative economy. Put theologically this is an understanding of an economy of grace. We are always told that you cannot get something for nothing. "Nothing comes from nothing," as Lear says. But, Michael Rowbotham objects, something for nothing is part of what life is based upon. Life itself is a gift, something for nothing. We are inheritors of the planet, and economy, culture, and communities; all of these are something for nothing.[46] That is the most basic economic fact.

Because this was the case social credit thinkers—but also Milton Friedman—advocated a citizen's income, which would be paid to people as a right. Income, they argued, should be distributed on the basis of the common cultural inheritance, i.e. the common ownership of the real resources of the community. All people are dependent upon common factors inherited from the past and held in trust for the future, said C. H. Douglas, including the land and natural resources, the fabric and infrastructure of buildings and communications, artistic traditions and the full range of intellectual property, the knowledge of skills and processes built up by countless generations of the past.[47] The priority of grace is, then, the first thing, and a citizen's income is a way of saying that grace has consequences in the real world—that it only means anything when worked out in the world of flesh, bodies, and societies—the central message of the Gospel of John, and, we could add, of Athanasius, in his battle with the Arians, which was precisely not, as Gibbon described it, a dispute over an iota!

From this account of reality as gift I turn to another implication of thinking of creation as a whole, namely the need for limits.

---

46. Rowbotham, *The Grip of Death*, 317.
47. Hutchinson, *Money*, 135.

Growth and limits

Every major economy today is founded on the premise of continual growth and the rationale usually provided for this is to extend the benefits Western consumers enjoy to everyone: expand the size of the cake so that everyone can have more. In fact, there are aspects of the system itself that demand growth. Machinery requires mass consumption, and ever new markets, if expenditure on outlay is to be justified. The competition between firms likewise leads to growth as firms need to outcompete each other in order to survive.[48] Finally, and most importantly, growth is demanded by the system of interest. If we borrow money to finance plant and machinery, we have to make a profit to pay back the loan and the interest. Failure to make a profit threatens the entire system. It means that less money for investment is available, which may mean job losses, which in turn means that consumers have less money to spend, leading to further cut-backs and job losses and so on. The financial markets also play their part. Andrew Simms comments: "The power of an investment bank like J. P. Morgan which expects 20 percent return on its money is like having a giant financial whip over the head of the economy, telling it to grow."[49]

The need for growth is also written into economic anthropology. The second half of the twentieth century saw people who had struggled to move from subjects to citizens redefined as consumers. This move was essential if the engine of growth was to continue. The advertising industry—now worth $500 billion annually, and backed up by government subsidies and tax breaks, and billions more in lobbying and public relations spending—has grown in order to persuade us that consumption is vital and that enough is never enough.[50]

48. "Under the lash of competition," writes Ernest Mandel, "the capitalist mode of production . . . becomes the first mode of production in the history of mankind the essential aim of which appears to be unlimited increase in production, constant accumulation of capital by the capitalization of the surplus value produced in the course of production itself." *Marxist Economic Theory*, 133.

49. Simms, *Cancel the Apocalypse*, 403.

50. As Leon Rosselson brilliantly satirizes in his song "We sell everything,"

The problem with the need for constant growth is that it is inconsistent with a finite world. The discipline of economics does not recognize this because it has retained the Newtonian worldview that was dominant when it emerged. This is evident in the circular flow model of production and consumption that lies at the heart of standard economic modeling, in which the economy is seen as a closed system of exchange between households and firms.[51] Nicholas Georgescu Roegen pointed out that this was inconsistent with the first and second laws of thermodynamics for economics sixty years ago. Economics has to take account of the fact that all energy degrades, which means that there are practical limits to efficiency so that increased efficiency is no "get out of jail free" card.[52] His student, Herman Daly, has for forty years sought to adumbrate the implications of this for economic thinking. "Throughput" is the number of people times their use of resources. Both are sharply in-

and as the Yes Men satirize in their spoof advertisements.

51. Zencey, "Energy as master resource," 75.

52. Simms, *Apocalypse*, 19.

creasing—indeed, rocketing off the graph. He argues that it means that the idea of growth has to be replaced by that of development. "Standard growth economics ignores finitude, entropy and ecological interdependence because the concept of throughput is absent from its preanalytic vision, which is that of an isolated circular flow of exchange value."[53] The economy grows in physical scale but the ecosystem does not. Therefore, as the economy grows it become larger in relation to the ecosystem.[54] Limitless growth is therefore not a possibility, and in any case, as has become clear over the past three centuries, it leads to "violence, waste, war and destruction."[55]

Daly has used the notion of the plimsoll line—the carrying capacity of a boat, which was introduced in 1872 because of the number of overloaded ships that were sinking. In the same way the planet, it is argued, has a carrying capacity. The planetary boundaries sketched in the first chapter suggest that this is a reasonable analogy, most obviously in relation to food, fresh water, and basic resources for manufacturing, but more seriously in relation to biodiversity and climate change.

As we saw in the third chapter, Christianity understood life-destroying forms of behavior in terms of sin as a "power" under which we are "bound." The question is not primarily of the extraordinary viciousness, wickedness, or even selfishness of particular human beings, but of the way in which we all collectively get trapped in life-denying forms of behavior. A good example of this is the way in which human beings can destroy the complex ecological balance that sustains them. The economist E. F. Schumacher argued that, "Nature always. . . knows when to stop. Greater even than the mystery of natural growth is the mystery of the natural cessation of growth . . . The system of nature, of which man is part, tends to be self-balancing, self-adjusting, self-cleansing."[56] "Sin," in this context, is not knowing when to stop. The practice that follows from this realization is at the center of ancient Greek ethics

53. Daly, *Beyond Growth*, 33.
54. Daly, *Steady State*, 180.
55. Berry, *What Matters?*, 44.
56. Schumacher, *Small is Beautiful*, 122.

and was taken up by St. Paul: it is the centrality of moderation, of respect for limits, both because we do not survive without them but also because (and I take it this is the burden of the story in Genesis 3) limits are proper to our humanness. Where we ignore them we lose ourselves both morally and, if Emmott and Anderson are right, absolutely.[57]

A second problem with the growth model is that it prioritizes only one vision of the good life and obscures all others. More people are defining themselves first and foremost by how they consume and are striving to own or use ever more stuff, whether in fashion, food, travel, electronics, or countless other products and services.[58] Life is understood in terms of "endless fun, entertainment, escape, money, sex; and perpetual distraction from the pain and pleasure of being fully human."[59] Aristotle already understood that a life without limits was no life and condemned us to triviality and loss of humanity.[60] A person who has been

57. For many years Herman Daly has proposed a steady state economy, that is, an economy with constant stocks of people and artifacts maintained at some desired, sufficient levels by low rates of maintenance throughput. For this, he argues, three institutions are needed: An institution for stabilizing population (distributable birth licenses); an institution for stabilizing the stock of physical artifacts and keeping throughput below ecological limits (depletion quotas), and a distributist institution limiting the degree of inequality in the distribution of constant stocks among the constant population. Daly, *Steady State*, 53. I turn to the last of these recommendations shortly. Andrew Jackson and Ben Dyson argue that a steady state economy is not possible under present monetary arrangements. These transfer wealth towards those with higher incomes, forcing people to borrow to keep up. The need to pay off debt, which is further increased by asset price bubbles such as the exponential rise in house prices, drives further production. Without a debt-based money system there would be no money for investment and so a zero-growth economy would become a negative-growth economy of recession, unemployment, and the same pressures on government described earlier. Jackson and Dyson, *Modernising Money*, 165. What this shows, of course, is not that a steady state economy is impossible, but that a debt-based money system has to be replaced if we are to survive, a question I address in the next chapter.

58. Assadourian, "Re-engineering Cultures to Create a Sustainable Civilization," 113.

59. Cited in Hutchinson, *Money*, 60.

60. Aristotle, *Politics*, 1257b25ff.

seduced by the consumer value system, wrote Havel, is a demor-
alized person, and to structure a whole society around consumption means a profound crisis of human identity. The only thing
that can challenge it is living within the truth.[61]Historically,
societies developed social mechanisms such as saving accounts,
marriage, norms of social behavior, and government, to prevent
people trading away long-term well-being for the sake of short-
term pleasures. Affluence, Claus Offe argues, is eroding and undermining these commitment devices.[62]

The fact that the Euro-Atlantic model cannot be generalized means that it requires social exclusion by its very structure.
It requires lack of equity both within and between nations—this is
the third problem with the consumerist vision. Politics, therefore,
says Wolfgang Sachs, is at a crossroads. "The choices are either affluence with persistent disparity or moderation with prospects of
equity. If there is to be some kind of prosperity for world citizens,
the Euro Atlantic model needs to be superseded, making room for
ways of living, producing, and consuming that leave only a light
footprint on the earth."[63]

Accepting limits to growth would mean that it was no longer
possible to conflate needs and wants. Molly Scott Cato talks of a
provisioning economy, as opposed to a growth economy, the task
of which would be to meet the needs of the whole human community for both survival and quality of life whilst being ecologically
sustainable.[64] This would have implications for health provisioning. In this respect the Cuban model, in which, some advanced
procedures might not be available, and the emphasis would be on
preventive medicine, is at least worth thinking about not least because, according to the World Health Organization, Cuba's health
services score far higher than those in the United States, and its
population is healthier![65]

61. Havel, *Power of the Powerless*, 45.

62. Cited in Jackson, *Prosperity without Growth,* 161.

63. Sachs, "Development and decline," 125

64. Cato, *Bioregional Economics,* 85.

65. Murphy and Morgan, "Cuba," 338.

The aim of proposals such as these is to create the vision of a life lived differently, a life where economic growth, competition, and material consumption are replaced as the central objectives of society by a renewed sense of spiritual meaning, and social and environmental harmony.[66]

I turn now from creation to anthropology and the economic implications of the way we understand what it means to be human.

The competitive individual

The person generally taken as the founder of modern economics, Adam Smith, makes particularly clear that economics rests on an anthropology.[67] Although Smith was the author of the *Theory of Moral Sentiments*, which was in part a theory of what today we would call "empathy," his assumptions in his more famous and influential book were thoroughly individualist: it is not to the benevolence of the butcher and the baker that we look, but to their self-interest. This individualism remains a key part of economic and much political theory up to the present. Thus in *The Limits of Liberty* the Nobel Prize-winning economist James Buchanan argued that the idea of the public good is just not meaningful because human beings are all self-interested and the market expresses people's preferences much better than voting.[68] Hence the

66. Cato, *Economics*, 205.

67. Karl Heinz Brodbeck argues that at the root of modern economics is Descartes's move to begin with the self, the isolated individual, which establishes methodological individualism as the rule for social science, and which applies above all to economics. *Herrschaft*, 53. Brodbeck argues that Keynes retains this Cartesian starting point. That may be, but Locke, who had an enormous influence on eighteenth-century thinkers like Smith, begins with the idea of property as deriving from the labor anyone invested in something (he is thinking of America, and thinking of it as *terra nullius*). Society exists to protect the property of the individual. Hobbes and Locke "fastened on social theory the presumption that individual self-interest is clear and compelling, while the public or social interest is thin and unsubstantial." Sabine, *History*, 447.

68. Buchanan, *The Limits of Liberty*. The Nobel Prize in economics seems to imply moral and ethical illiteracy!

elision of capitalism and democracy, which we have seen in North American rhetoric over the past forty years.

It is no accident that Hayek, the father of neoliberalism, dismissed any idea of morality apart from that between intimate acquaintances (in this following W. S. Jevons). For Hayek, strangers have no moral claim on us and there is no form of human solidarity that implies that we should help and sustain one another. That stance is itself a moral standpoint, and in ancient terms would have been classed as cynical. The chief feature of *Homo economicus*, write Herman Daly and John Cobb, is extreme individualism. What happens to others does not affect *Homo economicus* unless he or she has caused it through a gift. "Even external relations to others, such as relative standing in the community, make no difference. In addition, only scarce commodities, those that are exchanged in the market, are of interest. The gifts of nature are of no importance, nor is the morale of the community of which *Homo economicus* is a part."[69]

Bound up with individualism is the assumption that everything in human society works better through competition, which is supposed to be good for us because it encourages efficiency amongst producers and brings prices down for what have become known, in the present phase of capitalism, as "consumers." Trade between nations is based on competition, ignoring the fact that they start from grossly unequal positions—like having a race where the most powerful competitors start from three-quarters of the way around the track. Colin Tudge argues that neoliberal economics owes a great deal to a perverse reading of Darwin that believes that we compete, and we have to compete, because that is how we are made. The latest version of this myth is provided by Richard Dawkins's hugely successful *The Selfish Gene*, which argues that we are survival machines—"robust vehicles blindly

69. Daly and Cobb Jr., *For the Common Good*, 87. Streeck notes that mainstream economic theory is based on "a kind of anthropological act of faith." *Buying Time*, 136. Hayek dismisses the idea of social justice as "quasi religious," but his own position is in fact more accurately described in this way, involving as it does "awe in the face of the operations of the market," and a very strong, not to say fatalistic, secularized account of providence.

programmed to preserve the selfish molecules known as genes
. . . They are in you and me; they created us, body and mind; and
their preservation is the ultimate rationale for our existence."[70]
In that case we are part of a universe in which all altruism is
specious. Even if we seem to be acting for others we are actually
seeking our own preservation. Such an idea underwrites the idea
that we are all "rational utility maximizers" and that there is no
alternative to the neoliberal economy. The whole of life is one big
punch-up and we are part of a nature that is, as Tennyson put it
in 1849, "red in tooth and claw."

Dawkins's reading of Darwin is now decidedly passé. Tudge
argues that the idea of the selfish gene is not science at all, but
rhetoric, springing from an assortment of philosophical, political,
and sociological prejudices. It suggests that life is one big punch
-up but in fact, he argues, life is a constructive dialogue. The best
survival tactic, essential in an age of extremely dangerous climate
change, is cooperation. The selfish gene theory suggests that DNA
is what rules us, but far more important is metabolism, the chemical cycle that keeps life going. Life did not arise through tooth-
and-claw competition but through collaboration. Human beings,
like many other animals, are primarily cooperative. Sociality un-
derpins morality and we are inclined to be unselfish much more
than we are to be solipsistic—exactly the argument which Kropotkin took from Darwin a century ago.[71] If we want a metaphor
for DNA, Tudge argues, it is not "boss" but librarian. "The whole
process is *not* primarily competitive. It is cooperative. The essence
of the relationship between DNA and the rest of the system is *not*
one of master and servants, but of dialogue."[72] In fact, "Nothing
can survive without everything else. Every living thing that aspires
to exist at all must master the arts of survival—but the best survival tactic by far, and indeed the sine qua non, is to cooperate."[73]

70. Dawkins, *The Selfish Gene*, 2.

71. Tudge, *Why Genes are Not Selfish and People are Nice.*

72. Ibid., 92.

73. Ibid., 94. Hahn and Hart remark, analogously, that the premise of *Homo
economicus* is seriously undermined when neuroscientists show calculating

If this is right then competition is the practice to avoid, and co-operation the one to follow and this is not to adopt a self-defeating stance: where cooperation is tried, in cases like Mondragon or the Scott Bader Commonwealth, as well as in many aspects of the "war effort" in World War II, it works. By the same token competition is inherently limited: the "simple paradox" of competition is that its end is monopoly. As Giovanni Arrighi points out, capitalism oscillates between the two extremes of the supposedly ruinous effects of unregulated competition and excessive centralizing powers of monopolies and oligopolies.[74] Capitalism tends to monopoly, either through setting up corporations that dominate markets or by securing the monopoly rights of private property through international, commercial laws that regulate all global trade.[75]

The prioritization of competition over against cooperation is a choice, an option for a particular grand narrative, not driven by reason but by the mythic power of the idea of the struggle for existence. If we begin from the fundamental ecological principle that everything is connected to everything else, on the other hand, then competitiveness cannot be the ruling principle. Prioritizing competition ignores the fact that the economy is not the "sum of its parts" but a membership of parts inextricably joined to each other, indebted to each other, receiving significance and worth from each other and from the whole.[76] By the same token the idea that we are in the first instance individuals overlooks the obvious fact that humans are dependent on others at every level—dependent in their early and later years, dependent for the provision of all the goods needed for life, dependent on friendship and community. Not only that but in our very identity we are constituted by relationships—not just in childhood, but throughout our lives. So

<hr/>

reason to be limited to "one small section of the brain . . . the decisions which matter in life are determined elsewhere." Hahn and Hart, *Economic Anthropology*, 92.

74. Arrighi, "Towards a Theory of Capitalist Crisis."
75. Harvey, *Seventeen Contradictions*, 139.
76. Berry, *Home Economics*, 72.

the myth of the competitive individual flies in the face of human social and biological reality.

From the theological point of view (and not forgetting the Pauline or Pseudo Pauline use of the metaphor of the competitive race), radical individualism ignores the reality of grace. As Berry puts it, "Rats and roaches live by competition under the laws of supply and demand; it is the privilege of human beings to live under the laws of justice and mercy."[77] What the ideal of competition most flagrantly and disastrously excludes, he argues, is affection. "For human beings, affection is the ultimate motive, because the force that powers us, as Ruskin also said, is not 'steam, magnetism, or gravitation' but 'a Soul.' Pleasure is, so to speak, affection in action."[78]

I turn now to the articulation of relations between people in the economy, namely the question of justice.

Economics and the question of justice

Nothing is more remarkable than the complete absence from mainstream economic theory of the question of justice, and in this respect it is, in Alasdair MacIntyre's terms, paradigmatically, "after virtue." This absence follows clearly from Hayek's view of society and the human, which developed out of his opposition to Soviet communism, the attempt to produce a just society by regulation and compulsion. It deprives us of choice, which is central to Hayek's view of what it means to be human. Freedom, on his account, is the heart of human dignity, and freedom means choice, and choice implies an absence of regulation. The social welfare state, which tries to redistribute wealth from rich to poor, to see that the shares of the cake allocated to all are less unequal than they might be, is not only misguided, sapping of moral fiber for the poor, but also morally wrong. It has simply misunderstood what it means to be human. The idea of social

77. Berry, *What are People For?*, 91.
78. Ibid., 96.

justice is a quasi-religious superstition that represents the gravest threat to the values of a free civilization.[79]

Wolfgang Streeck makes the distinction between social justice and market justice. The first is based on cultural norms and follows collective ideas of fairness, correctness, and reciprocity. The latter is the distribution of the output of production according to the market evaluation of individual performance, expressed in individual prices. Hayek's agenda was to comprehensively replace social justice with market justice, and the present situation where corporations or hedge funds can sue governments for loss of profit or breach of contract represents its realization.

The idea of social justice has roots equally in Greek and biblical thought. For Aristotle justice is to see that each has their due. Aristotle argues that justice is a kind of mean, whilst injustice is excess and defect, contrary to proportion, of the useful or hurtful. The unjust person is driven by greed, and therefore breaches equality and proportionality. Justice is primarily a political virtue, found amongst free and equal people. The very idea of justice only makes sense within a community with a shared idea of the common good. A society like ours, Aristotle would argue, which cannot agree on an idea of the common good, or which is indifferent to the question, is bound to be unjust. It actually rules out for itself the very preconditions for knowing what justice is. To be just, on his account, is to know that no man is an island sufficient unto himself, to know that I am, at the deepest level, a community animal. Survival in the community, Aristotle implies, is only possible when each takes only what they need and makes sure that others have what they need.

Suum cuique is, of course, consistent with extremely hierarchical societies, but hierarchy is problematized if we allow human equality. In this respect Western liberal societies are highly conflicted, believing at one and the same time in an abstract equality, but also in meritocracy, and comfortable with the most extreme forms of inequality, both within and between nations. Thomas Piketty has put the question of inequality back at the center of

79. Hayek, *Law, Legislation and Liberty*, vol. 2, 230.

economic analysis.[80] Neither equality nor inequality "just happen" he points out. Under assumptions of progress made during the "development decades" (1955–75) the idea was that everyone would more or less become equal as a rising tide lifted all boats. This has not happened: inequality is back at mid-nineteenth century levels, or worse. The history of inequality, Piketty argues, is shaped by the way economic, social, and political actors view what is just and what is not, as well as by the relative power of those actors and the collective choices that result. There is no natural, spontaneous process to prevent destabilizing, inegalitarian forces from prevailing permanently.[81] The experience of France in the Belle Epoque proves, he writes, that no hypocrisy is too great when economic and financial elites are obliged to defend their interests.[82] The resurgence of inequality after 1980 is due largely to the political shifts of the past several decades, especially in regard to taxation and finance.

The decline in inequality during the twentieth century was due partly to the impact of two world wars and partly to inflation. There was no gradual, consensual, conflict-free evolution towards greater equality. The shocks were destruction caused by two world wars, bankruptcies caused by the great depression, and above all new public policies enacted in this period from rent control to nationalizations and the inflation-induced euthanasia of the rentier class living on government debt.[83]

Today inequality is driven not primarily by inherited wealth but by salary differentials.[84] Some CEOs earn more than a thousand times what their lowest-paid employees earn. It is rather naive, Piketty comments, to seek an objective basis for their high

80. Piketty, *Capital*, 16.

81. Ibid., 21.

82. Ibid., 514.

83. Ibid., 275.

84. Today in France the richest 10 percent command 62 percent of total wealth while the poorest 50 percent have only 4 percent. In the United States the most recent survey indicates the top decile owns 70 percent of America's wealth, while the bottom half claimed only 2 percent. Ibid., 257.

salaries in individual productivity.[85] In fact, comparative studies show that there is no correlation between vast salaries and company performance. These salaries are set incestuously by corporate compensation committees whose members usually earn comparable salaries.[86]

Such inequality is problematic for several reasons. It fails to recognize that every society is a body, in which all are mutually interdependent. Second, it is as well evidenced as possible that all the major killer diseases affect the poor more than the rich; that the poor are less healthy, die younger, and have a higher incidence of both mental disorder and physical illness than the rich. Third, it is doubtful if it is socially sustainable. Piketty suggests that if it got to a stage where the top decile appropriated 90 percent of each year's output, revolution will likely occur unless some peculiarly effective repressive apparatus exists to keep it from happening.[87] Even in terms of the system, an inegalitarian spiral cannot continue indefinitely: ultimately there will be no place to invest the savings, and the global return on capital will fall, until an equilibrium distribution emerges.[88]

A Christian reading of *suum cuique* problematizes inequality still further, because, as we saw in the last chapter, it is based on the notion that each human being is a sister or brother of the Human One. Why does exploitation matter? Why do we feel outraged by stories of children in Asia sewing footballs for a few pennies a day? The answer lies in our understanding of what it means to be human. What is outraged is an intrinsic dignity, which in turn calls for a basic equality of treatment between persons. The Eucharist (when not fetishized) adumbrates as a sign the view that the world is gifted to all creatures and is to be shared equally between them. Equality as God's creature demands equality of resource allocation. Although he accepted a hierarchical society as given, Aquinas argued for economic justice in terms of the just wage and the

85. Ibid., 330.
86. Ibid., 331.
87. Ibid., 263.
88. Ibid., 366.

just price. The attempt to see that people were properly rewarded for their labor, and that prices should not be either depressed or inflated was an important anticipation of what later came to be called social justice.

Daly argues that the goal for an economics of community is not equality, but limited inequality. If complete equality is the collectivist's denial of true differences in community, then unlimited inequality is the individual's denial of interdependence and true solidarity in community.[89] A factor of one to ten, he feels, is about the limit for a sustainable society. Unlimited inequality is inconsistent with community, no matter how well off the poorest are. "Even relative poverty breeds resentment, and riches insulate and harden the heart. Conviviality, solidarity and brotherhood weaken with economic distance. Political power tends to follow relative income and cannot be allowed to concentrate too far in either a theocracy or democracy without leading to a plutocracy."[90] The remedy for this—and this was the burden of the prophets of Israel from first to last—is the practice of justice at the heart of the body politic:

> Did not your father eat and drink
>
> And do justice and righteousness?
>
> Then it was well with him.
>
> He judged the cause of the poor and needy;
>
> Then it was well.
>
> Is this not to know me? says YHWH. (Jer 22:15–16)

The contest between market justice and social justice is, if Streeck is right, the fundamental political and moral contest of our age. In his view, the 1 percent, the plutocrats of the world, hold the levers of power and there is little chance of overturning them. What Berry, Daly, and Schumacher appeal to, by contrast, is the moral common sense of getting on for three millennia, articulated

89. Daly and Cobb, *Common Good*, 331.

90. Daly, *Beyond Growth*, 214.

in accounts of what it means to be human, and in particular in calls not just for mercy and compassion, but for a recognition that human beings are fundamentally equal. It is this moral imperative which Hayek, in Nietzschean fashion, scorned and sought to oppose, which underlies the whole demand for social justice.

This consideration of competition and cooperation now leads us to an understanding of how economic action is coordinated, what we usually call "the market."

The myth of the market

For Hayek and the neoliberals the "market" becomes a metaphysical principle that enables societies to manage without central control, and that seeks to put all resources, even the most fundamental, under private ownership. All that is required is a minimal state, which exists to protect private property rights and must not intervene in markets. The market will always allocate resources better than governments and so increase human well-being more than governments can. It is now argued by some academics, and by right-wing think tanks, that governments have no legitimate rights to create law as democracies oppress those with wealth. Voting is a mechanism for indicating choice vastly inferior to that supplied by the market where the expenditure of cash indicates real preferences in society.[91]

This view is theorized in the form of the "Efficient Markets Hypothesis" (EMH), which assumes that governments can never outperform well-informed financial markets. The only exception is where mistaken government policies, or a failure to define property rights adequately, leads to distorted market outcomes.[92]

To this account of the virtues and efficiency of the market I shall make four objections. The first is that the EMH assumes— what is clearly not the case—that there can be no such thing as a bubble in the prices of stocks or houses. In fact, recent studies

---

91. Murphy, *Courageous State*, 51.
92. Quiggin, *Zombie Economics*, 49.

show that prices of financial assets do not behave as the theory of consumption-based asset pricing predicts.[93] Stock market bubbles have been a major cause of market failure and embarrassment since the seventeenth century. The dot-com bubble of the 1990s, based on the over estimation of the value of new technology, was just the latest of these.

Amartya Sen defends the need for markets as a form of basic freedom, but then goes on to note that there "may" be circumstances in which markets do not function optimally, in which case the point is to help them to function with greater fairness.[94] But the point is—my second objection—that markets *never* function fairly—the dice is always loaded in favor of those with more wealth and power. Those with greater abilities benefit more and exercise greater economic power than do those with lesser abilities.[95] Wealth and power are redistributed from government to private enterprises, from workers to capitalists, and from poor to rich.[96] It cannot be said too strongly that there are no such thing as markets either in the classic or the neoliberal sense: There are *people*, and very powerful corporations, betting, bigging up and crying down, speculating on currencies, driving thousands into unemployment, and making fortunes for the fraction of the world's citizens who own stocks and shares. This activity is strictly speaking parasitic because not only does the state (i.e., ordinary taxpayers) pay the cost of much of the infrastructure, from education to transport to disposal of waste, not only does it step in to bail out the banks at the cost of billions to the taxpayer, but it also intervenes repeatedly to protect, for example, oil and gas interests. At the same time the so-called private sector depends on education, health care, and a transport infrastructure provided by the state. Where it is not provided by the state, millions "fall through the net," with the bizarre result, for example, that the United States has worse health indices than Cuba. As this shows, leaving economics to "the market" de-

93. Ibid., 53.
94. Sen, *Development as Freedom,* 148.
95. Albert, *Parecon,* 56.
96. Cited in ibid., 76.

feats the common good. When public services are privatized the most profitable activities are undertaken first and those which make a loss are then dropped

Third, if society is subordinated to the market social or environmental costs are not factored in.[97] As David Korten puts it, "Markets don't tell people with substantial incomes to consume no more than their rightful share of ecosystem resources. They don't tell retailers not to sell guns to children. They don't tell producers their wastes must be recycled. They don't give priority in the allocation of scarce resources to the basic needs of those with little or no money before providing luxuries for those who have great wealth. They generally do the exact opposite."[98] Belief is widespread among economists, comments Daly, that internalization of externalities, or the incorporation of all environmental costs into market prices, is a sufficient environmental policy, but market equilibria coincide neither with ecological nor with ethical boundaries.[99] The market cannot by itself keep aggregate throughput below ecological limits, conserve resources for future generations, avoid gross inequities in wealth and income distribution, or prevent overpopulation.[100] What neoliberalism in fact does is to treat the market as a categorical imperative, as an end in itself. In doing this it fundamentally traduces accounts of the human good forged over millennia, quite

97. Polanyi argued that to allow the market mechanism to be sole director of the fate of human beings in their natural environment, indeed even of the amount and use of purchasing power, would result in the demolition of society: Robbed of the protective covering of cultural institutions, human beings would perish from the effects of social exposure; they would die as the victims of acute social dislocation through vice, perversion, crime, and starvation. Nature would be reduced to its elements, neighborhoods and landscapes defiled, rivers polluted, military safety jeopardized, the power to produce food and raw materials destroyed. Polanyi, *Great Transformation*, 73. Keith Hart says that Polanyi had all the attributes of a great prophet, except that his prophecies were not fulfilled. That was in 1999. The ecological crisis in my view reverses that judgement. *The Memory Bank*, 198.

98. Korten, *When Corporations Rule the World*, 98.

99. Daly, *Steady State*, 69.

100. Ibid., 89.

as fundamentally as Nazism did, and with potentially fatal consequences for the planet.

Lastly, markets are not socially neutral, as Smith and Hayek imagine. They "shape our culture, foster or thwart desirable forms of human development, and support a well-defined structure of power. Markets are as much political and cultural institutions as they are economic . . . They make us unsympathetic egoists."[101] Markets are, says Michael Albert, a vote of no confidence in the social capacities of the human species. They organize our creative capacities and energies primarily by threatening our livelihoods and bribing us with luxury beyond what others can have.[102]

The outcome of all these arguments is that to have a "total market"—still the reigning ideology—is disastrous. In terms of practices it may be that, as John Quiggin suggests, a mixed economy is the best we can do, or, as Albert prefers, a decentralized, managed economy, but in any case the present system is completely incapable of dealing with the planetary emergency—in fact, it is largely its cause.[103] Because that is the case I now turn to the question of economic democracy—the subjection of economic activity to political control.

Economic democracy

The present economic model, as we saw in the last chapter, is a severe threat to democracy through the lobbying system, and the way in which money translates into power, which Hansen describes as the biggest obstacle to dealing with climate change.[104] Only

101. Ibid., 67, citing Sam Bowles.

102. Ibid., 65.

103. Quiggin suggests that it seems likely that markets will do better than governments in planning investments in some cases (those where a good judgement of consumer demand is important, for example) and worse in others (those requiring long-term planning, for example). The logical implication is that a mixed economy will outperform both central planning and laissez faire, as the twentieth century suggested. *Zombie Economics*, 68.

104. Wendy Brown's example of the influence of Monsanto in the writing of the Iraqi constitution is a stark example.

political and corporate elites inhabit the decision-making halls of capitalist globalizers, argues Michael Albert. The idea that the broad public of working people, consumers, farmers, and the poor and disenfranchized should have a proportionate say is considered ludicrous.[105] In the previous chapter, I argued there that if we are serious about political democracy we need economic democracy as well. The biggest challenge to the realization of such democracy, as Adam Smith already suggested, is taming the corporations. The power and reach of corporations is a key part of what is meant by globalization. More than half of the 100 largest corporations have sales bigger than the combined economies of all but the top ten countries. The top 200 have one quarter of world trade but they employ less than 1 percent of the world's work force. Five firms control 50 percent of the car market, electrical goods, aerospace, and steel. The poorest forty-nine countries, with 10 percent of world population, have 0.4 percent of world trade. The control of food is especially important. Two firms control 70 percent of world trade in grain and corporations are engaged in an aggressive attempt to patent seeds and other life forms. All this means a more homogenized world—the so-called McDonaldization of culture.

Following a bizarre ruling in the United States in 1886, which resulted from the huge amount of money railroad companies had to fight things through the courts, corporations are regarded legally as "persons" so they have all the rights of individuals in law. But, as Berry comments, "Unlike a person a corporation does not age."

> It does not arrive, as most persons do, at a realization of the shortness and smallness of human lives; it does not come to see the future as the lifetime of the children and grandchildren of anybody in particular. It can experience no personal hope or remorse, no change of heart. It cannot humble itself. It goes about its business as if it were immortal, with the single purpose of becoming a bigger pile of money . . . The WTO enlarges the old idea of the corporation as person by giving the global

105. Albert, *Parecon*, 3.

corporate economy the status of a super government
with the power to overrule nations.[106]

Susan George has documented the lobbying interests of corporations (there are fifteen to twenty thousand lobbyists in Brussels),
their creation of "institutes," "foundations," "centers," and "councils"
to promote often dangerous products and cast doubt on scientific
critical studies. WTO rules and other trade treaties allow corporations to sue sovereign governments if the company chooses to
claim that a government measure will harm its present, or even
its "expected" profits. Countries, by contrast, are not able to sue
corporations. Corporate claimants demand up to $100 million in
compensation, which has to be paid by the taxpayer. And who are
these corporate claimants? Researchers in Zurich found that 147
companies control 40 percent of the economic value of 43,000 other
registered companies. Forty-eight of these are banks, hedge funds,
and other financial corporations. Their close interconnectedness
means they are "prone to systemic risk." George concludes:

> It's not just their size, their enormous wealth and assets
> that make the TNCs dangerous to democracy. It's also
> their concentration, their capacity to influence, and of-
> ten infiltrate, governments and their ability to act as a
> genuine international social class in order to defend their
> commercial interests against the common good.[107]

Their overall aim is to demolish notions such as the public interest,
public service, the welfare state, and the common good in favor
of higher corporate gains in terms of both money and power and
rules tailored for corporate purposes.

The economist Robert Reich argues that given the existing
rules of the market, corporations "cannot be socially responsible,
at least not to any significant extent . . . Super capitalism does not
permit acts of corporate virtue that erode the bottom line. No corporation can voluntarily take on an extra cost that its competitors

106. Berry, *What Matters?*, 188.
107. George, *State of Power.*

don't take on."[108] For Hahn and Hart corporations are the main obstacle to implementing global justice.[109]

David Korten argues that a first step toward removing corporations from the political sphere would be to eliminate all tax exemptions for corporate expenditures related to lobbying, public education, public charities, or political organizations of any kind. The ultimate goal, however, should be a flat prohibition on for-profit corporations involvement in any activity intended to influence the political process or to "educate" the public on issues of policy or the public interest.[110] There are few actions we might contemplate with comparably far-reaching positive consequences, he says, than the elimination of corporate personhood. Global taxation measures—harmonizing corporate taxes, preventing companies from shifting their money to tax havens and levying a tariff on all international currency transactions—would forestall one of the world's gravest impending problems: the erosion of the tax base as states offer ever more generous terms to the ultra rich in order to attract their money.[111]

Only the effort to prioritize social justice over market justice, to give priority to Staatsvolk over Marktvolk, would make it meaningful to speak of democracy today, Streeck argues. Neoliberalism is incompatible with a democratic state in that a democracy must be able to modify the distribution of economic goods resulting from market forces.[112] In other words, what is required is the subordination of economic activity to democratic political control. In the previous chapter I argued for a world of smaller but federated political units, so I turn now, finally, to the relation of local and global in the economy.

108. Cited by Orr, "Governance," 281.

109. Hahn and Hart, *Economic Anthropology*, 168.

110. Korten, *Corporations*, 309.

111. Monbiot, *Captive State*, 355.

112. Streeck, *Buying Time*, 57, 174.

Local and global

Rather than there being a global economy, into which all smaller economies are articulated, I shall argue that the economy should be primarily local and only then global. This is the heart of the idea of relocalization, championed, amongst others, by the Transition Movement, which seeks to prioritize social entrepreneurship over the present private-profit model, and which asks first how to sustain the local economy and to help it flourish. Daly talks of an economics for person-in-community, (as opposed to an economics for the atomized individual). The key question is that of scale: how many persons simultaneously living at what level of per capita resource use is best for community, where community includes concern for the future and nonhuman species as well as presently living humans?[113] As we saw in chapter four, Daly argues that rather than thinking first of "the nation" we have to think of "a community of communities." The goal of an economics for community is to restore to communities at lower levels the power to determine their own affairs (which was also a key goal of Social Credit).[114]

A local economy, Wendell Berry argues, rests upon two principles: neighborhood and subsistence. In a viable neighborhood, he says, neighbors ask themselves what they can do or provide for one another, and they find answers that they and their place can afford. "This and nothing else is the practice of neighborhood. The practice must be, in part, charitable, but it must also be economic and the economic part must be equitable; there is a significant charity in just prices."[115]

Local economies challenge the power of supermarkets, increasingly international, if not global players, which Andrews Simms describes as "extractive industries"—because all of their profits ultimately go to shareholders. Local economies will have shorter supply chains and help keep real wealth within the community. They will not import products they can produce for themselves

113. Daly and Cobb Jr., *Common Good*, 241.
114. Ibid., 293.
115. Berry, *What Matters?*, 191.

or export local products until local needs have been met. Keynes already agreed with this in his celebrated remark that goods should be homespun and finance primarily national.[116]

Molly Scott Cato appeals to the notion of bioregions—areas naturally defined by rivers, mountains, or other large geological features that historically have supported local economies and food systems. In her account of this we can see many analogies with the small federated political units I have been arguing for in the past two chapters. In the United Kingdom she analyzes perhaps twenty bioregions, and argues that they could be the basis for a reformed economy. Each bioregion would have the task of provisioning its inhabitants—this would include regulations regarding land use, and power to introduce tariffs and taxes. This would make possible much greater economic democracy, effectively what Berry intends when he writes that "Without prosperous local economies the people have no power and the land no voice."[117]

Ways need to be found to make industry of all kinds more accountable to local communities. This was one of the concerns of Guild Socialism, which wanted to see the ownership of industry vested in the state, but administered locally by guilds which embraced all workers in the industry—managers and workers. Payment would be based on being part of the whole, rather than as remuneration for hours worked or in relation to productivity.[118]

The priority of the local would not mean world trade would cease, but it would mean that it was not the driver of the world economy as it is at present (when this isn't finance). Instead of the ludicrous situation where countries export to each other exactly equal amounts of butter or pork or cars, world trade would rest on the exchange of what different economies cannot provide for

116. "I sympathise with those who would minimise, rather than those who would maximise, economic entanglement between nations. Ideas, knowledge, art, hospitality, travel—these are the things which should by nature be international. But let goods be homespun whenever it is reasonably and conveniently possible; and above all let finance be primarily national." "National Self-Sufficiency," 756.

117. Berry, *What Matters?*, 193.

118. Hutchinson, *Money*, 136.

themselves (as Ricardo seems to have imagined). The problem with Ricardo's theory of comparative advantage is that it presupposed both equality between trading partners and capital immobility. The former did not apply when he was writing, and never has applied, and with regard to the latter we now live in an age of extreme capital mobility, a factor which has helped ruin many Third World economies. In fact, as Rowbotham points out, the world trade that is supposed to benefit everyone involves wildly excessive transportation and the neglect of domestic need. The doctrine of "free" trade (i.e, trade rules framed by corporations for their own benefit) has everywhere "led not to prosperity but directly to a poverty far worse than the original state from which the country started."[119]

Cato envisages that networks of bioregions would be responsible for energy strategy and planning policy. Below the bioregion there would be community participatory resource planning— somewhat as it happens in Port Allegre today. All communities would need to embrace an ethic of responsibility so while we claim a right to the resources of our bioregion this does not allow us to consume excessively when this might threaten the global systems on which we all depend. Hence the basic norms of ecological citizenship should be established on a global and equitable basis within the framework of the contraction and convergence model.[120]

Networks of bioregions would in turn answer to a national (or a regional) government, which would be responsible for defense and for allocating carbon rights. At this level there would be a diversity of forms and structures, ranging from state-owned enterprises in strategic sectors through worker cooperatives and small-scale private enterprises depending on the relevance or not of economies of scale and the preferences of those working in the sector.[121]

Globally some kind of beefed up UN economic organizations—the Bretton Woods Institutions as Keynes intended them,

---

119. Rowbotham, *Grip of Death*, 137.

120. Cato, *Bioregional Economics*, 199.

121. Ibid., 107.

and not as they have become—might be responsible for employment rights, minimum wage, and carbon emission limits.[122]

At this level, too, Piketty suggests a progressive global tax on capital which would provide a way to avoid an endless inegalitarian spiral and control global capital concentration.[123]

To the objection that the proposals for an alternative economy are utopian I reply, first, that nothing is so wildly utopian as to try and build a sustainable world on the basis of greed and competition, but also, second, that proposals such as I have outlined are actually being modeled on the ground the world over. As I have already suggested, it is not that we have to wait for one great cataclysmic revolution to overthrow the old order. Rather, the world is already being remade, and the question is exactly when this remaking will outflank and transform the present world order, based on hierarchy and violence. Every small step to trade differently, to refashion banking, to find a new way to exchange, is a step towards the realization of this different order. Nothing on earth is forever—including neoliberalism and corporate rule. Both critique and the working out of concrete alternatives are essential to hastening their demise. This applies also to money and finance, to which I now turn.

122. Ibid., 198. Albert suggests the Bretton Woods Institutions should be replaced by an International Asset Agency, a Global Investment Assistance Agency, and a World Trade Agency. These should be transparent, participatory, and bottom up with local democratic accountability. Albert, *Parecon*, 5.

123. Piketty, *Capital*, 515.

Chapter Seven
Money and Value

Money value can be said to be true only when it justly and stably represents the value of necessary goods, such as clothing, food and shelter, which originate ultimately in the Great Economy. Humans can originate money value in the abstract, but only by inflation and usury, which falsify the value of necessary things and damage their natural and human sources. Inflation and usury and the damages that follow can be understood, perhaps, as retributions for the presumption that humans can make value.

—WENDELL BERRY

What is money?

"Papa! what's money?"

The abrupt question had such immediate reference to the subject of Mr Dombey's thoughts, that Mr Dombey was quite disconcerted.

"What is money, Paul?" he answered. "Money?"

"Yes," said the child . . . "what is money?"

Mr Dombey was in a difficulty. He would have liked to give him some explanation involving the terms

> circulating-medium, currency, depreciation of currency,
> paper, bullion, rates of exchange, value of precious metals
> in the market, and so forth; but looking down at the little
> chair, and seeing what a long way down it was, he an-
> swered: "Gold, and silver, and copper. Guineas, shillings,
> half-pence. You know what they are?"
>
> "Oh, yes. I know what they are," said Paul. "I don't mean
> that, papa. I mean, what's money after all?. . ."
>
> "What's money after all!" said Mr Dombey, backing
> his chair a little, that he might the better gaze in sheer
> amazement at the presumptuous atom that propounded
> such an inquiry.
>
> "I mean, papa, what can it do?" returned Paul . . .
>
> Mr Dombey drew his chair back to its former place, and
> patted him on the head. "You'll know better by and by,
> my man," he said. "Money, Paul, can do anything."[1]

We are all familiar with Dickens's ironic morality tale, and it
makes us smile. But here is J. K. Galbraith, at the end of his history of economics, explaining the problem with Milton Friedman's
monetarism:

> There was a further, more grievous difficulty with the
> Friedman prescription . . . and that was that no one knew
> with certainty what, in the modern economy, is money.[2]

In this chapter I attempt to unpick the cat's cradle that is money, and
pick up suggestions as to how it might be better understood and
deployed—what practices we should follow in regard to this form
of social relation. I begin by asking about the origin and meaning
of money and go on to the nature of money in the contemporary
economy, which is indivisible from (what is dealt with in the next

1. Dickens, *Dombey and Son*, 1.
2. Galbraith, *A History of Economics*, 272.

section) debt. I turn then to discuss usury and speculation, and the way both these practices create inequality within society. I discuss the idea that money is a measure and a store of value, and Philip Goodchild's important idea that rather than committees determining interest rates we need a committee that assigns values. This, he argues, is what money is supposed to do. I then turn to a number of current schemes and proposals for reforming the money system, some of which, like WGR in Switzerland, are well established and that could, with sufficient political momentum, become normative.

The origin of money

Mr. Dombey begins answering his son's question by reference to coins, and especially to gold, silver, and copper. Adam Smith gives what is now regarded as a classic account of the origin of money as beginning with the division of labour. Once people specialize, "every man lives by exchanging" and the disadvantages of this soon make themselves felt so that "in all countries . . . men seem to have been determined by irresistible reasons to give preference . . . to metals above every other commodity."[3] Eventually, according to this story, precious metal is what counts above all as money.

Credit notes, rather than bags of gold and silver, circulated for many centuries, and became more common in the eighteenth. The advantages of a notional equivalence of such and such a number of notes with such and such an amount of gold, something of intrinsic value, were vehemently argued by David Ricardo. Without such an equivalence, he said, money "would be exposed to all the fluctuations to which the ignorance of the issuers might subject it."[4] He had no problem with bank notes, so long as they were fully convertible into silver and gold.[5] In the United States the second president, John Adams, agreed. Every bank bill issued

3. Smith, *The Wealth of Nations*, 1.4, 21.
4. Ricardo, *The Works and Correspondence of David Ricardo*, vol. 4, 59.
5. So Galbraith, *Money*, 37.

in excess of stocks of silver and gold, he said, "represents nothing, and is therefore a cheat upon somebody."[6] Gold and silver, on this account, are intrinsically valuable and they are used to provide a universal equivalent for other goods.

The idea that money evolves from barter gains some plausibility from the fact that when currencies break down, as in Weimar Germany, barter is used to obtain goods. However, anthropologists tell us that no pure barter society has ever been found.[7] In fact, as Polanyi suggests, early societies seem to rely either on redistribution or on reciprocity. Contemporary anthropologists trace the origins of money either to wergeld, or to money of account.

Wergeld is payment to atone for crimes. The English word "to pay," Graeber tells us, comes from the word to pacify or appease.[8] When William the Conqueror arrived in Britain he found a sophisticated system of wergeld in place. Societies like Saxon Britain had tallies for offenses which involved commuting them with money: this was a way both of avoiding blood feuds, and establishing societal mores at the same time. What this shows, says Geoffrey Ingham, is that society is a moral community before it is a market. The codification of values necessary for wergeld to function means that money has its origin in law.[9]

The second approach argues that "money" began with accounting systems in the ancient world. Money, says David Graeber, "is not the product of commercial transactions. It was created by bureaucrats to keep track of resources and move things back and forth between departments."[10] In ancient Mesopotamia there was an accounting system that kept track of the relation between crops and labor. "Rents could be paid at the official silver rate, in barley, which was then redistributed by the central temple and place authorities to other workers. Money was the very means by which society was organized and managed by a hierarchy of value (money of account)

6. Cited in ibid., 29.
7. Graeber, *Debt*, 29.
8. Ibid., 60.
9. Ingham, *Nature of Money*, 93.
10. Graeber, *Debt*, 39.

which measured the flows and allocation of resources and the pivotal temple-farmer, creditor-debtor relation."[11] Rents and taxes were calculated in money of account but were paid in commodities and labor services. It follows that money is not a "thing," or a commodity, but a way of calculating proportions, of saying that one of x is equivalent to 6 of y.[12] Somewhat analogously Keith Hart suggests that money is "a source of collective and individual memory, a way of tracing our relations with people." Money is a convenient way of keeping track of our various relations.[13]

Whichever of these origins we accept, the key thing is that *money is primarily a social relation.* It is socially and politically constructed. In his magisterial account of "the rule of money," Karl Heinz Brodbeck explores this at length, arguing that we are socialized by both speech and money which, as Hamann already saw, run together. Subjectivity and rationality are altered once accounting through money becomes normal. Meaning is produced through socialization (in this Brodbeck is close to Findlay). All forms of knowledge, all forms of law and property, and the personal identity of people, are the products of a converging social process. The most important form of this process is communication. In this communications process calculation through money constitutes a strange new meaning. We see this in Greek philosophy and in natural science.[14] Money produces meaning and identity as social facts, as Shakespeare noted in Timon of Athens, in a passage quoted by Marx.[15] The value which is thus constituted

11. Ingham, *Nature of Money,* 95.

12. Graeber, *Debt,* 52.

13. Hart, *The Memory Bank,* 15.

14. Brodbeck, *Herrschaft,* 1006. Quite independently Seaford argues that both Greek philosophy and Greek tragedy are related to the emergence of a money economy, the former because it makes abstraction easier, the latter because it foregrounds the individual. *Money and the Early Greek Mind.*

15. Timon of Athens, Act IV, scene 3:

> Gold? yellow, glittering, precious gold? No, gods,
> I am no idle votarist: roots, you clear heavens!
> Thus much of this will make black white, foul fair,

is mere appearance, it is illusionary: "value" is marked by money, but then money comes to establish value.[16] It is only because everybody believes in the value of money, and so is compelled to measure their endeavors through money, that money has power as value—even if this power is grounded in a circular illusion that only rests on faith in this value.[17] This situation brings into being a society dominated by avarice, the subordination of all other forms to the value marked by money—this is its "lordship."[18]

The confusion between signifier and thing signified is at the heart of our difficulties with money. "Money" is the name we use to speak of our way of measuring social relations. It is a signifier.

> Wrong right, base noble, old young, coward valiant.
> Ha, you gods! why this? what this, you gods? Why, this
> Will lug your priests and servants from your sides,
> Pluck stout men's pillows from below their heads:
> This yellow slave
> Will knit and break religions, bless the accursed,
> Make the hoar leprosy adored, place thieves
> And give them title, knee and approbation
> With senators on the bench: this is it
> That makes the wappen'd widow wed again;
> She, whom the spital-house and ulcerous sores
> Would cast the gorge at, this embalms and spices
> To the April day again. Come, damned earth,
> Thou common whore of mankind, that put'st odds
> Among the rout of nations.

Marx comments "the divine power of money lies in its character as men's estranged, alienating, and self disposing species-nature. Money is the alienated ability of mankind." *Economic and Philosophic Manuscripts*, 131.

16. Brodbeck, *Herrschaft*, 369, 871. More narrowly David Harvey speaks of money as a representation of the value arising from the social relation between the laboring activities of millions of people around the world that requires material representation as it is, itself, immaterial and invisible. *Seventeen Contradictions*, 26.

17. Brodbeck, *Herrschaft*, 375.

18. Of course "Herrschaft" has to be translated "rule," but the stronger term "lordship," which is also possible, brings it into connection with Karl Barth's account of "the lordless powers" and has stronger implications of absolute rule.

But it becomes the thing signified. "Money" itself—whether gold and silver, coins, or numbers entered on a computer—becomes identical with value. This puts the cart before the horse. Value, socially determined, comes first. It is then signified in a thousand ways (in jewelery, fashion, architecture, etc.); "money" is the signifier used in exchange. The question is how to prevent this signifier becoming the signified.[19]

For "money" to operate as a signifier, the chartalist account of money argues, firm authorities are necessary: money rests on the authority of a particular state. "States confer the quality of valuableness by accepting . . . tokens as payment for taxes and using them to make their own purchases. Money is the measure and not the thing measured—i.e., it is abstract value. Moneyness is conferred by money of account which cannot be produced by the free play of economic interests in the market."[20] It is the power of the state that solves the problem of trust in large anonymous markets. It is social and political legitimacy that makes it possible to trust strangers.[21]

British bank notes "promise to pay the bearer" the sum of—whatever the note denominates, implying that we might be able to go to the Bank of England and obtain so many grammes of gold. This has been untrue since 1931, when the UK came off the gold standard. Better, Jackson and Dyson argue, to treat money as a token, issued by the state—the chartalist position. Notes, in fact, get their value from what they can be exchanged for in the economy.[22] In the US, notes and coins are not considered liabilities, but

19. In Sparta Lycurgus's rejection of gold and silver coinage, and the use of iron doused in vinegar for coins, was an attempt to keep money as a signifier. However, it was only possible due to the rejection of trade and the subjection of the helots. Our question is—how is it possible to have money as a signifier in a trading economy?

20. Ingham, *Nature of Money*, 49. Chartalism was itself a response to an earlier nineteenth-century idea that understood money as an expression of the national spirit. Brodbeck, *Herrschaft*, 147. Aquinas opts for a form of chartalism. *Summa Theologiae*, 2a 2ae 77.2ad2.

21. Ingham, *Nature of Money*, 74.

22. Jackson and Dyson, *Modernising Money*, 313.

as an asset of the federal reserve, and then of the holder—a more commonsensical position.

If social relations must be considered as the reality of money, what kind of relations are we thinking of? In contemporary rhetoric the operations of the market are founded on "trust" but Ingham draws attention to the role of coercion: "Flogging, imprisonment and branding with red hot coins were the penalties for not paying taxes in the money issued and accepted by the state."[23] That is to say, the social relation that is money is from the start one of inequality and power.

Graeber argues that the existence of virtual credit money and coinage oscillate throughout history. The dominance of coinage in the axial period is bound up with the need to pay armies—especially armies covering vast territories, like that of Alexander.[24] When coinage dominates, the social relationality of money is lost sight of, and it quickly becomes valuable in itself and people take to hoarding it instead, or using it to make more money. There is an obvious reason for doing this, because money is power, but, whether it takes the form of silver and gold, or of paper, it is a very fragile form of power, as the hoards that Romano British families buried in the fourth century, or the fortunes of Weimar or of the American industrial barons in 1929, remind us. One function of the Midas story is to remind us that money is not, in fact, intrinsically (i.e., as a commodity) valuable.

Money and debt

According to the myth that Adam Smith evidently accepted, "money" is essentially precious metal. For a long time now it has been realized that, as concerns modern money at any rate, this is nowhere near the truth. When banks make loans to customers, for example for mortgages, they create money. This is not money borrowed from savers, as many imagine. Without loans made to

23. Ingham, *Nature of Money*, 55, appealing to the work of Wray.

24. The drain on the State to pay armies is a key theme of Thucydides's *Peloponnesian War*.

people and debts incurred money is not, in the present system, created. For some time, 97 percent of money, at least in Britain, has been created in this way, by commercial banks, by way of loans.[25] Between 1970 and 2012 banks in the UK increased the money supply from £25 billion to £2050 billion, an eighty-two–fold increase. This was the effect on the money supply of a high demand for credit combined with a lack of regulation.[26] The worries Ricardo and Adams expressed, and which they sought to ward off by insisting on the convertibility of paper notes into gold, seems to be instantiated. "Money" is loans built on loans, "entirely abstract, and quite empty of meaning."[27] The rush by governments to bail out the banks was to keep this abstract architecture intact, to prevent a worldwide loss of faith in the financial system that would plunge society everywhere into chaos. The effect of this has been decades of "austerity," which have seen social spending slashed even as the "wealth" (i.e., money in the bank) of the richest 10 percent has spiraled upwards, as we saw in the last chapter.

The creation of money by commercial banks has given them a power that they never had before. They have become extremely wealthy—to the tune of £1 trillion worth of interest-bearing assets—and money is power. But also since the Bank of England guarantees bank deposits, the government effectively turns bank loans into state-issued money and so commercial banks, rather than the central bank, determine the money supply.[28]

Money is created as debt, and this involves relations of inequality and power, as David Graeber above all has emphasized. By and large when we talk of debt we think of owing money but we are also familiar with debts of gratitude, of honor, and so forth. Some anthropologists speak of "primordial debt"—the debt we owe simply for being alive, and to all previous generations—akin to the notion of the cultural inheritance that, I argued in the last chapter, underwrites an economy of grace.

25. Jackson and Dyson, *Modernising*, 48.
26. Ibid., 113.
27. Rowbotham, *Grip of Death*, 13.
28. Jackson and Dyson, *Modernising*, 80.

Graeber is certainly right to highlight the role debt plays in religion, and above all in Christianity. Jesus teaches his disciples to pray, "Forgive us our debts as we forgive our debtors." In the eleventh century Anselm of Canterbury constructed a hugely influential theology of the atonement based on the idea of satisfying debts—a debt which could only be paid by a "God-man." In this theology all humans are in debt, but God pays the debt for them (a payment which requires a death) and this is the reality of grace. The religious appeal to debt rests on the ubiquity of "owing" people something: I owe my life to my parents; my education or training to my community; my food to the labor of others, and so forth. Graeber points out that Mafiosi build their empires by putting people into their debt. We can then think of society as a complex network of debts, which it is relatively easy to signify in money. As he argues, a profound ambivalence attends the idea of debt: on the one hand, I owe all the most important things, and ultimately my life, to others. On the other hand, debt keeps me in subjection. If I am in debt I am not your equal: to restore equality I need to repay my debt. A debt, Graeber argues, is simply a promise, and society is a series of promises that we make to one another. Surely, he asks, if democracy is to mean anything it would mean everyone has an equal say in what sort of promises we make as a society, how we weigh them against each other, and, when circumstances change, which have to be honored and which can be renegotiated. As it is, not all of us have to pay our debts: only some of us do.[29]

But are societies necessarily built on debt? Graeber proposes that there are three ways of organizing society, which he calls "actually existing communism," exchange, and hierarchy. What he means by "communism" is the fact that people will, in most circumstances, do to others as they would be done by—what Kropotkin referred to as "mutual aid" and what Colin Tudge argues for on the basis of how our DNA works, as I illustrated in the previous chapter. In this situation the very idea of paying for services is offensive. He cites the story of an Inuit hunter who rejects the very idea of payment and says, "Up in our country

29. Graeber, *Promises Promises*, Lecture 10.

we are human! And since we are human we help each other. We don't like to hear anybody say thanks for that. What I get today you may get tomorrow. Up here we say that by gifts one makes slaves and by whips one makes dogs."[30] Rather than seeing himself as human because he could make economic calculations the hunter insisted that being truly human meant refusing to make such calculations.[31] This is a recognition of the interdependence that grounds all human society, which does not have to be construed in terms of debt. We do not ask who owes what to whom: in functioning (as opposed to dysfunctional) families, this is how relationships operate. It is money, says Graeber, which distinguishes a debt from an obligation or a promise. Money tabulates debts. "A debt is just the perversion of a promise. It is a promise corrupted by both math and violence."[32]

In the alternative proposals for money that I suggest at the end of the chapter I am asking whether money necessarily tabulates debts. I noted above that conventionally money and banking relies on trust, but that this rhetoric conceals the exercise of power. In some alternative proposals, however, trust, or mutual aid, is reinstated as the meaning of money. I shall be asking whether these alternative proposals might be realizable.

As opposed to "communism," exchange is the situation where everyone keeps accounts and where the dependence that follows the incurring of a debt can be canceled when the debt is repaid. The logic of the market is the logic of exchange—except that inequality is written in to all the societies we know, and market societies increase inequality.

Hierarchy, meanwhile, is formed when debt is unpayable, and, as in feudalism, only support or esteem is possible by way of return.[33] These three forms of relationship, Graeber argues, are not accounts of different types of society, but logics that are al-

---

30. Graeber, *Debt*, 79. R. L. Stevenson depicts a similar ethic amongst the eighteenth-century Highland clans in *Kidnapped*.

31. Graeber, *Debt*, 79.

32. Ibid., 391.

33. Ibid., 119.

ways operating in any society. On the other hand, Graeber shows that there have been, continue to be, and therefore there could be in the future, societies that are not founded on the payment of debt and exchange.

Under the current monetary system, as we saw in the previous section, for there to be money there must also be debt, and since the economy does not function without money it is in fact predicated on debt. Money, says Ingham, cannot be said to exist without the simultaneous existence of a debt it can discharge. The origin of the power of money is in the promise between the issuer and the user of money. Money would disappear if everyone paid his or her debt.[34]

This point about the nature of money is instantiated, Graeber argues, when we have "national debts," in which case "money" is circulating government debt. Were the debt paid off those who control money would be in a quandary, as Alan Greenspan realized when faced with a potential budget surplus. Hence the ambivalence of politicians, who both speak of cutting down the national debt but also need to maintain it. Debts today, especially in the debate about austerity, are "power dressed up in a mantle of morality."[35]

So government debt is needed, but it is also stoked up by the fact that bank lending to purchase assets such as housing or land, which have either a limited supply or an absolute limit, push up prices and create asset bubbles. People therefore need to borrow more and more, until the bubble bursts, when they are left with negative equity. As Jackson and Dyson point out, recessions also increase private debt, as people need to borrow more in order to make ends meet. "This trend can be seen in the UK with the increasing prominence of payday loans and similar schemes in the wake of the financial crisis and subsequent recession."[36]

The whole system of money as debt is ecologically unsustainable. Debt is a claim on future production, and it grows according to arithmetical rules. Future production, in contrast, confronts

34. Ingham, *Nature of Money*, 83.

35. Graeber, *Promises Promises,* lecture 10.

36. Jackson and Dyson, *Modernising,* 159.

ecological limits and cannot possibly keep pace.[37] As money (i.e., debt) is created, nonrenewable energy resources are depleted. As the EROI ratio worsens we continually generate less and less GDP for each additional debt pound or dollar.

The problem is that while debt can endure forever; wealth (understood in its Aristotelian sense as that which sustains life) cannot, because its physical dimension is subject to the destructive force of entropy. Since wealth cannot grow as fast as debt, the one to one relation between the two will at some point be broken— there must be some repudiation or cancellation of debt.[38]

Usury

The Jubilee laws in Deuteronomy and Leviticus, now well known through the work of the Jubilee debt campaign, are the Israelite version of debt remission provisions that were familiar throughout the ancient world. Usury was banned because it lay behind the growth of debt slavery. The remission codes were a way of insisting that any workable economy had to return and be based on "the things that make for life." Usury was, and is, forbidden, says Berry, "because the dispossession and privation of some should not be regarded by others as an economic opportunity, for that is contrary to neighbourliness; it destroys the community. And the greed that destroys the community also destroys the land. What the Bible proposes is a moral economy the standard of which is the health of properties belonging to God."[39]

The early Church Fathers, followed by Muslim teachers, all banned interest outright.[40] However, as states became centralized,

37. Costanza et al., "Building a sustainable and desirable economy," 137.

38. Daly, Beyond Growth, 179.

39. Berry, What are People For?, 99.

40. Usury contravenes Scripture and breaks all the laws of charity (Tertullian C. Marc 4.17; Cyprian Strom 2.18; Chrysostom Hom 57 on Matt; Nyssa Oratorio c Usuarios). Augustine regards it as a crime (Augustine, On Ps 128). The Council of Nicea (325) ordered usurious clergy to be deposed, and the Council of Carthage (345) condemned its practice by laity. Later Councils

in medieval Europe, so rulers, and even popes, found the need to borrow money. Aquinas, in the thirteenth century, set the tone for much later teaching in repeating Aristotle's condemnation of usury as unnatural. Money is made for exchange, and to lend it on interest is to sell what does not exist. This leads to inequality and is contrary to justice.[41] Though usury is sinful, however, it is not sinful to take a loan so long as this is done for a good cause.[42] (This prevarication enabled Jewish moneylenders to be simultaneously employed and vilified.) Developing economies soon made it difficult to exist without taking interest. In the fifteenth century, Franciscan schemes to help the poor found it necessary to charge a small amount of interest to cover expenses. Despite this, the medieval canonists all condemn usury and place it alongside adultery, theft, and murder. It was allowed only to cover actual losses, or the profit forgone by making the loan.

In 1524 Luther's great tract *On Trade and Usury* appealed to the medieval tradition. Usury is "grossly contrary to God's word, contrary to reason and every sense of justice, and springs from sheer wantonness and greed." Twenty years later, however, and writing from the merchant city of Geneva, Calvin argued that the biblical texts relating to usury have to be understood in their context, that conditions have changed, and that restrictions on usury were too severe. Both Protestants and Catholics now distinguished between loans for production and consumption, and argued that in the former case capital was productive. Usury was neither contrary to Scripture nor to natural law, but must be used only under the strictest conditions so that the poor are not oppressed. Benedict XIV reiterated scholastic warnings against usury in 1745, and usury laws remained on the statute books throughout Europe for another two centuries (in England until 1854), but fell everywhere

---

reiterated this, the third Lateran Council (1179) denying usurers the sacrament or Christian burial, and the second Council of Lyons (1274) forbidding the letting of property to foreign usurers.

41. Aquinas, *Summa Theologiae*, 2.2 Qu 78, Art 1; Aristotle, *Politics*, 1.3,1.10.

42. Aquinas, *Summa Theologiae*, 2.2 Qu 78 art 4.

into desuetude. Within Protestantism attacks on usury ceased and the market place came to be seen as a moral battlefield where the righteous could prove their mettle. When Bentham wrote his *Defence of Usury* in 1787 he argued that money was on a par with any other form of goods. When not legalized it forces people into criminal practices, and the usury laws expose a useful class of people to unnecessary suffering and disgrace.

The principal justification of usury is pragmatic. Appeals are made to the tremendous advances achieved by capitalism. These could not have happened, it is argued, without interest, which is necessary to attract investors to make their capital available. Interest can be regarded as a charge on services, or a kind of danger money for putting capital at risk. But Aquinas's contention that usury leads to the growth of inequality has been confirmed by careful contemporary studies. Brodbeck argues that interest institutionalizes avarice, and represents a systematic misuse of the trust on which society is based.[43] The present operations of interest lead to a systematic transfer of wealth from those who have less to those who have more, and the need to repay debt both destroys societies, through the imposition of "austerity," and leads to the reckless consumption of natural resources (to meet interest payments). A fair rate of interest would have to be determined by responsible bankers, acting also as community members, in the context of their community, local nature, and the local economy.[44] Such a determination, says Berry, can take place only in a bank which is locally owned, conforming in scale to the size and needs of the local community, and by bankers who are aware that the prosperity of the bank is not and can never be separated from the prosperity of the community.[45] This is analogous to Keynes's argument that interest should be kept low for productive enterprises (but high for speculative ones).

43. Brodbeck, *Herrschaft*, ix.
44. Berry, *What Matters?*, 13.
45. Ibid., 14.

Speculation

The classic way of making money out of money was through interest, but with the rise of modern banking financial speculation has often been more profitable, though at the expense of frequent frauds, bubbles, and collapses. According to Varoufakis it was the US Federal Bank's decision to offer high interest rates that attracted global finance to invest its money in New York that launched the advent of finance capitalism, which in turn led to the frenzy of derivative trading in the 1990s and following.[46] These days hedge funds are a major way of maximizing returns on investment. To "hedge" is to seek to reduce risk whilst getting a good return on investment. Normally, when people buy shares they hope they will rise in value—that would be the classic story of investing in what seems a good scheme. But hedge funds often "short sell," i.e., sell stock in the hope the price will fall and then buy it back at a lower price. The hedge fund keeps the difference. Hedge funds trade in equities, foreign currencies, bonds, or commodities. This form of betting can bring whole countries to their knees, as George Soros did with the United Kingdom in 1992.[47]

The difference between the way hedge funds and Ponzi schemes operate is not as great as might be imagined. Ponzi schemes (named after a convicted fraudster Charles Ponzi) get people to invest, pay handsome dividends in the hope of attracting other investors, and then at some point make off with the loot—though Minsky claimed that Ponzi schemes were not necessarily criminal. Certainly Bernie Madoff, who ran the biggest Ponzi scheme ever, and ended up with 150 years in jail, never planned to scarper. Well known on Wall Street, he attracted vast investments, but was unable to keep up the promised returns. He was paying dividends out of the new investments he attracted. When these began to falter (because of loss of confidence in the market at large) the whole scheme collapsed. The problem with the schemes

---

46. Varoufakis, *And the Weak Suffer What They Must?*, 87. Varoufakis uses the myth of the Minotaur to describe it.

47. Ibid., 128–29.

is that what is owed to investors can only be paid if the assets can be sold for more than what is owed. The scheme depends on confidence—as does all speculation. Nick Leeson, who brought about the downfall of Barings, and also ended up in jail, was a highly successful trader—but he got his bets wrong, or, to put it more accurately, he was wrong-footed by the Tokyo earthquake.

Financial deregulation by most nations now allows fund managers to make instant international investments and withdraw profits at will, in any country, in any sector, and in any company anywhere in the world. This investment is often short term—from a few hours to a few days or weeks. Firms spend vast sums on better internet technology because it enables them to speculate on foreign exchanges almost simultaneously.[48] Stock markets no longer exist primarily to fund industrial investment, Michael Rowbotham points out, but to extract wealth from the productive economy. Hedge funds act in a predatory way.

> Asset stripping has destroyed thousands of smaller companies with a sound financial basis, which were producing a livelihood to many honest people who have then been cast into unwarranted poverty. The market in stocks and shares, far from being a justifiable and respected mechanism for the distribution and joint ownership of industry, has become little more than an arena for gambling, manipulation, dishonesty, deception and rank fraud.[49]

The 2008 crash was caused by the practice of bundling mortgages together into "collateralized debt obligations" and then selling these off as secure investments.[50] Those in charge of the money markets insisted that nothing could go wrong. Goldman Sachs

48. Rowbotham, *Grip of Death*, 164.

49. Ibid., 166.

50. The way these work is that the bank receives an up-front payment, and the investors receive a stream of income over the life of the financial instrument. "The bank's profit comes from fee for arranging the loans, instead of collecting the interest as the loan is repaid. When you securitise a mortgage you don't care about the risk, because you are going to pass it off." Jackson and Dyson, *Modernising*, 89,

said that the possibility of default happening was comparable to winning the lottery twenty-one or twenty-two times in a row. That this happened twice in nine years, comments Mark Blyth, shows that these claims are nonsense.[51]

As we saw in the first chapter, Antony Giddens believes hedge funds are an important part of our response to climate change, but this kind of speculation trades precisely on the distinction which Aristotle made between the real economy and money as a mathematical function that has no limit. This is illustrated by current foreign exchange dealing, which is worth fifteen times world GDP.[52] What are called "derivatives" allow banks to trade things such as movements in interest rates or currencies. A derivative is a contract, a bet that pays out based on how a particular asset performs over a particular time period.[53] *Derivative* is the proper word, Richard Murphy argues, because it drags resources from the real economy to those who manipulate the cash, which is then siphoned off to tax havens. This cash can be used to undermine the value of a currency, as happened in the UK in 1992, or to force a change in a government's policies by aggressive intervention in bond markets.[54] Internally it distorts both the labor and the housing markets. It is, says Murphy, a truly feral economy that undermines genuine democratic possibilities of tax and regulation. The power the new form of finance capital has given to bankers and speculators has, as Ann Pettifor notes, led to a situation where democracies are held to ransom by offshore capital and corporations. "The effective capture of the supine nation state by global bankers and financiers means that taxpayers are obliged to finance and maintain public legal and judicial systems in the service of . . . private wealth."[55]

51. Blyth, *Austerity*, 33.
52. Murphy, *Courageous State*, 199.
53. Blyth, *Austerity*, 27.
54. Murphy, *Courageous State*, 201.
55. Pettifor, *Production*, 38.

Hyman Minsky has argued that the creation of money as debt is inherently unstable.[56] Periods of stability, he argued, led to greater risk taking on debt—that is, stability was itself destabilizing. There are psychological reasons for this. Success boosts confidence, and long periods of stability lead to overconfidence—commentators on the South Sea Bubble were already aware of this. Ben Bernanke, at the Federal Reserve, talked of "the great moderation" months before the 2008 crash. This was an example of 'disaster myopia', the systemic underestimation by decision-makers of the chances of disaster or collapse.[57]

This way of operating an economy is deeply damaging. As Thomas Piketty has shown, it leads to vast increases in inequality, and gives us a world where the top 1 percent or 0.1 percent effectively controls the levers of all global wealth and power; it results in the imposition of austerity which can have devastating results for millions of people, as we see in the example of Greece; and it lies behind the growth that in turn pushes us over the limits of planetary boundaries.

Money, wealth, and value

"There is no wealth but life," said Ruskin. We are accustomed to say of a person that they are "wealthy" if they own houses, posh cars, and have large bank accounts. But it was another function of the Midas parable to point out that money is not wealth—it is parasitic on life; it does not produce it. Those who speak of "prosperity" and "economic growth" in a world of degraded farms, forests, ecosystems, and watersheds, polluted air, failing families, and perishing communities have not understood this.[58]

In the second chapter I set out John Findlay's argument about the origin of values in the way in which people communicate wants and assign importance to them, a social process which results in

56. Ingham, *Nature of Money*, 161.
57. Jackson and Dyson, *Modernising*, 132.
58. Berry, *What Matters?*, 181.

"a relatively fixed firmament of values." How does money relate to this realm of value? An obvious starting point for answering this question is to think about gold, which has always been not just a measure and store of value, as money is supposed to be, but has been ascribed value in itself. This is not entirely irrational. Gold is precious because it is beautiful and doesn't oxidize, and it is used in jewelry, and thus says something about the ego, attractiveness, and then, in hierarchical societies, about marks of class distinction. Thus, the origin of value would be the ego. Very early, however, moralists wanted to say that true value was found in virtue rather than in appearance, which called the worth of gold into question. So gold is taken to represent a spurious, superficial value.

Locke, followed by Adam Smith and Marx, located the source of value in labor, which is to say, in the life of a human being. In its origins money of account was directly related to human work and subsistence. In ancient Mesopotamia the accounting system was based on the value equivalence of the shekel weight of silver and the monthly consumption unit of a gur of barley. "It seems probable that this equivalence was based on the redistributed barley ration necessary to sustain a labourer and his family."[59] In other words, the fundamental value was the life of that class that kept everybody else alive. Money (the silver shekel) was a way of measuring that. To treat labor as a (and not necessarily the) source of value is not irrational—in fact in one way it conforms to Ruskin's dictum that wealth is life. The problem is that in all class societies different people's time is assessed at completely different levels and money comes to signify that difference of value.[60] This means that all sorts of other factors supervene on the idea of labor as the source of value—under what Marx calls "primitive accumulation" this would be armed force, which quickly congeals into hereditary hierarchies and especially monarchies.[61]

59. Ingham, *Nature of Money*, 95.

60. The idea of a citizen's income, paid simply in virtue of being a member of the community, and currently being trialed in Finland, is designed to overcome this problem, at least to some degree.

61. The medieval system of the just wage was a recognition of labor as a

Use values are often suggested as the origin of value, and therefore of wealth. "Wealth" might be fertile land, clean water and air, ecological health, and the capacity of nature to renew itself.[62] Derivatively value attaches to things (e.g., agricultural instruments) or practices (farming) that help sustain life. But as the Mesopotamian example shows, and as remains true to this day, such fundamental use values have rarely commanded much respect, or at least attracted much financial remuneration. Some argue that since all productive activity comes from some form of energy, then energy is the true wealth, the true source of value, and money and financial instruments are simply markers for it, a claim on a certain amount of energy.[63] But this is too reductively materialist an account of productivity.

Today pleasure is an important value, as signified by the high earnings of "entertainers" and the astronomic prices paid for art. Again, through the centuries this has been the exception and not the rule. Velazquez, one of the greatest artists who ever lived, sat with the Court Dwarfs on public occasions, and the Emperor addressed Haydn as "Es"—the form used for children. Only just over a century ago Van Gogh could die in penury.

Money is supposed to be a measure and store of value. But the crash of 1929, and the buried hoards of Romano British society, both show that money (i.e., cash, the signifier) cannot store value. When we speak of money as a measure of value what we are thinking of is "exchange value"—the measuring and relative valuing

---

source of value but the accompanying belief in a hierarchical society nullified it.

Attempts to find a just wage and a just price have never been quite abandoned. Until 1994, in Britain, there was a Milk Marketing Board that brought together leaders of the dairy industry and government ministers each autumn to fix the price of milk for the coming year. What was hammered out was a living wage for dairy farmers; what was considered to be a fair reward for working 365 days a year, ten hours a day. Under the nostrums of neoliberalism the Milk Marketing Board was considered a bar to competition, and abolished. The result has been that the dairy industry has gone into free fall and milk is sold for less than the price of bottled water. The minimum wage and the living wage are both nods to labor as the source of value.

62. Berry, *What Matters?*, 4.

63. Hagens, "Energy, credit, and the end of growth," 30.

THE WORLD MADE OTHERWISE: PRACTICES

of chalk and cheese. The problem is that when we use money to do this money quickly becomes itself the source of value—signifier becomes signified. It then comes to determine all aspects of policy-making, as we see with "austerity." "Decisions on the use of land and other natural resources, on methods of childcare, care in the community, education and care of the environment are based upon the availability of money."[64]

David Harvey argues that money and value go together. This is because without money and the commodity transactions it facilitates, value could not exist as an immaterial social relation. In other words, according to him, value could not form without the aid of the material representation (money) and the social practices of exchange. The relation between money and value is dialectical and co-evolutionary—they both emerge together—rather than causal.[65] Historically this is impossible—Homer , for example, and probably some parts of the Hebrew Bible, long predate the invention of cash, which is presumably what Harvey means by a "material representation." And, as I argued in the second chapter, value precedes the emergence of money, and the fundamental values—life, freedom, human equality—are independent of it. The cultural codes which express value go back to the very dawn of humanity, long before even money of account.[66]

64. Hutchinson, *Money*, 51. As she points out, the education system is then geared to reinforce belief that money is value,.

65. Harvey, *Seventeen Contradictions*, 27.

66. The need to affix value to something material has a curious relation to the theological idea of the "real presence" in the Eucharist. It is clear in the Messianic Writings that what is important is the network of relationships and the vision according to which the community lives. The community centered on a story which it retold around a meal. Those unable to be present through illness were included by sending them a food parcel afterwards, as Justin Martyr tells us (*Apology*, 1.67). In the eighth century AD, however, we get the first controversy about how the bread and wine used in the Eucharist should be understood. Some people want to say that they are "really" the body and blood of Christ, and we begin to get stories of bleeding hosts and all the rest of it. This is fetishism exactly as Marx understood it. Where what once mattered were the reconciliatory relationships of the community (ascribed to "Spirit"), value is now attached to an object, which must be kept in a locked box—and it is this object which is then taken to the sick, and later adored. This form of fetishism

A cynic, said Oscar Wilde, is someone who knows the price of everything and the value of nothing—a remark that has long been applied to economists. The point about real wealth is not that it needs vast vaults to hoard it, but that it is priceless—it cannot be brought under the money calculus. To do so is to make a fundamental mistake. Those who wish to defend forests or fields by putting a price on them fail to see this. They turn them into commodities like any other, and sooner or later they will meet the fate of commodities, and be parcelled up, sold, and exploited. "When everything has a price and the price is made endlessly variable by an economy without a stable relation to necessity or to real goods, then everything is disconnected from history, knowledge, respect, and affection—from anything at all that might preserve it—and so is implicitly eligible to be ruined."[67]

Marx argued that under the money system what counts are commodities and not people. What connects people is the cash nexus. Marx calls this reification. "Things" determine social relations and thus dominate the life of society. Not only does this reify, says Marx—i.e. treat people as objects—but it is fetishism—the primitive worship of things. Once the money system has become dominant people cannot penetrate the reifying process. The money form conceals the social character of private labor and the social relations between producers. Money becomes the direct incarnation of all human labor.[68]

The confusion in capitalism as to whether use value or exchange value was fundamental was one of the reasons for the development of a purely subjective theory of value. Already in the nineteenth century Carl Menger claimed that exchange value was all that there was, and this was purely subjective.[69] Nietzsche an-

---

is still with us, though perhaps changes in the understanding of money will lead to changes here too.

67. Berry, *What Matters?*, 8.

68. In this connection Marx quotes Revelation 17:13 and 13:17: "These are of one mind and give over their power and authority to the beast. . . . And no one can buy or sell unless he has the mark, that is the name of the beast or the number of its name."

69. Brodbeck, *Herrschaft*, 660.

nounced the death of God, and therefore the end of all traditional values. Henceforth the "noble" human being was to understand himself as the source of all value.[70]

Value is so capricious, says Keith Hart, that it can be whatever people will pay for something that catches their fancy. "Money and art, especially when exchanged for each other, rest on values that are insubstantial or only as substantial as the shifting desires of the people who exchange them. Money, like art, is subjective."[71] To fix value in precious metals is an attempt to escape this subjectivity, but the absurdity of it constantly strikes people, as in Timon's speech, quoted earlier. We can see this as soon as we start to compare prices, asking, for example, how many pounds of potatoes, or small saloon cars, or paintings by Chagall, a Trident submarine is "worth." The language of value simply disintegrates before these comparisons.

The confusion between money and value, the fact that money quickly moves from signifying value to being value, is behind Jesus' warning that it is impossible to serve both God and Mammon (Matt 6:24). "Mammon" is money as the source of value, taking a person over and changing their values, centering them on power and prestige.[72] In a money economy, says Brodbeck, it is not that religious and moral orientations disappear, but they are subsumed like everything else under the striving for money. Virtually all religions, he says, have capitulated to money, and we find in all of them clear traces of the way a very earthly god has displaced the God believed in.[73]

"Mammon," says Walter Wink, must be understood as a set of delusional assumptions that embraces us and gives us our worldview. We cannot serve both God and Mammon because money functions as the core of an alternative belief system. Prayer consists in time, attention, and devotion but when all this is given to money then we have idolatry. The prohibition of idolatry, the

70. Nietzsche, *Beyond Good and Evil,* para. 260.

71. Hart, *Memory Bank,* 237.

72. Pieris, *An Asian Theology of Liberation,* 15–16.

73. Brodbeck, *Herrschaft,* 900–1.

insistence on monotheism, were not doctrinal niceties, but rooted in an awareness of the way in which making values not rooted in the living God destroyed both individual and society.

How to address the corruption of value that follows from a money economy? Since money is supposedly a measure of value, Philip Goodchild proposes that in any economy the Central Bank should have a committee that would assign values, a sort of marketing board extended over the whole economy. The problem with this proposal is that its model is still the bureaucratic or technocratic one of a committee of experts who would do the evaluation for society as a whole. We saw in chapter 5 that Christiano grounds human dignity on the fact that all humans are "experts in the realm of value." Goodchild says, in a somewhat similar way, that the capacity to make effective evaluations is an intrinsic good that all should desire. Just as, in Fishkin and Van Reybrouck's proposals, committees appointed by lot would propose legislation, so evaluation committees could propose "evaluative credits"—effectively saying what labor and goods were worth.[74] Michael Albert's worker and industrial boards, setting wages, prices, and the desired amount of production, effectively function like this. What this proposal does is to take seriously the notion of "money" as a measure of value. "Money" (i.e., whatever unit we choose to signify value) is nothing but a signifier. If value were democratically assigned it would not be left to "the market," which, as we saw in the last chapter, is actually a way of seeing that the strong flourish "and the weak suffer what they must." This proposal, if adopted, would subsume money to value, instead of the other way around. Since money is a convention, there is no reason why this should not happen. To dismiss this as ludicrous is simply to insist that the subordination of society to "the market" which, as Polanyi says, is a very recent phenomenon, must continue forever—or at least until a six-degree temperature rise makes all life—even the life of hedge funds and stockmarkets—those "mortal gods"—impossible. As it happens, all over the world there are many attempts—some very well established—either to conceive money differently or to

74. Goodchild, *The Theology of Money*, 247.

organize monetary affairs differently. It is to these I turn in the last four sections of this chapter.

Keeping money local

Between 1925 and 1930 the Swedish economist Brynjolf Bjorset recorded over 2,000 schemes for monetary reform.[75] We live in a similar period today. There is a huge literature on "alternative money," and a good many experiments. J. K. Galbraith thought that all such schemes were on a hiding to nothing. "There are some economic lessons that are never learned," he wrote:

> One is the need for the most profound suspicion of innovation in matters concerning money and more generally the field of finance. The thought persists that there must surely be some as yet undiscovered way of solving great social problems without pain, but the simple fact is that there is not. Ingenious monetary and financial designs, without known exception, turn out to be, if not innocuous, then frauds on the public or, frequently, on their perpetrators themselves.[76]

But why should we accept this? Money is a social creation. It has in fact changed profoundly since the abandonment of the gold standard in 1971. Why should we believe that in this area of human experience nothing can change? Given the enormously destructive nature of modern finance, surely some better way of organizing things can be found? If money is a social convention it can be changed. If we keep the current debt-based monetary system, financial crises will continue to occur, with the costs passed on to ordinary people and businesses. There is no justification for this when the changes that need to be made are both beneficial and relatively simple to enact.[77]

---

75. Rowbotham, *Grip of Death*, 212.

76. Galbraith, *History*, 99.

77. Jackson and Dyson, *Modernising*, 283.

I shall consider three sets of alternatives to present arrangements, beginning with experiments in various kinds of local currency.

Many towns and cities have Local Exchange Trading Schemes (LETS). These schemes enable people to assess value between each other. A local "currency" is denominated (in Exeter it is an "Exe") and people offer goods or services through which they earn Exes, which can then be used to purchase the other goods and services on offer.[78] Keith Hart thinks this might be a model for the future. With the internet, he says, one can imagine swaps taking place within networks of infinite size and global scope. This would enable people to engage in direct exchange.[79] Of course one problem with this is that it is a way of avoiding tax, but LETS schemes have argued that their currency is not really money, but a way of recording nonmarket exchanges between friends, not unlike domestic services within the family.[80] Were LETS schemes to become general, any government would need to find a way either to tax them, or to find an alternative tax base (for example by taxing polluting activity). It is also true that LETS schemes highlight the difficulty of establishing value without any accepted measure. How much is any particular kind of work "worth"? Every LETS exchange raises this question and in my experience, in negotiating value all the usual power dynamics come into play.[81]

Time banks operate in a somewhat similar way to LETS. People list their skills—including especially caring and listening skills. When they give an hour this is registered centrally and people can then participate in an informal economy. It is another

78. In Exeter LETs categories include arts and crafts, building and decorating services, children's activities and care, domestic and household, including cleaning and hairdressing, food preparation, and some small holding produce, tool hire, including a chain saw, ladders, and a sailing dinghy, various forms of alternative medicine, lifts and removals, and some forms of tuition.

79. Hart, *Memory Bank*, 279.

80. Ibid., 282.

81. Ingham argues that as the LETS chits cannot store value there is less incentive to drive a hard bargain, which in turn further inhibits the production of stable prices. Ingham, *Nature of Money*, 185.

way of trying, first, to operate outside the logic of the market, and second, to recognize as valuable skills that the market does not value. Andrews Simms gives the example of a time bank operating in three British prisons where prisoners can use credits to earn different types of support for themselves or their families.[82] In Ithaca, in the US, an hour is valued slightly above the minimum wage, and participants are encouraged to value their services equally, though some professionals are allowed to charge more. The idea is to keep value within the community by tying transactions to a close circuit motivated by local interest.

The objection to this is that it simply formalizes, and brings within an economic orbit, the practice of good neighborliness, which still in many communities is what makes life worth living. Do we really need "schemes" to promote this?

82. Simms, *Cancel the Apocalypse,* 147.

Many towns and cities are experimenting with local currencies. In Britain this includes Totnes, Bristol, Lewes, Exeter, and Brixton.[83] Local currencies, it is argued, lead to greater social inclusion, more jobs, stronger local governance, more civic engagement, and bet-

83. Britain's second city, Birmingham, and Liverpool, are now considering a local currency.

ter health outcomes. The aim of these currencies is to boost the local economy, to keep money circulating within that, rather than leaching out to multinational board rooms through supermarkets and chain stores. Local currencies don't replace conventional money but lubricate parts of the social economy where the cost or lack of formal currency is an obstacle.[84]

The problem with such schemes, as Geoffrey Ingham puts it, is that real social money should give access to education, healthcare, and housing.

The creation of extensive monetary spaces, he says, requires social and political relations that necessarily exist independently of any network of exchange transactions. The extension of monetary relations across time and space requires impersonal trust and legitimacy. Historically this has been the work of states.[85]

Beyond this, Andrew Simms draws attention to the priority of the big banks over local or community banks—particularly obvious in the United Kingdom. In Germany the small or community banking sector has 70 percent of the market. These local banks, he points out, are the foundations of Europe's dominant economy. In the United States, Oregon, Washington, Massachusetts, Maryland, Illinois, Hawaii, and Virginia have all either produced legislation to establish their own state banks or are investigating doing so.[86]

Two banks that grew out of response to the 1930s Depression offer particularly impressive examples of alternatives to conventional banking. In Switzerland two businesses started a "Wirtschaftsring Genossenschaft," the WIR (basically a "business friendly society") to help each other out when credit was hard, or impossible, to obtain. Its purpose is to encourage participating members to put their buying power at each other's disposal and keep it circulating within their ranks, thereby providing members with additional sales volume. As far as possible members trade with each other. Today it has 62,000 members and assets of 3 billion Swiss Francs. It is credited with helping to keep the

84. Ibid.,146.

85. Ingham, *Nature*, 187.

86. Simms, *Apocalypse*, 163.

Swiss economy stable. It does not charge interest and so does not propel growth. It does not seek to replace the Swiss Franc, but understands itself strictly as a complementary currency of mutual help and, it has been argued, such a scheme could be of immense value in countries strapped by "austerity," like Greece. It is a way of circumventing interest and to that extent does something to take power from the central banks. In this scheme the WIR Franc is a signifier. It only works, of course, because it is matched against the conventional Swiss Franc, but this is not so much to do with conventional money as value but with chartalism—with the trust engendered by a particular political community. This is ultimately what "money" is—a signifier of the confidence and cooperative nature of a community, an affirmation of faith in its productive capacity. Conventional economics gets this precisely in reverse—it begins with the amount of "money" a community can produce and then says whether it is healthy or not. This disconnects money from real value and is ultimately (through producing climate change, despoiling the planet, and wrecking communities) ruinous.

The Land, Labour and Capital (JAK) Bank was started in Denmark in 1931, for similar reasons, but closed by the government after a couple of years. It restarted in Sweden after World War II and now has 38,000 members and savings of 130 million euros. It makes interest-free loans to members administered through branches staffed largely by volunteers. The board of directors is elected annually by members, who are each allowed only one share in the JAK bank. Subscribers accumulate savings points rather than interest, and these are used to determine eligibility for loans. The bank is a non-profit organization, and the recipients of loans are charged an administration fee to cover wages and related costs. The main point is "to promote dialogue about how to achieve a fair and sustainable economy, as much as it is about financing loans through savings."[87] Both the WIR and the JAK reestablish money as a form of mutual aid founded on trust. Though dependent on national currencies, or the Euro, they nevertheless give us a clue to

87. Hart, *Memory Bank*, 285.

thinking of a world where money might not be "mammon" but a positive and creative form of social relation.

Similar schemes are to be found in Latin America. What we find, when the many subtly varying approaches to making our own money system are put together on a map, writes Andrew Simms, is a hidden architecture of a different way to run an economy. The question is, he asks, whether this hidden architecture can accommodate and bear the weight of our livelihoods should conventional banking fail.[88]

Positive money

In 1865 Abraham Lincoln addressed the US Senate thus:

> Government, possessing the power to create and issue currency and credit as money and enjoying the right to withdraw both currency and credit from circulation by taxation and otherwise, need not and should not borrow capital at interest as a means of financing governmental work and public enterprise. The government should create, issue and circulate all the currency and credit needed to satisfy the spending power of the government and the buying power of consumers. The privilege of creating and issuing money is not only the supreme prerogative of government, but it is the government's greatest creative opportunity.
>
> By the adoption of these principles, the long felt want for a uniform medium will be satisfied. The taxpayers will be saved immense sums of interest, discounts and exchanges. The financing of all public enterprises, the maintenance of stable government and order progress, and the conduct of the Treasury will become matters of practical administration. The people can and will be furnished with a currency as safe as their own government. Money will cease to be the master and become the servant of humanity. Democracy will rise superior to the money power. [89]

88. Simms, *Apocalypse*, 149.
89. Rowbotham, *Grip of Death*, 221.

What Lincoln was proposing has become known today as "positive money," which means that governments, and not commercial banks, create money (which is what people intuitively believe is the case anyway). The question is how to stop the power to create money being abused and to that end Andrew Jackson and Ben Dyson propose an independent body, the money creation committee, which would take decisions over how much new money should be created, while the elected government of the day should make decisions over how that money will be spent.[90] In Britain the Committee would include the governor and two deputy governors of the Bank of England but other members of the committee would be vetted by a cross-party group of MPs. Parliament (rather than the Executive) would therefore exercise oversight over the creation of money. The central bank would create new money via the MCC and lend it to commercial banks, which would then lend this money to businesses in the productive economy (but not for mortgages or financial speculation).[91] Banks, which would not be protected from failure, and would thus have an incentive, as they used to have, to operate cautiously, would bid for the funds provided by the Central bank in an auction. Good judgement would likely be rewarded.

This plan would introduce a permanent debt-free, stable, state-issued money supply that is not dependent on banks lending. Money would predominantly be spent into the economy debt-free. "Thus money will exist without a corresponding debt—there will no longer be a need for the rest of the economy to rent the medium of exchange from the banking sector."[92]

As Jackson and Dyson insist, the idea is perfectly feasible and could be easily achieved. It would have the immense advantage of removing one of the key drivers for constant growth—the creation of money through loans (i.e., debt). The question might be whether it was sufficiently ambitious. "We have to escape," writes David Boyle, "from the old idea that money is one, indivisible, totemic,

90. Jackson and Dyson, *Modernising*, 204.

91. Ibid., 208.

92. Ibid., 261.

semi divine, golden truth—issued from on high by an infallible Federal Reserve and handed down to a grateful populace. Complementary currencies can reveal to us that, even in the poorest places, there are vast living assets—ideas, skills, time, love even—that can turn our ideas of scarcity on their heads."[93]

Ann Pettifor criticizes the positive money campaign for retaining the quantity theory of money approach—the idea that the amount of money available is what is crucial, an idea that cannot account for credit. She wants a return to Keynes's original proposals—controls on capital mobility, variable interest rates, dependent on whether money is being used for productive or for speculative purposes, and public expenditure financed by loan issuance. She is not against the creation of money by private banks as long as this is for productive purposes. This vests money creation in borrowers, not in technocrats. The important thing, she argues, is to impose controls on private banks.[94] However, in her understanding money as a system of mutual debts is perfectly acceptable—which overlooks the power dynamics of indebtedness—and she believes money is indeed a store of value, where I have argued it has a tendency to corrupt the true nature of value, which long predates it. Goodchild has grasped the point that whatever it is that mediates exchange and sets a value on things ("money") has to be subordinate to older, wider, and much more important systems of value.

Social credit

Social credit also sought to bring money creation under communal scrutiny and control, and it had a much less centralized vision than positive money. Douglas also wanted to see money as credit rather than as debt and he envisaged a National Credit Office (NCO). Using government statistics this would compute, on a quarterly or yearly basis, the total value of the nation's assets, production and imports, and the total value of all assets consumed in the previous

93. Cited in Simms, *Apocalypse*, 149.
94. Pettifor, *Production*.

period. By maintaining a steady ratio between purchasing power in the hands of the community and real wealth (the actual potential capacity to supply goods and services) it would ascertain a just price.[95] He proposed that new money would be fed into the system as consumer credit, either in the form of the national dividend or through producer-owned guilds. The control of credit would lie with the local community rather than in private hands.[96]

The premise of the scheme, as we saw in the last chapter, was that wealth both belongs to and is created by the whole community, resting on all previous generations, and responsible to generations to come. Social credit, says Frances Hutchinson, seeks to counter economic globalization by securing control over the institutions of finance by local communities, enabling values other than money values to resurface.

> It runs counter to the prevalent misapprehension that capitalism in general and its financial institutions in particular, just happen: that, like the constellations and planets in the very waves of the sea, some blind force dictates the direction of economic progress; and that any form of agitation against what happens naturally is at best utopian, most likely misguided and always a thorough nuisance to serious authority going about its lawful business.[97]

As with the WIR and JAK banks, social credit seeks to rethink money in terms of mutual aid. Since money is not a thing but a social construction, why should this not be possible?

Keynes drew attention to the ideas of Silvio Gesell, who proposed money that would oxidize if not used. "Only money that goes out of date like a newspaper, rots like potatoes, evaporates like ether, is capable of standing the test as an instrument of exchange of potatoes, newspapers, iron and ether," he wrote.[98] "With electronic monies," says Harvey, "this is now practicable, in ways that

95. Hutchinson, *Money*, 140.
96. Ibid., 141.
97. Ibid., 172.
98. Cited by Harvey, *Contradictions*, 35.

were not possible before. An oxidization schedule can easily be written into monetary accounts such that unused monies (like unused airline miles) dissolve after a certain period of time. This cuts the bond between money as a means of circulation and money as a measure and even more significantly as a store of value."[99]

Keith Hart considers the sorts of proposals made by positive money as too old fashioned and too bound to the state. His idea is that "we should look for the meaning of money in the myriad acts of remembering that link individuals to their communities." Money, in its many forms, is a way of keeping track of these connections as well as the principal instrument of collective memory. "To an increasing extent it will be possible for people to enter circuits of exchange based on voluntary association and defined by special currencies of the sort pioneered by LETS schemes. At the other extreme, we will be able to participate as individuals in global markets of infinite scope, using international monies of account, such as the dollar, electronic payment systems of various sorts or even direct barter via the Internet."[100] He thinks that money, like language, will become a subjective capacity of the individual, and personal credit the counterpart of the private idiolect that each of us speaks.[101]

However, for it to happen, both usury and speculation would have to be taken out of the equation. If that happened, as many of the world's religions advocate, one of the principle causes of inequality would be removed at a stroke. Alternative means of funding pensions, and of providing capital for enterprise, would have to be found. One way of doing this would be by providing a citizen's income recommended, let us recall, not only by "alternative" thinkers but by Milton Friedman, and currently being trialed in Finland. "The focus would then have to be on what really matters, which is the continuous creation of use values through social labour and the eradication of exchange value

99. Ibid., 35.
100. Hart, *Memory*, 319.
101. Ibid., 322.

as the principal means by which the production of use values is organised."[102] This could make possible not only a reconfiguration of how exchange is organized but the ultimate dissolution of the power of money over social life. Harvey speaks of the possibility of a moneyless economy, by which he seems to mean an economy where the means of circulation is not at the same time a store of value, as Gesell proposed. However, while this might be our utopian aim, "the intermediate step of designing quasi money forms that facilitate exchange but inhibit the private accumulation of social wealth and power becomes imperative."[103]

Also crucial is the recognition that state taxation is not a penalty but a recognition of our mutual indebtedness—a way of expressing solidarity. The competitive individualism I outlined in the previous chapter is, of course, designed to challenge any such idea (the Republican Party in the United States regards taxation as "theft"). It claims that "it's just not human nature!" An Augustinian reading of sin can also feed in to so-called "realist" thinking, which dismisses any scheme to do things radically differently as wildly utopian. Kropotkin, Tudge, and Graeber, on the other hand, all represent a different reading of human nature, which Tudge, a biologist, roots in human biology, and which an alternative reading of the Christian Scriptures to that proposed by the Augustinian tradition can also support. Can the world really be made otherwise? Despite the many dire features of our present political and economic landscape—manifesting only too clearly stupidity as sin, or the kind of maniacal commitment to destruction that characterized Western fascism and today characterizes Islamic fundamentalism, I believe this is possible and in the final chapter I will look at the successes social movements have achieved and consider the possibility that the "blessed unrest" throughout the world might create a "world made otherwise."

102. Harvey, *Contradictions*, 36.
103. Harvey, *Contradictions*, 35, 36.

Chapter Eight

Feeding Ten Billion

Biology will not be flouted; and unless we keep morality and
aesthetics firmly in view, then they will go by the board. The
idea that human values simply install themselves by default is
another illusion. In agriculture as in all things, human values
must be written specifically into the act.

—COLIN TUDGE

I BEGAN THIS BOOK with Stephen Emmott's play *10 Billion*, which
is the world population the United Nations calculated would be
reached by the end of the century (this has now been revised upwards to 11.5 billion) and I have noted a number of times that
famine is likely to be the most serious consequence of climate
change. I also reminded readers that for Adam Smith agriculture
was a central part of economics, but that this has now become
a sideshow—relegated to "agricultural economics." The question
of how people are to be fed is not a sideshow, however—hence
a chapter on farming in a book on how to respond to the likely
consequences of climate change. I begin by outlining what we
know about the current situation vis à vis the production of food,
drawing both on the food and agriculture organization reports,
and on Worldwatch reports.

The Food and Agriculture Organization (FAO) figures for
2015 show that the world already produces plenty of food—roughly

a third more for each of us than in the 1960s. Even after feeding to livestock a third of global grain production, 90 percent of all soy meal, and a third of the fish catch, there is still a global average of roughly 2,800 calories available per person per day.[1] So distribution is still the problem, rather than production. At the same time, 795 million people still suffered from hunger in 2015, 2 billion are afflicted by the "hidden hunger" of micronutrient deficiencies, and over 1.9 billion are obese or overweight. Non-communicable diseases (NCDs) associated with imbalanced diets have increased so rapidly as to have overtaken infectious diseases as the number one cause of global mortality.[2] This is the present reality but it is also clearly important to take heed of projections of drought issued, for example, by the Hadley Centre, which point out that the area of the earth's surface suffering from extreme drought has trebled from just 1 to 3 percent in a decade. They predict that such drought conditions will affect over 8 percent of the land surface by 2020 and 30 percent by 2090.[3] The IPCC noted in its fifth assessment report in 2014 that crop yields could decline by 0.2 to 2 percent per decade over the remainder of the century, even as demand increases by 14 percent per decade. Sandra Postel, one of the world's leading experts on water, notes that 10 percent of the global food supply depends on unsustainable use of groundwater. A large share of the world's people depend on irrigated farms located where renewable water is not very abundant. China has nearly 20 percent of the world's population and 21 percent of total irrigated area but only 6.5 percent of the world's renewable freshwater—and most of that supply is in the southern part of the country.[4]Aquifers, which water some 38 percent of global agricultural fields, are increasingly overtapped.[5]

Climate change is already affecting food supply, and staple crops like rice and maize are likely to be badly affected. The FAO

1. Cited in Smith et al., *Realizing the Right to Food,* 4
2. Frison et al., *From Uniformity to Diversity,* 8.
3. Simms, *Apocalypse,* 230.
4. Postel, "Sustaining fresh water and its dependents."
5. Gardner, "Mounting losses of agricultural resources," 68.

notes that in each of the IPCC's projected climate-change scenarios the geographic distributions of crop species will be affected faster than they are able to migrate and adapt. Changes in crops' life cycles, migration patterns, and population distributions have already been documented. One change, such as a later flowering time, can have repercussions in other parts of the food system because the processes and species involved have coevolved and are highly interdependent. Shifts in the ranges of pests and pathogens are also predicted, demanding that crop species develop immunities to unfamiliar biotic stresses.[6] Shrinking glaciers will affect people in areas fed by the Ganges, whilst, conversely, sea level rises may take much fertile land out of production. Hunger is not the only result: revolutions have often followed famines (as they did in 1789), and the current conflict in Syria is linked to a three-year drought in the north of the country, where most food is grown. Thus, though it is true that food production has soared in the past sixty years, constant gains in production cannot be taken for granted. Particularly serious is the fact that the world's two most populous nations have lost the ability to feed themselves.

Fish provides food for around a half of the world's people but this is threatened by ocean acidification. Increasing acidity means that marine species cannot build shells and skeletons from calcium carbonate. This threatens the plankton at the base of the marine food chain.[7] Given only a two-degree Centigrade increase in global temperature by 2050, this would result in a huge depletion of fish stocks, already marked in many places in the world. Putting this together what this means, according to Oxfam, is that hunger "may be the defining human tragedy of this century."[8]

6. Guimarães, ed., *Second report on the state of the world's plant genetic resources for food and agriculture*, 183–98. In Burkina Faso average temperature has risen by 0.8° C since 1975 and this has made agriculture well nigh impossible. "Across the region, rainfall is increasingly erratic and increasingly intense. The rain cuts into the ground and washes away the little humus it contains." L. van Eeckhout, "Winds of Change blast Burkina Faso," *Guardian Weekly*, July 10, 2015.

7. Lovejoy, "Climate Change's Pressures on Biodiversity," 69.

8. Renton, *Suffering the Science*, 10.

These issues around food supply mean that farming and ocean conservation is a matter of crucial importance. Which practices must we follow to see that the world's people are fed? This is not simply a technical question. Over this question people have been sharply divided for getting on for a century, one side following an industrial logic, and putting their money on technological wizardry, the other on the continuance of good husbandry and traditional skills. The fundamental assumptions outlined in the previous two chapters constitute the underlying terrain of the debate. Whichever side one takes, however, the issue of the commons, both land and sea, is obviously crucial, and it is here I begin. I am extending what was said in chapter six, and considering it primarily in relation to the production of food. I then turn to the contest between two systems of production—looking back to the contest between two economies that structures Deuteronomy, but also drawing on current work by scientists working on agroecology. I consider the question—increasingly widely mooted in the churches at the moment—as to whether we should all become vegan or vegetarian, and conclude by looking at the issue of food sovereignty versus corporate control.

The land is mine

In Leviticus 25:23 we read: "The land shall not be sold in perpetuity, for the land is mine; with me you are but migrant workers and tenants."

Veerkamp calls this "perhaps the most important verse in Scripture."[9] The denial of absolute possession of the land, on the ground that "the land is mine," means that there are no absolute property rights, and that therefore no class structure is other than provisional. Land, for the biblical writers, is not a form of private property, with its exclusive character and absolute right of use and abuse. Israel did not have this right, at least according to the authors of Leviticus. The land is gift and trust—part of the "wealth"

9. Veerkamp, *Autonomie*, 98.

which Social Credit, building on earlier notions of the common treasury, identified as the common human inheritance. Bas Wielenga comments: "The land is the aim of YHWH's ways with Israel. It is and remains his gift, and the fruits of its soil are his blessing. It is meant to be the basis of a new society, of fellowship in freedom and equality. Such a gift is necessarily demanding. The fellowship in freedom is threatened by the development of inequality and class contradictions in society."[10] In contemporary society issues about both the care and ownership of the land follow from this understanding of the land as a gift to be held in common.

As regards care of the land, misusing it is one of the key factors in civilizational collapse. Part of the reason for Rome's decline was that it lost its granaries in North Africa through over-intensive cultivation. Today, too, land degradation, soil erosion, and salination are of major concern. Soil is formed at a rate of one inch every 250 to 1,200 years, John Madeley tells us. It takes 3,000 to 12,000 years to make agriculturally fertile land. It is being lost at a rate of 7 million hectares a year (the size of Ireland) due to soil degradation. Another 25 billion tonnes are washed down the world's rivers each year. Overgrazing accounts for 35 percent of all erosion; mismanagement like repeated conventional tillage accounts for 27 percent; water erosion and wind erosion are other factors.[11] In addition the growth of cities and roads constantly takes more land, often grade one, out of use. On the whole, as Colin Tudge notes, the best land is already cultivated. Land henceforth brought into cultivation will be marginal. The cities are eating into it and they tend to occupy land which is best for farming.[12] Tarmac is the land's last crop.

According to Genesis 2:15 humans are set in the world to serve (*abad*) and to keep (*shamar*) it. Serving, according to whoever it was who wrote the "servant songs" of Isaiah, and according to Jesus, is the true vocation of humanity—that way of acting in which we find our humanness. The Redactor (who is always our teacher—"Redactor is Rabbenu") put Genesis 2 after Genesis 1,

10. Wielenga, *Long Road to Freedom*, 125.

11. Madeley, *Food for All*, 134.

12. Tudge, *So Shall We Reap*, 37.

thus decisively qualifying what might be meant by "have dominion" (which in any case denotes the kind of activity a shepherd has with regard to his or her sheep which—I speak from experience—entails constant care). Service of the earth is manifested in what Berry calls "kindly use." The verb *shamar*, which can mean "to keep" (as in, "Keep my commandments" or "Am I my brother's keeper?") can also mean "observe" and Ellen Davis suggests that this includes the idea that human beings have not only to keep the garden but "to learn from it and respect the limits that pertain to it."[13] Davis points out that the earliest prophetic writings likewise presuppose an understanding of land as gift and that they read from that the idea that misuse of the gift of land, including maltreatment of those who work the soil, will ultimately undo every political structure, no matter how sophisticated, stable, and powerful it appears to be.[14] Jesus' practice of sharing food and using it as a sacrament of inclusion suggests that he understood this. Certainly, thanksgiving for food was such a characteristic act that it was then that the disciples at Emmaus recognized him when he gave thanks at the beginning of the meal in breaking and sharing bread. Such "thanks giving" is not a pious act but a recognition that The NAME is the source of all things and that therefore we are called to holiness of life. It was not just a simple domestic ritual; it was a domestic ritual that had implications for economics, politics, farming, and everything else. Indeed, everything hangs on it.

Meanwhile, alongside poor care, farmland is being bought up in dozens of countries by foreign investment firms, biofuel producers, large-scale farming operations, and governments. Since 2000, agreements have been concluded from foreign entities to purchase or lease more than 36 million hectares, an area about the size of Japan. About half of this area is intended to be used in agriculture.[15] An article in the *Journal of Peasant Studies*, which collated data from FAO reports on seventeen countries, found that food production is just one of the reasons for land

13. Davis, *Scripture, Culture, and Agriculture,* 30.
14. Ibid., 121.
15. Gardner, "Mounting losses of agricultural resources," 70.

grabs. Others are to find land to grow biofuels, other climate change mitigation strategies, and demands for natural resources by new centers of capital.[16] Land grabbing is worst in Africa, but also affects Latin America and Eastern Europe. The financial crisis has turned land into a highly profitable investment—more profitable than gold. Investment funds are amongst the large investors, along with states and multilateral agencies. The main beneficiary is the population of the land-grabbing countries.[17]

We know that all economies begin to lie as soon as they assign a fixed value to land, writes Wendell Berry. "People who have been landless know that land is invaluable; it is worth everything . . . Whatever the market may say, the worth of the land is what it always was: it is worth what food, clothing, shelter, and freedom are worth; it is worth what life is worth."[18] Land, in other words, is priceless, and the land-grabs are part old-fashioned colonialism and part manifestation of that colonization of culture by money that Karl Heinz Brodbeck documents in *The Rule of Money*.

Industrial agriculture

The contest over how the future is to be fed broadly proposes "two ways"—terminology I derive from Deuteronomy, which, as we saw in the second chapter, sets before its hearers "a way of life and a way of death." These are between industrial agriculture, which is supported by most governments, corporations, and many big farmers (the NFU in the UK, for example), on the one hand, and what is called in the US agrarianism, what Colin Tudge calls enlightened agriculture or, to use an older term, agroecology, on the other.[19] In this section I look at industrial agriculture.

16. Borras Jr. et al., "Land grabbing in Latin America and the Caribbean."

17. La Via Campesina, Notebook No 3, April 2012.

18. Berry, "The Agrarian Standard," in Wirzba, ed., *The Essential Agrarian Reader*, 29.

19. The term *agroecology* was first used in Germany in 1928. Wezel et al., "Agroecology as a science."

On the face of it the case that industrial agriculture is the shape of the future is incontrovertible. In Britain, Jules Pretty tells us, 10 percent of farms produce 80 percent of the food. In Europe just 12 percent of all farms produce 60 percent of all agricultural output and a mere 1 percent rear 40 percent of all animals.[20] There has been a huge rise in output over the past eighty years, with three times the amount of wheat and barley per hectare and more than twice as much potato and sugar beet, and double the amount of milk per lactation. This is truly impressive—and it is these kinds of increase which have made possible the more than doubling of the global population since 1960. However, as has been very well documented, this comes at a cost.

Industrial agriculture began with the attempts to harness steam power to agricultural tasks at the end of the nineteenth century (memorably described in Hardy's *Tess*) but really took off with the mass production of the Fordson tractor in 1919. After 1945, in a war-ravaged world, the emphasis was on growing enough food for people, many of whom had been hungry or starving for four years. This process reached a climax in the "green revolution" of the late 1960s, heralded as the way "the starving millions" were to be fed. By the 1980s, however, on the back of subsidized agriculture, there was a crisis of overproduction, with "butter mountains" and "wine lakes," and farmers began to be paid for taking food out of production or growing crops for fuel. In many areas of Europe, ancient and productive resources like apple orchards were grubbed up in the interests of keeping agricultural prices stable. Overproduction drove prices down, farmgate prices fell, and farmers were told that they had to diversify and find out how to be profitable. The rationale of agriculture changed: for a spell farmers in Britain, at any rate, were told that they were chiefly park keepers—keeping the countryside looking nice for the valuable tourists who flocked there at weekends—and that growing food was not the issue. Meanwhile, growing globalization meant that food was now part of a global market in which all farmers competed with each other. Competition meant that costs had to

20. Pretty, *The Living Land*, 4.

be cut, which meant, in the North, cutting labor, which was the most expensive item. The impact of this, Colin Tudge points out, was that more machines were used, but this meant there was less good husbandry, which meant simpler systems, which meant monoculture instead of polyculture.[21] Out of this process has emerged a practice that produces vast quantities of food, poorly distributed (that is, left to the market which, as Amartya Sen has shown, can aggravate famines), and practices that actually damage the sustainability of the food system.

The values behind industrial agriculture are spelled out by the UK's National Farmers' Union, which the magazine *Ethical Consumer* branded, at the end of a two-year study, an "agribusiness lobby group."[22] The theme song of the NFU is that farming is "a business like any other." Like any other business it has a "bottom line," and it is assumed that it is possible to farm well just by following the rules of money: cutting costs, maximizing turnover, adding value, maximizing profit. It is wedded to technological advances, which involve reduction in labor: ever bigger machines, automated milking parlors, and ever newer pesticides. Industrial agriculture wants to "follow the science," but the science it has in mind is industrial chemistry, not biology and ecology. When feeding the human family ought to be a cooperative exercise, instead industrial agriculture, in its support for global trade, pits every farmer against every other farmer—because it is wedded to "the market"—which leads to bad practice, impoverishment, and a race to the bottom.[23] As argued in chapter six, a proper balance

21. Tudge, *Is Agroecology Natural?*

22. *Understanding the NFU: An English Agribusiness Lobby Group.* The NFU challenged some of the facts, but their support for free trade, their opposition to the ban on neonicotinoids, their support for GM, and their links with both supermarkets and firms like Syngenta are not contested.

23. Berry, *Sex, Economy, Freedom and Community,* 47. In almost all regions and at almost all times, says Brian Donahue, "whole-hearted engagement with the market has led farm families to narrowly specialized, extractive practices, to mounting debt, and either to outright failure or to . . . sell out and try something else" ("The Resettling of America," 40).

between what people earn and what they pay can only be brought about by regulated markets.[24]

The impact of this approach is spelled out in a report by the International Panel of Experts on Sustainable Food Systems (iPes)—an international research center based at the University of Louvain, and co-chaired by Olivier de Schutter, former UN Rapporteur on the right to food.[25] The report considers the situation of world food systems at present as "perilous." Indeed, in the view of its authors, "there may be no greater risk than sticking with industrial agriculture and the systematic problems it generates."[26] It notes that industrial agriculture does indeed produce a lot of food, but it is only a crude cost-benefit analysis that could call it efficient because of the problems involved in it. The report looks at both industrial agriculture and agroecology in terms of productivity, environmental, socioeconomic, and nutrition and health outcomes.

In terms of productivity, the high-yielding varieties introduced through the green revolution have started to plateau, whilst monocultures have over and over again proved vulnerable to disease. Mass pesticide use is increasingly producing herbicide resistant weeds (210 as of 2016). Soil fertility is depleted so that huge expenditures on inorganic fertilizers are required .

In terms of environmental outcomes, industrial food systems, which include the transport and packaging of food in a global market, as well as the production of chemical fertilizer and pesticides, contribute around 30 percent of global greenhouse gas emissions. Food production is outsourced by wealthy nations, which threatens the food supply of the producing countries. About 20 percent of land is currently degraded and this continues at a rate of 12 million hectares a year. It is estimated that 50 percent of irrigated arable land will be salinized by 2050. "Externalities" include the contamination of water supplies with agricultural pesticides, or

24. "When farmers have to sell on a depressed market and buy on an inflated one, that is death to farmers, death to farming, death to rural communities, death to the soil, and death to food." Berry, *Home Economics*, 125.

25. Frison et al., *From Uniformity to Diversity*, 15–27.

26. Ibid., 43.

poisoning vast swathes of ocean so that they no longer support marine life, as happened in the Gulf of Mexico.[27]

Rachel Carson pointed out in 1961 that the development of pesticides to deal with insects, weeds, rodents, and other "pests" led to an escalation in which bacteria and insects evolved, so stronger pesticides were needed and so forth. "The chemical war is never won, and all life is caught in its violent crossfire."[28] As crude a weapon as the cave man's club, says Carson, "the chemical barrage has been hurled against the fabric of life—a fabric on the one hand delicate and destructible, on the other miraculously tough and resilient, and capable of striking back in unexpected ways."[29] Over the past ten or fifteen years bee populations have been decimated around the world. Research consistently points to the use of neonicotinoids, but industrial agriculture insists that they are necessary to keep up yields.[30]

Industrial agriculture is leading to a loss of biodiversity which, according to the second Planetary Boundaries Report, which I cited in the first chapter, is the domain in which the world has moved furthest beyond what could be considered a safe operating space.[31] Concentration on a few main plant varieties has resulted in the loss of 75 percent of plant genetic diversity, and 20

27. As long ago as 1972, testimony to the United States Congress noted that "the large agricultural firm is . . . able to achieve benefits by externalising certain costs. The disadvantages of large-scale operation fall largely outside the decision-making framework of the large farm firm. Problems of waste disposal, pollution control, added burdens on public service, deterioration of rural social structures, impairment of the tax base, and the political consequence of a concentration of economic power has typically not been considered as costs of large-scale by the firm. They are unquestionably costs to the larger community." Scott, *Seeing Like a State,* 293.

28. Carson, *Silent Spring,* 25.

29. Ibid., 256.

30. According to the Millennium Ecosystem Assessment (2005), the presence of pollinators tends to be significantly lower in monocultures than in fields containing diverse forage and nesting sites. The economic value of pollination is approximately 9.5 percent (€153 billion) of the value of global agricultural production for human food.

31. Steffen et al., "Planetary boundaries."

percent of livestock breeds are under threat. The importance of this can be illustrated by what happened when India's rice crop was devastated by a virus in the 1970s: scientists examined 17,000 varieties of rice before finding one wild rice strain that was resistant. The Irish potato famine could have been avoided if there had been more varieties of potato.[32]

We can add that industrial agriculture is inhumane, because it involves keeping animals in ways in which they should never be kept. In the US there are feedlots for 20,000 cattle, and applications for huge cattle and pig lots are being launched in the UK, all of which deprive animals of their natural habitat and feeding patterns. The sole justification for this is profit. Philosophers pour scorn on Descartes's arguments that animals are merely machines, but industrial agriculture—in the teeth of what stock keepers have known for thousands of years—insists on treating them as such. As Schweitzer argued, respect for life is a continuum, and inhumane practices in regard to animals generate inhumane practices elsewhere.

In terms of socioeconomic outcomes the high cost of chemical inputs threatens farm incomes. Industrial agriculture seeks to employ fewer and fewer people (currently 1.5 percent in the UK). Reductions in farm labor may entail a loss of knowledge that may become increasingly important in a context of rising environmental and pest stresses. For example, herbicide-tolerant GM cropping systems that promise labor-saving, simplified forms of crop management are now facing major issues of weed resistance and there may well be a need to return to hand weeding.[33] The commitment to global trade has exposed low income countries to the volatilities of the commodity markets. Large scale land-grabs have generally further impoverished poor communities and led to the breakdown of local systems of governance.

32. Madeley, *Food for All*, 140. Pesticide exposure has been linked to increased incidence of Alzheimer's disease, asthma, birth defects, cancer, learning and developmental disorders, Parkinson's disease, and sterility. Frison et al., *From Uniformity to Diversity*, 29.

33 Frison et al., *From Uniformity to Diversity*, 25.

Finally, industrial agriculture has grown mainly energy rich but nutritionally poor crops, which has been linked to the rise in obesity throughout the world, and the variety of food available in the West is not available in low-income countries, so it is the needs of only one small portion of the world's population that is being met.

What all this amounts to is that industrial agriculture is only "efficient" if loss of soils, damage to biodiversity, pollution of water, and harm to human health are ignored. In the West at present it gives us "cheap" food, but, as Jules Pretty says, food is not cheap. "We actually pay three times for our food: once at the till, a second time through taxes that are used to subsidize farmers and a third time to clean up the environmental and health side effects."[34]

Nature, said Carson, has introduced great variety into the landscape, but man has displayed a passion for simplifying. "Thus he undoes the built-in checks and balances by which nature holds the species within bounds."[35] Aldo Leopold spoke of a "Pax Germanica of the agricultural world."[36] The damage caused by agriculture, highlighted by the iPES report, springs from a worldview that thinks of the soil as an extractable resource, uses living things as if they were machines, and imposes "scientific, that is, laboratory, exactitude upon living complexities that are ultimately mysterious."[37]

The hubris in such technocratic process involves the kind of stupidity I mentioned in the first chapter, which believes that science and technology can always get us out of trouble. It is true, of course, that science and technology have achieved extraordinary things over the past century and a half, but everything is double edged—new problems attend every advance and, in every area, but especially in farming, a contempt for the craft wisdom built up over millennia is involved, inextricably linked to the drive for profit. Farming builds on more than 12,000 years of practice and experimentation. By constantly observing the results of their field

34. Pretty, *Agri-Culture*, xvi and 52.
35. Carson, *Silent Spring*, 27.
36. Leopold, *A Sand County Almanac*, 199.
37. Berry, *The Unsettling of America*, 90.

experiments and retaining those methods that succeed, writes James Scott, farmers have discovered and refined practices that work, without knowing the precise chemical or physical reasons why they work. In agriculture, as in many other fields, practice has long preceded theory. "And indeed some of these practically successful techniques, which involve a large number of simultaneously interacting variables, may never be fully understood by the techniques of science."[38]

As an example of this kind of hubris Tudge points to the attempt to produce strains of rice that include Vitamin A. This is done by introducing carotene but, says Tudge, this is one of the commonest molecules in nature. It is abundant in green leaves of all kinds, including spinach.

> Traditional farming always included horticulture. The vegetable patch and the occasional fruit tree were and are standard. So long as people have horticulture they have all the vitamin A they need. Obsessive monoculture, in which there is no room for local produce to feed local people, is a modern aberration, another example of obsessive commercialism. It is in many ways pernicious, socially, economically, ecologically; and the blindness of children is only one of the consequent evils.[39]

In traditional societies vitamin A deficiency does not exist. It is caused by the imposition of Western economics. "Yellow rice is the heroic, Western, high-tech solution to the disaster that heroic, Western commercial high-tech has itself created."[40]

Can GM Technology feed the world?

Although GM has so far contributed next to nothing in feeding the world, it is constantly cited by industrial agriculture enthusiasts and by politicians as the key to doing so, and so it requires a section

---

38. Scott, *Seeing Like a State,* 306.
39. Tudge, *So Shall We Reap,* 269.
40. Ibid., 270.

to itself. GM technology involves the insertion of an alien gene into a plant to give it a certain trait, for example vitamin enrichment or drought tolerance. It bypasses conventional breeding and brings about combinations of genes that would not occur naturally. No one knows the upshot of this technology.[41] The Soil Association points out that there is available a less invasive technique known as market-assisted selection, which allows plant breeders to select desirable genetic traits that are then brought out using conventional breeding.[42] The iPes Report cites studies found, over a thirty-year study, that average organic yields are equivalent to conventional agriculture, and 30 percent higher in drought years.[43] The main problem, however, is that it puts too much power over food into too few hands. Control is the central issue.

With the election of Pope Francis the newspaper *USA Today* carried a feature on his likely attitude to GM crops.[44] The new Pope is a chemist by training, we are told, and therefore "pro science," comes from Argentina, where GM is widely used, and is an advocate of the poor, and will therefore support food policies that provide food for the hungry. In the background here is the 2009 consultation of the Pontifical Academy of Science on GM. It did not, as *USA Today* claims, come out with a "ringing endorsement" of GM technology, but first noted the potential of the technology

41. Madeley, *Food for All*, 59.

42. Simms, *Apocalypse*, 253.

43. A 2007 study with a global data set of 293 examples found that on average, in developed countries, organic systems produced 8 percent lower yields than conventional agriculture. However, the same study found that in developing countries, organic systems outperformed conventional farms by as much as 80 percent. Similarly, a review of 286 projects in fifty-seven developing countries, found that farmers had increased agricultural productivity by an average of 79 percent by adopting "resource-conserving" agriculture. The Rodale Institute found, on a thirty-year comparison of organic corn and soybean with conventional production in tilled systems in the US, equivalent yields on average, and higher yields for organic in drought years. Similar results were obtained in a ten-year experiment with wheat. Frison et al., *From Uniformity to Diversity*, 31.

44. David Gibson, "The story behind Pope Francis' Election," *USA Today*, March 14, 2013.

for helping to address world hunger, second called for GM technologies to be "cost free" for poorer regions, and third, encouraged
"more widespread use of sustainable and sound agricultural practices to help the lives of the poor." Four speakers at the conference
had ties to Monsanto and were predictably enthusiastic about the
technology, but the African delegation warned that GM technology could not solve Africa's food crisis. On the contrary, the African
Bishops warned, using GM risked "ruining small landholders,
abolishing traditional methods of seeding and making farmers dependent on the production companies." Argentine farmers wrote
to their countryman, Pope Francis, in May 2014. "In Argentina,"
the farmers write,

> monocultures of soya and other genetically-modified
> seeds have been advancing at a tremendous pace. Al-
> though imperceptible to those living in towns, the trag-
> edy is that they have decimated rural populations. The
> area covered by these monocultures has now reached
> the terrifying figure of 24 million hectares, and they oc-
> cupy a large proportion of our agricultural land. What
> is at risk here is not Food Sovereignty, which was lost
> years ago, but the food security of the population. These
> unfamiliar green deserts are governed by biotechnol-
> ogy and the patenting rights applied to life by the mul-
> tinational corporations. Nothing is sacred to them, and
> they have displaced millions of people who are now
> uprooted and deterritorialised.[45]

The authors go on to call for the Pope to back a locally based and
people-centered agriculture—an agriculture that already feeds
two-thirds of the world's population. As they note, what farmers
need is not GM, but peace and security. Here the arms export industry of the so called "advanced" countries comes into play. It is
by arming conflict that we make food production impossible.

The Vatican is quite clear that the production of food, like
the ownership of water, is part of the human common good that

45 "Why Genetically Modified Crops Pose a Threat to Peasants, Food
Sovereignty, Health, and Biodiversity on the Planet." Published by the ETC
(Erosion, Technology and Concentration) Group, Montreal, August 4, 2010.

cannot be subordinated to the profit motive. The hallmark of genuine science, as opposed to the spurious corporate-financed variety, is an absolute commitment to the common good, which of course means shared research. The development of GM has been associated with shocking manipulation of scientific evidence. Arpad Pustzai's research was independently funded. When his work found evidence of a connection between GM and cancer he was pulled off it, and drummed out of the discipline. In France in 2012, again, a paper that found similar results was retracted after intense pressure from scientists, all of whom were found to have connections with the GM industry. Monsanto has brought over 400 lawsuits against farmers for misusing seeds. Ultimately what we need is government, public-good-funded research. The idea that the private sector undertakes this more "efficiently," or that governments cannot afford it in an age of austerity (whilst it can afford weapons of mass destruction capable of blasts twenty times more powerful than Hiroshima) is not necessity but part of neoliberal mythmaking.

In 2000 the director of Novartis—one of the world's biggest biotech companies—told a meeting in Norwich: "If anyone tells you that GM is going to feed the world tell them that it is not . . . to feed the world takes financial and political will—it's not about production but about distribution."[46]

In reality, Colin Tudge comments, genetic engineering has so far contributed nothing that can truly be said to be of any significant use at all in feeding the world. "Agriculture is primarily craft. Science is the gilt on the gingerbread."[47] The enthusiasm for genetic engineering on the part of politicians and the industrial agriculture lobby reflects a particular set of values. It is, writes Brewster Kneen (a beef farmer himself),

> a vehicle, in practice, of an attitude of domination and
> ownership, as expressed in the assumption that it is pos-
> sible, reasonable, and morally acceptable to claim owner-
> ship over life. The claim that it is possible to own life, at

46. Cited in Madeley, *Food for All*, 64.
47. Tudge, *So Shall We Reap*, 264–65.

least to the extent of being able to claim a patent on a life process or life form, is so outrageous socially and ethically as to be hardly worth debating.[48]

The alternative approach, agroecology, to which I now turn, represents a different set of values.

Agroecology

Against industrial agriculture can be set agroecology, or enlightened agriculture. Enlightened agriculture is "commonsense agriculture rooted in good husbandry; traditional in structure, yet making all the use it chooses to of the very best science and where appropriate the highest technology; guided by biological reality (ecology, physiology) and by the human values of kindness, autonomy and justice."[49] The kind of contribution "the very best science" could make might be, for example, in the use of biochar, which is produced when biomass is heated without oxygen. It increases yields, helps soil retention of nutrients, and holds carbon in the soil. It can help combat global climate change in this way, and also by providing an alternative to inorganic fertilizers.[50]

At the heart of agroecology is an understanding that on-farm genetic diversity, local knowledge systems, and context-specific management practices are integral and inseparable components of resilient farming systems. It enhances soil's productivity and protects the crops against pests by relying on the natural environment such as beneficial trees, plants, animals, and insects.[51] The iPES report calls it "a universal logic for redesigning agricultural systems in ways that maximize biodiversity and stimulate interactions between different plants and species."[52] The report emphasizes that

48. Kneen, *Farmageddon*, 29.
49. Tudge, *So Shall We Reap*, 380.
50. Gathorne-Hardy et al., "Biochar as a soil amendant."
51. Smith et al., *Realizing the Right to Food in an Era of Climate Change*, 15.
52. Frison et al., *From Uniformity to Diversity*, 7.

it rests on a different worldview to industrial agriculture and on different values.

Tudge argues that the small mixed farm is the key to the future of all humanity because, in mixing crops and livestock "agriculture mirrors nature; and nature works."[53] What he means by "nature" here are the ecological systems that have evolved and endured through dramatic shifts of climate over millions of years. Four things have made this possible, Tudge argues: diversity— plenty of species and plenty of genetic variation; synergy—what one creature excretes another regards as provender, and so on and so forth, ultimately to the advantage of all; recycling—everything goes round and round and anything that leaves the system sooner or later comes back in again; finally, natural ecosystems in general are low-input. No wild ecosystem makes use of fossil fuel. "All is powered by the sun (with a bit of help from gravitation via the tides, and some geothermal heat)."[54] These principles are the basis of agroecology.

The Quaker Report agrees with Tudge in finding that the best defense against unpredictability is diversity. The vast majority of diversity within and between species, the report argues, is maintained by farmers on-farm in the form of landrace varieties and crop wild relatives adapted to local conditions. Agreeing with Jim Scott, the report argues that small-scale farmers continually develop better ways of managing resources and overcome local challenges by synthesizing local and scientific knowledge systems and applying them to changing circumstances.[55] While vulnerable to the effects of climate change, small-scale farmers are highly responsive to change. They have the advantage of local knowledge, which includes environmental and ethnobotanical knowledge (which tends to be highly sophisticated in the case of specific crops important to household food security and income), detailed histories of what has worked under what conditions based on generations of direct observation, and an understanding

53. Tudge, *So Shall We Reap*, 83.
54. Tudge, *Agroecology*, 4.
55. Smith et al., *Right to Food*, 11.

of how to integrate local and scientific knowledge systems. Local knowledge, the report argues, informs the selection of farm management practices such as soil and water management, pest control, and crop selections, rotations and combination, reflecting local resource endowments and the nutritional and cultural requirements of local people. Local knowledge exchanged through informal networks is selectively applied and modified by farmers according to their own unique and changing circumstances.[56] Small-scale farmers embody Berry's dictum that land that is in human use must be lovingly used. "It requires intimate knowledge, attention, and care . . . This law, which is not subject to repeal, is the justification of the small, family worked farm, for this law gives a preeminent and irrevocable value to familiarity, the family life that alone can properly connect a people to a land."[57]

Small mixed farms also generate more robust rural communities and on the whole employ more people. Given that ten billion people cannot all live in cities and find things to do there the question of human community, and what people are meaningfully going to do, is quite as urgent as the question of how people are to be fed. We do not want 50 percent of the population farming, says Tudge—the percentage of the mid-nineteenth century—but how about 10 percent?[58] One of the things that traditional farming provides is more satisfying and productive work, one of the key problems society has lacked since the Industrial Revolution. To some extent this is already underway in the growth of community food systems and rural partnerships around the world, which both develop more vibrant local communities and are involved in massive

56. Ibid., 11.

57. Berry, *Home Economics*, 164.

58. "As the cities grow it doesn't occur to politicians that agriculture benefits from more people as cities after a certain point do not. Or that the countryside could and should and traditionally did provide the principal solution to urban squalor and all the horrors that go with it." Tudge, *So Shall We Reap*, 47. Tudge has developed the idea of 10 percent in farming in lectures over the past few years, and gives many examples of how this can be achieved in *Six Steps Back to the Land*.

increases in agricultural productivity using locally adapted and sustainable technologies.[59]

The iPES report already mentioned argues that a fundamental shift towards diversified agroecological farming can deliver simultaneous benefits for productivity, the environment, and society. If we think of the negativities of industrial agriculture, agroecology answers all of them: it is more sustainable (it involves some use of diesel, but not pesticides); it does not have the externalities associated with pesticides; it does not run the risk of making antibiotics unusable; its livestock are by and large pasture fed; it has the potential to reverse soil degradation and rebuild soil fertility; and it employs more people, offering potentially satisfying work to those who need it.[60] Thus, cumulatively, it does not pose a threat for coming generations—quite the contrary. Ah—but can it feed ten billion? This is the question that is always posed. I cited above the studies that found that organic crops outperformed conventional ones and GM crops under drought conditions. Other studies have found that total outputs in diversified grassland systems are 15 percent to 79 percent higher than in monocultures; that there is a two to four time higher resource efficiency on small-scale agroecological farms; that there are 30 percent more species and 50 percent higher abundance of biodiversity on organic farms; and that there is around 50 percent more beneficial omega 3 fatty acids in organic meat and milk.[61]

These findings are already anticipated by a study of eighteenth-century Indian agriculture that found rice yields in India

59. The Skidelskys contemptuously dismiss these as "just middle class baubles, the modern equivalent of French courtiers playing at milk maids" (Skidelsky and Skidelsky, *How Much is Enough?*, 176). But for small farmers they can make all the difference and as Solnit notes, "A farmer's market selling the produce of local farmers isn't an adequate solution but ten thousand of them begin to be." *Hope in the Dark*, 147. Massingham (*The Wisdom of the Fields*) also notes the crucial importance of local markets for small farmers, as does the iPES Report.

60. It is true, of course that child labor and slave labor is involved in some Third World farming, and that if there was a large increase in people working in agriculture, and they were paid a living wage, the price of food would go up.

61. Frison et al., *From Uniformity to Diversity*, 31–40.

were 3,600 kg per hectare; the best 130 villages were 8,200 kg per hectare. This was higher than what was obtained by the green revolution. This was put down to care in tending fields and techniques such as intercropping and fallow. Intercropping results in more efficient utilization of resources (light, water, nutrients) by plants of different height, provides insurance against crop failure, provides effective cover to soil, and reduces the loss of soil moisture and helps keep pest and weeds under control.[62] Henry Massingham, in 1944, found a peasant smallholder in Somerset who rented four and a half acres of extremely steep land who grew fruit and vegetables of superlative quality, kept a pony, pigs, sheep, 130 fowl, and thirty hives of bees. This, he said, was the kind of husbandman who could feed a hundred million people and teach a generation "stuffed with illusions and false values."[63]

In terms of environment a growing body of evidence shows that diversified agroecological systems build healthy ecosystems where different plants and species interact in ways that improve soil fertility and water retention. They perform particularly well under environmental stress and deliver production increases in the places where additional food is most needed.

In terms of safety, diversified agriculture also holds the key to increasing dietary diversity at the local level, as well as reducing the multiple health risks from industrial agriculture (e.g., pesticide exposure, antibiotic resistance).

Of course, agroecological practices, though crucial, cannot work without the kind of alternative economic system I sketched in chapter six. The iPES report points to the burgeoning initiatives now forming around alternative food and farming systems, from new forms of political cooperation to the development of new market relationships that bypass conventional retail circuits. What holds agroecology back is the mismatch between its huge potential to improve outcomes across food systems, and its much smaller potential to generate profits for agribusiness firms, and I shall return to this in the final section of this chapter.

62. Madeley, *Food for All*, 26.
63. Massingham, *The Wisdom of the Fields*, 140.

The two systems of industrial agriculture and agroecology are underpinned by different value systems. In the first profit is the goal, and it reflects money as an absolute value. In the second reality is apprehended as gift. This understanding, I argued in chapter six, is the fundamental economic reality, and in terms of values and virtues gratitude is not simply an emotion, nor an individual trait, but an expression of a fundamental worldview, what Christians call a response to grace. Taken seriously it reorients all our practices, and especially our economy and therefore our farming.

What shall we eat?

Until the second half of the twentieth century in a few parts of the world (Europe, North America, Australasia) humans have always gone hungry. Flora Thompson (in *Larkrise to Candleford*) calls the generation of the 1880s in the United Kingdom "the besieged generation": what besieged them was hunger. The rural poor in this country in the nineteenth century never knew what it was to have a full stomach. The one topic of conversation in Thompson's North Oxfordshire hamlet was the pig kept in the backyard: the pig meant food in the lean months after Christmas. Ronald Blythe, in *Akenfield*, tells us that the young country boys flocked to the army in 1914 partly because it meant regular food. The agricultural historian Joan Thirsk tells us that one in six years in the sixteenth century in Britain was a general famine. Still today one-sixth of humanity goes hungry every day. David Harvey thinks that facts like these—actually he points to the great famine in China at the time of "the great leap forward" that killed 20 million people—should warn us against giving up on the global market.[64] But the assumption that food should be transported long distances, that Britain does not need a dairy industry because it can get milk "more cheaply" from Poland, or even that it has no need of a farming industry whatever, because food can all be supplied by trade, suggests, as Ellen Davis puts it, "a lack of prescience about peak oil,

---

64. Harvey, *Seventeen Contradictions*, 125.

not to mention terrorist and climatic threats to regional food security. It is now becoming evident to many that our current practices of moving food around the world have a short future; the lifestyle choice will soon be prohibitively expensive."[65]

The supermarket society in which we live is the only society in the whole of human history in which food security has not been a problem. I suspect that it is only in this society that the sense of food as gift has been lost, so that harvest suppers and grace before meals no longer have the resonance they once did. Thankfulness for food is strongly linked with a knowledge of the fragility of the food supply. The key story of the Hebrew Bible, the exodus, turns on famine, and a threat to survival. The stories of the wilderness wanderings in the book of Numbers constantly return to hunger and thirst, contrasting it with the well-fed slavery of Egypt. For the supermarket society food insecurity is not even a memory, but this society, even today, does not include the majority of human beings and since it is entirely dependent on oil it will not last much longer even for us.

Food security is partly a problem because of the weather: poor summers, unseasonal rainfall, frosts at the wrong time and so forth; partly because of pests, as anybody who tries to grow brassica knows; but even more because not all that much of the world is actually suitable for growing. Fertile land is finite. Arable land constitutes one-tenth of our world; meadows and pastures one quarter; forest and woodland one third; urban areas, deserts and ice caps the final third. Historically humans have dealt with this by diversifying their food sources. Humans have eaten the most unpromising things, including insects, molluscs, and the guts of animals which these days are routinely discarded (tripe and onions anyone?). Land not suitable for arable farming has been grazed. Ruminants convert cellulose, which humans cannot eat, into meat, which they can.

> Hedgerows, chemically speaking, are made of sugar. Yet
> all of this cellulose is useless for creatures like human
> beings, or lions or wolves, who cannot digest it. Still,

65. Davis, *Scripture, Culture, and Agriculture*, 28.

> though, these omnivores and specialist predators can
> join the feast, simply by eating the herbivores that can
> digest cellulose . . . Thus, for us, the specialist herbivores
> provide the entrée to nature's best stocked larder.[66]

As Colin Tudge, the author of this remark, points out, vegetarian-
ism is not an option for many people in difficult environments,
including high latitudes and semi-deserts. It is difficult to envisage
a vegan Inuit culture. Many people argue, and I agree, that those
of us in the supermarket society should greatly reduce the amount
of meat we eat. (Simon Fairlie proposes putting VAT on meat.) In
general, it seems to me, in feeding ten billion it is imperative to
follow Tudge's recipe: "to give the best, most suitable land to pulses,
cereals and tubers (that is, to arable farming); to fit in horticulture
in every spare pocket—and be prepared to spend a lot of time and
effort on it, and to invest capital for example in greenhouses; and to
allow livestock to slot in as best it can."[67] But this is a very different
argument to the idea that we destroy the planet if we keep eating
meat. Simon Fairlie, a smallholder and dairyman himself, makes a
good case for a more positive assessment of livestock given the milk
and cheese produced (and the world's largest dairy producer is not
rainy Britain, but India), and above all the pig, which recycles waste
(and we are told that a third of all food bought is thrown away in
the UK.[68] We don't have to accept the statistic, but certainly there is
enough to support armies of pigs).

Awareness of the fragility of the food supply teaches us thankfulness, part of the apprehension of reality as gift that I mentioned
as underpinning agroecology. Thankfulness for food is something
that characterizes most peasant cultures, and was once part of daily

66. Tudge, *So Shall We Reap,* 75.

67. Ibid., 357. The most important form of food are the staples: rice, maize,
and wheat. About 600 million tonnes of each are grown each year but about a
third of the wheat, and two thirds of the maize, are fed to livestock. Staples are
the principal sources of energy, mainly carbohydrates, but also fat and protein.
"They provide humanity with roughly half of our daily calories and two thirds
of our protein, so that all other crops and even the most conspicuous and economically important livestock are minor by comparison." Ibid, 79.

68. Fairlie, *Meat: A Benign Extravagance.*

life in Christian Europe. The fundamental thankfulness involved in eating is one of the most secure things we know about Jesus of Nazareth. The central ritual act of Christianity is now most commonly known as "the Eucharist," from the Greek verb *eucharisteo*, to give thanks. It stems from a key action at the last supper where Jesus, following conventional Jewish practice, broke bread and gave thanks. Crucially, in the story of the supper at Emmaus, the disciples did not recognize Jesus until he gave thanks. This reveals thanksgiving as an absolutely characteristic, identifying action on Jesus' part. Grounded as he was in the traditions of his people Jesus was a thankful human being, someone who attached special significance to giving thanks, and who for that very reason taught his disciples to ask for their daily bread—the opposite of taking it for granted or abusing it.

Thankfulness should characterize both our farming and our eating. To be thankful as a farmer is to treat both land and animals with profound respect. To be thankful as a consumer is to know and appreciate the effort and love involved in food production, and to honor the Creator who has given us the world in which we live. It is also to understand what it means to be human not apart from creation but as part of it, indeed, according to Paul (in Romans 8), as a sacramental part of it—conscious of the destiny of all material reality in a way other creatures are not. If we read Genesis 3 together with the wilderness stories, Davis suggests, we can see that accurate knowledge of God, the world, and our place in it—in short, wisdom—is available only to those who eat with restraint.[69]

But should we eat meat? One FAO report (since qualified by another) suggested that ruminants were driving global warming through the amount of methane they produce, and the cry went up—from some vegetarians—that this showed that all meat eating should be abandoned. But there is a great deal of "wild" meat—rabbits, squirrels, deer, and increasingly, in the UK, wild boar—which has to be culled if crops and trees are not to be seriously damaged. What are we to do with the cull? If we are reduced to keeping animals in zoos then, Simon Fairlie suggests, something profound

69. Davis, *Scripture, Culture, and Agriculture*, 78.

is lost. Pure arable farming, he argues, unlike mixed farming, "removes an entire order from the system. Moreover, it is the order which is closest to humanity, which gallops and gives birth and suckles, which feels pain and anger and joy." "By declining to eat meat we abandon our status as predator, ostensibly to take on the more humble role of middle rank herbivore, but increasingly to assume the roles of manager and absentee landlord."[70] Certainly in Peter Singer's prescriptions there is more than a whiff of neo Platonic dissatisfaction with bodies as we have them, an assumption that it is time to redesign them. "The natural world," Fairlie remarks, is controlled by God, while the technological world is managed by scientists. "Both are tyrannical, but as tyrants go, the former has a better record than the latter."[71]

Fairlie argues for a permaculture livestock economy, which would be self-reliant, organic, and low carbon. We would eat much less meat, but what we eat would be fresher. Pigs would once again be allowed to eat food waste; farms would grow a wider range of livestock and crops, working together. Animals, plants, fungi, and all the myriad variety of other organisms complement each other and feed off each other. Human beings are part of this chain, both in life and death, "bound in the bundle of life with the Lord your God," as Abigail puts it (1 Sam 25:29). Ecology, and therefore agroecology, thinks about the connectedness of all things: humans are not excluded from this. In our food and farming we have to understand ourselves as part of a whole, to understand where we fit in, and this includes our relation to the animals. They should certainly not be exploited but it may be, as our evolutionary inheritance suggests, that our mutual dependence involves eating meat.

Food sovereignty vs corporate control

So far I have spoken about food security, but the worldwide peasant organization, Via Campesina, calls instead for food sovereignty.

---

70. Fairlie, *Meat*, 222–223, 231.

71. Ibid., 295.

Once again we are back with the "two ways" as illustrated in the table below, which also sets out the difference between industrial agriculture on the one hand and farming based on the small mixed farm on the other.[72]

Issue	Dominant Model	Food Sovereignty Model
Trade	Free trade in everything	Food and agriculture exempt from trade agreements
Production priority	Agroexports	Food for local markets
Crop prices	"What the market dictates" (leave intact mechanisms that enforce low prices)	Fair prices that cover costs of production and allow farmers and farmworkers a life with dignity
Market access	Access to foreign markets	Access to local markets; an end to the displacement of farmers from their own markets by agribusiness
Subsidies	While prohibited in the Third World, many subsidies are allowed in the US and Europe—but are paid only to the largest farmers	Subsidies that do not damage other countries (via dumping) are okay; i.e., grant subsidies only to family farmers, for direct marketing, price/income support, soil conservation, conversion to sustainable farming, research, etc.
Food	Chiefly a commodity; in practice, this means processed, contaminated food that is full of fat, sugar, high fructose corn syrup, and toxic residues	A human right: specifically, should be healthy, nutritious, affordable, culturally appropriate, and locally produced
Being able to produce	An option for the economically efficient	A right of rural peoples
Hunger	Due to low productivity	A problem of access and distribution; due to poverty and inequality
Food security	Achieved by importing food from where it is cheapest	Greatest when food production is in the hands of the hungry, or when food is produced locally
Control over productive resources (land, water, forests)	Privatized	Local; community controlled
Access to land	Via the market	Via genuine agrarian reform; without access to land, the rest is meaningless
Seeds	A patentable commodity	A common heritage of humanity, held in trust by rural communities and cultures; "no patents on life"
Rural credit and investment	From private banks and corporations	From the public sector; designed to support family agriculture
Dumping	Not an issue	Must be prohibited

72. Peter Rosset, "Food Sovereignty: Global Rallying Cry of Farmer Movements."

Monopoly	Not an issue	The root of most problems; monopolies must be broken up
Overproduction	No such thing, by definition	Drives prices down and farmers into poverty; we need supply management policies for US and EU
Genetically modified organisms (GMOs)	The wave of the future	Bad for health and the environment; an unnecessary technology
Farming technology	Industrial, monoculture, chemical-intensive; uses GMOs	Agroecological, sustainable farming methods, no GMOs
Farmers	Anachronisms; the inefficient will disappear	Guardians of culture and crop germplasm; stewards of productive resources; repositories of knowledge; internal market and building block of broad-based, inclusive economic development
Urban consumers	Workers to be paid as little as possible	Need living wages
Another world (alternatives)	Not possible / not of interest	Possible and amply demonstrated (see resources below)

Food sovereignty is essentially about insisting that food should not be controlled by the global market but should first and foremost serve local populations.[73] Trade liberalization has led to an influx of cheap food imports into the developing world, which is putting farmers there out of business. A Kenyan study says that liberalized trade, including WTO agreements, benefits only the rich while the majority of the poor do not benefit but are instead made more vulnerable to food insecurity.[74] Countries such as South Korea, which can be completely self-sufficient in their staple, rice, should not be forced to open their gates to rice from the US or elsewhere, argues Helena Norberg Hodge. This is not free trade but forced trade. Far from benefiting these countries, such trade threatens the viability of farmers and their communities while undermining their food security. It does not benefit Western farming either, because growing for export leads to monocultures.[75]

73. Rosset, "Food Sovereignty: Global Rallying Cry of Farmer Movements."
74. Madeley, Food for All, 120.
75. Norberg-Hodge et al., Bringing the Food Economy Home, 103.

In farming, as elsewhere (as we saw in chapter six), what we find is the growth of corporate control. Vertically integrated corporations now monopolize almost every aspect of farm production and distribution, from seeds, fertilizers, and equipment to processing, transport, and marketing. Four biotech companies own 44 percent of patents on the world's most important food crops. Agrifood TNCs have market concentration that spans chemical fertilizers, pesticides, seeds, grain sales, livestock production, processing, shipping, and retail. Six corporations account for 85 percent of world trade in grain; eight for between 55 to 60 percent of world coffee; seven for 90 percent of tea; three account for 83 percent of cocoa. Through its ownership of grain elevators, rail links, terminals, and the barges and ships needed to move grain around the world, Cargill controls 80 percent of global grain distribution. Four other companies control 87 percent of American beef and another four 87 percent of American cereal. Syngenta, DuPont, and Monsanto account for nearly two-thirds of the global pesticide market, almost one-quarter of the global seed market, and 100 percent of the transgenic seed market.

Cargill's turnover in 2000 was $48 billion, equal to the GDP of the twenty-eight poorest countries. Cargill's goal is to double every five to seven years but the achievement of this goal requires the occupation of more and more territory and the expulsion of whole societies from their settlements and their commons. It has tried to convince developing countries that self-sufficiency is not a practical answer to their problems. By controlling germplasm from seed to sale TNCs are moving to monopolistic control of the food chain that allows them to extract maximum profit.[76] The biblical vision of self-perpetuating fruitfulness, says Davis, collides with the profit strategies of corporations.[77] They represent the culture of Canaan in the present context, by following which, according to the Deuteronomists, the downfall of Israel was caused. The logic of empire, as Davis says, is centralization of information and social control; its essential processes include overriding the culture

76. Madeley, *Food for All*, 122–23.

77. Davis, *Scripture, Culture, and Agriculture*, 52.

of local populations and appropriation of goods. "Good farming and good speech are both forms of local knowledge, skills held in community and developed from the cradle by imitation, use, trial and error. Both involve a sense of propriety, fitness, that does not derive from abstract rules or purely scientific reasoning."[78]

Through patenting TNCs seek to exploit a valuable Third World resource. They argue that they can only afford to invest large sums of money in breeding activities if their investment is protected. Third World farmers have to pay for "improved" varieties. The WTO agreement on Trade Related Intellectual Property Rights (TRIPS) globalizes the patent system. The agreement, which came into force in 1995, grants corporations the right to protect their intellectual property. But this threatens the sovereignty of small-scale farmers. The creation of dependency, says Brewster Kneen, is an ancient colonial practice, serving the interests of the colonizers at the expense of the colonized. It is not hard to imagine seed in the role of colonizing troops, the occupiers of the land, dictating that the peasants will now produce agricultural commodities, process them, and send them back to be purchased by those among the colonized peoples who can afford them.[79]

The Campbell's Soup firm noted that most of the soup in Asia is still homemade, "so our growth potential in this region brims with promise . . . In Mexico our opportunities have been significantly broadened with the passage of NAFTA. With doors opened wide to trade Mexico's 85 million people beckon as a highly attractive market." "Efforts at forging a consumer monoculture," writes Helena Norberg Hodge, "are effectively an attack on billions of people, mostly in the South, who must be made to reject their own individual, ethnic and cultural identities."[80]

Corporate control of the food system is bound up with industrial agriculture. For example, "the political imperative of export-led agriculture could not exist without the development of

78. Ibid., 152.
79. Kneen, *Invisible Giant,* 205.
80. Norberg-Hodge et al., *Bringing the Food Economy Home,* 29.

highly specialized commodity cropping and vice versa."[81] The iPES Report looks at eight "lock ins" that keep industrial agriculture in place. In the first place industrial agriculture is self-reinforcing because the investments it requires have to see a return. At the same time high labor costs and cheap fuel costs drive the reliance on technology. In the West cheap food has become an expectation that no politician is willing or able to challenge, but this relies on large volumes of uniform commodities. Following the emergency in Europe after World War II, a "feed the world" narrative developed, first by NGOs, but then taken up by agribusiness, which persuades both politicians and the public that it is their task. Political priorities are driven by five-year election cycles, and short-term bottom-line results are the main consideration for investors. Thinking holistically is difficult when research is increasingly privately financed, and when government, research, and farmers are all asking different questions. Above all there is a concentration of power, so that changing the food system is first and foremost a political task. The iPES Report notes the difficulties in the way of establishing an alternative food system model because it requires fewer external inputs, relies on locally adapted seeds, and favors local production and short value chains. The companies that currently control the world food system can therefore be expected to resist attempts to change the food system.[82] Here subsidiarity, and the reframing of democracy, including economic democracy, which I discussed in chapters four to six, are relevant.

No matter how urban we are, says Berry, our bodies live by farming. In the West politicians and economists, based in urban centers, have forgotten this. The giant agro chemical firms, for whom batteries of lawyers are even more important than batteries of chemists, chiefly view farming as a means to profit. If they are aware of the dangers of crossing planetary boundaries, it is as a chance to make greater profits. Just as it was for Elijah, and just as it was for the Deuteronomists, what this means for us is a choice between two ways, and two quite different value systems

---

81. Frison et al., *From Uniformity to Diversity*, 41.

82. Frison et al., *From Uniformity to Diversity*, 58.

and the practices that follow from them. As I argued in chapter six, economics fundamentally rests on an account of value that (chapter seven) can be corrupted by the dominant understanding of money. Two things are necessary to the preservation of a rich and healthy food supply for all in the coming century or centuries. The first is the restoration of an idea of the common good, especially as applied to science, which is corrupted if it is understood principally as a means to make a profit. The second is a respect for the knowledge and practices of farming communities that rest on millennial cultures. There are many signs that a move to a different paradigm is underway. Local food policy councils are looking to rethink food provisioning at a regional level both in North America and the UK. Here and there public procurement is being used to support local produce. This picks up on the bioregional idea of "foodsheds," "self-reliant, locally or regionally based food systems comprised of diversified farms using sustainable practices to supply fresher, more nutritious food stuffs to small scale processors and consumers to whom producers are linked by the bonds of community as well as economy."[83] Many attempts at developing shorter supply chains are emerging. The iPES Report concludes with a section on "Pathways of Transition" and it is to the realization of that transition—in the teeth of "the powers that be"—that I turn in the final chapter.

83. Pretty, *Agri-Culture,* 117.

TRANSITION

Chapter Nine

The World Made Otherwise

> Between the realisation of the status quo and the utopia of un-
> limited possibilities lies the field of really possible alternatives.
>
> —ULRICH DUCHROW AND FRANZ HINKELAMMERT

"THE WORLD MADE OTHERWISE" is the title of Ton Veerkamp's great account of the grand narrative of Scripture, *Die Welt Anders*. Scripture, he argues, is from first to last a vision of a world made otherwise than that based on hierarchy, domination, and the rule of money and violence. The vision lasted into the fourth century, when the church became the cult of empire. Augustine, as we saw in chapter six, transformed the biblical eschatology, which looked for different structures here and now, into a hope for life hereafter, and so disabled the revolutionary impact of the church. For this to be truly possible the Bible had to be silenced, and we saw in the fifth chapter the radical consequences of vernacularization, and the fruitless struggles to stem that tide.

The grand narrative of the church was transposed to the narrative of liberty, equality, and fraternity in the eighteenth century, and then into the vision of a world free from capital, ruled by ordinary people ("the proletariat"). All those narratives, Veerkamp believes, have collapsed:

> The wall is down. Marx and Engels wrote in the Communist Manifesto: "A spectre is abroad in Europe—the

spectre of communism." On 9 November 1989 that spectre vanished. And the grand narratives were washed away like sewage. There is no longer a seventh day to look forward to: the American Francis Fukuyama announces "the end of history." Jacques Derrida talks of the "new gospel" in his 1993 book "The Ghost of Marx." According to Matthew the old gospel must be proclaimed to all people "and then comes the end." Fukuyama's gospel of freedom and democracy is in fact announced to all peoples—with bombs. The end of which Fukuyama speaks is the end of all alternatives, to help those who, themselves heartless, dwell in the heartless world. No alternative will be given to them except that which has become real, no more "God" except the true "God of merchandise," that is gold, as Marx, that pale ghost, made clear in the 19th century. The end is no new grand narrative, but rather the destruction of all grand narratives. It offers people and nations homelessness in their world.[1]

Divested of the ritual trappings of the churches, writes Melucci, the sacred becomes a purely cultural form of resistance that counters the presumptions of power by affirming the right to desire—to hope that the world is more than what actually is. The voice of the possible, however, is soon reduced to silence, as institutionalization and routinization take over.[2] Of course we believe in political equality, writes Wolfgang Streeck, but where is the energy for this going to come from given decades of re-education in which cultural politics (gay marriage, the symbolic "gendering" of everything) takes the place of aspirations to justice? Where is the "revolutionary subject" any longer?[3] He thinks that the advocates of market justice, with all the power money brings, are able to corrupt the majority and that this will very likely lead to anarchy or the spread of a serf mentality.

These melancholy visions suggest that there is no realistic hope for dealing with the kind of social disintegration the crossing

1. Veerkamp, *Welt Anders,* 422.
2. Melucci, *Challenging Codes,* 171.
3. Streeck, *Capitalism,* 192.

of planetary boundaries will very likely bring. In this book I have argued, to the contrary, that the humane values that have been adumbrated over the past two and a half thousand years, since well before the axial age, but given a decisive turn then, will win out, leading to fresh expressions of polity and economy (and therefore, naturally, of farming). As we saw in the first chapter, scientists like Brad Werner, and writers like Naomi Klein, argue that the only effective way to deal with the problems we face is through social movements. I have considered people's organizations as part of the process of educating for democracy but I turn now to consider the claim that social movements can help shape a more humane future. If my argument in the first chapter is right, then this is not simply an "academic" matter, but a matter of the utmost importance. How effective are social movements? What hope do they really offer? In the contest between market values and democratic values, how likely are the latter to win out?

In chapter five I looked at participatory democracy, which Fishkin understands as just another variant of mass democracy. What social movement activists understand by it is quite different. Carole Pateman, in a classic book, appealed to studies which showed that *significant changes in human behavior can be brought about rapidly only if the persons who are expected to change participate in deciding what the change shall be and how it shall be made.*[4] The importance of this argument for addressing the transgression of planetary boundaries is obvious and it is fundamental to my argument. We learn to participate by participating, Pateman argues, and feelings of political efficacy are more likely to be developed in a participatory environment. Experience of a participatory authority structure might also, she thought (here agreeing with Bauman), lead to diminishing tendencies towards non-democratic attitudes in the individual.[5] Participatory practices are at the heart of my account of a political reality that can sustain humanizing values and it is these I turn to in this final chapter. I first look at the successes social movements have already had in changing society and

4. Pateman, *Participation and Democratic Theory,* 63 (my italics).
5. Ibid., 105.

consider the claim that they constitute a "prefigurative politics."
I turn to their relation to anarchism, and then look more closely
at the Transition movement, which began in Britain but is now
established in Europe, North America, and Australasia. I evaluate its key theme of resilience before turning to a review of what
Christianity might have to offer to the sustaining of our humanity,
and lastly, what it might have to offer if attempts to change direction fail, and we have to cope with "a new dark ages."

Social movements and prefigurative politics

Social movements were not, of course, invented by sociologists in
the 1990s. The groups Norman Cohn documents in *The Pursuit of
the Millennium* were all social movements, as were the Donatists
in the fourth century, and doubtless countless other groups in
ancient times. Probably the church in the first two centuries is
best understood as a social movement. Throughout history, says
Manuel Castells, such groups are the producers of new values and
goals around which the institutions of society are transformed,
creating new norms to organize social life.[6] Social movements
are the sources of social change, he argues, and therefore of the
constitution of society.[7] Unlike trade unions, say, they do not
represent just one segment of the population but seek to change
society as a whole. David Graeber talks of a "prefigurative politics"—the idea that the organizational form that an activist group
takes should embody the kind of society we wish to create.[8] Precisely this is how Paul understood ecclesia as he set it out to the
small and fractious group in Corinth (1 Cor 12). Unfortunately,
for most of its existence the church has modeled hierarchical (and
now managerial) ideas of society.

It is worth pausing a moment to think of who was and is involved in the North American movements mentioned above. The

6. Castells, *Networks of Outrage and Hope,* 9.

7. Ibid., 12.

8. Graeber, *The Democracy Project,* 23.

civil rights movement, of course, began with the injustice suffered by black, largely African origin, populations in the United States. It then attracted student groups of all ethnicities in support. It learned from Gandhi, and was committed to nonviolence, but also used the street theater of long marches, mass demonstrations, and so forth. Both Gandhi and King were geniuses in the use of profound cultural symbols to create liberative theater. King avoided polarizing politics. Instead he used references to the themes and values of the heritage of the white American elites of that period, such as the relationship between individual liberty and a sense of responsibility towards the community. It was these values that provided him with a base to argue the full legitimacy of the demands for civil rights.[9] The movement learned from Quaker traditions of appeals to the "sense of the meeting" with pauses for reflection, issues laid aside for future discussion, and decisions made by consensus.[10] Václav Havel spoke of the preparedness to stand up for the truth as "the living humus from which genuine political change springs," and both Gandhi and King, and their followers, instantiate this.[11]

The peace movement, at least in the UK, was a largely middle class movement—Bertrand Russell was one of its leading spokesmen. It began with protest marches and then proceeded, again through theater—the theater of fence cutting and, in a small number of very effective cases, of inflicting damage on an airplane or nuclear submarine—which brought huge publicity through the court cases which followed. In Britain the burgeoning feminist movement mounted its own protest by surrounding the American bomber base at Greenham Common, a protest which lasted for nineteen years, and helped bring about the withdrawal of the planes. At its height it involved as many as 50,000 women. The peace movements, wrote Alberto Melucci, with their highly symbolic content, have achieved much more

9. Della Porta and Diani, *Social Movements,* 76.

10. Polletta, *Freedom is an Endless Meeting,* 197.

11. Havel, *Power of the Powerless,* 50. We can also think of Tertullian's claim that "the blood of the martyrs is the seed of the church."

in changing military policies and East-West relations than have decades of political negotiation.[12]

Building on the suffragette movement of the early years of the twentieth century, second-wave feminism might be said to have begun in 1962 with the publication of Betty Friedan's *The Feminine Mystique*. She gave voice to the outrage of educated women who were forced to stay at home, and were unable to find work in which their education and talents could be used. The movement began by attacking gender discrimination in the workplace, which was included in the US Civil Rights Act of 1964. It then adopted the much more ambitious goal of overthrowing patriarchy, adding the idea that "the personal is the political" to the political lexicon. Although the movement was divided on class and racial lines it was by and large non-hierarchical, and did things collectively and experimentally.[13] In the United States the movement gained momentum from the anti-Vietnam war protests. The FBI paid it the compliment of viewing it as "part of the enemy, a challenge to American values," as well as potentially violent and linked to other "extremist" movements.[14] Consciousness raising, which had already been part of the civil rights movement, now became part of the women's movement as well. More militant tactics included using class action lawsuits, formal complaints, protests, and hearings to create legal change.

Although, of course, there is still massive discrimination against black people in the United States, although there are still nuclear arsenals, and although women have not yet attained full equality anywhere, nevertheless these three movements have without any doubt brought about profound cultural changes that everybody in the West benefits from.[15] Together, these movements—at

12. Melucci, *Challenging Codes*, 194.

13. Collins, *When Everything Changed*.

14. Rosen, *The World Split Open*, 245–46.

15. Wendell Berry believes people in movements too readily learn to deny to others the rights and privileges they demand for themselves, and that they seek to remedy or control effects while leaving causes in place. It is hard to see how this applies to these movements, unless he is thinking of fundamental economic change. *In the Presence of Fear*, 36.

least, those in the democratic polities mentioned in chapter five—came to be characterized by a subculture of nonviolent direct action, defined by egalitarian, feminist, pacifist, and ecological values and by internal procedures centered on consensus decisionmaking and efforts to create community.[16] An attitude that turns away from abstract political visions of the future towards concrete human beings and ways of defending them, wrote Havel, "is quite naturally accompanied by an intensified antipathy to all forms of violence carried out in the name of 'a better future', and by a profound belief that a future secured by violence might actually be worse than what exists now."[17] Francesca Polletta talks of "an evolving culture of radical protest," fed by popularization of ideas about self-development from psychotherapy and Eastern religions, acceptance of the idea that the personal is the political, a willingness to see culture and everyday life as sites of radical change, all of which, she says, contributed to a personalist political stance. "To make the self the arbiter of political choices was a way to bridge differences of political opinion among people who lacked strong traditions of church, community or long standing left politics." There was a convergence of new left and new age politics.[18]

Della Porta and Diani note that although the civil rights movement was, in origin, anything but middle class, the "new social movements" (NSMs) by and large had a middle-class identity and that "substantial barriers" seem to persist against a more systematic cooperation between NSMs and the working class.[19] "Although there is no obvious reason why concerns for public goods like clean environment [and taking action about planetary boundaries: TG] should be the preserve of the middle classes the way these preoccupations are organized by new middle class activists seems to prevent working class involvement."[20] One study traced the roots of middle-class involvement to the fact that the activists involved

16. Jasper, *The Art of Moral Protest,* 188–90.

17. Havel, *Power,* 71.

18. Polletta, *Freedom,* 197.

19. Della Porta and Diani, *Social Movements,* 15, 17.

20. Ibid., 53.

worked in jobs like teaching or social work, dedicated to maximizing noneconomic values.[21] The class base of NSMs marks them off from people's organizations. NSM norms, it is argued, are influenced by the experiences of their educated middle-class members, such as belief in the power of information to convert others, the value of individual expression, and the importance of egalitarian process, and this cultural difference is one of the reasons community organizations distance themselves from them.[22]

In contrast to people's organizations there is often a strong utopian dimension in NSMs that means movements are not limited to the selection of practical goals. Rather, it makes it possible to think of aims and objectives that the dominant culture tends to exclude from the outset, and thus movements disseminate concepts and perspectives that might otherwise have remained marginal.[23] Holding to, and living out, alternative values is central to this (as it was for the church in the first and second centuries). If power is exercised by programming and switching networks, says Castells, then counter-power, the deliberate attempt to change power relationships, is enacted by reprogramming networks around alternative interests and values.[24] Contemporary social movements are not concerned primarily with a more or less disruptive public confrontation against the authorities. Instead, their modus operandi is to fashion new meanings for social action.[25] Recent forms of collective action, Melucci argued, largely ignore the political system and generally display disinterest towards the idea of seizing power. "It appears that the traditional goals of taking political power and gaining control over the state apparatus have given way to a desire for immediate control over the conditions of existence and to claims to independence from the system."[26]

21. Cotgrove and Duff, "Environmentalism, Middle Class radicalism and Politics."

22. Swarts, *Organizing*, 51.

23. Della Porta and Diani, *Social Movements*, 72.

24. Castells, *Networks*, 14.

25. Melucci, *Challenging*, 203.

26. Ibid., 104.

NSMs may not take power, but they certainly effect change. It is not uncommon, writes David Meyer, for governments to create new institutions, such as departments and agencies, in response to activists' demands. Social movements spawn dedicated organizations that generally survive long after a movement's moment has passed. Moreover, social movements change the people who participate in them, "educating as well as mobilizing activists, and thereby promoting ongoing awareness and action that extends beyond the boundaries of one movement or campaign ... To paraphrase a famous scholar: activists make history, but they do not make it just as they please. In fighting one political battle, they shape the conditions of the next one."[27] Social movements may become institutionalized, but if so, says Sidney Tarrow, they will nevertheless have changed the terrain and helped to prepare the ground for something better.[28]

I turn now to the relation these movements have to anarchism, especially as illustrated by the Occupy movement.

Anarchism and social movements

The Occupy movement, which briefly garnered so much media attention in 2012, and which led to some highly publicized resignations at St. Paul's in London, began, at least partly, at the instigation of David Graeber. His vast and entertaining ethnography of direct action is an account of the meaning and methods of anarchism and there are obvious links to the social movements just mentioned.

Anarchists have a bad name because of the violent behavior of a few people who claimed that name during the nineteenth century, as fictionalized by Dostoevsky in *The Devils*, and by Joseph

27. Meyer, "How Social Movements Matter."

28. Tarrow, *Power in Movement*, 274. For all their achievements social movements are not without their problems. If they are in for the long haul ordinary people with work or family requirements may not be able to sustain their participation. The "movement society," Tarrow argues, may actually be increasing the participation gap between rich and poor, the well-networked and the relatively isolated, and those with full-time occupations and those with disposable income and free time. Ibid., 269.

Conrad in *The Secret Agent*. Today some anarchist groups, like Black Dwarf in London, continue to pursue pretty bruising behavior in demonstrations. But Graeber has nothing but scorn for any form of violence: it is, he says, a form of active stupidity, "a way of clapping one's hands over one's ears and refusing to be reasonable."[29]

What sort of social relations is it possible to create among those who wish to make their lives a refusal of the logic of capitalism, even as they necessarily remain inside it?[30] Anarchists, says Colin Ward, appealing to Kropotkin, are people who make a social and political philosophy out of the natural and spontaneous tendency of humans to associate together for mutual benefit. Anarchism is just the name given to the idea that it is possible and desirable for society to organize itself without government, which is to say, without structures of control.[31] He agrees that the problems we face cannot be dealt with by tweaking the system. Instead, he argues that spheres of free action need to be extended until they make up most of social life.[32] Such spheres might be instantiated by the LETS schemes mentioned in the seventh chapter, but they cover very few of the other areas of daily life (going to work, using transport, going to a doctor's surgery, for example).

In a much more socialist direction Richard Day looks for the transfer of the means of production—the soil, the mines, the factories, the means of communication, and the means of existence—"from the hands of the individual capitalist into those of the communities of producers and consumers."[33] He privileges direct action for the construction of sustainable alternatives over revolution and reform.[34] Here again we can think of some of the initiatives

---

29. Graeber, *Democracy*, 257.

30. Graeber, *Direct Action*, 262.

31. Ward, *Anarchy in Action*, 15. Martin Buber, hardly an anarchist, said the problem was not government but rather the need not to have domination. *Paths in Utopia*, 43.

32. Ward, *Anarchy in Action*, 123.

33. Day, *Gramsci is Dead*, 119.

34. Ibid., 215.

mentioned in the sixth chapter, and of Martin Large's proposals for mutualization as, perhaps, fulfilling an anarchist agenda.

Anarchists, Graeber tells us, envision a world based on equality and solidarity, in which human beings would be free to associate with one another to pursue an endless variety of visions and projects but no one would have the ability to call on armed men to show up and say, "I don't care what you have to say about this, shut up and do what you're told."[35] We act like anarchists, he says, every time we come to an understanding that wouldn't require physical threats as a means of enforcement.[36] Anarchists believe, he argues, that the ultimate form of power is the power of the imagination. It is the imagination—vision—that creates social movements that can change the reality in which we live.

Anarchists reject states and the systematic forms of inequality states make possible. They neither seek to get governments to institute reforms nor seek to seize power for themselves but rather seek to build a new society in the shell of the old.[37] In part they seek to do this by creating local assemblies and setting up the foundations of an alternative economic and political system. In other words, their practice is a form of participatory democracy and it is this which constitutes prefigurative politics.

Francesca Polletta argues that the social movements of the 1960s showed people that decentralized and participatory organizational forms could work, powerfully, creatively, and with immediate impact.[38] In these movements it turned out that "freedom is an endless meeting"—politics was precisely the kind of local debate which Jefferson, Tocqueville, or Ellis imagined. "Far from a utopian retreat from the rough and tumble of real political contention, participatory democracy within the movement helped powerless people contend politically."[39]

35. Graeber, *Democracy*, 188.
36. Ibid., 295.
37. Graeber, *Direct Action*, 217.
38. Polletta, *Freedom*, 44.
39. Ibid., 205.

Although the conventional wisdom is that participatory democracy is worthy in principle but unwieldy in practice, in fact, Polletta argues, there are solidary, innovatory, and developmental benefits to it.[40] The practices of participatory democratic decision-making build solidarity by pressing participants to recognize the legitimacy of other people's reasoning—precisely what Fishkin wants in deliberative democracy. An etiquette of deliberation was developed in the 1960s, taken up by Occupy, and the Transition movement, which, "by routinizing interaction and domesticating attendant emotions, generated trust in the process."[41]

Building on the culture of these movements, the Occupy movement also saw its activities (which included squatting, rent strikes, and debtors' assemblies), as a way of "laying the groundwork for a genuinely democratic culture, and introducing the skills, habits, and experience that would make an entirely new conception of politics come to life."[42]

So, as Carole Pateman argued, participation can change political culture. But what about the difficulties? First, Jo Freeman's celebrated paper *The Tyranny of Structurelessness*, written in 1970, explored the limits of pedagogy and friendship as models for democratic relationships.[43] "With the women's movement the notion of sisterhood was simply inadequate to gloss over the very real differences of interest among women. Despite their common aspirations for radical equality, their views of how to achieve equality were too diverse for consensus."[44] This, says Polletta, is the participatory

40. Ibid., 7.

41. Ibid., 191. Polletta remarks, "A 1960s activist would be surprised by the procedural paraphernalia that accompanies democratic decision making today. There are formal roles in the process—timekeeper, staker, facilitator, vibes watcher and sophisticated hand signals: agreement with point made; concern about whether the deliberative process is proceeding according to form; blocking a decision—non support, reservations, blocking, withdrawal. In some segments of the movement field participatory democracy has come close to being institutionalised."

42. Graeber, *Democracy*, xviii.

43. Polletta, *Freedom*, 148.

44. Ibid., 151.

democratic dilemma. "The very relationships generating the trust and respect that democracy requires may also come with norms that undercut the democratic project."[45] We have to ask about the limits of consensus, and how far it can take us.

The critique of Occupy was that the process became the goal, and a kind of group narcissism developed that meant that nothing followed from the protests. Instead of being prefigurative, the process became the goal and nothing of any consequence followed.

More fundamentally comes the problem I raised in the fourth chapter, concerning the relative importance of order and freedom as goals of any polity. Those who prioritize order can say, quite justifiably, that anarchism, of the kind recommended by Kropotkin, Ward, or Graeber, does not face up to the difficulty of dealing with those who want to "bend the banana straight for the benefit of mankind," as Günther Grass put it—dictators, whether religious or secular, who are able to inspire millions of people to impose their will on others by indiscriminate mass terror. It also does not face up to the difficulty of the Camorra, or the Mexican drug gangs, or the assassins who murder environmental activists in Brazil. Anarchism rests on a vision of a redeemed society, but we have daily, and indeed hourly, reminders that we are not currently redeemed. So is the aspiration to change the world within the shell of the old delusionary daydreaming? To test this question further I look in more detail at the Transition Movement.

Transition

Those familiar with the Transition Town movement will see many resonances between it and the account of social movements and of anarchism just given. The Transition Town movement started in Totnes, England, in 2006 and has since spread throughout the country and to Europe, Scandinavia, North America, Australasia, and Asia, with more than 1,000 initiatives in all. Transition is a social movement that specifically arises in response to the threat

45. Ibid., 221.

posed by the transgression of planetary boundaries. Originally the transition envisaged was from an oil-dependent to a non-oil-dependent society. Driven by the peak oil analysis, it asked what work people were going to do, and how they were going to feed themselves, when oil was no longer cheap and abundant. As the determination to extract every last drop of oil from tar sands, the Arctic, deep sea beds and so forth, becomes apparent, the emphasis has shifted more to addressing climate change. Its focus is cultural. "It is about asking what the culture of your community would need to be like to be as resilient as possible in the face of great change. It goes beyond reducing energy and planting trees and needs, ultimately, to seep into the culture of place: how a place thinks of itself; what it takes pride in. This is the depth of the change Transition initiatives are attempting to effect."[46] By focusing on community it attempts to change social and *therefore* political and economic structures: building community, or regenerating community, comes first.[47] One of the key aspects of transition is that it does not understand itself as a militant organization. Hopkins speaks of it as "a creative, engaging, playful process, wherein we support our communities through the loss of the familiar and inspire and create a new lower energy infrastructure which is ultimately an improvement on the present."[48]

Rather than beginning with a grim portrayal of the future, Hopkins hopes to sketch "a picture of the future so enticing people instinctively feel drawn towards it."[49] It seeks to be hopeful and constructive. It understands itself to be not about campaigning against things but working for a world that has embraced its limitations. Unlike Naomi Klein, Wolfgang Streeck, and Castells, Transition does not believe that fear is a useful driver: any approach that seeks

46. Hopkins, *The Transition Companion*, 79.

47. Cf. Melucci: "No liveable future can be imagined unless we change our social relations and the circulation of information before simply improving our technical apparatuses." *Challenging*, 163.

48. Hopkins, *The Transition Handbook*, 50. Solnit emphasizes the importance of playfulness in movements seeking a world otherwise. *Hope*, 62.

49. Hopkins, *Handbook*, 79.

to engage a significant proportion of the population in responses to energy descent, writes Hopkins, "has to instil in people a sense of optimism regarding the possibility of change rather than berate them for their wicked ways."[50] This sense of optimism is instilled partly by "unleashing" the creativity, motivation, and knowledge of communities. A study of Transition initiatives around the world published in 2012 found that many groups prioritized positivity, fun, conviviality, and sense of community.[51]

How effective a strategy is this? William Gamson's *The Strategy of Social Protest* found, in an examination of social movements, that the groups that were most successful in achieving policy outcomes developed centralized and hierarchical forms of organization.[52] Without some degree of formal organization, he found, movements frequently fade away or dissipate their energies.[53] The noncentralized leadership described by Graeber and other anarchists, however, describes the ethos of Transition initiatives. The movement attempts to be open and consensual. It shares the repertoire of discussion and debate developed in the North American movements referred to above. It attempts to create a participant driven and bottom-up democratic process and thus invites comment and debate to enable the movement to evolve. In this way it constitutes a "prefigurative politics" preparing the ground for a more genuinely democratic society. In its *processes* it provides that "primary education for democracy" that Tocqueville saw in North American wards and Tom Ellis in parish councils. How far it changes mass perceptions of political culture is another matter however: in my experience it largely remains the domain of a small group of highly committed activists. Even in Totnes, the center of the movement, full of highly talented and engaged people working

50. Ibid., 92.

51. Feola and Nunes, "Success and failure of Grassroots Innovations for addressing climate change." Other characteristics identified by this survey, such as "the need for outreach projects such as education and awareness-raising in the community" apply to any group whatsoever, outside a cult.

52. Tarrow, *Power*, 123.

53. Tarrow, ibid., 124.

at Transition full time, ordinary citizens can be completely vague about what Transition stands for.[54]

Transition emphasizes optimism, and the Transition Network blog is relentlessly upbeat—perhaps in response to the idea that all of us are secretly "in denial," hanging over an abyss of despair.

Unlike people's organizations it does not acknowledge anger as an important motivation. This seems to me to be limiting. Optimism and confidence are frequent accompaniments to protest, says Castells, but so are anger, indignation, fear, compassion, and a sense of obligation.[55] Appealing to the theory of affective intelligence, he argues that fear and enthusiasm are the emotions most relevant to social mobilization. Fear is overcome by anger. "Concretely speaking: if many individuals feel humiliated, exploited, ignored or misrepresented, they are ready to transform their anger into action, as soon as they overcome their fear. And they overcome their fear by the extreme expression of anger, in the form of outrage, when learning of an unbearable event suffered by someone with whom they identify."[56] People seeking a new kind of world order are often convinced of the need for militant action. Capitalism will never fall on its own, says David Harvey. It will have to be pushed:

> The accumulation of capital will never cease. It will have to be stopped. The capitalist class will never willingly surrender its power. It will have to be dispossessed. To do what has to be done will take tenacity and determination, patience and cunning, along with fierce political commitments born out of moral outrage at what exploitative compound growth is doing to all facets of life, human and otherwise, on planet Earth. Political mobilisations

54. Communication of one of my students, born and brought up in central Totnes, whose neighbors have no clear idea what Transition is about. My experience in speaking to clergy in Totnes deanery in 2012 was similar.

55. Tarrow, *Power*, 154.

56. Castells, *Networks*, 15. Streeck agrees that "fear can be a good counsellor." *Buying Time*, 163.

sufficient to such a task have occurred in the past. They
can and will surely come again.[57]

The major social movements that I reviewed earlier, which gave rise
to the social movement literature, were all "protest movements." In
order for mobilization to occur, says Melucci, the following factors must be present: a collective identity, the identification of an
adversary, the definition of a purpose, and an object at stake in
the conflict.[58] The irreducible act that lies at the base of all social
movements, says Tarrow, is contentious collective action that
brings ordinary people into confrontation with opponents, élites,
or authorities.[59] But this is not true of Transition, which does not
identify an adversary, does not think in terms of conflict, and for
which the local community is the primary referent.

In 2008 the Trapeze Collective in Leeds, a socialist action
group, took issue with Transition about its tactics. While it is clearly
important to support projects for sustainability, they argued, they
should not be confused or conflated with tackling the root causes
of climate change or peak oil's energy scarcity. Meaningful social
change, they argued, comes through political organizing, rupture
and struggle, and a lot of mobilizing at the local level. They wanted
"high-impact actions that shake people to question the habits of
high consumer lifestyles, cheap flights and unnecessary car jour-
neys and the political systems that facilitate them." The idea of
Transition Towns is to create a model that everyone can agree to.
But if everyone can agree with an idea then what exactly is going to
change, and how is it different to what went before?[60]

Hopkins replied that Transition is determinedly inclusive
and non-blaming. A successful transition, he said, will by necessity be about a bringing together of individuals and organizations
rather than a continued fracturing and antagonizing. Transition
was designed to appeal as much to the Rotary Club and Women's

57. Harvey, *The Enigma of Capital*, 260.

58. Melucci, *Challenging*, 292.

59. Tarrow, *Power*, 7, 8.

60. http://www.paulchatterton.com/2009/08/17/the-rocky-road-to-a
-real-transition-reprinted-with-new-preface/.

Institute as to the authors of the Trapeze report. Transition's refusal to engage in confrontational approaches to change has been a conscious decision from the outset. It is designed in such a way as to come in under the radar. Transition is positive and solutions focused. It is undogmatic and it allows space for people to explore how change will affect them personally.[61] Here he agrees with Solnit, who believes that new movements have "an ease with difference that doesn't need to be eliminated and that differences can be a strength, not a weakness."[62]

The problem with including both the Rotary Club and the Trapeze collective is that one will very likely be in favor of neoliberalism, which is currently crucifying the people of Greece, as it has done the people of many Third World countries, and the other will be vehemently opposed to it. The irenic gesture ducks the issue of deciding between them. In fact, of course, Transition is working for a quite different economy to that of neoliberalism, and recognizes the damage neoliberalism does, both to people and to planet. But here the strategy of London Citizens seems both more honest and more realistic: to vehemently oppose the policy and equally strenuously to refuse to demonize the opponent and to keep dialogue open with them as far as possible.

Three years after the exchange with the Trapeze collective, in response to queries from within the Transition movement about action over cuts in public services, Hopkins argued that to embrace activism as a dynamic force actually weakens transition rather than strengthens it. Transition, he said, is not another deep green left-wing campaign group. A transition group comes together to pursue an explicit mission, to make the community more resilient, more viable, more diverse, more entrepreneurial, and happier. Transition is not a campaigning organization. It does not have any party political allegiances and indeed includes people from all political perspectives. Rather than lobbying or campaigning the focus is on making change happen on the ground, on helping the

61. Hopkins, "The Rocky Road to a Real Transition." It emerges that Transition is less undogmatic than it thinks it is!

62. Solnit, Hope, 146.

economy of this place become more robust and reduce its impact. In the face of the slashing of public services it is even more urgent that we are successful in arguing the case of economic localization and resilience, and that we model it in practice, creating new viable businesses, influencing council decisions, creating broad networks of organizations, working with local business, bringing investment and expertise into support this.[63]

Hopkins's stance finds some support from Melucci's account of social movements. New social movements, he says, have a bottom-up and disenchanted approach, compared to the purist tradition of Left militantism. They act at their own specific level, aiming at precise, concrete, and unifying goals. For this core of the movement, the institutions and the market are not traps to be avoided but instruments to be utilized to the extent to which they enable the achievement of environmentalist goals. Better accustomed to wielding the same weapons as their adversaries, these actors may perform a modernizing role within the institutions, while their behavior towards the outside translates into institutional support or "alternative" entrepreneurship.[64] Transition aims at culture change but it has to be said that, in the UK in 2017, Jeremy Corbyn's "Momentum" movement, which uses more precisely targeted means of effecting change—for example by mobilizing student voters—seems, for the moment, to have done more by way of culture change than ten years of Transition mobilization.

The politics of a transition away from fossil fuels is ultimately moral, authors writing for the Worldwatch Institute argue. They look to the delegitimization of the use of fossil fuels in the same way that slavery and smoking tobacco were delegitimized.[65] In this process they look to acts of local resistance which contribute to a new normative belief. Resistance, too, is what Naomi Klein calls for in face of the wrecking tactics of the Trump administration and its use of what she calls "the shock doctrine," which she finds

63. Hopkins, "Transition and Activism."

64. Melucci, *Challenging*, 166. The emphasis on social entrepreneurship in Transition tends to bear this out.

65. Princen, Manno, and Martin, "Keep them in the ground," 165.

analogies to throughout the world. Resistance implies struggle, and evokes the sacrifice of "resistance groups" against fascism during World War II. We have to ask, in relation to the Transition strategy, whether more could be learned from satyagraha, Gandhi's nonviolent resistance, or refusal of cooperation. The problems I sketched in the first chapter, as climate scientists like Kevin Anderson cannot emphasize strongly enough, are screamingly urgent. The question of whether no violent direct action is needed, for example in relation to fracking, or the erection of new coal fired power plants, has to be on the cards. Gandhi's program was both positive, and based on the search for truth—here, an analogy with Transition—but also rested on noncooperation. The potential of this for bringing about social change has not yet been sufficiently explored as part of the response to the ecological crisis.

Social movements, argue both Melucci and Graeber, stake out the territory of a prefigurative politics. If we are to survive humanly, however, we have to move from the prefigurative to the realized, and I have suggested ways in which this might happen both in terms of different construals of democracy and of economics. Only this will reverse the new feudalism sketched by Crouch and reclaim territory that is now "post democratic." That process, like every other humane advance in history, will be driven by humane values, of the kind given voice to by Isaiah, Jeremiah, Jesus of Nazareth, and Paul, as well as by the prophets and teachers of many other traditions (but not by Nietzsche!). This returns us to the third chapter, the account of the virtues, and the question how they are learned. We saw there that education, broadly conceived, has a key role. Although "education" is far more than school and university the current contest over the nature and content of secondary and tertiary education is still crucial. In a country like the UK education is seen largely as a preparation for "business"—which means business as usual—the priority of profit, the emasculation of democracy, the sanctification of retributive justice, the use of nuclear deterrence. Finland, by contrast, which has no seat at the Security Council, and does not have to play the power game, and which has the best educational scores worldwide, is pursuing a genuinely democratic and humane primary and secondary school education, based on different values, which could be the seed bed of a different kind of society.[66] Changing the nature of education is, of course, a political task and cannot be attained by Transition methods.

Transition culture

In the guide to the 2010 Transition Conference people were told that critical thinking was central to Transition initiatives. Participants were urged to promote the questioning of assertions and to try to promote values of scientific reasoning so as to give people the critical tools vital to the successful design of communities. They were told to avoid the creation of any sacred cows, keeping all assumptions open to ongoing questioning. They should work to avoid perceptions of being hippy or excessively rooted in alternative culture, and ensure that the project remains accessible to as wide a range of people as possible.[67] Like so much excellent advice, this is not always followed.

Much of the Transition vernacular is borrowed from psychotherapy or ecopsychology. Inner Transition, we are told in the *Transition Companion*, draws on three distinct strands: insights of psychology and psychotherapy that seek to understand the roots of human destructiveness and dysfunction and to enable the healing of the wounded and wounding human psyche. Ecopsychology argues that our relationship to the earth has a significant bearing on our psychology. The second involves insights from teachings and writings about the transformation of consciousness, often drawn from Eastern traditions. The third major strand comes from the many peoples who still remember and practice "Earth centred wisdom."[68] Unlike the BBCOs Bretherton documents, Judaeo Christian influence is virtually zero. When a Transitioner

66. As emphasized in the film *Demain*, C. Dion and M. Laurent, 2017.
67. *2010 Transition Network Conference Guide,* 38.
68. Hopkins, *Companion,* 141.

THE WORLD MADE OTHERWISE: TRANSITION

from Norwich mentioned as sources of inspiration Marxist theory, Noam Chomsky, Naomi Klein, and the history of Levellers and Diggers, Hopkins replied that this was "almost certain to relegate Transition to being seen as yet another deep green, left wing campaign group."[69] But for many people (I put up my hand) most or all of these things name spiritual resources more than they identify being part of a left-wing campaign group. For some (I could not say how many) they are more significant spiritual resources than "teachings and writings about transformation of consciousness" or "Earth centred wisdom." What is missing from these latter resources is social analysis, and it could be that this is related to Transition's determined blindness to class and the almost complete absence (in contrast to London Citizens, where it derives from the prophetic tradition) of the rhetoric of justice.

The three roots of inner Transition sketched out in the *Transition Companion* are part of a certain (though far from universal) demotic, very much adopted by Transition, and it is worth recording, in the interests of the "rigorous critique" recommended in the earlier document, that not everyone accepts it as, shall we say, "gospel." Beginning with Philip Rieff in 1966 many critics have worried that the function of therapy is not to help change the status quo but to reinforce it.[70] For William Epstein, psychotherapy is a romantic denial of reality that in its most common expression realizes the dominant preferences of contemporary society.[71] Similar doubts accompany the centrality of the work of Carl Jung to ecopsychology, rooted as it is in the nature philosophy of late–nineteenth-century German thought and what Richard Noll has called the "Central European cauldron of neopa-

69. Hopkins, "Transition is not a left wing campaign group."

70. "The outcome of psychotherapy is undoubtedly in part at least about improving a person's capacity to cope and function successfully in their given context. In this sense it is about conformity and adaptation and serves to reinforce the status quo." Pilgrim, *Psychotherapy and Society*, 22.

71. Epstein, *Psychotherapy as Religion*, xi. For Epstein (4), "The entire field is pseudoscience and best understood as an elaborate mysticism only differentiated from frank religion, even its crackpot fringes, by a seemingly modern orientation and the cant of science."

gan, Nietzschean, mystical, hereditarian volkish utopianism out of which national socialism arose."[72]

People new to Transition are often directed to positive thinking books like *Find Your Power*. Once again, ought we to take this uncritically? Self-help books advocate the twelve steps which Transition, at least in the beginning, appealed to. These are essentially a series of maxims and mandates. The problems discussed, says Wendy Kaminer, don't seem nearly as formidable as the problems of the poor and the uninsured chronically ill. In her view the books market authority in a culture that idealizes individualism but not thinking, and shy away from critical social analysis.[73]

Rieff talks about Jung's "elaborately Romantic contempt for 'mere intellect.'"[74] An anti-intellectual demotic is characteristic of Western society and despite the splendid advice quoted at the beginning of this section, Transition is not always free of it. Thus, reviewing Klein's *This Changes Everything*, Hopkins complains in the first instance that it is too long. People, he tells us, no longer read big books.[75] Although I cited Neil Postman's mordant analysis of the television culture in the first chapter, this seems to me in equal measure patronizing and mistaken. In a rather mystifying way early Transition literature encouraged communities to "learn from the elders." Well, if we go back one generation in the UK (and doubtless in the rest of Europe and certainly in other parts of the world, and especially contemporary Latin America) we have miners, steelworkers, farmworkers, dockers—people who worked a ten-hour day and then went to WEA classes (where

---

72. Noll, *The Jung Cult*, 21. There is also a worry about Jung's account of evil as a nonmoral or premoral good, which has important consequences when we are trying to work out what is wrong with society and what we ought to do about it. Cf. Epstein, *Psychotherapy as Religion*, 191, 196.

73. Kaminer, *I'm Dysfunctional, You're Dysfunctional*, 165.

74. Rieff, *The Triumph of the Therapeutic*, 98.

75. Similar things were said in my Transition training. This seems to me a spineless abdication of intellectual responsibility. Schell reminds us that Mandela organized political discussions and read literature (especially Shakespeare) in prison, read for correspondence degrees, and that Polish activists established a flying university. *Unconquerable World*, 253.

they were taught by, amongst others, Tawney and Polanyi) and to local libraries in the evening to work through Marx and Hegel, Spinoza and Locke—the whole tradition of Western political and philosophical thought. That tradition of valuing and embracing hard intellectual work has not in fact been destroyed by the internet and television as the tens of thousands of copies of Klein's books sold, and discussed in book clubs, and the debate they stimulate, indicates.

Having said all this, my own experience is that the heart of Transition, as Hopkins suggests in *The power of just doing stuff*, and as London Citizens finds, is in the practical realization of alternatives. These projects build bridges between people from very different backgrounds, with very different intellectual stances. Still, Hopkins is right to ask for rigor, and a healthy Transition should hold him, and the movement as a whole, to it.

Resilience

Resilience is a key word in Transition thinking and literature.[76] The theme of resilience is prominent in ecology but it underlies older forms of agricultural writing: the ideas were perfectly familiar, for example, to Albert Howard or Henry Massingham. It is defined as "the capacity of a system to absorb disturbance; to undergo change and still retain essentially the same function, structure and feedbacks . . . to undergo some change without crossing a threshold to a different system regime."[77] Two things that are always stressed are the importance of diversity and understanding a system as a whole. These principles are especially formalized in permaculture, which Rob Hopkins, a permaculturist by trade, describes as "the design glue" for a sustainable and resilient culture. The elements for such a culture include local food production, energy generation, water

76. As might be expected, it has also been taken over by the political right and by big business, where it means simply adaptive adjustment. It is applied in the same sense to individuals resisting neoliberalism. Streeck, *Capitalism*, 39–40 Neither Transition nor I understand resilience in this sense.

77. Walker and Salt, *Resilience Thinking*, 32.

management, meaningful employment, and so on. Permaculture helps assemble those things in the best way possible.[78]

Design is a key word. Ecological design, David Orr argues, opens genuine possibilities for greater local control over energy, food, shelter, money, water, transportation, and waste recycling. It is the most likely basis for revitalizing local economies powered by home-grown efficiency and locally accessible renewable energy while eliminating pollution, improving resilience, and spreading wealth.[79] He instances the Mondragon cooperative, the Transition towns movement, and the Evergreen project in Cleveland as projects seeking to transform complex systems called cities and city regions into sustainable, locally generated centers of prosperity, powered by efficiency and renewable energy. "Resilience means redundancy of major functions, appropriate scale, firebreaks between critical systems, fairness, and societies that are robust to error, technological accidents, malice, and climate destabilisation. In short, it is human systems designed in much the same way that nature designs ecologies from the bottom up."[80] Sociologically translated, this means that communities with vibrant patterns of interaction survive much better than those where relationships are breaking down.[81]

Beyond this, however, and in my judgement more crucial, there is an important spiritual dimension to resilience that is not captured by this approach. To begin with, Frank Furedi draws attention to the way in which the village of Aberfan survived the catastrophe of the loss of almost all of its children when a coal slag overwhelmed the village school. He cites a study that is perturbed by the fact that counseling was not offered to the survivors. "Instead of exploring the resilience of this Welsh mining community, commentators are far more likely to treat the survivors as hidden victims whose emotional needs were ignored by a

78. Hopkins, *Companion*, 98.

79. Orr, "Governance in the long emergency," 289.

80. Ibid., 290.

81. As show studies of victims of the 1995 heat wave in Chicago and the experience of the Cuban emergency. Solnit, *Paradise*, 149, 265.

clamorous officialdom."[82] He points out that this culture was built on at least two centuries of oppression and suffering that had led people to develop an immense spiritual strength in dealing with disaster. This could not be supplied by "counseling." All kinds of communities across the world, rural, industrial, developed, and undeveloped, have this kind of spiritual resilience. It may be (a key theme of late–nineteenth-century sociologists like Tönnies and Durkheim) that the atomization of society during industrialization dealt a blow to these cultures, though in Britain during World War II it seemed in pretty good shape.

The same could be said about Viktor Frankl's experiences in Dachau and Auschwitz. Frankl found that maintaining a sense of meaning, believing that the suffering that he and his fellow inmates were undergoing was not meaningless, was what made the difference between survival or not. Bettelheim, who had a much more transient experience of the camps, found something similar. The Gestapo sought to destroy people's autonomy by forcing prisoners to adopt childlike behavior, forcing them to merge themselves into an amorphous mass, and destroying all capacity for self-determination, all ability to predict the future and thus to prepare for it. "What was implied, for survival, was the necessity to carve out, against the greatest of odds, some areas of freedom of action and freedom of thought, however insignificant. The two freedoms, of activity and passivity, constitute our two most basic human attitudes, while intake and elimination, mental activity and rest, make up our most basic physiological activities."[83] Redolent of the discussion of the virtues in chapter three, John Davenport finds that "dispositions of character that constitute virtues are resilient against outward misfortune and thus shield us at least partly from the effects of disaster, preventing us from becoming wholly miserable in their wake. Aristotle's normative theory of

82. Furedi, "The Silent Ascendancy of Therapeutic Culture in Britain," 21.

83. Bettelheim, *The Informed Heart*, 148. Dostoevsky, who spent a year in solitary confinement prior to being sent to Siberia, wrote to his brother Mikhail that he had discovered "infinite reserves of toughness and vitality." It was a discovery, writes his biographer, of the resilience of the human spirit. Frank, *Dostoevsky*, 21.

the virtues depends crucially on their providing stability against misfortune to their agent."[84]

Spiritual and cultural resilience, that is to say, rests on profound, culturally shaped, understandings of meaning and purpose, and especially on a well-developed response to the question of suffering in human life. Most, if not all, traditional cultures provide ways of thinking about, wrestling with, and coming to terms with tragedy, and these, ultimately, are the roots of our resilience. This is really crucially important in contrast to the "positive thinking" culture that offers a shallow and ultimately mendacious account of human experience that cannot cope with disaster, or indeed even with the normal tribulations of human life.[85]

Paul's extraordinary poem about faith, hope, and love in his Letter to the Corinthians, these days mostly familiar as a reading at church weddings, is actually about the spiritual conditions of resilience. Paul says faith—belief in the fundamental goodness and wisdom of The NAME, and hope—refusal to be overcome by bitterness or despair even when assaulted by the might of Empire— are at the heart of a community that seeks a world made otherwise. Hope's statements of promise, wrote Moltmann in 1964, stand in contradiction to reality and lead existing reality toward a promised and hoped-for transformation.[86] The letter Paul wrote to a group he had never met, at the heart of empire in Rome, can best be summarized in the phrase "another world is possible." At its heart is a hope that embraces not just human realities but all things (Rom 8). Against the "realism" of the market—of Antony Giddens and Dieter Helm—hope alone is to be called "realistic," Moltmann ar-

---

84. Davenport, *Will as Commitment and Resolve*, 177.

85. This is, of course, the point of Aldous Huxley's 1932 satire where people deal with any distress by taking "soma" tablets. The "Savage" (i.e., human beings) wants God, poetry, real danger, goodness, sin, the right to grow old and ugly and impotent, the right to have syphilis and cancer, the right to have too little to eat, etc., over against the "comfort" of the brave new world. Huxley is reflecting on true humanity, and therefore also on "resilience." The emphasis on "happiness" of the positive thinking culture misses this entirely, and indeed is uncomfortably susceptible to Huxley's critique.

86. Moltmann, *Theology of Hope*, 18.

gued, "because it alone takes seriously the possibilities with which all reality is fraught."[87]

Paul goes on to talk not only about faith and hope but about *agape*, "love," which is not the emotion at the heart of the pop song industry but that disposition that is prepared to be crucified rather than opt for violence, which lives by forgiveness, and which (and here there is a resonance with Hopkins's desire to include all comers) seeks inclusion rather than exclusion. This letter to a small group of "mullers" is a message of guidance and encouragement to social movements of all times.

Paul writes over and over again about community. The militant labor movement was really strong in Europe but it didn't stop fascism and war, writes Alinsky. The Christian church is entrenched in Europe but it didn't stop fascism and war. "We must learn from this that only . . . in the pooling of all the strength of every people's institution and in the awakening of our people to participation lies hope of salvation on earth."[88] Brian Martin argues that the experience of people power against repression provides a template for the sort of governance most likely to be effective in crises. The kind of thing Transition is doing in thinking about what alternatives might look like, and building broad-based coalitions in communities is key, in his view, to responding to threats intelligently.[89] In India the value of intergroup networks in areas plagued by communal violence has been shown. Indian cities with positive connections between Hindus and Muslims prevented ethnic riots whereas those without solid interreligious relations could not stem the rising tide of violence.[90] Combined with disaster preparedness, the mutual responsibility and resilience characteristic

87. Ibid., 25. Naomi Klein argues that a politics of hope is essential to counteract the current "politics of fear" that appeals to "nostalgic nationalisms." *No is Not Enough*, 113.

88. Alinsky, *Reveille*, 202.

89. Martin, "Effective crisis governance," 278.

90. Green, "Shaping community responses to catastrophe," 369.

of well-networked communities have proved essential in times of war or climate disaster.[91]

These dimensions of resilience—solidarity, compassion, an ability to cope with tragedy, a sense of purpose, and an understanding of faith, hope, and *agape*—seem to me to be the real heart of "inner transition." They do not embrace all the values and virtues that I have explored as fostering life but they underpin them all—which is perhaps why Aquinas distinguished them as "theological virtues" as opposed to the civic virtues he took from Aristotle.

Church and Transition

Is the church a Transition movement—a movement that believes in and works for a transition from one state to another? I am not asking here whether the church supports the Transition movement that began in Kinsale and Totnes: that question can come later. Rather, what is the church's raison d'être? Any stranger "going to church" on a Sunday trying to find out might come to the conclusion that it was a meeting of the religiously inclined—primarily (in the UK at least) of the middle class religiously inclined. If the stranger asked worshipers about the content of their faith she might find that many of them had inherited, chiefly through the older liturgies, an Augustinian eschatology, according to which we hope to live by grace, keep evil at bay as far as we can, and look for the realization of justice and truth only in the next life. Any transition that may occur is purely personal. The task of the church, on this account, is witness to the love of God, often said to be known in the fact that "God sent God's Son to redeem us by dying for our sins."

If the stranger were sufficiently motivated to consult a book on church history she would then be surprised at the overtly political nature of much of that history, which laid direct claim to political power in the high middle ages and which, for more than a thousand years, understood itself as supplying the ideological legitimation

91. Ibid., 370.

for empire. If she began reading Scripture she would be even more surprised. Here we come to a contemporary *crux interpretum*. The "third quest" for the historical Jesus seems to have returned us to the conclusions of the first, that Jesus was an eschatological prophet, who looked for the imminent arrival of God's rule, or kingdom, and who taught his disciples to do the same. The calling of "the twelve" was a sign that the new age was about to dawn. The great feedings, the miracles, the parables, all have the same single meaning: God's rule is imminent. Although Jesus was crucified as a messianic pretender he had absolutely no political agenda—and that goes for the church too. All we are concerned with is God's grace for the sinner.[92] Now this eschatological prophet seems to have next to no connection with the prophets of Israel, who from first to last were political busybodies, and who spoke up *against* injustice and *for* the values and virtues that followed from the God of life. Despite the fact that Jesus quoted Isaiah 61, the announcement of Jubilee, according to Luke, he seems otherwise to have had no knowledge of the prophetic tradition, and to have understood the exodus on a purely personal level. This reading strains belief. If we take Scripture as a whole, and if we read the Messianic Writings (aka the New Testament) in the light of the Hebrew Bible and vice versa, then I think we come up with a quite different picture. Is the church a Transition movement? Yes it is. Its founding narratives include a movement from slavery to freedom and from death to life. They insist from first to last on the need to care for the poor, oppressed, and marginalized—that is not an anachronistic trendy liberal reading of Scripture but a strict account of the significance of the *gerim*—migrant workers or aliens—in Torah. Israel, and the Jews Jesus and Paul, worship the God of life who opposes whatever brings death in the world gifted to God's creatures. To worship this God is to be called to the same celebration and opposition—celebration of life in care for the earth, in care for the poor, in care for justice, in food and relationships, including sexuality, resistance to the power structures that impoverish and destroy. There is a Yes and a No, and the Yes comes before and

92. I am thinking in the first instance of the five-volume work *A Marginal Jew*, by John Meier.

is more important than the No. The Yes takes the form of worship, but also of solidarity, compassion, kindness, and generosity way out beyond the church. "Church" translates *ekklesia*, the word used for the citizens' assembly in Athens. "Ekklesia" probably, in turn, translates *quahal*, the gathering of the tribes of Israel, usually to address a threat. The word Jesus, or the first community, used to describe the community that recognized Jesus as embodying God's Word, was a political word. This does not mean that Jesus founded a political social movement, but it certainly means he did not simply convene a meeting for worship either. Ekklesia, as Paul uses the term, is the seed bed for a new, liberated, humanity—liberated from ethnic hatreds, from class domination, and even (on my reading, though not on John Meier's) from gender hierarchy (Gal 3:28). The seed bed— not the realization of. Ekklesia, as Paul sets out the argument in Romans 9–11, exists as an invitation and a sign for all people—not to get them to sign up to a list of fundamental articles or even any of the creeds, but to learn the practices of life.[93] It is called to live out a prefigurative politics of the affirmation of life, the heart of which is thankfulness and living by forgiveness. The superscription of all the Messianic Writings is—"another world is possible!" At the same time the solidarity to which it is called is a solidarity in resistance to everything which opposes the God of life. So, not just charity— kindness, practical help, and generosity to those who suffer. That, of course—but also solidarity in the quest to see that whatever it is that causes that suffering changes (Desmond Tutu's stand in the struggle against apartheid would be a model for this).

The prefigurative politics ought to extend to the organization of the church—though it hardly does so anywhere. The church's orientation, said Helmut Gollwitzer, resonating with the thought of Colin Ward and David Graeber already cited, is that of an "anarcho-socialist, decentralized, democratic group," whose existence

93. Barth wrote to his to his Czech friend Hromadka that "our attitude should be one in which, with our Word and for the sake of God we can be in helpful solidarity with man as such, and therefore with those of the left and the right, those who suffer and those who strive, the righteous and the unrighteous, Christians and atheists, the followers of humanism A, B, C, and D." *Letters 1961–8*, 82.

creates "repercussions and correspondences" in the world.[94] From the church's deed and word "those outside" need to learn "that things can be different, not merely in heaven but on earth, not just some day but even now, than those to which they think they must confine themselves in the formation and administration of their law."[95] That there is a real identity between Christ, the kingdom of God, and the church means that the community has an exemplary function within world history, for example in the way in which it structures itself on the law of service which is fundamental to the being of the church.[96]

Of course, given the reality of the church—hierarchical, wedded to the status quo, glorifying military power and conquest—all this is a bizarre caricature of what ekklesia is intended to be, but as I noted in chapter 5, Scripture—the founding documents of Christianity—rises up against it, even though anyone who actually preaches, let alone practices, what it has to say will probably be thrown out of the church/synagogue as Jesus himself was (for daring to take Isaiah 61 seriously!).

So, is the church a transition movement? Yes it is—from structures of death to those of life, at the personal, social, and political levels. Should it support transition movements (including the current Transition movement)—yes it should. Not to try and convert them or "Christianize" them—God forbid!—but simply in virtue of the call to solidarity with everything that makes for life that is part of ekklesia's foundation and, of course, in sympathy with fellow anarchist movements.

Staying human amidst collapse

Social movements and people's organizations represent moves against the dominance of "business as usual"—big money, politics in bed with the corporations, cynicism or carelessness about

94. Gollwitzer, "The Kingdom of God and Socialism," 89.
95. Barth, *Church Dogmatics*, IV/2, 721.
96. Ibid., 692, 820.

the future. If there is any hope for the future, say Brad Werner and Naomi Klein, it rests with these movements. Meanwhile, business as usual gives us everywhere a more and more reactionary politics in which the transgression of planetary boundaries is either denied or ignored. Perhaps the resilience that emerges is the traditional one based on power, prestige, position, and influence.[97] What remains of the radical left now operates largely outside of any institutional organized oppositional channels, in the hope that small-scale actions and local activism can ultimately add up to some kind of satisfactory macro alternative, says Harvey. "But to the degree that this left seeks to change the world without taking power, so an increasingly consolidated plutocratic capitalist class remains unchallenged in its ability to dominate the world without constraint."[98]

In chapter five I cited Luke Bretherton's acknowledgment that any people's movement needs a sense of irony and also an awareness that it is not the Messiah, not "the answer" to the problems we face. These are crucial to the work of any humanizing progressive movement. Looking at the heroism and generosity that often follow disasters, Rebecca Solnit argues that the "paradise" of a truly mutual and peaceful society "will never exist whole, stable, and complete." The realization of alternatives is improvisational and we make them up as we go along.[99] Transition—alongside all the other movements for the common good, like people's organizations and Via Campesina—represents a kind of guided improvization and as such is a hopeful way of realistically addressing the enormous challenges that present themselves as a result of crossing planetary boundaries. They are lighting candles rather than cursing the dark.

There is no guarantee that a new age, better than the last, is on the way, says Keith Hart. "Everything remains to be fought for; and the evidence of the last century is that the forces of counterrevolution, the drive of states and corporations to control society from the top and exclude most people from meaningful power,

97. Barr and Devine-Wright, "Resilient Communities," 6.

98. Harvey, *Seventeen Contradictions*, xiii.

99. Solnit, *Paradise*, 312.

will only be displaced by a mighty social movement or, to employ a much abused expression, a world revolution."[100] Havel, like Bahro, looked to an "existential revolution"—"a new experience of being, a renewed rootedness in the universe, a newly grasped sense of "higher responsibility."[101] These aspirations might sound vague, but they are the aspirations of millions of people seeking political and social alternatives across the planet. If there is a struggle, as Naomi Klein puts it, of "capitalism vs the planet," then there are also in every country social movements and people's organizations against the corporate takeover of life.

At the same time, to put this whole discussion of social movements in context, we have to remind ourselves of what we saw in chapter five, that there are only twenty or so long-standing democracies, and for the rest, the world is full of mafia-led states, "gangster capitalism," states where drug lords have more power than the government, states without any effective individual freedom, like China, and movements like ISIL and Boko Haram (also "social movements") that seek to restore not just a ferocious kind of patriarchy, but atavistic forms of rule. Transition would not last a day in any of these places, and they constitute the bulk of the world. In these places, ordinary people, living in the honeycomb of networks that makes up "civil society," often act cooperatively, as Kropotkin and Tudge argue, and they can respond to disasters with heroic generosity. Equally, as we know, daily life can be shaped by ancient pathologies like anti-Semitism, and by chauvinisms of all kinds, as we see today in Russia and Hungary, or by the psychosis of violence we see in the North American addiction to guns—a whole culture built on the myth of redemptive violence. In Europe the refugee crisis is everywhere provoking not just generosity and attempts to help but also large-scale hatred, fear, and attacks on "foreigners" egged on by a rabid and quasi-fascist press. As I argued in the third chapter, keeping human life human needs the work entailed in all the practices that maintain the virtues, patient social, political, and spiritual

100. Hart, *Memory*, 295.
101. Havel, *Power*, 92.

work, practices that I have tried to sketch in chapters four to eight. So our (justified) enthusiasm for social movements—springing from a humanist anthropology (which I would argue is strongly influenced by Christianity)—has to be tempered by this global reality. What this leaves us with is neither optimism, nor despair, but hope. The German theologian Jürgen Moltmann, who had the misfortune to be sixteen in 1944 in Hitler's Germany, and had to man anti-aircraft guns as the Allies firebombed Hamburg, knows about this. In the present situation of our world, he writes, facile consolation is as fatal as melancholy hopelessness:

> No one can assure us that the worst will not happen. According to the laws of experience it will. We can only trust that even the end of the world hides a new beginning if we trust the God who calls into being the things that are not, and out of death creates new life. Life out of this hope then means already acting here and today in accordance with that world of justice and righteousness and peace, contrary to appearances, and contrary to all historical chances of success. It obliges us solemnly to abjure the spirit, logic, and practice of the nuclear system of deterrence and all other systems of mass annihilation. It means an unconditional Yes to life in the face of the inescapable death of all the living.[102]

It is on the basis of this kind of hope that we engage in transformative action in the belief that humanity—a humanity marked by justice, compassion, mercy, and generosity, a passion for life, and in which fundamental human equality is honored—can be sustained.

Building arks

Suppose the efforts of all those working tirelessly in Transition and other like-minded organizations to bring about a genuinely sustainable society, is too little or too late to avert the worst effects of the transgression of planetary boundaries. In the first chapter I quoted Alasdair MacIntyre's invocation of "new Benedictine

---

102. Moltmann, *The Coming of God*, 235.

communities" within which moral life could be sustained in an age of barbarism and darkness.[103]

It seems to me that in the European Dark Ages the original Benedictine monasteries functioned as arks. That is, in the midst of an overwhelming tide of violent migrations they provided shelter, food, a place of spiritual security in a world where the old certainties had been lost. They were places of order, prayer, hospitality, and disciplined agricultural labor. They were frequently burned down, many or all of their occupants killed. And then they built them again. In their practices they nourished the virtues—in this case, both faith and hope—a key part of what it means to build an ark. Greer notes that the monks and nuns who kept the lamps of Western civilization burning voluntarily embraced a lifestyle even more impoverished than that of the peasants amongst whom they lived.[104] But when Rudolf Bahro said, "Dare to form communes," then the communes were not utopian hippy communities but, again, modeled on Benedictine insights. My sense is that our energy should go in to Transition-type initiatives, but at the same time we should "dare to form communes," because arks might be needed.

Ched Myers turns to the Benedictine model in his reflections on Sabbath economics. Benedict understood, he argues, that his culture was built on the concentration of wealth and exploitation. Thus, if his communities were to repent they must become as self-sufficient as possible. Second, that the root of wealth concentration was private property. Thus, if they wanted to resist the "temptations of the world" they must renounce exclusive ownership. Third, the exploitation of human labor was the root of all alienation. If their communities were to restore human dignity they must practice manual, that is, unalienated, labor.[105] Myers proposes that we reimagine the evangelical counsels for our own day, and this reimagining is, I think, a helpful way of thinking about the practice of the virtues that is a key part of ark building.

103. MacIntyre, *After Virtue*, 263.

104. Greer, *Long Descent*, 125.

105. Myers, *The Biblical Vision of Sabbath Economics*, 61–62.

An ark can only be built by a community. Jesus called people into a universal "imagined community," a utopian community, not rooted in kinship (Mark 3:31f), whose purpose was to provide a messianic "home," or rooting, for human beings or, in my present metaphor, an ark. In a society characterized by very stable, religiously undergirded, family ties Jesus calls into being a community of *voluntary* commitment, willing to take on the hostility of this society.[106] However, from the beginning this utopian community has found that it is necessarily parasitic on the "natural" community, that is, on the community structured in villages, towns, and cities in which human beings trade, defend themselves, procreate, and celebrate. Monasticism was from the start an affront to the natural community, in opting for celibacy, but very quickly came to live in symbiosis with it, and for some centuries made a vital contribution to it, as MacIntyre argued. My first claim, then, is that the voluntary or utopian community, which cannot survive without the natural community, nevertheless builds an ark for the natural community without which, in circumstances of emergency, it in turn cannot survive. Such community might involve experiments in collectivist living and co-housing which, Myers suggest, might be part of what the vow of poverty means today.[107]

Wendell Berry reminds us that community includes the nonhuman creation, as in the story of Noah. "A healthy community," says Berry, "is a form that includes all the local things that are connected by the larger, ultimately mysterious form of Creation. In speaking of community, then, we are speaking of a complex connection not only among human beings or between humans and their homeland but also between the human economy and nature, between forest or prairies and field or orchard, and between troublesome creatures and pleasant ones. All neighbours are included."[108] Building an ark, in other words, involves work that cares for biodiversity, and practices that respect rather than seek to dominate creation. It recognizes that these concerns

106. Yoder, *The Politics of Jesus*, 43.

107. Myers, *Biblical Vision*, 63.

108. Berry, *Sex, Economy*, 15.

are not sentimental or simply aesthetic but that they are bound up with our survival.

Secondly, I note that the Benedictine communities were structured not simply by commensality but by work, prayer, and the cultivation of the virtues. All these are essential to ark building. To begin with work: Benedict's insistence on manual labor was, of course, a challenge to a world where such labor was devalued, but it was also, I suspect, to do with the fact that in a disintegrating world, where supply chains are interrupted and the mechanisms of the market cannot be taken for granted, such work was necessary for survival. Such work will be cooperative. Cooperative work, Myers remarks, "strikes at the heart of alienated and alienating wage labour."[109]

Together with work comes prayer: *laborare est orare*. Forming communities that can carry people through really dark times cannot be accomplished by optimism, but only by a disciplined collective effort centered on a sober but hopeful spirituality, or as Christians would say, on a spirituality of cross and resurrection. Spirituality will be at the heart of it because humans do not live by bread alone but by every word that proceeds from the mouth of God, which is to say by an openness to the mystery of all reality, by practices of gratitude such as praise, and by refusing the nihilism that constantly confronts us, above all in violence. Prayer is the recognition that grace alone, which is to say, grateful ways of living, saves us.

Building an ark involves the practice of the virtues. I have already noted some of Myers's claims about the reworking of the vow of poverty for our day. As regards chastity he recommends a kind of consumer celibacy towards commodity fetishism. Chastity is not a private vow, but a discipline of collective accountability that embraces not just property but the use of time, space, vocational options, and above all, decision-making. "Nothing challenges our socialization into the fictive economy of the consumer more viscerally than accountability for how we earn and how we spend, because we actually (not hypothetically) have to give up

109. Myers, *Biblical Vision*, 63.

private control. More accurately, we are taking back control from the expectations of the market."[110] Interestingly, the Iona community rule involves mutual accountability for our use of money, time, and our use of the earth's resources. Chastity understood like this would involve an acceptance of limits. The Amish, says Berry, "have mastered one of the fundamental paradoxes of our condition: we can make ourselves whole only by accepting our partiality, by living within our limits, by being human—not trying to be gods. By restraint they make themselves whole."[111]

The vow of obedience originally meant single-minded attentiveness to the will of God. Today, Myers suggests, it might mean both a defensive strategy of noncooperation with the social and economic imperatives of public addiction and an offensive strategy of engagement with the political Powers. War tax resistance, for example, is "a household discipline of refusing to cooperate with the political economy of militarism, as well as an act of citizenship responsibility . . . more meaningful than voting."[112]Because public addiction is legal the vow of obedience may mean civil disobedience, as in the anti-globalization movement protests. Ark building, in other words, involves resisting the claim of capital to provide the narrative of the world.

Understanding ark building like this of course has political and economic consequences, which I have tried to set out in chapters four to eight. The communities that model these may practically, ethically, and spiritually help us to survive the global emergency. If I am right then a rigorous return to the traditions, practices, and virtues that Christians have nourished for so many centuries, but which at the same time the church has

110. Myers, *Biblical Vision*, 64.

111. Berry, *The Unsettling of America*, 95. The Roman Catholic insistence on priestly celibacy springs partly, of course, from a problematic understanding of sexuality, but also from a perception that single-minded work for the kingdom makes erotic relations difficult. Gandhi, for example, adopted celibacy (whilst still married) from the moment serious struggle began in India. There is a puzzle here (which Myers goes some way to resolving) in understanding how to welcome and integrate eros and constructive political action.

112. Myers, *Biblical Vision*, 65.

compromised so abjectly in relation to the present imperium, may be, to put it no more strongly, amongst the most important things that help to make and to keep human beings human in the dark ages already upon us.

Bibliography

Abramson, Paul, and Ronald Inglehart. *Value Change in Global Perspective.* Ann Arbor, MI: University of Michigan Press, 1995.

Achen, Christopher, and Larry Bartels. *Democracy for Realists: Why Elections Do Not Produce Responsive Government.* Princeton, NJ: Princeton University Press, 2016.

Albert, Michael. *Parecon: Life after Capitalism.* London: Verso, 2003.

———. "The Politics of a Good Society." *New Left Project.* http://www. newleftproject.org/index.php/site/article_comments/the_politics_of_a_ good_society.

Alinsky, Saul. *Reveille for Radicals.* New York: Vintage, 1969.

———. *Rules for Radicals.* New York: Random House, 1971.

Anderson, Kevin. *Real Clothes for the Emperor: Facing the Challenges of Climate Change.* Manchester: Tyndal Centre, 2012.

Anderson, Kevin, and Alice Bows. "Beyond 'dangerous' climate change: emission scenarios for a new world." *Philosophical Transactions of the Royal Society* 2011 (369) 20–44.

Annas, Julia. *The Morality of Happiness.* Oxford: Oxford University Press, 1993.

Aquinas, Thomas. *Summa Theologiae,* vols 1–61. Cambridge: Cambridge University Press, 1963–1980.

Archibugi, D., D. Held, and M. Köhler. *Re-imagining Political Community.* Cambridge: Polity, 1998.

Archibugi, Danieli. "Principles of cosmopolitan democracy." In *Re-imagining Political Community,* edited by D. Archibugi, D. Held, and M. Köhler, 198–230. Cambridge: Polity, 1998.

Arendt, Hannah. *Crises of the Republic.* New York: Harcourt Brace, 1972.

———. *Eichmann in Jerusalem: A Report on the Banality of Evil.* Harmondsworth: Penguin, 1977.

———. *The Human Condition.* Chicago: University of Chicago Press, 1958.

———. *The Life of the Mind:* vol. 1 *Thinking;* vol. 2 *Willing.* New York: Harcourt Brace, 1971.

————. *The Origins of Totalitarianism* London: Deutsch, 1968.

————. *On Revolution*. Harmondsworth: Penguin, 1973.

Aristotle. *Nicomachean Ethics*. Translated by J. A. K. Thomson, revised by H. Tredennick. Harmondsworth: Penguin, 1976.

————. *Politics*. Translated by T. A. Sinclair, revised by T. J. Saunders. Harmondsworth: Penguin, 1992.

Arrighi, Giovanni. "Towards a Theory of Capitalist Crisis." *New Left Review*, September 1978, 3–24.

Arrow, Kenneth. "Gifts and Exchanges." *Philosophy and Public Affairs* 1:4 (Summer 1972) 343–62.

Assadourian, Erik. "Re-engineering Cultures to Create a Sustainable Civilization." In *State of the World 2013*, edited by Linda Starke, 113–25. Washington, DC: Island, 2013.

Avila, Charles. *Ownership: Early Christian Teachings*. Maryknoll, NY: Orbis, 1983.

Bahro, Rudolf. *Avoiding Social and Ecological Disaster: The Politics of World Transformation*. Bath: Gateway, 1994.

————. *Building the Green Movement*. London: GMP, 1986.

Balakrishnan, Gopal. *The Enemy: An Intellectual Portrait of Carl Schmitt* London: Verso, 2000.

Barr, Stewart, and Patrick Devine-Wright. "Resilient Communities: sustainabilities in transition." *Local Environment: The International Journal of Justice and Sustainability* (May 2012) 1–8.

Barth, Karl. *Against the Stream*. Translated by R. Knox. London: SCM 1954.

————. *The Epistle to the Romans*. 2nd ed. Oxford: Oxford University Press, 1933.

————. *Church Dogmatics*, III/4. Edinburgh: T&T Clark, 1954.

————. *Church Dogmatics*, IV/2. Edinburgh: T&T Clark, 1958.

————. *Letters 1961–8*. Translated by G. Bromiley. Edinburgh: T&T Clark, 1981.

————. *Der Römerbrief*. 1st ed. Zurich: Theologischer Verlag, 1985.

Bauman, Zygmunt. *Modernity and the Holocaust*. Cambridge: Polity, 1989.

————. *Postmodern Ethics*. Oxford: Blackwell, 1993.

Bellah, R., R. Madsen, W. Sullivan, A. Swidler, and S. Tipton. *Habits of the Heart: Individualism and Commitment in American Life*. Berkeley, CA: University of California Press, 2008.

Bellamy, Richard, and Castiglione, Dario. "Between Cosmopolis and community: three models of rights and democracy within the European Union." In *Reimagining Political Community*, edited by D. Archibugi, D. Held, and M. Köhler, 152–78. Cambridge: Polity, 1998.

Benda, Julien. *The Treason of the Intellectuals*. London: Transaction, 2007.

Berry, Wendell. "The Agrarian Standard." In *The Essential Agrarian Reader*, edited by N. Wirzba, 23–33. Berkeley, CA: Counterpoint, 2003.

————. *The Art of the Commonplace*. Washington, DC: Shoemaker and Hoard, 2002.

————. *Home Economics*. New York: North Point, 1987.

————. *In the Presence of Fear*. Great Barrington, MA: Orion, 2001.

————. *Sex, Economy, Freedom and Community*. New York: Pantheon, 1992.

————. *Standing by Words*. Washington, DC: Shoemaker and Hoard, 1983.

————. *The Unsettling of America: Culture and Agriculture*. San Francisco: Sierra Club, 1996.

————. *What are People For?* San Francisco: North Point 1990

————. *What Matters? Economics for a Renewed Commonwealth*. Berkeley, CA: Counterpoint, 2010.

Bettelheim, Bruno. *The Informed Heart*. Harmondsworth: Penguin, 1991.

————. *Recollections and Reflections*. London: Thames & Hudson, 1990.

Bhatt, Chetan. *Liberation and Purity: Race, New Religious Movements and the Ethics of Postmodernity*. London: UCL, 1997.

Beinen, D., V. Rittberger, and W. Wagner. "Democracy in the United Nations System: Cosmopolitan and Communitarian Principles." In *Re-imagining Political Community*, edited by D. Archibugi, D. Held, and M. Köhler, 287–308. Cambridge: Polity, 1998.

Birol, F. *World Energy Outlook 2012*. Paris: IEA.

Blackledge, P., and K. Knight, eds. *Virtue and Politics: Alasdair Macintyre's Revolutionary Aristotelianism*. Notre Dame, IN: University of Notre Dame Press, 2011.

Block, G., and M. Drucker. *Rescuers: Portraits of Moral Courage in the Holocaust*. New York: TV, 1992.

Blyth, Mark. *Austerity: The History of a Dangerous Idea*. Oxford: Oxford University Press, 2013.

Bobbitt, P. *The Shield of Achilles*. London: Penguin, 2002.

Booker, Christopher, and Richard North. *Scared to Death: From BSE to Global Warming: Why Scares are Costing Us the Earth*. London: Continuum, 2009.

Borras, Saturnino, Jr., Jennifer C. Franco, Sergio Gomez, Cristobal Kay, and Max Spoor. "Land grabbing in Latin America and the Caribbean." *The Journal of Peasant Studies*, 39:3–4 (July–October 2012) 845–72.

Bradstock, Andrew, and Christopher Rowland. *Radical Christian Writings*. Oxford: Blackwell, 2002.

Braudel, Fernand. *Civilization and Capitalism 15th–18th Century*. Vol. 2, *The Wheels of Commerce*. London: Fontana, 1982.

Bretherton, Luke. *Resurrecting Democracy*. Cambridge: Cambridge University Press, 2015.

Brodbeck, Karl Heinz. *Die Herrschaft des Geldes*. Darmstadt: WBG, 2012.

Brown, Wendy. *Undoing the Demos: Neoliberalism's Stealth Revolution*. New York: Zone, 2015.

Buber, Martin. *A Believing Humanism*. New York: Humanity, 1999.

————. *Paths in Utopia*. London: Routledge Kegan Paul, 1949.

————. *Pointing the Way* New York: Humanity, 1999.

Buchanan, J. *The Limits of Liberty*. Chicago: University of Chicago Press, 1975.

Bull, Hedley. *The Anarchical Society: A Study of Order in World Politics.* London: Macmillan, 1977.

Burke, Edmund. *Reflections on the Revolution in France.* Harmondsworth: Penguin, 1969.

Busch, Eberhard. *The Barmen Theses Then and Now.* Grand Rapids: Eerdmans, 2010.

Cardinale, B. J., et al. "Biodiversity loss and its impact on humanity." *Nature* 486 (June 2012) 59–67.

Carr, E. H. *Nationalism and After.* London: Macmillan, 1945.

Carson, M., and G. Peterson, eds. Arctic Resilience Report. Arctic Council, Stockholm Environment Institute and Stockholm Resilience Centre, 2016. http://www.arctic-council.org/arr.

Carson, Rachel. *Silent Spring.* Harmondsworth: Penguin, 1965.

Castells, Manuel. *Networks of Outrage and Hope: Social Movements in the Internet Age.* Cambridge: Polity, 2012.

Cato, Molly Scott, and Jean Hillier. "How could we study climate-related social innovation? Applying Deleuzean philosophy to Transition Towns." *Environmental Politics* 19:6 (2010) 869–87.

Cato, Molly Scott. *Bioregional Economics.* Abingdon: Routledge, 2013.

Chatterton, Paul, and Alice Cutler. *The Rocky Road to Real Transition.* http://trapese.clearerchannel.org/resources/rocky-road-a5-web.pdf.

Christiano, Thomas. *The Constitution of Equality.* Oxford: Oxford University Press, 2008

Cicero. *On the Laws.* Edited by N. Rudd. Oxford: Oxford University Press, 1998.
———. *The Republic.* Translated by N. Rudd. Oxford: Oxford University Press, 1998.

Clastres, Pierre. *Society against the State.* New York: Zone, 1989.

Collins, Gail. *When Everything Changed: The Amazing Journey of American Women from 1960 to the Present.* New York: Little, Brown & Company, 2009.

Collingwood, R. G. *The Idea of History.* London: Oxford University Press, 1946.

Comaroff, Jean, and John Comaroff. *Of Revelation and Revolution.* Vol. 2: *The Dialectics of Modernity on a South African Frontier.* Chicago: University of Chicago Press, 1997.

Costanza, Robert, Gar Alperovitz, Herman Daly, Joshua Farley, Carol Franco, Carol, Tim Jackson, Ida Kubiszewski, Juliet Schor, and Peter Victor. "Building a sustainable and desirable economy-in-society-in-nature." In *State of the World 2013,* edited by Linda Starke, 126–42. Washington, DC: Island, 2013.

Cotgrove, S., and A. Duff. "Environmentalism, Middle Class radicalism and Politics." *Sociological Review* 28:2 (1980) 333–49.

Cottingham, J. *Why Believe?* London: Continuum, 2009.

Crisp, Roger, and Michael Slote. *Virtue Ethics.* Oxford: Oxford University Press, 1997.

Crompton, Tom. *Common Cause: The Case for Working with Our Cultural Values.* London: WWF, 2010.

Crouch, Colin. *Post Democracy.* Cambridge: Cambridge University Press, 2004.

Crutzen, P. J. "Geology of mankind." *Nature* 415 (2002) 23.

Dahl, R. E., and E. Tufte. *Size and Democracy.* London: Oxford University Press, 1974.

Daly, Herman, and John Cobb Jr. *For the Common Good.* London: Green Print, 1990.

Daly, Herman. *Beyond Growth.* Boston: Beacon, 1996.

————. *Steady State Economics.* London: Earthscan, 1992.

Day, Christopher. *Consensus Design: Socially Inclusive Process.* Oxford: Architectural, 2003.

Day, Richard. *Gramsci is Dead: Anarchist Currents in the Newest Social Movements.* London: Pluto, 2005.

Davenport, John. *Will as Commitment and Resolve: An Existential Account of Creativity, Love, Virtue and Happiness.* New York: Fordham University Press, 2007.

Davis, Ellen. *Scripture, Culture, and Agriculture: An Agrarian Reading of the Bible.* Cambridge: Cambridge University Press, 2009.

Dawkins, Richard. *The Selfish Gene.* Oxford: Oxford University Press, 1976.

DeFries, R., and C. Rosenzweig. "Toward a whole landscape approach for sustainable land use in the tropics." *Proceedings of the National Academy of Sciences,* USA, 107 (2010) 19627–32.

Della Porta, Donatella, and Mario Diani. *Social Movements: An Introduction.* Oxford: Blackwell, 1999.

Dennis, Kingsley, and John Urry. *After the Car.* Cambridge: Polity, 2009.

Diamond, Jared. *Collapse: How Societies Choose to Fail or Survive.* London: Penguin, 2005.

Dickens, A. G. *The English Reformation.* London: Fontana, 1967.

Dickens, C. *Dombey and Son.* London: Bradbury and Evans, 1846.

Donahue, Brian. "The Resettling of America." In *The Essential Agrarian Reader,* edited by N. Wirzba, 34–51. Washington, DC: Shoemaker and Hoard, 2003.

Dorling, Daniel. *Injustice: Why Social Inequality Persists.* Bristol: Policy, 2011.

Douthwaite, Richard, and Gillian Fallon, eds. *Fleeing Vesuvius.* Dublin: Feasta, 2010.

Douzinas, Costas, and Conor Gearty. *The Meanings of Rights: The Philosophy and Social Theory of Human Rights.* Cambridge: Cambridge University Press, 2014.

Duchrow, Ulrich. *Alternatives to Global Capitalism: Drawn from Biblical History, Designed for Political Action.* Utrecht: International, 1995.

Duchrow, Ulrich, and Franz Hinkelammert. *Property.* London: Zed, 2003.

————. *Transcending Greedy Money: Interreligious Solidarity for Just Relations.* New York: Palgrave, 2012.

Dunn, John. *Democracy: A History.* New York: Atlantic Monthly, 2005.

Eagleton, Terry. *The Idea of Culture*. Oxford: Blackwell, 2000.

Ehrenreich, Barbara. *Smile or Die: How Positive Thinking Fooled America and the World*. London: Granta, 2009.

Ellacuria, Ignazio. "Violence and non-violence in the struggle for peace and liberation." In *A Council for Peace, Concilium 195*, edited by H. Kung and J. Moltmann, 69–77. Edinburgh: T&T Clark, 1988.

Emmott, Stephen. *10 Billion*. Harmondsworth: Penguin, 2013.

Epstein, William. *Psychotherapy as Religion: The Civil Divine in America* Nevada: University of Nevada Press, 2006.

Esteva, Gustavo, Salvatore Babones, and Philipp Babcicky. *The Future of Development: A Radical Manifesto*. Bristol: Policy, 2013.

Fairlie, Simon. *Meat: A Benign Extravagance*. East Meon: Hyden House, 2010.

Feola, G., and J. R. Nunes. "Success and failure of Grassroots Innovations for addressing climate change: the case of the Transition Movement." *Global Environmental Change* 24 (2014) 232–50.

Figes, Orlando. *A People's Tragedy*. London: Pimlico, 1996.

Findlay, J. N. *Values and Intentions*. London: Allen and Unwin, 1961.

Fishkin, James. *When the People Speak: Deliberative Democracy and Public Consultation*. Oxford: Oxford University Press, 2009.

Fogelman, Eva. *Conscience and Courage: Rescuers of Jews during the Holocaust*. New York: Doubleday Dell, 1994.

Forrester, Duncan. *On Human Worth*. London: SCM, 2000.

Frank, J. *Dostoevsky: The Years of Ordeal*. Princeton, NJ: Princeton University Press, 1983.

Frankl, Viktor. *Man's Search for Meaning*. New York: Random House, 2004.

Frison, Emile, et al. *From Uniformity to Diversity: A Paradigm Shift from Industrial Agriculture to Diversified Agroecological Systems*. Louvain: iPES, 2016.

Fromm, Eric. *The Anatomy of Human Destructiveness*. Harmondsworth: Penguin, 1973.

Furedi, Frank. "The Silent Ascendancy of Therapeutic Culture in Britain." In *Therapeutic Culture: Triumph and Defeat*, edited by Jonathan Imber, 19–50. New Brunswick, NJ: Transaction, 2004.

Galbraith, J. K. *A History of Economics : The Past as the Present*. Harmondsworth: Penguin, 1989.

———. *Money: Whence it Came, Where It Went*. London: Deutsch, 1975.

Galston, William. "Liberal Virtues." *The American Political Science Review* 62:4 (December 1988) 1277–90.

Gans, H. J. *The Levittowners*. London: Allen Lane, 1967.

Gardner, Gary. "Conserving non-nonrenewable resources." In *Is Sustainability Still Possible?*, edited by Linda Starke, 6–12. Washington: Island, 2013.

———. "Mounting losses of agricultural resources." In *State of the World 2015*, edited by Linda Mastny, 65–78. Washington, DC: Island, 2015.

Gathorne-Hardy, A., J. Knight, and J. Woods. "Biochar as a soil amendant positively interacts with nitrogen fertilizer to improve barley yields in the UK." 2009. *IOP Conf.Series: Earth and Environmental Sciences 6.* doi 10.1088/1755-1307/6/7/372052.

Gellner, Ernest. *Nations and Nationalism.* Oxford: Blackwell, 1983.

———. *The Psychoanalytic Movement* London: Paladin, 1985.

George, Susan. *State of Power.* Amsterdam: TNI, 2014.

Geras, Norman. *Solidarity in the Conversation of Humankind: The Ungroundable Liberalism of Richard Rorty.* London: Verso, 1995.

Gerolymatos, A. *An International Civil War.* Yale: Yale University Press, 2016.

Gibbon, E. *The Decline and Fall of the Roman Empire.* London: Penguin, 1996.

Giddens, Anthony. *The Politics of Climate Change.* Cambridge: Polity, 2009.

Gilligan, Carol. *In a Different Voice.* Cambridge, MA: Harvard University Press, 1982.

Goodchild, Philip. *The Theology of Money.* London: SCM, 2007.

Goodwin, Jeff, and James Jasper. *The Social Movements Reader: Cases and Concepts.* Oxford: Blackwell, 2009.

Gombrich, E. H. *Art and Illusion.* Oxford: Phaidon, 1986.

Gollwitzer, Helmut. "The Kingdom of God and Socialism." In *Karl Barth and Radical Politics,* edited by G. Hunsinger, 77–120. Philadelphia: Westminster, 1976.

Gorringe, Timothy. *The Common Good and the Global Emergency.* Cambridge: Cambridge University Press, 2011.

———. *Karl Barth: Against Hegemony.* Oxford: Oxford University Press, 1999.

Graeber, David. *Debt: The First 5000 Years.* New York: Melville House, 2011.

———. *The Democracy Project: A History, a Crisis, a Movement.* London: Allen Lane, 2013.

———. *Direct Action: An Ethnography.* Edinburgh: AK, 2009.

———. *Promises Promises.* BBC Radio 4. April 2015.

———. *Toward an Anthropological Theory of Value: The False Coin of our Own Dreams.* New York: Palgrave, 2001.

Green, Paula. "Shaping community responses to catastrophe." In *State of the World 2013,* edited by Linda Starke, 363–73. Washington, DC: Island, 2013.

Greer, John. *The Long Descent: A User's Guide to the End of the Industrial Age.* Gabriola Island: New Society, 2008.

Grossman, Vasily. *Life and Fate.* New York: Harper & Row, 1985.

Guimarães, Elcio P., ed. *Second report on the state of the world's plant genetic resources for food and agriculture.* Rome: FAO, 2010.

Gutierrez, Gustavo. *Las Casas: In Search of the Poor of Jesus Christ.* Maryknoll, NY: Orbis, 1993.

Haas, Peter. *Morality after Auschwitz.* Philadelphia: Fortress, 1988.

Hagens, Nathan John. "Energy, credit, and the end of growth." In *Confronting Hidden Threats to Sustainability: State of the World 2015,* edited by L. Mastny, 21–36. Washington: Island, 2015.

Hahn, Chris, and Keith Hart. *Economic Anthropology.* Cambridge: Polity, 2011.

Hall, S. "The Multi-cultural Question." In *Un/settled Multicuturalisms*, edited by B. Hesse, 209–40. London: Zed, 2000.

Hansen, James. *Storms of my Grandchildren: The Truth about the Coming Climate Catastrophe and Our Last Chance to Save Humanity.* London: Bloomsbury, 2009.

Harvey, David. *The Enigma of Capital.* London: Profile, 2010.

———. *Seventeen Contradictions and the End of Capitalism.* London: Profile, 2014.

Hassner, Pierre. "Refugees: a special case for cosmopolitan citizenship?" In *Reimagining Political Community,* edited by D. Archibugi, D. Held, and M. Köhler, 273–86. Cambridge: Polity, 1998.

Hastings, Adrian. *The Construction of Nationhood: Ethnicity, Religion and Nationalism.* Cambridge: Cambridge University Press, 1997.

———. *A History of English Christianity 1920–1985.* London: Collins, 1986.

Hart, Keith. *The Memory Bank: Money in an Unequal World.* London: Profile, 1999.

Hauerwas, Stanley. *A Community of Character: Toward a Constructive Christian Social Ethic.* Notre Dame, IN: University of Notre Dame Press, 1981.

———. *In Good Company: The Church as Polis.* Notre Dame: University of Notre Dame Press, 1995.

Hauerwas, Stanley, and Charles Pinches. *Christians among the Virtues: Theological Conversations with Ancient and Modern Ethics.* Notre Dame, IN: University of Notre Dame Press, 1997.

Hauerwas, Stanley, and W. H. Willimon. *Resident Aliens.* Nashville: Abingdon, 1989.

Havel, Václav. *The Power of the Powerless.* London: Routledge, 2015.

Hawken, Paul. *Blessed Unrest: How the Largest Social Movement in History is Restoring Grace, Justice and Beauty to the World.* New York: Penguin, 2008.

Hayek, F. A. *Law, Legislation and Liberty: A New Statement of the Liberal Principles of Justice and Political Economy.* Abingdon: Routledge, 2013.

Hay, Colin, Michael Lister, and David Marsh. *The State: Theories and Issues.* Basingstoke: Macmillan, 2006.

Held, David. *Cosmopolitanism: Ideals and Realities.* Cambridge: Polity, 2010.

———. *Democracy and the Global Order.* Cambridge: Polity, 1995.

Helm, Dieter. *The Carbon Crunch.* New Haven, CT: Yale University Press, 2012.

Hegel, G. W. F. *Philosophy of Right.* Translated by T. M. Knox. Oxford: Oxford University Press, 1967.

Hendriks, Frank. *Vital Democracy: A Theory of Democracy in Action.* Oxford: Oxford University Press, 2010.

Hesse, B., ed. *Un/settled Multicuturalisms.* London: Zed, 2000.

Hill, Christopher. *The English Bible and the Seventeenth Century Revolution.* Harmondsworth: Penguin, 1993.

Hilton, Rodney. *Bond Men Made Free: Medieval Peasant Movements and the English Rising of 1381.* London: Methuen, 1973.

Himmelfarb, Gertrude. *The Demoralization of Society.* New York: Knopf, 1995.

Hobbes, Thomas. *Leviathan.* Oxford: Oxford University Press, 1996.

Hobsbawm, E. J. *Globalisation, Democracy, Terrorism.* London: Little, Brown, 2007.

———. *Nations and Nationalism Since 1780.* Cambridge: Canto, 1990.

Hoffman, John. *Beyond the State.* Cambridge: Polity, 1995.

Holloway, John. *Change the World Without Taking Power: The Meaning of Revolution Today.* London: Pluto, 2010.

Holmgren, David. *Future Scenarios: How Communities Can Adapt to Peak Oil and Climate Change.* Totnes: Green, 2009.

———. *Permaculture: Principles and Pathways Beyond Sustainability.* East Meon: Permanent, 2011.

Hopkins, Rob. "The Rocky Road to a Real Transition: A Review." Transition Network, May 15, 2008.

———. "Transition and Activism: A Response." Transition Network, May 30, 2011.

———. *The Transition Companion: Making Your Community More Resilient in Uncertain Times.* Totnes: Green, 2011.

———. *The Transition Handbook: From Oil Dependency to Local Resilience.* Totnes: Green, 2008.

———. "Transition is not a left wing campaign group." http://transitionnetwork. org/blogs/rob-hopkins.

Horton, John, and Susan Mendus. *After MacIntyre: Critical Perspectives on the Work of Alasdair MacIntyre.* Cambridge: Polity, 1994.

Hursthouse, Rosalind. *On Virtue Ethics.* Oxford: Oxford University Press, 1999.

Hutchinson, Frances. *What Everybody Really Wants to Know about Money.* Charlbury: Jon Carpenter, 1998.

Ignatieff, Michael. *Human Rights as Politics and Ideology.* Princeton, NJ: Princeton University Press, 2001.

———. "The Limits of Sainthood." *The New Republic* (June 18, 1990) 40–46.

Ingelhart, Ronald. "How solid is mass support for democracy—and how can we measure it?" *Science and Politics* (January 2003) 51–57.

Ingelhart, Ronald, and Christian Welzel. *Modernization, Cultural Change and Democracy: The Human Development Sequence.* Cambridge: Cambridge University Press, 2005.

Ingham, Geoffrey. *The Nature of Money.* Cambridge: Polity, 2004.

Jackson, A., and B. Dyson. *Modernising Money.* London: Positive Money, 2012.

Jackson, Tim. *Prosperity Without Growth: Economics for a Finite Planet.* London: Earthscan, 2009.

Jasper, James. *The Art of Moral Protest: Culture, Biography, and Creativity in Social Movements.* Chicago: University of Chicago Press, 1997.

Jaspers, Karl. *The Origin and Goal of History.* London: Routledge, 1953.

Johnson, K. D. *Theology, Political Theory and Pluralism: Beyond Tolerance and Difference.* Cambridge: Cambridge University Press, 2007.

Johnstone, Chris. *Find Your Power.* London: Brealey, 2006.

Jüngel, Eberhard. "Value Free truth: the Christian experience of truth in the Struggle against the 'Tyranny of Values.'" In *Theological Essays II,* 195–215. Edinburgh: T&T Clark, 1995.

Kahn, Paul. *Political Theology: Four New Chapters on the Concept of Sovereignty.* New York: Columbia University Press, 2011.

———. *Putting Liberalism in Its Place.* Princeton, NJ: Princeton University Press, 2005.

Kaldor, Mary. "Reconceptualising organised violence." In *Re-imagining Political Community,* edited by D. Archibugi, D. Held, and M. Köhler, 91–112. Cambridge: Polity, 1998.

Kaminer, Wendy. *I'm Dysfunctional, You're Dysfunctional: The Recovery Movement and Other Self-help Fashions.* New York: Random House, 1993.

Kant, Immanuel. *Critique of Practical Reason.* Translated by L. Beck. Indianapolis: Liberal Arts, 1956.

———. *Kant's Political Writings.* Edited by H. Reiss. Cambridge: Cambridge University Press, 1970.

———. *The Moral Law: Kant's Groundwork of the Metaphysic of Morals.* Translated by H. Paton. London: Hutchinson, 1948.

Keynes, J. M. *The Collected Writings of John Maynard Keynes,* vol. 9. Cambridge: Cambridge University Press, 1978.

———. *A General Theory of Employment, Interest and Money.* London: Macmillan, 1954.

———. "National Self-Sufficiency." *The Yale Review* 22:4 (June 1933) 755–69.

Klein, Naomi. *This Changes Everything: Capitalism vs the Planet.* Harmondsworth: Penguin, 2014.

———. *No is Not Enough.* London: Allen Lane, 2017.

———. *The Shock Doctrine: The Rise of Disaster Capitalism.* Harmondsworth: Penguin, 2007.

Kneen, Brewster. *Farmageddon.* Gabriola: New Society, 1999.

———. *Invisible Giant.* London: Pluto, 1995.

Knight, Kelvin, ed. *The MacIntyre Reader.* London: Polity, 1998.

Koonings, Kees, and Dirk Kruijt, eds. *Fractured Cities: Social Exclusion, Urban Violence and Contested Spaces in Latin America.* London: Zed, 2007.

Kohr, Leopold. *The Breakdown of Nations.* Totnes: Green, 2001.

Korowicz, D. "On the cusp of collapse: complexity, energy and the globalised economy." In *Fleeing Vesuvius,* edited by R. Douthwaite and G. Fallon, 12–39. Dublin: Feasta, 2010.

Korten, David. *When Corporations Rule the World.* Hartford, CT: Kumarian, 1995.

Kropotkin, P. *Ethics.* Dorchester: Prism, 1924.

———. *Fields, Factories and Workshops.* Nelson: London, 1912.

Kunstler, J. Howard. *The Long Emergency.* London: Atlantic, 2006.

Kung, Hans, and Jürgen Moltmann, eds. *A Council for Peace, Concilium 195.* Edinburgh: T&T Clark, 1988.

La Via Campesina. Notebook No. 3, April 2012. https://viacampesina.org/end/ wp-content/uploads/sites/2/2013/06/EN-notebooks6.pdf.

Ladner, A. "Switzerland: subsidiarity, power-sharing, and direct democracy." In *The Oxford Handbook of Local and Regional Democracy in Europe*, edited by John Loughlin, Frank Hendriks, and Anders Lindström, 196–220. Oxford: Oxford University Press, 2011.

Large, Martin. *Common Wealth: For a Free, Equal, Mutual and Sustainable Society*. Stroud: Hawthorn, 2010.

Le Goff, Jacques. *Medieval Civilization*. Oxford: Blackwell, 1988.

Lebow, V. "Price Competition in 1955." *Journal of Retailing* (Spring 1955) 1–7.

Lee, R., and R. Daly. "Foragers and Others." In *The Cambridge Encyclopaedia of Hunters and Gatherers,* edited by R. Lee and R. Daly, 1–22. Cambridge: Cambridge University Press, 1999.

Lehman, Paul. "Karl Barth: Theologian of Permanent Revolution." *Union Theological Seminary Review* 28:1 (1972) 67–81.

Leonard, Annie. "Moving from individual change to societal change." In *State of the World 2013*, edited by Linda Starke, 244–52. Washington, DC: Island, 2013.

Leopold, Aldo. *A Sand County Almanac*. New York: Ballantine, 1970.

Lijphart, Arend. *Patterns of Democracy: Government Forms and Performance in Thirty Six Countries*. 2nd ed. New Haven, CT: Yale University Press, 2012.

Linklater, Andrew. "Citizenship and sovereignty in the post Westphalian European State." In *Re-imagining Political Community*, edited by D. Archibugi, D. Held, and M. Köhler, 113–37. Cambridge: Polity, 1998.

Locke, John. *Two Treatises of Government*. Edited by P. Laslett. Cambridge: Cambridge University Press, 1960.

Loughlin, John, Frank Hendriks, and Anders Lidström. *The Oxford Handbook of Local and Regional Democracy in Europe*. Oxford: Oxford University Press, 2011.

Lovejoy, T. "Climate Change's Pressures on Biodiversity." In *State of the World 2009*, edited by Linda Mastny, 67–70. Washington, DC: Island, 2009.

Luther, Martin. *The Christian in Society, Luther's Works*. Vol. 46. Edited by R. Schultz. Philadelphia: Fortress, 1967.

———. *The Large Catechism*. Minneapolis: Augsburg, 1967

———. *Luther's Primary Works*. Edited by H. Wace and C. Bucheim. London: Murray, 1883.

Lynas, Mark. *Six Degrees*. London: Fourth Estate, 2007.

MacIntyre, Alasdair. *After Virtue: A Study in Moral Theory*. 2nd ed. London: Duckworth, 1985.

———. *A Short History of Ethics*. London: Routledge, 1967.

———. "How Aristotelianism can become revolutionary." In *Virtue and Politics: Alasdair Macintyre's Revolutionary Aristotelianism*, edited by P. Blackledge and K. Knight, 11–19. Notre Dame, IN: University of Notre Dame Press, 2011.

———. *The Tasks of Philosophy: Selected Essays.* Vol. 1. Cambridge: Cambridge University Press, 2006.

———. *The Tasks of Philosophy Ethics and Politics Selected Essays.* Vol. 2. Cambridge: Cambridge University Press, 2006.

———. "Where we were, where we are, where we need to be." In *Virtue and Politics: Alasdair Macintyre's Revolutionary Aristotelianism*, edited by P. Blackledge and K. Knight, 307–34. Notre Dame, IN: University of Notre Dame Press, 2011.

MacLean, N. *Democracy in Chains.* London: Penguin, 2017.

Macpherson, C. B. *The Real World of Democracy.* Toronto: Anansi, 1992.

MacCulloch, Diarmaid. *Reformation: Europe's House Divided.* Harmondworth: Penguin, 2003.

Macfadyen, Peter. *Flatpack Democracy.* Bath: Eco-logic, 2014.

Macy, Joanna. *Coming Back to Life: Practices to Reconnect Our Lives, Our World.* Gabriola: New Society, 1998.

McFadyen, Alistair. *Bound to Sin: Abuse, Holocaust and the Christian Doctrine of Sin.* Cambridge: Cambridge University Press, 2000.

Madeley, John. *Food for All.* London: Zed, 2002.

Madison, James, Alexander Hamilton, and John Jay. *The Federalist Papers.* London: Penguin, 1987.

Mandel, Ernest. *Marxist Economic Theory.* London: Merlin, 1968.

Maniates, M. "Teaching for Turbulence." In *Is Sustainability Still Possible?*, edited by Linda Starke, 255–68. Washington, DC: Island, 2013.

Marechal, Sylvain. *Manifesto of the Equals.* Translated by Mitchell Abidor. marxists.org 2004, 2016.

Marquardt, F. W. *Theologie und Sozialismus.* Munich: Christian Kaiser, 1972.

Martin, Brian. "Effective crisis governance." In *State of the World 2013*, edited by Linda Starke, 269–78. Washington, DC: Island, 2013.

Marx, K. *Economic and Philosophic Manuscripts.* Moscow: Progress, 1977.

Massingham, H. *The Wisdom of the Fields.* London: Collins, 1945.

Masson, Jeffrey. *Against Therapy.* London: Fontana, 1990.

Mastny, Linda, ed. *Confronting Hidden Threats to Sustainability: State of the World 2015.* Washington, DC: Island, 2015.

———. *Into a Warming World: State of the World 2009.* Washington, DC: Island, 2009.

Marx, Karl, and Friedrich Engels. *Collected Works.* Vol. 5. Moscow: Progress, 1976.

Meier, John. *A Marginal Jew.* 5 vols. New York: Anchor Doubleday, 1991–2016.

Melucci, Alberto. *Challenging Codes: Collective Action in the Information Age.* Cambridge: Cambridge University Press, 1996.

Meyer, David. "How Social Movements Matter." In *The Social Movements Reader: Cases and Concepts*, edited by Jeff Goodwin and James Jasper, 417–22. Oxford: Blackwell, 2009.

Meyer, D.; V. Jenness, and H. Ingram, eds. *Routing the Opposition: Social Movements, Public Policy, and Democracy.* Minneapolis: University of Minnesota Press, 2005.

Meyer, Thomas. *Identity Mania: Fundamentalism and the Politicisation of Cultural Differences.* London: Zed, 2001.

Mignolo, Walter. "From human rights to life rights." In *The Meanings of Rights: The Philosophy and Social Theory of Human Rights,* edited by Costas Douzinas and Conor Gearty. Cambridge: Cambridge University Press, 2014.

Mill, J. S. *On Liberty Etc.: Three Essays.* London: Oxford University Press, 1952.

Mollison, B. and Holmgren, D. *Permaculture One.* Tyalgum: Tagari, 1990.

Moltmann, Jürgen. *The Coming of God.* London: SCM, 1996.

———. *Ethics of Hope.* Minneapolis: Fortress, 2012.

———. *God in Creation* London: SCM, 1993.

———.*Theology of Hope.* London: SCM, 1965.

Monbiot, George. *Captive State: The Corporate Takeover of Britain.* London: Macmillan, 2000.

Monroe, K. R. "Cracking the Code of Genocide: The Moral Psychology of Rescuers, Bystanders, and Nazis During the Holocaust." *Political Psychology* 29:5 (October, 2008) 699–736.

Moore, Barrington. *Injustice: The Social Bases of Obedience and Revolt.* London: Macmillan, 1978.

———. *The Social Origins of Dictatorship and Democracy.* Harmondsworth: Penguin, 1977.

Moore, Jennie, and William E. Rees. "Getting to one planet living." In *State of the World 2013,* edited by Linda Stare, 39–50. Washington, DC: Island, 2013.

Moore, Kathleen Dean, and Michael P. Nelson. "Moving toward a global moral consensus on environmental action." In *State of the World 2013,* edited by Linda Starke, 225–33. Washington, DC: Island, 2013.

Mouffe, Chantal. "Democracy, human rights and cosmopolitanism: an agonistic approach." In *The Meanings of Rights: The Philosophy and Social Theory of Human Rights,* edited by Costas Douzinas and Conor Gearty, 181–92. Cambridge: Cambridge University Press, 2014.

Moyn, Samuel. *Human Rights and the Uses of History.* London: Verso, 2014.

———. *The Last Utopia: Human Rights in History.* Cambridge, MA: Harvard University Press, 2010.

Mumford, Lewis. *The Myth of the Machine: Technics and Human Development.* London: Secker & Warburg, 1967.

———. *The Pentagon of Power.* London: Secker & Warburg, 1971.

Murdoch, Iris. *The Sovereignty of Good.* London: Ark, 1985.

Murphy, Pat, and Faith Morgan. "Cuba: Lessons from a Forced Decline." In *State of the World 2013,* edited by Linda Starke, 332–42. Washington, DC: Island, 2013.

Murphy, Richard. *The Courageous State: Rethinking Economics, Society and the Role of Government.* London: Searching Finance, 2011.

Myers, Ched. *The Biblical Vision of Sabbath Economics.* Washington, DC: Church of the Saviour, 2001.

Naipaul, V. S. *Amongst the Believers.* Harmondsworth: Penguin, 1981.

Nierenberg, D., and B. Halweil. *Cultivating Food Security.* New York: W. W. Norton, 2005.

Nietzsche, F. *Beyond Good and Evil.* Translated by W. Kaufmann. New York: Vintage, 1966.

Noll, Richard. *The Aryan Christ: The Secret Life of Carl Jung.* New York: Random House, 1997.

———. *The Jung Cult. Origins of a Charismatic Movement.* London: Fontana, 1996.

Norberg-Hodge, Helena, Tod Merrifield, and Steven Gorelick. *Bringing the Food Economy Home.* London: Zed, 2002.

Nordhaus, William D. "To curb or not to curb: The economics of the greenhouse effect." Paper presented to the annual meeting of the American Association for the Advancement of Science, New Orleans, February 1990.

Norgaard, Kari Mari. *Living in Denial: Climate Change, Emotions and Everyday Life.* Cambridge, MA: MIT Press, 2011.

Norris, Pippa. *Democratic Phoenix: Reinventing Political Activism.* Cambridge: Cambridge University Press, 2002.

Northcott, Michael. *The Environment and Christian Ethics.* Cambridge: Cambridge University Press, 1996.

Nussbaum, Martha. *Cultivating Humanity.* Cambridge, MA: Harvard University Press, 1997.

———. *Political Emotions: Why Love Matters for Justice.* Cambridge, MA: Harvard University Press, 2013.

———. *The Therapy of Desire: Theory and Practice in Hellenistic Ethics.* Princeton, NJ: Princeton University Press, 1994.

Odum, H. T., and E. C. Odum. *A Prosperous Way Down: Principles and Policies.* Boulder, CO: University of Colorado Press, 2001.

Oliner, Samuel, and Pearl Oliner. *The Altruistic Personality: Rescuers of Jews in Nazi Europe.* New York: Macmillan, 1988.

Orr, David. *Earth in Mind: On Education, Environment, and the Human Prospect.* Washington, DC: Island, 1994.

———. "Governance in the long emergency." In *State of the World 2013,* edited by Linda Starke, 279–91. Washington, DC: Island, 2013.

Parekh, Bhikhu. *Redefining Multiculturalism.* Basingstoke: Palgrave, 2000.

Pateman, Carole. *Participation and Democratic Theory.* Cambridge: Cambridge University Press, 1970.

Patton, Paul. "History, Normativity, and Rights." In *The Meanings of Rights: The Philosophy and Social Theory of Human Rights,* edited by Costas Douzinas and Conor Gearty, 233–50. Cambridge: Cambridge University Press, 2014.

Pelagius. "On Riches." In *Radical Christian Writings*, edited by Andrew Bradstock and Christopher Rowland, 16–19. Oxford: Blackwell, 2002.

Pettifor, Ann. *The Production of Money: How to Break the Power of the Bankers.* London: Verso, 2017.

Pieris, Aloysius. *An Asian Theology of Liberation.* Edinburgh: T&T Clark, 1988.

Piketty, Thomas. *Capital in the Twenty-First Century.* Cambridge, MA: Harvard University Press, 2014.

Pilgrim, David. *Psychotherapy and Society.* London: Sage, 1997.

Plato. *The Laws.* Translated by T. Saunders. Harmondsworth: Penguin, 1970.

———. *Protagoras and Meno.* Translated by A. Beresford. Harmondsworth: Penguin, 2005.

———.*The Republic.* Translated by D. Lee. Harmondsworth: Penguin, 1974.

Polanyi, Karl. *The Great Transformation.* Boston: Beacon, 1957.

Polletta, Francesca. *Freedom is an Endless Meeting: Democracy in American Social Movements.* Chicago: University of Chicago Press, 2002.

Postel, Sandra. "Sustaining fresh water and its dependents." In *State of the World 2013*, edited by Linda Starke, 51–62. Washington, DC: Island, 2013.

Postman, Neil. *Amusing Ourselves to Death.* London: Methuen, 1986.

Pretty, Jules. *Agri-Culture: Reconnecting People, Land and Nature.* London: Earthscan, 2002.

———. *The Living Land.* London: Earthscan, 1998.

Preuss, Ulrich. "Citizenship in the European Union: A paradigm for Transnational Democracy?" In *Re-imagining Political Community*, edited by D. Archibugi, D. Held, and M. Köhler, 138–51. Cambridge: Polity, 1998.

Princen, Thomas, Jack Manno, and Pamela Martin. "Keep them in the ground: ending the fossil fuel era." In *State of the World 2013*, edited by Linda Starek, 161–71. Washington, DC: Island, 2013.

Putnam, Robert. *Bowling Alone: The Collapse and Revival of American Community.* New York Simon & Schuster, 2000.

Quiggin, James. *Zombie Economics.* Princeton, NJ: Princeton University Press, 2010.

Raworth, Kate. "Defining a safe and just space for humanity." www.oxfam.org/files/dp-a-safe-and-just-space-for-humanity-130212-en.pdf.20.

Rees, Ioan B. *Government by Community.* London: Knight, 1971.

Reilly, Robert. *The Closing of the Muslim Mind.* Wilmington, DE: ISI, 2010.

Renner, Michael. "The seeds of modern threats." In *Confronting Hidden Threats to Sustainability: State of the World 2015*, edited by Linda Mastny, 3–20. Washington, DC: Island, 2015.

Renton, Alex. *Suffering the Science: Climate Change, People and Policy.* Oxfam, 2009. https://d1tn3vj7xz9fdh.cloudfront.net/s3fs-public/file_attachments/bp130-suffering-the-science-summary_14.pdf.

Ricardo, David. *The Works and Correspondence of David Ricardo.* Vol. 4, Pamphlets 1815–23. Edited by P. Sraffa. Cambridge: Cambridge University Press, 1951.

Rieff, Philip. *The Triumph of the Therapeutic.* Harmondsworth: Penguin, 1966.

Robertson, James .*The Sane Alternative*. St. Paul, MN: River Basin, 1983.

Robbins, Lionel. *An Essay on the Nature and Significance of Economic Science*. London: Macmillan, 1932.

Rockström, Johan, et al. "A safe operating space for humanity." *Nature* 461 (2009) 429–36.

Rosen, Ruth. *The World Split Open: How the Modern Women's Movement Changed America*. New York: Viking Penguin, 2000.

Rosenau, J. "Governance and democracy in a globalising world." In *Reimagining Political Community*, edited by D. Archibugi, D. Held, and M. Köhler, 28–57. Cambridge: Polity, 1998.

Rosset, Peter. "Food Sovereignty: Global Rallying Cry of Farmer Movements." *Backgrounder* 9:4 (Fall 2003) 1–4.

Rousseau, Jean Jacques. *Political Writings of Jean Jacques Rousseau*. 2 vols. Edited by C. E. Vaughan. Cambridge: Cambridge University Press, 1915.

———. *Social Contract and Discourses*. London: Dent, 1913.

Rowbotham, Michael. *The Grip of Death: A Study of Modern Money, Debt Slavery and Destructive Economics*. Carpenter: Charlbury, 1998.

Ruskin, John. *Unto this Last*. London: Routledge, 1907.

Sabine, G. H. *A History of Political Theory*. London: Harrap, 1951.

Sachs, W. "Development and decline." In *State of the World 2013*, edited by Linda Starke, 125. Washington, DC: Island, 2013.

Sale, Kirkpatrick. *Dwellers in the Land: The Bioregional Vision*. Athens, GA: University of Georgia, 1991.

Saviano, Roberto. *Gomorrah: Italy's Other Mafia*. London: Pan Macmillan, 2008.

Sayers, Sean. "MacIntyre and Modernity." In *Virtue and Politics: Alasdair Macintyre's Revolutionary Aristotelianism*, edited by P. Blackledge and K. Knight, 79–96. Notre Dame, IN: University of Notre Dame Press, 2011.

Schell, Jonathan. *The Unconquerable World*. London: Penguin, 2005.

Schumacher, E. F. *Small is Beautiful: Economics as if People Mattered*. London: Collins, 1989.

Schumpeter, J. *Capitalism, Socialism, and Democracy*. New York: Harper Colophon, 1975.

———. *History of Economic Analysis*. London: Allen & Unwin, 1981.

Schüssler Fiorenza, Elizabeth. *Discipleship of Equals*. London: SCM, 1993.

Schweitzer, Albert. *Civilization and Ethics*. 3rd ed. London: A&C Black, 1955.

Scott, James. *Seeing Like a State: How Certain Schemes to Improve the Human Condition Have Failed*. New Haven, CT: Yale University Press, 1998.

———. *Two Cheers for Anarchism*. Princeton, NJ: Princeton University Press, 2012.

Scruton, Roger. *Green Philosophy: How to Think Seriously about the Planet*. London: Atlantic, 2012.

———. *The West and the Rest*. London: Continuum, 2002.

Seaford, Richard. *Money and the Early Greek Mind: Homer, Philosophy, Tragedy*. Cambridge: Cambridge University Press, 2004.

Segundo, J. L. *Evolution and Guilt.* London: Gill and Macmillan, 1980.

Sen, Amartya. *Development as Freedom.* Oxford: Oxford University Press, 1999.

Simms, Andrew. *Cancel the Apocalypse.* London: Little, Brown, 2013.

Simon, J. *The Ultimate Resource.* Princeton, NJ: Princeton University Press, 1981.

Skidelsky, Robert, and Edward Skidelsky. *How Much is Enough? The Love of Money and the Case for the Good Life.* London: Penguin, 2012.

Smith, Adam. *The Wealth of Nations.* London: Dent, 1977.

Smith, Chelsea, David Elliott, and Susan H. Bragdon. *Realizing the Right to Food in an Era of Climate Change.* Geneva: Quaker United Nations Office, May 2015.

Smith P., M. Bustamante, H. Ahammad, H. Clark, H. Dong, E. A. Elsiddig, H. Haberl, R. Harper, J. House, M. Jafari, O. Masera, C. Mbow, N. H. Ravindranath, C. W. Rice, C. Robledo Abad, A. Romanovskaya, F. Sperling, and F. Tubiello. "Agriculture, Forestry and Other Land Use" (AFOLU). In: *Climate Change 2014: Mitigation of Climate Change. Contribution of Working Group III to the Fifth Assessment Report of the Intergovernmental Panel on Climate Change,* edited by Edenhofer, O., R. Pichs-Madruga, Y. Sokona, E. Farahani, S. Kadner, K. Seyboth, A. Adler, I. Baum, S. Brunner, P. Eickemeier, B. Kriemann, J. Savolainen, S. Schlömer, C. von Stechow, T. Zwickel and J. C. Minx. Cambridge: Cambridge University Press, 2014.

Solnit, Rebecca. *Hope in the Dark: The Untold History of People Power.* Edinburgh: Canongate, 2005.

———. *A Paradise Built in Hell.* London: Penguin, 2010.

Spengler, Otto. *The Decline of the West.* New York: Modern Library, 1962.

Spiro, Melford. *Culture and Human Nature: Theoretical Papers of Melford S. Spiro.* Edited by B. Kilbane and L. Langness. Chicago: University of Chicago Press, 1987.

Spoor, Max. "Land grabbing in Latin America and the Caribbean." *The Journal of Peasant Studies* 39:3–4 (July–October 2012) 845–72.

Starke, Linda, ed. *Is Sustainability Still Possible? State of the World 2013.* Washington, DC: Island, 2013.

Steffen, W., et al. "Planetary boundaries: Guiding human development on a changing planet." *Science,* January 2015, 1–10.

———. *Trajectories of the Earth System in the Anthropocene 2018.* https://doi.org/10.1073/pnas.1810141115

Steiner, George. *Extraterritorial.* London: Faber & Faber, 1972.

———. *No Passion Spent: Essays 1978–1996.* London: Faber & Faber, 1996.

———. *Tolstoy or Dostoevsky: An Essay in Contrast.* London: Faber & Faber, 1980.

Stern, J. P. *Nietzsche.* London: Fontana, 1978.

Stout, Jeffrey. *Ethics after Babel: The Languages of Morals and their Discontents.* Cambridge: James Clarke, 1988.

Streeck, Wolfgang. *Buying Time: The Delayed Crisis of Democratic Capitalism.* 2nd ed. London: Verso, 2017.

———. *How Will Capitalism End?* London: Verso, 2016.

Sutherland, Keith. *The Party's Over.* Exeter: Imprint Academic, 2004.

Swarts, Heidi. *Organizing Urban America: Secular and Faith Based Progressive Movements.* Minneapolis: University of Minnesota Press, 2008.

Tainter, Joseph A. *The Collapse of Complex Societies.* Cambridge: Cambridge University Press, 1988.

Tarrow, Sidney. *Power in Movement: Social Movements and Contentious Politics.* 3rd ed. Cambridge: Cambridge University Press, 2011.

Taylor, Charles. *A Secular Age.* Cambridge, MA: Belknap Press of Harvard University Press, 2007.

———. *Sources of the Self: The Making of the Modern Identity.* Cambridge: Cambridge University Press, 1988.

Terence. *The Woman of Andros; The Self-Tormentor; The Eunuch.* Edited and translated by John Barsby. Loeb Classical Library 22. Cambridge, MA: Harvard University Press, 2001.

Thayer, R. L. *Life Place: Bioregional Thought and Practice.* Berkeley, CA: University of California Press, 2003.

Thomson, George. *Aeschylus and Athens.* London: Lawrence & Wishart, 1941.

Thompson, Janna. "Community Identity and World Citizenship." In *Reimagining Political Community,* edited by D. Arachibugi, D. Held, and M. Köhler, 179–97. Cambridge: Polity, 1998.

Tocqueville, A. de. *Democracy in America.* New York: Knopf, 1994.

Todorov, Tzvetan. *Facing the Extreme: Moral Life in the Concentration Camps.* London: Phoenix, 2000.

Toynbee, Arnold. *A Study of History.* Oxford: Oxford University Press, 1962.

Troyat, Henri. *Tolstoy.* New York: Harmony, 1967.

Tudge, Colin. *Is Agroecology Natural?* Campaign for Real Farming, http://www.colintudge.com/articles/article18.phpTudge.

———. *Six Steps Back to the Land.* Cambridge: Green, 2016.

———. *So Shall We Reap.* London: Penguin, 2003.

———. *Why Genes are Not Selfish and People are Nice: A Challenge to the Dangerous Ideas that Dominate Our Lives.* Edinburgh: Floris, 2013.

Turnbull, Colin M. *The Mountain People.* New York: Simon & Schuster, 1972.

Turner, Graham. "A comparison of The Limits to Growth with thirty years of reality." Sustainable Ecosystems. London: Commonwealth Scientific and Industrial Research Organisation, 2008.

Tyndale, William. *The Obedience of a Christian Man.* Harmondsworth: Penguin, 2000.

Understanding the NFU: An English Agribusiness Lobby. http://www.ethicalconsumer.org/portals/0/downloads/nfu%20an%20english%20agribusiness%20lobby%20group.pdf.

Urry, John. *Climate Change and Society.* Cambridge: Polity, 2011.

Vacca, Roberto. *The Coming Dark Age.* New York: Anchor, 1974.

Van Reybrouck, David. *Against Elections: the Case for Democracy.* London: Bodley Head, 2016.

Varoufakis, Y. *And the Weak Suffer What They Must?* London: Vintage, 2017.

Veerkamp, Ton. *Autonomie & Egalität: ökonomie, Politik, Ideologie in der Schrift.* Berlin: Alektor, 1993.

———. *Die Vernichtung des Baal.* Stuttgart: Alektor, 1981.

———. *Die Welt Anders: Politische Geschichte der Grossen Erzählung.* Berlin: Argument, 2012

Vellacott, Philip. *Euripides: Orestes and Other Plays.* Harmondsworth: Penguin, 1972.

Victor, P., and Tim Jackson. "The Trouble with Growth." In *State of the World 2015,* edited by Linda Mastny, 37–50. Washington, DC: Island, 2015.

Walker, Brian, and David Salt. *Resilience Thinking: Sustaining Ecosystems and People in a Changing World.* Washington, DC: Island, 2006.

Ward, Colin. *Anarchy in Action.* London: Freedom, 1983.

Webb, Janette. "Society Matters: Changing Environmental Attitudes and Behaviour in Scotland." *Sociology* 46:1 (February 2012) 109–25.

Weil, Simone. *The Need for Roots.* London: Routledge, 1958.

Wezel, A., S. Bellon, T. Dore, C. Francis, D. Vallod. "Agroecology as a science, a movement and a practice. A review." *Agronomy for Sustainable Development* 29:4 (December 2009) 503–15.

Wielenga, Bas. *It's A Long Road to Freedom.* Madurai: TTS, 1981.

Wilkinson, Richard, and Kate Pickett. *The Spirit Level: Why Equality is Better for Everyone.* Harmondsworth: Penguin, 2010.

Williams, Bernard. "Acting as a Virtuous Person Acts." In *Aristotle and Moral Realism,* edited by R. Heinamen, 13–23. London: UCL, 1995.

———. *Making Sense of Humanity.* Cambridge: Cambridge University Press, 1995.

Williams, Rowan. *Dostoevsky: Language, Faith and Fiction.* London: Continuum, 2008.

———. "Religious Faith and Human Rights." In *The Meanings of Rights: The Philosophy and Social Theory of Human Rights,* edited by Costas Douzinas and Conor Gearty, 71–82. Cambridge: Cambridge University Press, 2014.

Wink, Walter. *Engaging the Powers.* Minneapolis: Fortress, 1992,

Winstanley, Gerrard. *The Complete Works of Gerrard Winstanley.* 2 vols. Edited by Thomas Corns, Ann Hughes, and David Loewenstein. Oxford: Oxford University Press, 2009.

Wirzba, Norman, ed. *The Essential Agrarian Reader.* Berkeley: Counterpoint, 2003.

Wogaman, J. Philip. *Christian Perspectives on Politics.* London: SCM, 1988.

Wycliffe, John. *De Veritate sacra Scripturae.* Edited by R. Buddensieg. London, 1905–1907.

Varoufakis, Yanis. *And the Weak Suffer What They Must?* London: Vintage 2016.

Yoder, J. Howard. *The Politics of Jesus.* Grand Rapids: Eerdmans, 1972.

Young-Bruehl, E. *Hannah Arendt: For Love of the World.* New Haven, CT: Yale University Press, 1982.

Zencey, Eric. "Energy as master resource." In *State of the World 2013*, edited by Linda Starke, 73–83. Washington, DC: Island, 2013.

Žižek, Slavoj. "Welcome to the spiritual kingdom of animals." In *The Meanings of Rights: The Philosophy and Social Theory of Human Rights*, edited by Costas Douzinas and Conor Gearty, 298–318. Cambridge: Cambridge University Press, 2014.

Index

9 781532 648670